Interdisciplinarity and Higher Education

Interdisciplinarity
and
Higher Education

Edited by
Joseph J. Kockelmans

The Pennsylvania State University Press
University Park and London

Library of Congress Cataloging in Publication Data
Main entry under title:

Interdisciplinarity and higher education.

   Includes bibliography and index.
   1.   Education, Higher—Addresses, essays, lectures.
2.   Interdisciplinary approach in education—
Addresses, essays, lectures.   I.   Kockelmans,
Joseph J., 1923–
LB2325.I496   378   78-50066
ISBN 0-271-00200-X

Contents

Preface

The idea of preparing this anthology arose during a postdoctoral seminar on interdisciplinarity conducted under the auspices of the Interdisciplinary Graduate Program in the Humanities at The Pennsylvania State University in 1975–1976. The aim of the seminar was to promote among the participants a better understanding of the contemporary interdisciplinary movement through a discussion of basic issues: What is meant by interdisciplinarity? In what different forms is interdisciplinary work to be distinguished? What is to be expected from interdisciplinary projects in both research and education? Why should one engage in interdisciplinary efforts? What is the origin of this relatively new phenomenon? What are the effects this movement is likely to have on the organization and administration of the university?

In our investigation and discussion of the relevant literature it became clear that many authors make a number of assumptions that they do not always take care to explain in detail. Furthermore, not everyone uses the same terminology: the same term employed by different authors sometimes refers to two different nondisciplinary projects in either research or education or both. Finally, many authors presuppose that everyone concerned with interdisciplinarity already has a clear idea of its historical origin and development and of the historical development of the contemporary American university.

Realizing the unnecessary confusion to which this state of affairs almost inevitably leads, the participants in the seminar decided to write some essays with the aim of remedying this undesirable situation as much as possible by providing accurate information, making careful distinctions where appropriate, clarifying issues that tend to cause confusion, and making constructive suggestions. In this anthology, therefore, an attempt has been made to concretely illustrate the broad spectrum over which investigations about interdisciplinarity range and to provide the reader with a large perspective within which to understand the discussion on interdisciplinarity. Thus the anthology contains chapters on historical, epistemological, methodological, philosophical, and educational issues.

The first four chapters attempt to depict important aspects of the general perspective within which the actual debate about interdisciplinarity is taking place. My own chapters are of a philosophical character, whereas Wolfram W. Swoboda and Hans Flexner are concerned predominantly with historical issues. Rustum Roy and Muzafer Sherif devote their chapters to interdisciplinary efforts in the natural and social sciences, respectively. Vincent C. Kavaloski deals with interdisciplinary education, and Jonathan Broido makes a fresh start investigating methodological problems encountered in strictly interdisciplinary projects. Robert L. Scott treats typical problems everyone will eventually encounter when seriously engaging in interdisciplinary efforts in higher education. Finally, Hans Flexner and Gerard A. Hauser describe some recent paradigmatic cases of interdisciplinary innovations in general education at contemporary American universities and colleges. To facilitate a first orientation for the reader, a brief summary of the most important ideas developed in each chapter is presented next.

Carl Hausman's Introduction consists in a brief sketch of some well-founded as well as misdirected objections to interdisciplinary efforts in higher education. Its aim is to provide a broad framework from which to evaluate the varying approaches to understanding and establishing interdisciplinary projects and structures in universities.

"Science and Discipline" provides information about the history and philosophy of science insofar as they are immediately relevant to the discussion of interdisciplinary issues. The chapter begins with some historical observations about the meaning of the terms *science* and *discipline* and some reflections on the way these expressions are usually employed in the literature on interdisciplinarity. Some historicocritical remarks on the contemporary division of the sciences follow. Then an attempt is made to characterize the basic dimensions that can be distinguished in any given science, namely, the logical, epistemological, and methodological dimensions on the one hand and the ontological, historical, sociopolitical, educational, and administrative dimensions on the other. Finally, in view of the fact that the humanities play a special part in our educational system as a whole, a section is devoted to them. My primary concern is with giving the reader an idea of the complexity of the domain in which the discussion about interdisciplinarity is to take place. This is why I stress the fact that in regard to virtually all of the issues mentioned here, there is not yet common agreement even about the most basic problems. A careful examination of the literature on these topics clearly shows that this lack of unanimity among authors results from different sources, among them the complexity of the issues themselves. Thus it is understandable that the inherent complexity of the problems involved will reflect itself in the literature on interdisciplinarity, also.

In "Disciplines and Interdisciplinarity" Wolfram W. Swoboda attempts to provide a more concrete context for discussions on interdisciplinarity through a historical sketch of the evolution of disciplines and specialties in the entire Western world. Modern disciplines are intimately linked to the history of educational and research institutions, as they developed from the medieval university and the scientific academy of the late Renaissance. These institutions had their origins in special historical interactions among economic, social, and political forces, which also intervened periodically in the further growth of these institutions. Such general historical factors became especially influential with the technological revolution of the nineteenth and twentieth centuries and transformed the organization of knowledge from one based on "faculties" to one of specialized disciplines. Modern disciplines are therefore integral components of the centralized and bureaucratic machinery of our technological society, a relationship whose detailed interactions must be understood before interdisciplinary alternatives can be discussed fruitfully.

The main concern of Hans Flexner's chapter is with the development and use of knowledge in the various divisions of the university and in relation to both research and education. It deals with educational changes and reform, at first through the developing disciplines and their impact on the curriculum, but also, and increasingly, through extradisciplinary social, political, and economic forces. The chapter focuses on higher education in the United States and in the latter part examines two related notions, general education and interdisciplinarity. The former is viewed not only as a revolt against the fragmentation that has come to characterize liberal education but also as a major departure from traditional conceptions; the latter represents an attempt to reorganize and integrate knowledge along lines other than those defined by the present disciplines. It is not the intention of the author to minimize the contribution of the disciplines in this historical account, but rather to consider their value as well as their limitations in a society and an educational system marked by serious intellectual and social discontinuities. The proliferation of knowledge delineated throughout the chapter is thus seen as both a major source of disintegration and a challenge to the badly needed reassessment and eventual achievement of common goals and values.

"Why Interdisciplinarity?" begins with a plea for a more uniform terminology. Although it is still too early to set aside all discussion and debate about the proper terminology and settle on a definitive set of labels, nonetheless a suggestion is made with respect to a terminology that seems to be both adequate and unambiguous. On the basis of these terminological distinctions three different types of interdisciplinarity are then described in detail: interdisciplinarity in the strict and limited sense, crossdisciplinarity, and transdisciplinarity. The reasons for these three forms suggested in the literature are then discussed. In each case some critical reflections are added, which focus on problems to be taken up in later chapters.

Rustum Roy analyzes the rapid growth of interdisciplinary research organizations on the American university campus and traces it to the increasing demand from society for universities to be more relevant to its problems. Drawing on extensive experience in initiating interdisciplinary structures for both teaching and research, principally in the physical sciences, Roy presents the potential of and limitations on such units on a campus. Extensive data on the field of materials research, the largest and prototypical interdisciplinary field in American higher education, are analyzed to show that very limited success can be claimed for such organizations. Possible courses of university reorganization are suggested. Finally the author presents recommended models for interdisciplinary organizations for the short term, as well as for the long-range future of American higher education.

The thesis of Muzafer Sherif is that any single one of the social sciences, psychology, sociology, and the rest, cannot validly develop in scope and depth without crossborrowing from the others. This interdisciplinary borrowing is not a matter of choice but a necessity to achieve the needed scope and depth within each discipline. The physical sciences have been practicing such crossborrowing in their development without a fuss; so has psychology, especially in the case of sensory processes. It is the immature ethnocentrism of social disciplines that is responsible for the debate about crossborrowing, which is a futile controversy. The failure of crossdisciplinary scientific projects and enterprises in grappling with urgent practical matters is due to ill-conceived and incorrect applications of these undertakings. The chapter contains a number of suggestions for the effective application of interdisciplinary borrowing and cross-validation of realistic hypotheses and generalizations.

Vincent C. Kavaloski begins his chapter by stating that interdisciplinary approaches to education have been justified on the grounds that they promote integration of knowledge, freedom of inquiry, and intellectual curiosity. These three desiderata are among the basic concerns of traditional and contemporary humanistic education. Thus interdisciplinary education contains within itself the promise of humanism.

This high promise, however, is seriously threatened by an objectivist epistemology presupposed in many contributions to the interdisciplinary movement. By confining itself to the objective content and ignoring the educational process, the interdisciplinary movement has often unwittingly borrowed from conventional disciplinary education an objectivist conception of the world. In this perspective human knowledge is conceived of as being a preexisting stuff or commodity, so that teachers appear as dispensers and students as passive receptacles of this stuff. In such a schema the humanistic promise of integration, freedom, and creativity is subverted. In the extreme cases education is reduced to the narration of dead materials. The alternative to narrative education is dialogical education, which commits itself to relentless self-reflection by both teachers and students as co-inquirers engaged in the ever-unfinished historical task of the humanization of man and his environment.

Jonathan Broido is concerned with the methodology of strict interdisciplinarity. The major difficulty of methods proposed for interdisciplinary efforts consists in their failure to preserve the unique outlook and substantive concern of the disciplines involved. Structuralist methodology has hitherto failed to preserve the empirical, referential uniqueness of the disciplines, whereas the unity-of-science movement failed to preserve the unique structural ingredient in the relevant subject matters.

Broido argues that strict interdisciplinarity must use disciplinary entrenchment even though it is aimed at overcoming it to some degree. Thus it must explain one disciplinary enterprise from the vantage point of another without destroying its legitimacy. Such an explanation, if possible, may involve some strong logical tools, but they need not threaten the philosophical presuppositions of the disciplines; they often can be used to show that even when one disciplinary enterprise is explicable in terms of the minimal conceptual framework presupposed by another, the original enterprise has significant instrumental advantages in solving particular problems over its alleged explication (instrumental justification).

Consequently the basic features of instrumental interdisciplinarity are considered. This proceeds in three stages: the exploration and mapping of the minimal conceptual frameworks presupposed by the disciplines involved, the application of different disciplines to particular problems that are considered beyond the proper territory of these disciplines, and the instrumental comparison of the utility of egocentrically expanded disciplines with respect to problems that could present a common challenge. Finally the chapter provides clues to the solution of some structural methodological problems that are involved in accomplishing interpretative tasks of strict interdisciplinarity.

Robert L. Scott is concerned with personal and institutional problems encountered in being interdisciplinary. The previously outlined history and the previously projected goals of interdisciplinarity have pointed to, but not directly addressed, certain specific problems and dilemmas, both personal and institutional, that are inevitable within academic structures. These dilemmas are discussed in detail on the bases of the following theses:

1. Nearly everyone already believes in interdisciplinary education.
2. Nearly everyone believes in specialization.
3. Interdisciplinarity may occur on various levels of higher education and consequently involves choices of levels for concentration.
4. Interdisciplinarians must persuade others to cooperate with them.
5. Interdisciplinary research and education must be administered.
6. Higher education involves students and students must be involved.

Hans Flexner and Gerard A. Hauser devote the first part of their chapter to a brief account of interdisciplinary contexts, goals and objectives, curricular and instructional arrangements, and faculty/administrative practices and strategies. The major part of the chapter is concerned with three paradigms. The first represents one of the very few programs that seriously involve faculty, students, and administrators from many of the graduate and professional units of a major university known for its long-time commitment to disciplinary as well as interdisciplinary research and education. The second paradigm represents one of the most radical and comprehensive curricular, instructional, and organizational innovations undertaken by any college in recent years. Finally, the Interdisciplinary Graduate Program in the Humanities, established at The Pennsylvania State University in 1973, is described.

From the preceding summary it will be obvious that the chapters brought together in this book neither exhaust the subject nor constitute a harmonious unity. Those who contributed to this volume believe that such a unity may not be expected at this initial phase of development. Interdisciplinarity has come to mean many things to many people. Anyone who tries to brush aside all heterogeneity underestimates the complexity of the issues and risks being accused of either dogmatism or ignorance. Yet one should realize also that much of the seeming contradiction found in this volume is just that. Depending upon the disciplines selected for discussion and the dimensions considered in each case, different solutions were to be expected for problems that might at first have seemed to be identical. Upon closer inspection it will become clear that here, as elsewhere, different circumstances require different attitudes.

Each author has had full opportunity to express his personal ideas, and the editor has explicitly encouraged each to do so. It seems to us as a group more important at this moment to lay out in detail the richness of opportunity and challenge opened up by interdisciplinary innovations than to seek ways in which the ongoing development might be brought to some form of synthesis. The book is not meant to deliver the solution for all interdisciplinary problems but rather to arouse interest in their cause and to elicit a meaningful dialogue.

Those who have contributed to the book wish to express their gratitude to the National Endowment for the Humanities for providing them with the framework within which this anthology could develop and, above all, to Professor Stanley F. Paulson, Dean of the College of the Liberal Arts, and Professor Thomas F. Magner, Associate Dean for Research and Graduate Studies, for their encouragement and support.

Joseph J. Kockelmans

Introduction
Disciplinarity or Interdisciplinarity?

Carl R. Hausman

What is the purpose of a book of essays on interdisciplinarity? The answer to this question depends in part on determining what is meant by *interdisciplinarity*. And determining this meaning is one of the functions of this book. But it is not its main function, which is to present varying approaches to the problems of understanding and establishing interdisciplinary efforts, projects, and structures in universities. In these introductory remarks, we shall focus on this main function. Assuming for the moment that there is a general though perhaps vague common agreement about the meaning of *interdisciplinarity,* we shall take as our initial task a brief sketch of some well-founded and some misdirected objections to interdisciplinary efforts in higher education.

The concept of interdisciplinarity and the controversies over its meaning and functions are of relatively recent origin. In the United States some of the earliest debates occurred at the University of Chicago in the 1930s. In Europe the significance and appropriateness of interdisciplinary study and research were not disputed before the 1950s. However, quite apart from such recent controversies, interdisciplinary study itself has a long history. In one sense the term can be applied to the earliest institutions of formal education.

Certainly Plato's Academy was not organized according to rigidly held disciplinary boundaries, though there were distinctions among subjects of study, such as mathematics, music, or dialectical reasoning. But these were viewed hierarchically as progressive, interdependent stages leading from an initial preparation requiring an understanding of nature and the human soul to a final training that was ideally to culminate in wisdom. And since the time of these earliest efforts at organizing the educational process, recurrent attention has been given to developing systems that include interdependent as well as independent fields of study.

The more recent, explicit concern about the importance of interdisciplinary study can be traced to developments in education initiated in the middle of the nineteenth century. At that time universities began to be organized administratively into schools and faculties along disciplinary lines. Administrative structures reflected this proliferation, and the boundaries between administrative units hardened even more than the boundaries between disciplines. Furthermore, disciplines began to proliferate: within what we now think of as the social sciences there arose the new, distinct fields of economics, psychology, sociology, anthropology, linguistics, political science, etc.; within the humanities distinct fields were newly identified as English, speech, religious studies, etc. Each discipline internalized its aim, and each discipline became increasingly specialized, so that study within it became rather rigidly compartmentalized in terms of its autonomous principles. As compartmentalization of disciplines increased, so did their administrative support structures. In most universities since World War II the various disciplines have been represented by relatively autonomous, independent departments. Administrative divisions required budgetary divisions providing financial support for the separate groups and the separate departments. It was inevitable that each department and group was forced to become competitive for resources.

These two factors, the autonomy of disciplines—each with its own integrity—and administrative competition, cause much of the resistance to interdisciplinary study. Thus one current reason for objecting to interdisciplinarity is pragmatic. It is partly because they require resources that new disciplines are resisted and new interdisciplinary efforts are opposed. Their needs threaten the support required for the maintenance as well as the growth of established disciplines. This pragmatic issue is obvious. However, we shall treat it together with the other development, which is theoretical. The theoretical consideration of disciplinary rather than administrative autonomy and integrity is more fundamental, and it represents a possible justification for practical resistance to interdisciplinary efforts.

It may be argued, then, that each of the current disciplines represented by distinct administrative units has its own integrity and autonomy, which must be preserved. What now are defined as traditional disciplines are distinguished by natural boundaries required by the nature of knowledge itself. Each has its own intrinsic principles, and each has developed in accord with methodologies and assumptions that are neither translatable into those of any of the other disciplines nor traceable to a more fundamental discipline. Of course, this conception of a field of study itself does not preclude the possibility of new disciplines, each with its own intrinsic principles and methodologies. Nor does it preclude the possibility that a combination or common set of the principles and methodologies of the established disciplines might be developed independently of these areas. Yet the extensive commitment to the preservation of established disciplines entails two ways in which interdisciplinarity is resisted for theoretical reasons. The first way of resisting is expressed simply as intellectual indifference. Those deeply engaged in a single discipline often ignore questions about the presuppositions and boundaries of their own field. Only if they reach the outer limits of their methods and principles of inquiry, when dealing with fundamental problems, would they recognize a need to broaden their perspectives. Such recognition is especially significant for our topic, and it must be pursued at least briefly. But before doing so, we should consider the second way of resisting.

This second way consists in a mobilized, active opposition to interdisciplinary study. Advocates of what is established deliberately oppose the claims of such new developments. One reason is that some advocates of new interdisciplinary developments, in their determination and zeal to defend their purposes, actively try to impose nontraditional concepts on their colleagues. They believe that they must prove themselves. However, because they do not yet possess defining principles or an acknowledged, preconceived domain of data that can constitute their subject matter, their opponents remain skeptical. After all, it has become impossible even in a single discipline for students to gain a thorough knowledge and understanding of its data and methods. Thus the interdisciplinarian is charged with being a generalist, "a jack of all trades and master of none." Or he is charged with amateurism and encroachment in areas outside his specialty, if he has one. He in turn charges the traditionalist disciplinarian with stultifying conservatism, lack of vision, and inflexibility bred of vested interests.

There is something to be said on both sides of this dispute. In order to see what is positive on both sides, let us look more closely at the resistance to interdisciplinary efforts. We may then provide a framework for suggesting what we believe is a proper approach to interdisciplinary study, as well as for treatment of the issues discussed in the succeeding chapters of this book. We shall argue that support for interdisciplinarity may be artificial or natural, and it is only the artificial support to which its opponents are justified in objecting.

Perhaps the most readily understandable reason for resisting interdisciplinary movements is found in situations in which the movement is artificial in the sense that it is imposed by administrative fiat, based on the view that a new interdisciplinary structure is more economical or more convenient for such matters as determining needs for faculty positions. These situations may be the expression of a deep concern—sometimes verging on desperation—about criticism, both explicit and implicit, from students, society, and some faculty. In times of rapidly changing social and economic problems, there are increased pressures on universities and colleges to be immediately responsive to social change and to apparent new needs of students. Although we know on reflection that student demands are sometimes fickle if not whimsical, and that what appears to be a social or economic need in one year may have vanished a few years later, faculties and administrations find it difficult to resist these pressures, particularly when appropriations for institutions of higher learning are controlled by groups that believe themselves keenly aware of whatever at the time are believed to be current social needs.

In any case, responses to such pressures have led to attempts to redesign curricula, to introduce experimental and what are called "innovative" courses, and sometimes to calls for "new" realignments of disciplines and reorganization of academic structure. Those who are anxious to be *au courant* are in the forefront of these attempts. However, the forefront often has little unity and singleness of purpose. And those who find value in traditional, established ideals of education react negatively to the experimenters, as do those who represent established and fundamental professions, such as those of the basic natural sciences, the classics and the humanities, and the long-standing social sciences. For they see these attempts as expressions of fear and faddishness and as a danger to substantive education. Insofar as interdisciplinary study represents nothing more than such an expression, it deserves to be resisted. Some of the discussions in this book will show that interdisciplinarity is more than an expression of despair.

The second situation that provokes resistance to interdisciplinary efforts gives greater weight to the theoretical issue and is more difficult to assess. This situation again centers on artificiality, but it is one in which interdisciplinary efforts are artificial not because of

compliancy or desperation but because they are intellectually motivated attempts to be different. In such cases the interdisciplinary
effort may be undertaken by those who wish to be innovative simply
because they admire innovation or because they disvalue what is
static. It seems plausible to expect disciplines to change. Without
change they would not progress. And some of us would like to be in
the forefront of progress. Yet interdisciplinary efforts based on the
desire to change and progress do not necessarily grow naturally out
of concerns common to more than one discipline or out of needs
recognized when problems seem insoluble from the perspectives of
single disciplines.

It should be obvious when we look at the history of thought that
disciplines have evolved. A discipline such as physics is in the twentieth century dramatically different in content and in acceptable
methodology from physics in the time of Newton. It is so different
that it would be difficult to say precisely where its outer boundaries
are to be drawn. Does biophysics or materials research belong to
physics or to some other independent discipline? Similar observations could be made about every field of study whose advocates view
it as an established discipline. Is there some rigorous way to define
psychology so that it is clearly a behavioral science, a biological science, or a speculative, theoretical understanding of mental processes? Should history be classified as social science or among the
humanities? Is philosophy fundamentally a mathematical-logical inquiry, a form of literary expression, or a critical return to ordinary
language?

Examples such as these suggest that established disciplines are
not invariably and perpetually controlled by clearly defined and universally accepted principles. Specialists in the disciplines define their
disciplines according to what they accept as data and the way these
data should be approached, and these differences align the discipline with other disciplines—developmental psychology with biology,
history with philosophy, certain kinds of philosophy with mathematics, biophysics with biology.

Of course, subdivisions and conflicting conceptions within established disciplines are not in themselves interdisciplinary fields. But
the point is that the evolution of subfields and methods within the
larger contexts of accepted disciplines often includes stages in which
there are new connections among disciplines, and because of these
new alignments new disciplines are initiated. Two notable examples
of this are the development of biochemistry and social psychology.
Both disciplines grew out of the interactions among established

fields, and both still depend upon and serve as bases for some of the work being done in other fields. They arose as interdisciplines, and they arose naturally.

This origin of new disciplines out of interactions among established disciplines is instructive. What occurs may be called "natural" not because it was a response to administrative or bureaucratic pressure to loosen the boundaries of the established fields, and not because it was based on a decision of specialists to abandon narrowness and be different, but rather because it was a response to developments intrinsic to the established discipline. The natural origin of new disciplines is a function of inquiry that is directed toward problems and that grows out of theoretical requirements that are discovered by inquirers whose eyes are set directly on a subject matter rather than on a self-conscious determination to abandon narrowness in inquiry. A similar point is sometimes made about the creating of art. The artist who leads and sometimes transforms a tradition does not work out of a sheer desire to be creative, which would in itself be merely a desire to be different and thus, like artificial interdisciplinary efforts, risk leading only to eccentricity. Instead the creative artist works with his eye on the possibilities of his medium and the exigencies of a general task to be done.

It might be concluded from this characterization of natural interdisciplinary effort that deliberate attempts to design interdisciplinary programs are misguided, that they all are artificial. We might conclude that the only respectable and realistic way to engage in interdisciplinary efforts is from within established disciplines, letting each specialist break out of his boundaries as necessity leads him to do so. However, the issue is not so simple. There is a complexity in what we have called interdisciplinary effort that is not obvious in what has been said thus far. In the remainder of this introduction we shall sketch the main features of this complex issue of interdisciplinarity in order to suggest why deliberate efforts not only need not be artificial but, under some conditions, are essential to the occurrence of natural interdisciplinary efforts. We shall single out four distinct issues, the responses to which may support deliberate attempts to promote interdisciplinary education. These issues concern (1) differences in conceptions of the aims of higher education, including different conceptions behind the curricula of different kinds of institutions of higher learning, (2) whether teaching or research is the context for interdisciplinary efforts, (3) the kind of disciplines considered to be appropriate for interdisciplinary relations, and (4) the various, sometimes conflicting, meanings of the term *interdisciplinary*.

The first problem has to do with the variation in conceptions of the proper function of institutions of higher education. What is understood as a natural development of interdisciplinary interests differs according to these conceptions. If the main function of a college or university is thought to be professional, with curricula and research centering in the professional schools, then interdisciplinary efforts most likely are viewed as properly concentrated in extraprofessional, general-education programs designed to broaden students' education. If the main function is to provide a basic liberal arts education, then interdisciplinary efforts most likely are viewed as integral to the curriculum, because this function is correlated with, if not identical with, a conception of general education that implies integration as well as specialized study. In contrast to the former conception, whose aim is to broaden the focus of the curriculum, here the aim is to generate a unifying focus out of divergent components of a curriculum. In either case, however, interdisciplinary efforts in some form are accepted, whether only because of the necessity of broadening students' education in the most economical way or because of a felt need to unify. Whether interdisciplinarity in such settings is natural or artificial depends upon the response one makes to the second issue, which arises once we notice that the point about general or liberal education presupposes a distinction we have not yet made.

In considering interdisciplinarity that arises out of general education needs, we have turned from the context of research to the context of teaching. And in this context naturalness or artificiality may be different. The first kind of interdisciplinary effort is conceived as the study, simultaneously, of several disciplines that are not part of the program for majors. In this setting, interdisciplinary efforts are directed toward courses that bring together two or more fields such as those of the humanities, the social sciences, the physical sciences, or the biological sciences. These courses normally are relatively fixed in content and approach and are common to students from different disciplines. As such, they are not intended to break new ground in research or to extend one discipline beyond its boundaries. The pursuit of this form of interdisciplinary effort is not an expression of natural necessity found within a discipline. And prima facie it seems most directly related to what has been called *artificial,* since it may be simply a convenient way to pack into a relatively short learning period several different areas to which students may be exposed. If this is the design of such courses, then they might as well be offered as a series of minicourses, each in a different discipline. Such interdisciplinary efforts are best referred to as *multidisciplinary,* a term to be mentioned below and to be explored later in this book.

However, it may be that such efforts are not simply convenient packages but are thoughtful attempts to integrate several disciplines by finding principles that are common to more than one field and that make possible a certain depth of understanding of the different fields. It is this endeavor that guides the second setting, unification of liberal education. If this is the case, then interdisciplinary study may serve as a model of the possibility of interactions among specialists from different fields. A course or set of courses of this kind not only would introduce a student whose major is in a single discipline to a cluster of subjects outside his discipline, but more importantly, would suggest to him the possibility of discovering principles more fundamental than those of his chosen discipline. And awareness of this possibility could be a valuable basis later for the student's ability to develop in what has been called a natural interdisciplinary effort.

This point calls attention to the fact that interdisciplinary research and teaching may interact. Accordingly, interdisciplinary teaching may follow trends in research all of which are not bound exclusively to general education needs. The evolution of a discipline leads to new concepts and methods that are appropriately treated in instructional settings, whether in lecture, seminars, or the laboratory. Until the newness of the concepts and methods wears off and the change has been established, the change and what is taught are taken to be interdisciplinary. Once the newness has worn off, what was interdisciplinary is regarded as a discipline, as in the case of psycholinguistics, biochemistry, or social psychology. Such developments are what we have called natural, and they highlight the need to stimulate instruction that is interdisciplinary in reflecting a natural growth of disciplines as these are defined in terms of research. Like general-education interdisciplinary courses, this instruction, although derivative from research developments, may serve to stimulate those who will put their course work to use in research and who may see beyond strict boundaries of subject matter and methods and extend these boundaries into new domains.

The evolution of new disciplines makes some disciplines seem to be more interdisciplinary than others, if only because they are at the time in transition and include interactions and realignments of various established disciplines. Yet there are long-standing established disciplines that seem to be inherently more interdisciplinary than others. Perhaps the most obvious example of such a discipline is philosophy, particularly when it takes the form of reflective critiques of other fields such as philosophy of science, philosophy of art or aesthetics, or philosophy of religion. And certainly philosophy has the longest tradition of any formal discipline that might be considered essentially interdisciplinary. But there are others. Literary criticism, which may be viewed as a subdiscipline of literature or letters, is an example of a discipline that necessarily calls on methods and data from other disciplines, such as psychoanalysis, anthropology, philosophy, and history. And as theories of criticism change, so does literary criticism vary the disciplines on which it draws. Anthropology too seems to be linked to other distinct disciplines, primarily some of the natural and social sciences.

Of course, these disciplines have their own distinctive characteristics. Nevertheless, they draw upon and sometimes extend other disciplines. They seem inherently to be integrative. And they may be viewed as appropriate focal points for understanding and perhaps promoting natural interdisciplinary efforts. If this is so, then it is not necessarily artificial to engage in deliberate attempts to develop programs that are interdisciplinary when they develop out of or with their focus in inherently interdisciplinary disciplines. The purpose of such attempts would be to promote natural interdisciplinary developments in knowledge. What they must guard against are artificial schemes, imposed structures, and bureaucratic machinery to force realignments. Instead, these attempts should establish a setting the main purpose of which is to discourage administrative restrictions on formal interaction among faculty from different disciplines, specifically, such requirements as generating student credit hours in a discipline as the main basis for appropriating funds, or the adherence to reward structures that favor productivity only in narrowly specialized accomplishments.

A formal setting for interdisciplinary work, if it is to avoid artificiality and at the same time promote natural developments, must maintain a flexible organization that serves as an arena or sounding board for faculty to try out ideas, to come together from different disciplines when need or new interests draw them together. And this organization should serve as at least a temporary home for students who want to look outside the boundaries of their degree-program discipline.

The last problem is that of deciding just what the term *interdisciplinary* means. How one interprets the term, of course, is important to the kind of interdisciplinary organization or program one may envisage. And, more important here, how one interprets the term affects one's view of whether interdisciplinary efforts are artificial or natural. *Interdisciplinary* has at least the following references: multidisciplinary, transdisciplinary, crossdisciplinary. Subsequent chapters in the book treat these variations on the common term *interdisciplinary*. Suffice it to say here that it is more likely that if interdisciplinary is construed as multidisciplinary, as a juxtaposing of established disciplines, one is likely to view interdisciplinary efforts as artificial. On the other hand, the kind of efforts we have recommended seems to require some commitment to a natural evolution of disciplines under what may be called "transdisciplinarity," that is, to a recognition and attempt to view different disciplines as related through some principle of interaction more fundamental than any one of them. To be sure, such a principle is more abstract than that which falls under it. To this extent, it cannot be an immediate condition of natural growth. To treat it as such would be to risk an artificiality that parallels the kind that is so easy to succumb to administratively. However, while such a transcendent principle is not a direct theoretical base or condition for change in any one of the disciplines to which it is relevant, it may serve as a model or archetype of possibilities at the outer reaches of any of these disciplines. By being alert to it, persons within a discipline may be disposed to openness and acceptance as well as to efforts in working with representatives of other disciplines. If this kind of cooperation is acknowledged as a real possibility, then a natural evolution of disciplines through interdisciplinary interaction is less likely to be resisted, and it just might be stimulated.

Science and Discipline

Some Historical and Critical Reflections

Joseph J. Kockelmans

The discussion on interdisciplinarity is an integral part of the contemporary discussion of all our systematic, theoretical endeavors, their possible applications, their effects on man and his environment, their educational and administrative implications, and their sociopolitical meaning and function. It seems to me, therefore, that the literature on interdisciplinary efforts can be properly understood only within the perspective of this much larger framework. From that perspective it becomes immediately clear that interdisciplinarity is not the solution for all of our problems; on the other hand, neither is all the literature on interdisciplinary issues irrelevant. Admittedly, certain well-meaning scholars who have been concerned about our systematic, theoretical endeavors have been much too optimistic with their suggestion that interdisciplinary projects and programs will automatically solve a number of important problems. Yet neither can it be denied that others have too easily dismissed all attempts at interdisciplinary innovations as trivial pursuits.

In the pages to come I shall focus on some of the major issues with which contemporary science confronts us. It is not my intention to engage in detailed historical investigations that perhaps could elucidate the origins of the actual situation as we now know it. Neither is it my intention to evaluate and pass judgment on events of the past. My purpose is to reflect critically on *certain* historical events in an attempt to understand their meaning and implications and in so doing to shed some light on the complexity of the actual situation and point to a number of problems and issues for which we still do not yet have a universally acceptable solution, although different authors have suggested possible solutions or alternatives for some of them. In this way I hope to be able to briefly characterize the scene in which most of the dialogue about interdisciplinary issues will be enacted in subsequent chapters.

The reader will find in the literature on interdisciplinarity that almost every author frequently uses the expressions *science, discipline,* and *interdisciplinarity,* and that each attaches a meaning to these expressions that to some degree reflects his philosophical perspective and conception of his own discipline, as well as the sociopolitical outlook that codetermined his view on the social meaning and function of research and education. Although these differences of perspective and outlook do exist, it is true also that the authors agree in many respects, some of which are very important in the debate on interdisciplinarity.

In this chapter I will attempt first to define the concepts of science and discipline so as to stress points of agreement among authors. Then I will attempt to explain how these terms will be employed in the discussions to follow. Next some critical reflections will be added on the historical aspect of the division of the sciences and on the three basic dimensions that can be distinguished in any given science or discipline. Because the humanities have a rather typical function in our educational system, I will devote a special section to them, concluding the chapter with a brief summary of its major points.

Science[1]

The term *science* is derived from the Latin *scientia* (from the verb *scire:* to know) and refers to what is characteristic for someone who knows. Taken as such, science is synonymous with knowledge. As a technical term the Latin *scientia* was used to translate the Greek *episteme,* which was used for the type of knowledge that has the following characteristics: universality, necessity, precision, rigor, and systematicness, and which thus implies the employment of well-defined methods. In the modern era the term *science* was used to characterize a type of knowledge that is neither prescientific nor "common" nor philosophical in character. The sciences are now generally divided into formal and empirical sciences, and the latter are often subdivided into natural and social (or human) sciences.

The word *science* indicates primarily the habitual disposition of those who have devoted themselves to methodical and systematic research in a certain domain, as well as the intentional correlate (object) of that disposition. In addition the term has a number of secondary meanings, according to which it can refer to the totality of all that can be known about a certain realm of phenomena, or to that which has actually been recorded systematically in texts of some kind for communication and education.

In the past most authors have assumed that the various sciences flow from a double cognitive interest, on the one hand a theoretical, speculative interest (man's desire to know) and on the other a practical or pragmatic interest (man's desire to control his environment). In view of the fact that the sciences are human creations, they are inherently temporal and historical phenomena that are continuously in development; this development is guided by factors flowing from the two interests that motivate all of our scientific efforts. Along with the historical development taking place in each branch of the sciences, there is development in the manner in which one conceives of the meaning and function of the sciences, the inner orientation just mentioned notwithstanding. This latter development is, among other things, connected with changes in the sociopolitical situation of the scientists, as well as with developments in the realm of the philosophical positions from which one reflects upon the history of the sciences. The domain in which philosophical issues concerning the sciences are discussed is called theory of science, philosophy of science, or epistemology.

The conception of science that is predominant in the Western world originated from attempts made by a number of pre-Socratic thinkers to come to an all-encompassing, cosmological conception of the world. These speculations, developed by various thinkers between Thales and Zeno, led to reflections on the nature and limits of man's knowledge by the Sophists, by Democritus (who distinguished the phenomena from reality), and particularly by Plato and Aristotle. The latter not only tried to determine the nature of man's knowledge but also to account for the division and unity of the sciences that had gradually developed.

Plato distinguishes between two realms of knowable things, the empirical world of changeable things, known by opinion or *doxa,* and the world of unchangeable and eternal ideas, known through *episteme.* In *Republic* (VII, 534 A) Plato defines *episteme* as perfect knowledge, which is of a higher order than discursive knowledge (*dianoia*) and opinion (*doxa*). Its typical characteristics are immutability and perfection.

In Aristotle the term is used in a much broader sense.[2] Aristotle allows for a number of sciences, which are to be related to one another in a systematic fashion. He defines *science* taken as habitual disposition as follows: "We suppose ourselves to possess unqualified scientific knowledge of a thing . . . when we think that we know the cause on which the fact depends, as the cause of that fact and of no other, and, further, that the fact could not be other than it is. . . . Consequently the proper object of unqualified scientific knowledge is something which cannot be other than it is." (*An. Post.* I, 2, 71b7 ff.) In the *Nicomachean Ethics* he stresses once more that genuine scientific knowledge is concerned with what is incapable of being otherwise. Therefore the object of scientific knowledge is to be characterized by necessity. Science is concerned with what invariably will always remain the same, notwithstanding the continuous changes in the things for which our scientific knowledge is relevant. In the same context Aristotle points out that scientific knowledge (which can be divided into various sciences) is itself part of a much larger intellectual framework implying the arts, practical wisdom, philosophical speculation, and intuitive reason. (*Nic Eth*, VI, 3, 1139b14 ff.)

In Aristotle's view a thing is known scientifically if it is known through its causes. Our scientific knowledge is perfect if it is developed systematically through demonstration aiming at the explanation of the thing's causes (*scientia propter quid, dioti*). There are less perfect forms of scientific knowledge in which one merely describes what is the case without being able to fully explain things in terms of their causes (*scientia quia, hoti*).

A new conception of science took shape in the modern era under the influence of ideas developed by Francis Bacon in his *Novum Organon* (1620) and by Descartes in his investigations concerning method.[3] Bacon stressed the necessity of experience and experiment as well as the employment of systematic inductive methods, whereas Descartes focused on the rational element in the scientific enterprise and on the necessary use of mathematics and logic. Both these conceptions became integral parts of what we now call modern science as developed by Galileo, Newton, and many others. It is important to note that for these authors the sciences are still part of a much larger scientific framework, implying in addition to the sciences practical wisdom as well as philosophical speculation. It is understandable that the sciences are called philosophical disciplines, in the sense that they too are part and parcel of man's quest for knowledge and wisdom.

For Kant every doctrine that constitutes a system, i.e., a whole of cognition, is to be termed a *science*.[4] On the other hand, a body of learning that does not (yet) constitute a system is called a *doctrine*. If the principles of the system are axioms of the *empirical* connection of our cognitions in a whole, one speaks of a historical doctrine which has a merely descriptive as well as a historical side.

If the principles of a doctrine are axioms of the *rational* connection of our cognitions in a whole, we speak of a science, particularly in cases where the doctrine would treat its subject wholly according to principles a priori.

> That only can be called science proper whose certainty is apodictic: cognition that can merely contain empirical certainty is only improperly called science. A whole of cognition which is systematic is for this reason called science, and, when the connection of cognition in this system is a system of causes and effects, rational science. But when the grounds or principles it contains are in the last resort merely empirical, and the laws from which reason explains the given facts are merely empirical laws, they then carry no consciousness of their necessity with them (they are not apodictically certain), and thus the whole does not in strictness deserve the name of science.[5]

It is important to recognize here that Kant takes the term *science* predominantly in an objective sense; a science is a whole of ordered knowledge, to be characterized by its systematicness, which flows from the application of rational principles. Second, it is clear that for Kant there is a sharp distinction among science, philosophy, and the arts. Philosophy has a foundational function of sorts in regard to the sciences, whereas the sciences have a guiding function in regard to the arts. Kant's philosophical reflections on the sciences originated what we now call *philosophy of science*. Contemporary philosophy of science is not a homogeneous field; there are several, often conflicting trends and schools. It is far beyond the scope of this book to undertake a discussion of these different conceptions.

Today the word *science* is still being used in different but related senses. The term is sometimes used as synonymous with knowledge. Most of the time, however, it is reserved for a special kind of knowledge to be distinguished from mere belief, opinion, and art. This special kind of knowledge is acquired through study and inquiry and leads to an acquaintance with a certain body of learning. In all of these instances the term refers to a habitual disposition on the part of the one who knows. Most often one finds the term being used in an objective sense to refer to the intentional correlate (object) of this disposition. In such cases the term refers to a body of knowledge that constitutes a harmonious whole of some kind, a system of interrelated insights in regard to a certain realm of phenomena, acquired through the critical application of methods on the basis of certain principles.

Discipline[6]

The word discipline is derived from the Latin *disciplina* (instruction of disciples). In classical antiquity *disciplina* and *doctrina* were corresponding expressions, both of which referred to an educational setting of some kind. Originally the two words were used synonymously or nearly so. They referred to the activity and content of the kind of education that is primarily oriented toward the acquisition of knowledge, as well as to the habitual disposition resulting from that education. Cicero uses *ars* as synonymous with *disciplina,* so that the expressions *artes liberales, disciplinae liberales,* and *doctrinae liberales* all have the same meaning.

In the Middle Ages the term *doctrina* was reserved basically for education in Christianity, the Christian faith, or the habitual disposition resulting from this education. *Doctrina sacra* stands for the teachings of the Church taken either as a whole or with respect to certain basic elements. The term often indicates Christian theology. Although in the same period *disciplina* was commonly used as synonymous with *ars,* the term *disciplina* was used also in the sense of *scientia* (*episteme*). Yet in this case *disciplina* refers to science with the connotation of being the result of pedagogical or school activity.

Boethius introduced the distinction between the quadrivium as the *disciplinae liberales* (arithmetic, geometry, astronomy, and music) and the *trivium* as the *artes liberales* (grammar, rhetoric, and dialectic). The former proceed *disciplinariter* (methodically with rigor and strictness) and thus stand closer to the theoretical sciences (philosophy) and constitute a necessary propaedeutic in regard to all pursuit of the truth.

In the later Middle Ages the term *disciplina* acquired four related meanings:

1. The seven liberal arts, insofar as they are taught at the university.
2. Any subject matter taught at the university.
3. Those branches of learning which proceed methodically with rigor and strictness, predominantly the logical and mathematical disciplines.
4. Science.

In contemporary English the word refers to the instruction imparted to disciples or scholars; it thus refers to the educational process that implies both teaching and learning. Second, the term expresses the subject matter of that process and thus a branch of instruction or education: a science or an art in its educational aspect. Third, the term is used for the instruction itself, having as its aim to bring a pupil to proper conduct and action; particularly the training of scholars to proper and orderly action within the realm of a science, by instructing and exercising them in the same.

Science Versus Discipline

Although the terms science and discipline are very often used synonymously, the word *discipline* contains a reference to the educational process in which students are introduced to the various branches of knowledge. In view of the fact that the term *interscientific* is very seldom if ever used, whereas the term *interdisciplinary* is now accepted in almost all Western languages, one must keep in mind that in the debate on interdisciplinarity, the educational dimension plays an important role. Thus one may expect that the literature will be concerned partly with typically educational, partly with administrative issues. On the other hand, because of the synonymy of the two words, in some instances the issues appear to be concerned with typically scientific problems. In order to avoid misunderstanding, we shall try to use the term *discipline* predominantly as implying a reference to the educational process associated with one of the branches of scientific knowledge.

Scientific Disciplines and Rational Discourse[7]

Scientific disciplines are the intentional correlates of a kind of theoretical knowledge that must be characterized by its sense of criticism. In his scientific activities the scientist carefully watches all of his steps and evaluates them on the basis of precisely defined principles. The methods he employs are determined in such a way that it is continuously possible to expand the realm of knowledge in a systematic fashion. The principles used to organize a realm of investigation and the insights that are relevant to it, the criteria of validity, and the research methods are usually not taken from a domain outside the scientific discipline but constitute an integral part of the development of scientific knowledge itself. Most of these principles, criteria, and methods are at first to a large extent implicit in a given piece of scientific research. At a later stage they are made explicit, critically analyzed and examined, and ultimately subjected to a rigorous process of validation and justification. At first each science begins with a number of ideas, criteria, principles, and methods that are put to work in regard to a certain realm of phenomena. At that stage of the development of a science these ideas, criteria, principles, and methods still have the character of presuppositions. At a later stage these presuppositions are made the subject matter of critical analysis and investigation in so-called foundational research. In this second type of research once again ideas, criteria, principles, and methods are put to work; in a later stage they too can be made the subject matter of a new type of foundational research. Thus even foundational research is never more than of relative validity. It tries to explain and justify presuppositions in the light of more fundamental assumptions, without being capable of ever reaching a final stage, a realm of absolutes.

For many centuries both philosophers and scientists were convinced that the final justification of the assumptions made in scientific research was to be given by philosophy. During that same period in history no sharp distinction between science and philosophy was ever made. After the middle of the nineteenth century science and philosophy grew apart, and it is now generally accepted that some distinction between the two must be made, although there is little agreement on the questions of how one should conceive of the distinction and the grounds on which it ultimately rests. Most philosophers and scientists today agree that the sciences constitute a legitimate subject matter for philosophical reflection, but here again there is no universal agreement on the question of how the expression *philosophy of science* is to be understood. According to some, philosophy of science is concerned with all the legitimate problems with which the phenomenon *science* confronts us today. Most authors who write on philosophy of science, however, apply the term in a more limited sense to those reflections that have to do with logical, methodological, and epistemological aspects of the sciences only. Of the latter some will claim explicitly that these are the only problems that should be dealt with in philosophy as far as the sciences are concerned, whereas others will leave room for problems of a more ontological nature that they feel should be dealt with in philosophy but not in philosophy of science proper.

There are philosophers and scientists today who share the opinion that research on the foundations of the sciences is an integral part of each science, and that the thesis that one of the functions and tasks of philosophy of science consists in clarifying and justifying the foundations of the sciences rests on a misconception of the meaning of both science and philosophy. Obviously it does not follow from this view that the historical development of the sciences no longer confronts philosophy with important and fundamental problems; yet these problems have no immediate connection with the *foundations* of the sciences, if the latter expression is understood in a limited and technical sense. According to these authors the sciences themselves are really autonomous, and science and science alone is capable of dealing with its own foundational problems. The problems that the sciences pose to philosophy are of a quite different nature, and all of them center around the basic questions of the meaning and function of science in a man's life: What is science? How does it relate to religion, morality, art? What is the precise relationship between science and action, between science and socio-political praxis? How can one explain the relationship between scientific constructs and the structures of the things they try to explain? What are the implications of the intrinsic historicity of science? Do the sciences have a teleological dimension? In what sense can one speak of progress in science? What are the limits of scientific knowledge? Whereas foundational questions are formulated and examined with the help of mathematical, logical, and methodological procedures in a general epistemology, the latter questions are of a strict philosophical nature and thus cannot be adequately dealt with except on the basis of a general ontology.

The large realm of science is divided and subdivided into a number of relatively independent sciences. Most people make a distinction between three basic domains: the purely *formal* sciences and the empirical sciences, the latter consisting of the *natural* and the *social* or human sciences.

The *formal sciences* consist in mathematics and formal logic. There is no universal agreement as to how these two formal sciences are related to one another, or how they should be distinguished from one another. Both types of sciences are concerned with formal systems, i.e., abstract frameworks in which one can constitute a class of statements (to be formulated in a certain language) on the basis of two kinds of specifications, namely, the specification of a subclass of the class under consideration consisting of the axioms of the system, and the specification of rules for deduction. In view of the fact that all logical and mathematical theories can be presented in the form of such systems, one might perhaps say that both mathematics and logic can be derived from one fundamental discipline or science that is concerned with the study of purely formal systems.

Demonstration occupies a central place in the purely formal sciences. Here nothing will be accepted that cannot be demonstrated on the basis of the chosen axioms and rules of deduction. For many centuries people have believed that these were to be accepted on the basis of immediate intuition. Due to the development of non-Euclidean geometries and the discovery of certain paradoxes, this position has now been abandoned. The only criterion of validity for a formal system still accepted is the principle of noncontradiction, and this is obviously a purely formal principle.

To prove the validity of a purely formal system on the basis of this criterion, one develops the system deductively while making use of absolutely nothing except the axioms of the system and its rules of deduction. One then tries to show that this system cannot lead to a contradiction. In order to do the latter it must be shown that one cannot derive in this system any arbitrary statement. Until now it has been impossible to show the noncontradiction of any known formal system; one had to limit oneself to showing that the known systems do not contain any *known* contradictions. If in the pursuit of this research certain systems appear to imply contradictions, one attempts to resolve them by relevant changes in the axioms or the rules of deduction. One hopes to solve the fundamental problem eventually through a more careful study of the concept of formal derivation and the logical mechanisms that give rise to contradictions (logic of natural deduction and combinatory logic).

Many people today are convinced that it is impossible to explain the mode of functioning as well as the mode of progression in the realm of the purely formal sciences merely by means of logical analyses. Logical analysis is insufficient for dealing with the historicity of the existing mathematical and logical theories, all of which developed over a long period of time in a certain order of succession. The existing formal systems give us, as it were, merely a momentary snapshot of a process and its inherent correlate, which develop on the basis of a kind of necessity that appears to be intrinsic in them. This leads us to the idea that perhaps even in the realm of the formal sciences it is incorrect to speak of an absolute criterion of validity valid for all times; the criteria of validity themselves seem to develop along with the development of the ever-new formal systems. In its historical development this form of theoretical thought is continuously in search of its subject matter as well as its methods. Mathematical entities are not given in advance in a special kind of intuition; they are progressively discovered in a constructive process that is and remains open-ended toward the future. This is the reason why at any stage of its development it can never claim to have secured its validity and the effectiveness of its procedures definitively. Its methods will become more and more precise to the degree that ever new subdomains will be constructed. The principle of non-contradiction merely indicates the limits of what is still acceptable, but it does not indicate positively the direction in which new progress can be accomplished.[8]

In the realm of the *empirical sciences of nature* physics occupies a central place, not only because of the impressive results to which its research has led over the centuries but also because of the fact that physics more than any other empirical discipline shows us in what the typical scientificity of the empirical sciences precisely consists. Contrary to the formal sciences, which discover their own subject matters while constructing them, physical research is oriented toward an external object given in experience, the ontic universe as directly or indirectly given in perception. Physics tries to explain the ontic universe with the help of theoretical constructions that are analogous to those constructed in the formal sciences and that also to a high degree are mathematical in character.

The basic problem encountered in the natural sciences is the question of precisely how these two basic elements, the experimental component and the formal theory, are to be related to one another. The history of these sciences has shown clearly that one cannot account for this relationship in terms of some theory of induction, in that scientific theories are not the result of a generalizing process that takes its point of departure from individual cases. A scientific theory is the result of an intellectual, productive process, which may have been suggested by empirically established relationships or may have been structured with the help of models discovered through experience, but which essentially is independent of experience and is guided by organizing principles of a purely formal nature. But if the theoretical part of an empirical discipline is indeed independent of experience and in this sense a priori, then one must ask the question of how such an a priori construct can be used to explain real physical phenomena.

Many authors, following ideas first suggested by Carnap and other members of the Vienna Circle, believe that this basic problem can be solved by a careful logical analysis of the language of physics. By making a distinction between a theoretical and an observation language and relating these two languages to each other by means of bridge principles of some kind, one can then explain in what sense, how and why, the formal constructs can be employed to explain real physical phenomena. Yet according to others this attempt to solve the basic problem failed because it appeared to be impossible in principle to formulate a criterion of empirical significance, as presupposed in this approach. Thus some authors have tried to avoid the difficulty by assuming that a certain model is to be constructed to mediate between the purely formal structure and the data of observation and experiment. Most recently, however, several authors have pointed in a totally different direction for an answer to this problem.[9]

According to them, almost all classical treatises on the philosophy of *empirical* science have been modeled after metamathematics. Accordingly, scientific theories are taken to be classes of statements; our philosophical reflections should focus on a careful study of the logical relations between the elements of these classes. Yet this approach to empirical science is not very fruitful; this statement-view of empirical theories leads to insurmountable difficulties in regard to theoretical functions; and this approach is totally inadequate as a way of explaining the dynamic aspect of scientific theories with which the history of science is concerned.

Thus it is important in philosophical reflections concerned with theories of empirical science to add a new type of reflection to the commonly used logical ones. These new reflections make use of symbols for model-theoretical entities, i.e., for basic mathematical structures, for the physical systems to which a given structure can be applied, for the class of specific laws, for the class of auxiliary hypotheses, etc. In this "structuralist" approach to theories of empirical science one can then show how the universal and existential statements with which logic is concerned make use of basic mathematical structures and in what sense these mathematical structures can be applied meaningfully to some fragment of the world. In such an approach it can be shown also how the "structuralist" investigations that are mainly concerned with our "knowledge that" should be related to a study of the human activities from which the logically interpreted entities flow; the latter is primarily concerned with our "knowledge how." By using this "structuralist" approach to theories of empirical science it is possible to determine *with precision* the meaning of the claims of certain historians in regard to "paradigms," "normal science," and "scientific revolutions."[10]

The *social* or *human sciences* confront us with a very special problem in that they are concerned with man's individual and social actions, which can be understood genuinely only within the context in which they occur. These contexts are contexts of meaning, so that man's actions and the situations in which they take place cannot be understood properly except by conceiving of them on terms of meaning (*Sinn*). Many philosophers and social scientists are of the opinion that one can legitimately place the meaning of the actions and the contexts of meaning in which they occur between brackets so that from an epistemological, methodological, and logical point of view the social sciences can be put on a par with the natural sciences. Many other authors believe that in so doing one deprives these actions of their genuine meaning.[11]

The discussion concerning the epistemological status of the social sciences has been in progress for many years now. A great number of philosophers and scientists have taken an active part in it. If we limit ourselves for a moment to the actual situation as we find it today, it seems we must make a distinction between at least four major trends in the philosophy of social science. The first is quite commonly found among American social scientists and has been given its most comprehensive and systematic justification in the works of Carnap, Popper, Hempel, Nagel, Rudner, Brodbeck, Rescher, Stegmüller, and many others. A second conception has been suggested by Schutz, Strasser, Natanson, Cicourel, and other phenomenologists who take their point of departure in Husserl's phenomenology. A third trend is to be found in the hermeneutic movement; it has received its clearest expression in the works of authors influenced by the philosophical ideas of Heidegger and Gadamer. A fourth conception of social science is defended by the so-called Frankfurt school and can perhaps be labeled by the expression *critical sociology* (Habermas). The first conception is historically related to the ideas first developed by Mill, Comte, Spencer, and Durkheim. The second view has many aspects in common with ideas developed by Brentano, whereas the third conception originated via Weber in Dilthey's publications. The last view has its origin in a Kantian critique of Marx.

A first fact to be noted here is that these four views were developed in "splendid isolation." Where a serious confrontation of these views has been attempted, the debate has not led to a generally acceptable conclusion. This has been due mainly to misunderstanding and in some instances to lack of firsthand information concerning the most recent literature on the issue. Second, whereas for most protagonists of the first view all *basic* issues have been settled by now, many scholars representing the fourth view argue that at the moment we are not even one step beyond the problematic as found in Dilthey's works at the beginning of the century. It should also be realized that the situation is much more complex than the preceding description may suggest. Actually in each of the four positions there are a number of subdivisions to be added; also the debate concerning the so-called separatist thesis has led to a number of alternative options that run parallel to the four distinctions mentioned.

Among those who defend the first view, many authors argue that the social sciences are empirical sciences in the same sense in which physics is an empirical science. Others hold that the human sciences, contrary to most physical disciplines, are inexact sciences. There are authors who believe that the social sciences indeed are empirical sciences, but in a sense quite different from that materialized in the natural sciences. There are phenomenologists who defend the view that an empirical science of man is impossible and that a phenomenological science of man has to *take its place*; however, there are other phenomenologists who with Husserl defend the view that a phenomenological science of man as a regional ontology is *to be added* to the empirical sciences of man.[12]

Given this extremely complex situation it is not to be expected that a generally accepted solution for these problems will be found in the near future.

The Pluridimensionality of the Nonformal Sciences[13]

For centuries scientists have devoted their efforts to research or teaching in the various branches of learning. While teaching or doing research many of them have reflected upon the meaning and function of their own work. Over the past two hundred years many philosophers have concerned themselves with issues related to the sciences, mainly the epistemological, logical, and methodological issues with which the various sciences confront man. Since the middle of the nineteenth century different trends of philosophy have suggested various solutions for the problems encountered in this vast domain.

Furthermore, a great number of educators, pedagogues, and administrators have always asked questions about when and how to introduce students of various age groups and development to the different branches of learning. Curricula for elementary schools, high schools, colleges, and universities have always to some degree reflected the stage of development of the society for which they were proposed, as well as developments in the realm of scientific research. Although obviously no one has ever denied the historical, social, and political dimension of the sciences, nonetheless these dimensions were not examined systematically and critically for their own sake until the beginning of this century. Since then psychology, sociology, and political science have begun to devote serious attention to the personal, social, and political dimensions present in each science. Philosophers concerned with the sciences have gradually broadened their perspective in order to include these dimensions in their reflections, in addition to the epistemological problems with which they were originally concerned.

Since the middle of the nineteenth century the discoveries made in the sciences have found a wide range of application. The influence of modern technology on man, society, and the environment cannot easily be overestimated. What concerns us in this connection particularly is the influence this development has had on the university. Several new colleges had to be added to those which formerly constituted the university, and literally countless departments and programs were added to the curriculum. This development not only affected the structure of the university but also profoundly changed its meaning and function in society. The interdisciplinary movement has found its most significant application in these new departments and programs.

In the preceding section the epistemological dimension of the sciences was discussed, showing that it is impossible to separate epistemological issues completely from the historical dimension of each science. The following discussion of the social and political aspects of the sciences will include only the nonformal sciences, in view of the fact that the formal sciences are not concerned with real beings but merely with ideal entities which these sciences themselves reveal while constructing them. The influence of these sciences on man and society has been enormous, but this influence has to a very large degree been indirect, i.e., via the empirical sciences.

For many centuries the sciences showed a monarchical organization. They constituted a system of subordinated members under the direction of one leading science. Theology played a leading role for many centuries. It was then displaced by philosophy, which occupied this privileged position in the seventeenth, eighteenth, and nineteenth centuries. During this long period each science in the system affected man and society mainly through the science that functioned as the "queen" in the system. In the nineteenth century the empirical disciplines one by one secured their independence, while trying to recapture the position that theology and philosophy had occupied in the system in the preceding centuries. This process of gradual emancipation is extremely complex, in that it appears to be connected with developments in Western religions and religious institutions, with developments in philosophy since the time of Descartes, with the growing awareness that each science indeed is autonomous, with institutionalization and professionalization in the various branches of learning, witl the application of scientific insights through technology, and thus with the fact that each science has gradually become a sociopolitical force in the development of Western society.

Today this ongoing process is still not fully understood. In some sense it is obviously true that each science is autonomous; yet it is true also that because of the sociopolitical implications (not to mention the basic human implications) of each science, the development of the sciences as well as their application to nature and human society is in need of guidance. Now it is by no means clear where this guidance should come from. One thing, however, is certain: it most certainly cannot come from any one of the sciences, be it physics, sociology, economics, or political science. Nor can it come from philosophy, if the latter be identified with either idealism or scientism. For an idealist philosophy is at root no more than an ideology, which may unite and give direction to some, while dividing and alienating all others; a scientistic philosophy obviously cannot guide the sciences, precisely because it is in itself inherently dependent upon at least one of them, logic, physics, psychology, or sociology. In both instances philosophy is dogmatic, and dogmatism is precisely the opposite of what is at the root of the various autonomous sciences.

Many people will say that this guidance has to flow from the will to gradually further the process of rationalization that should take place in human societies. Yet it is doubtful whether every scientist and every human being today is willing to posit rationality as a goal. But even if all of them were to subscribe to this goal, the view defending it would still not be a very illuminating one. For what does "rationalization" mean? History teaches us that each society of the past has tried to define this general idea in a different way. Furthermore, many people will argue that the goal of all societies and all of the sciences is not the rationalization but the humanization of the members of that society and of all its institutions. But even if one substitutes humanization for rationalization, little is gained, because humanization does not stand for an ideal that can be determined in advance. There was a time when peoples and nations looked toward a religion or a philosophy for the standards by which a so-called ideal society could be conceived of and materialized. But this time has gone. In our contemporary society people no longer share the same religion, nor do they subscribe to the same philosophy. In open societies we know that the humanity of man is to be determined time and again by the human beings who at each moment of time constitute a given society, and live in a world which they find in a situation no longer completely in their power. An open society will be human to the degree that for each era and for each spatial situation, the individuals and the groups have learned to achieve the humaneness of man within the limited possibilities of that situation. It is in that overall perspective that the meaning and function of science is to be determined time and again. In such a society philosophy has no leading function, if by this one means that philosophy should set the goal and determine the means adequate to achieve such a goal. In such a society philosophy limits itself to reflecting upon the experiences after they have been made, in order to understand their genuine meaning by projecting them upon the totality of all possible meaning of which each society at any given moment in time can legitimately conceive. The result of these critical reflections may then illuminate the members of a society and indirectly guide them in setting the society's priorities and establishing the means to materialize them.

As for the natural sciences, including biology, most people will still maintain today that in principle they are primarily concerned with the advancement of theoretical knowledge. Currently there is a very close relationship between science and technology, not only in the sense that science makes technology possible, but also in the sense that technology has become an integral part of the sciences. Furthermore, most people will still defend the view that the natural sciences occupy a socially neutral position, in the sense that they do not immediately serve a political institution, a nation, or a particular class. Yet here too the development of each science depends to a high degree upon the society to which the scientists engaged in these sciences belong. In our contemporary society the natural sciences find themselves in a delicate position: on the one hand, there is an effort to defend the autonomy of scientific research; on the other hand, most research has become so dependent on technology and the cooperation of a great number of scientists and so extremely expensive that it can only be undertaken with funds made available by either government or by industry. Usually both government and industry will promote those research projects which immediately serve their own causes, so that the autonomy of the sciences appears to be jeopardized.

It has been suggested that in this case a distinction should be made between scientific research proper and the conditions and circumstances under which it develops. One could then say that the sciences should maintain full autonomy in regard to the former, while negotiating their position in regard to the latter. Yet it is difficult to see what is gained by means of such a distinction. The fact is that basic research is no longer guided by a goal intrinsic to scientific research itself, namely, the advancement of our theoretical knowledge, but by extrinsic factors connected with priorities and goals of either government or industry.

Others have argued that the view according to which the natural sciences are or should be autonomous merely refers to an ideal that never has been materialized and never will be; thus basically this view is no more than a myth. The reason for this opinion is that there always have been a great number of extrascientific factors (religious, philosophical, personal, social, professional, economical, political) that have promoted some kinds of research while preventing others either from being developed or accepted. Given this necessary state of affairs, these people argue, a new science should be developed to help society determine which large research projects should be promoted, what priorities are to be established, and how much funding at any given time will be made available to each project selected. In their opinion this is the only way to make sure that a nation's research policies will remain rational, reasonable, and humane. It is in connection with these reflections that expressions such as politics of science, research politics, and *Wissenschaftspolitik* have been created. The basic concern of those who devote themselves to these problems is to prevent the natural sciences from becoming the "slaves" of military and economic speculation, and to make certain that they will continue to play a leading role in a society's genuine emancipation.

In the social or human sciences the situation is much more complex. We have seen already that today there is no common agreement on the epistemological status of these sciences. But let us assume for a moment that the basic problems involved here could be solved to everyone's satisfaction. The question of precisely what is the meaning and function of these sciences in regard to society would still remain.

In the period between the two world wars there was a widespread movement defending the view that all social and political problems can and should be solved by carefully planned applications of the insights of the social sciences to those problems. Yet although many have defended social technocracy, most scientists and philosophers maintain that contrary to popular misconceptions justified in part by the early history of the social sciences, and partly by the claims made by nineteenth-century positivism, social science does not have as its objective the determination or modification of social values, the proposal of reforms, the design and administration of welfare programs, or the direct promotion of a better social order, and most certainly not the establishment of society's goals and priorities. These are obviously very important objectives, but they are the task of the citizens, the politicians, administrators, legislators, educators, social workers, clergymen, and labor leaders. Social science is, strictly speaking, concerned only with the pursuit and foundation of theoretical knowledge about man and society. In this type of knowledge, which comprises generalizations drawn from empirically verified investigations of social phenomena, the social scientist strives to understand these phenomena, to explain them, and to achieve some reasonable predictions about them. However, according to other authors, both these conceptions are unacceptable in that both rest on a misunderstanding of the relationship between theory and praxis on the one hand and between science and philosophy on the other. In their opinion the progressive refinement of technological and managerial rationality tends to eliminate the public discussion of practical political issues by the citizens, although such a discussion has been the basic premise of the classical democratic doctrine. Today public affairs (including the decision about priorities in regard to scientific research) are increasingly controlled by specialized elites merely interested in technical efficiency; thus the role of the citizens has been reduced to the decision between alternative administrative suggestions made by teams of specialists.

And so in regard to the social sciences we find ourselves in a situation in which there is neither common agreement on the epistemological status of these sciences, nor on the questions involving their social and political meaning and function.

Each science has its inherent educational dimension. In our Western world the development in the realm of the sciences has been reflected gradually in the way we educate and train the younger generation, as well as in the manner in which we structure the various institutions of learning, from elementary schools to universities. Formerly the task of educator and administrator was in principle relatively simple; one introduced the students gradually to almost everything that was known at the time. Today it is totally impossible for one human being to know everything that has been discovered in the various sciences. Thus for each given discipline one must decide precisely what is to be taught, when, and in what order.

Formerly there seldom was a great difference between a well-educated man and a well-trained scholar. Today, particularly at the college and university level, it is becoming more and more difficult to know how to educate someone well, while training him for scientific research in the field of his choice. In former times people were educated while they were being prepared to be able to engage in independent and creative research in a given field. Today more and more people enter the various institutions of higher education asking to be prepared for the profession or vocation of their choice. Where formerly the university created well-educated scholars, today the university must also prepare people for a vocation or profession, the standards of which are no longer determined by the university. In the past, colleges and universities were erected by churches or governments. The goal to be achieved by the educational process as well as the means by which this goal was to be accomplished were largely determined by the sponsoring bodies.

Now this is no longer universally the case, and it is particularly true that in colleges and universities supported by governments that defend democracy, the institutions of higher education are left without guidelines in regard to goals and means. In former days higher education was enormously selective and elitist; today most colleges and universities admit great numbers of students regardless of creed, class, race, and even background knowledge. Today many students do not come to an institution of higher learning with the intention of earning the highest degree in a given field. Many of them leave the university after a few years with or without a certificate or a degree of some kind.

From these reflections it will be clear that both educators and administrators find themselves confronted with enormous problems for which they have to have a solution, although the possible answers are still heavily debated. What we know is that as far as almost all of the important issues connected with the sciences are concerned, there is no universal agreement, and that this lack of agreement does not have its root in ignorance, bad faith, or lack of interest, but flows necessarily from the complexity of the issues themselves.

Given this state of affairs, educators as well as administrators tend to try to maintain a status quo, particularly in view of the fact that any change one wishes to suggest involves dealing with issues that are still debated and legitimately debatable. Yet on the other hand it is obvious that educational procedures and administrative patterns developed for situations which no longer exist must be changed if our institutions of higher learning are to fulfill their basic function.

The Humanities[14]

To this point virtually nothing has been said about the humanities. And yet, according to one conception of interdisciplinarity, the humanities are central to all genuinely interdisciplinary effort. The meaning of the term *humanities,* then, must be defined here and their function with respect to interdisciplinary activities must be clarified.

There is abundant literature on the humanities dealing with their cultural, philosophical, educational, historical, administrative, social, and political aspects. Here, however, I shall limit my remarks to what is immediately pertinent to the problems addressed in this book.

It is difficult to determine today what the expression *the humanities* precisely signifies. In addition, many believe at present that the humanities are confronted with very serious problems. Obviously, everyone knows that to speak of the humanities is to speak of literature, the fine arts, history, rhetoric, and philosophy, and not of mathematics, physics, biology, or any other science. Yet this common agreement notwithstanding, it remains difficult to determine what the term *humanities* precisely means, in view of the fact that part of the work which people who engage in the various disciplines of the humanities actually do is qualified as scientific. Many scholars therefore suggest that it is not correct to try to determine the meaning of the expression either by circumscribing a certain subject matter or by indicating methods to be used in dealing with a given subject matter.

Furthermore, there are two historical factors which have often made a proper understanding of the primary concern of the humanities rather difficult. In the Latin language since Cicero's time the word *humanitas* has had a normative function. It has been used for the qualities, dispositions, and modes of behavior that human beings should develop in themselves in order to behave humanely. And over the centuries there have been a number of authors who have maintained that the humanities have an immediate function in regard to the development of the *humanitas* in man. Since the early Middle Ages the humanities have concerned themselves predominantly with Latin (and Greek) literature and philosophy. As a consequence it has often been said that a concern with classical antiquity is one of the basic characteristics of the humanities. Most authors today no longer subscribe to either of these views. It does not seem to be correct to link the humanities closely to any conception of humanism or to hold that the humanities' concern should be identified with the concern of classical philology. Yet, as will be shown, it is not correct either to deny that the humanities have some kind of normative function or to argue that concern with classical antiquity should be excluded from the concern of the humanities.

A number of people today believe that the humanities are in serious difficulty. At first it is hard to understand why this could be so. The humanities have always had a central position in higher education since the time of Cicero, if not since the days of Socrates. In addition, many philosophers, historians, authors, and critics have presented impressive arguments from which precisely the opposite thesis seems to follow, namely that the humanities must have a central part in every educational setting. Upon closer inspection it becomes clear that the alleged difficulty is connected with the contemporary notion shared by many, that the function of the humanities can and should be taken over by the social sciences. Many contemporary humanists, however, believe that this view is unfounded.

In an attempt to unravel some of these problems, in the sections to follow I shall make a few observations on the history of the humanities, discuss the actual situation of the humanities in higher education today, and conclude with some critical observations that attempt to relate the entire discussion to the interdisciplinarity issue.

Some Historical Observations[15]

The term *humanities* is derived from the educational program which Cicero introduced under the general heading *humanitas*. Cicero was concerned mainly with the education of the ideal orator; Gellius, on the other hand, identified *humanitas* with the Greek conception of *paideia*, the liberal education used in preparing a free man for manhood and citizenship. The Greek notion of *paideia* was then reformulated by other Roman authors and gradually developed into a basic educational program. Augustine and other Christian writers adapted the program to the fundamental ideas of Christianity. This new program then became the foundation for education in the early Middle Ages. The term *humanities*, however, gradually fell from use and was replaced by the expression *artes liberales*.

In the fifteenth century the Italian humanists revived the term *humanities*, suggested by Cicero, and introduced the distinction between the *studia divinitatis* and the *studia humanitatis*, the latter including grammar, rhetoric, poetry, history, and moral philosophy. All of these subjects were studied in the Latin language, and the *studia humanitatis* focused almost exclusively on the Greek and Latin civilizations.

In subsequent centuries the study of Greek and Latin and knowledge of the ancient literatures of the Mediterranean remained an essential element of education. During that period the expression *the humanities* became practically identical with humanistic scholarship and classical philology. It was mainly through the discovery of new continents and new civilizations, as well as the development of science and technology, that it became gradually clear that although knowledge of the classical tradition remains an important element in the education of Western man, nonetheless it is true also that a well-educated person cannot limit himself to a careful study of classical antiquity alone. The French Encyclopedists criticized the classical conception of the humanities severely; yet the program of classical studies continued to provide the basis for the liberal education of the eighteenth and nineteenth centuries in Europe as well as in the New World. Those who were engaged in teaching the humanities thought that their task consisted in educating younger people in the best that had been thought, said, and done about almost all of the great concerns of man, and that (in the West) the program of classical studies should have a privileged position in these efforts.

The Humanities in the Twentieth Century[16]
In the first part of the twentieth century the entire educational system of the West underwent a profound change that was to lead to our contemporary conception of education and the place the humanities have in this much larger whole. Several factors influenced this enormous change. First of all, there is the proliferation of our scientific knowledge. Although people such as Leibniz and Kant were still familiar with virtually everything known at that time, today it is impossible to know everything, even in one isolated province of learning. Second, our advanced knowledge in the various fields demands specialization. Thus each university must determine precisely how each student is to be introduced to the various subjects of learning in view of the limited time that each person remains within the university setting. Third, there is the development of the behavioral and social sciences, which at first sight seem to be concerned with the same subject matter as the classical humanities. Thus the distinction between the humanities and the social sciences has become problematic and has been ardently debated. Fourth, the university has become an institution that is primarily professionally oriented. Students come to the university because they wish to be trained for a professional career and a well-paying job, which will give them pres-

tige and a secure position in society. Most well-paying jobs demand a relatively high degree of specialization in applied science. Thus the university created options and degrees geared toward this need. In most of these options there is not much room for a humanist education. The interaction of these developments, together with other factors, has made the humanities' place within our educational system problematic.

In contemporary American universities the expression *the humanities* refers to a group of disciplines that cannot be included in the divisions of the natural and the social sciences, nor in those disciplines taught in most professional schools. The humanities today comprise history, literature, the fine arts, rhetoric, and philosophy. The term is universally used to refer to one of the administrative divisions of colleges and universities. Most authors believe that the humanities provide a distinct kind of knowledge. However, as for the latter claim, there is no agreement about precisely how this kind of knowledge is to be defined.

We have seen already that some authors have tried to characterize the humanities through reference to their subject matter, whereas others have tried to achieve a similar goal by claiming that the humanities employ a typical kind of analysis and criticism not used by the sciences. Still other authors hold that the humanities are to be distinguished from other disciplines by the kind of experience on which they are based and to which they appeal. And some authors feel that the humanities are to be distinguished by the goals one attempts to reach by engaging in them. By now it is generally accepted that the humanities should not be characterized by reference to either subject matter or method. Furthermore, any reference to a goal to be achieved by the humanities can easily be misunderstood, in that one may receive the impression that the humanities try to indoctrinate people. It is quite obvious that if the humanities have a goal at all, it is connected with a quest for the liberation of man, certainly not for his enslavement.

In the early Middle Ages most authors were concerned primarily with creating a harmonious unity between Christianity and the classical conception of *paideia*. In the Renaissance an attempt was made to make a clear distinction between Christianity and what was then believed to be the essence of the genuinely human. In the nineteenth century, when the distinction between the humanities and the social sciences had not yet been made explicitly, a proper demarcation between the humanities and the *natural* sciences was sought. The humanities were then no longer conceived of as the basis of an educational program, but rather as a fundamental dimension of our world of knowledge (Dilthey, Rickert, Cassirer, etc.). In the twentieth century, on the other hand, many authors have tried to determine the relation between the humanities and the *social* sciences.

According to some contemporary authors there is no basic difference between the humanities and the social sciences. Some believe that the difference between the two must be sought not in subject matter or method but in the direction in which they move in providing analysis, description, and explanation. The sciences are concerned with unity, uniformity, simplicity, and necessity, whereas the humanities stress creativity, novelty, originality, and uniqueness. The humanities focus on those aspects of human experiences which cannot be accounted for fully by the natural processes and social forces or structures studied by the various sciences, namely, the meaning and value of human achievement. In view of the fact that the humanities themselves are not primarily concerned with certainty and truth but try to evoke wonder and admiration, they are normative as well as descriptive (Ronald Crane).

Others are of the opinion that the distinction between the humanities and the sciences consists in the fact that they stress different dimensions or functions of language. The sciences are to be characterized by a language that is designative and cognitive, the humanities by a language which tends toward the expressive and evaluative (William T. Jones).

In both these views, the general-arts theory and the language-function theory, it is not denied that there is some distinction between the humanities and the behavioral and social sciences; yet it is believed that this distinction is not radical and basic, in that the humanities and these sciences are complementary to each other and must supplement each other.

According to other authors there is a *radical* difference between the humanities and the sciences. Some defend this difference on the ground that the world of learning must be divided into the humanities or arts on one side and the sciences on the other; the humanities consist of the fine arts, concerned with making, and the liberal arts, concerned with learning; the sciences, on the other hand, are to be divided into natural and social sciences; both are concerned with explanation, prediction, and control. The distinction between the arts and the sciences reflects a basic split within the structure of the human mind. The sciences are the expression of rational understanding, whereas the arts are the work of the imagination. Where the sciences employ concepts such as fact, law, theory, prediction, cause and effect, and communicate their insights through an impersonal, referential, and objective language, the humanities use concepts such as appearance, reality, destiny, free will, happiness, peace, the good, or tragedy, expressed in a language that is dramatic, emotional, and purposive (Albert W. Levi).

Others have tried to clarify the basic difference between the humanities and the sciences by means of a distinction between the natural world and the world of the sciences and correlatively between a natural logic and a scientific logic, each of which flows from a different kind of experience (H.B. Veach).

Yet all of these differences notwithstanding, the authors involved agree unanimously on the role and function of the humanities in higher education. In their view the humanities constitute the basis of a general and liberal education, which as nonvocational and nonprofessional aims at the maturation of the person as individual and as citizen. Literature is, according to many, still the core of the humanities. Its focus is no longer exclusively on the classical languages and their literatures. Today the mother tongue occupies the central position; sometimes other living languages and their literatures are added; in a very few instances the classical languages are still included in the humanities programs in the United States. New methods and new affinities with other disciplines have been discovered and applied. In addition, many works of other languages and cultures are used in translations. The traditional pattern set by the study of the classics is maintained, so that the works studied today include all the "great books" of Western civilization from Homer to contemporary authors, comprising literature in the narrow sense, as well as philosophical, political, and religious works. These works are studied because of significance of content and distinction of expression as well as their aesthetic qualities. In this study of the great books the stress is not on specialization in a particular field or era, but rather on the general education that flows from a close contact with the great works of the past.

In some universities the humanities are no longer taught by the various academic departments; instead, unified courses or programs in the humanities are being offered as a better way of meeting the real needs of the students. In view of the fact that these courses require specially trained teachers, in some instances interdisciplinary graduate programs in the humanities have been created to prepare teachers for undergraduate teaching in the humanities.

Critical Reflections: The Humanities and Interdisciplinarity
We have seen that the expression *the humanities* refers to a group of
educational disciplines that aim toward the maturation of the person
both as an individual and as a citizen. The humanities include concern with languages, literatures, the fine arts, history, rhetoric, and
philosophy. All of these disciplines have in common that they try to
acquaint a student with his cultural heritage and help him find an
appropriate response or attitude in regard to it.

We have also seen that today the humanities are confronted
with serious difficulties. These problems seem to flow from three
different but somehow related sources. The question of what is to be
understood by the humanities, and of what their precise educational
function should be, has become problematic because, as far as subject matter is concerned, the humanities appear to overlap with some
of the behavioral and social sciences. Regardless of how one resolves
this first difficulty, there is and remains the problem that those who
teach the humanities for the most part were trained as scientists and
not specifically as teachers of the humanities. Third, in most universities today the same courses in the humanities are offered to students who will eventually major in one of the humanities or the
parallel social sciences as to those students who major in other non-
related fields.

As for the first problem, the relationship between the humanities on the one hand and theology, philosophy, and some sciences on
the other has always been somewhat paradoxical. This has been so at
least since the time of the Renaissance. In addition, what we now call
the humanities has never had an exact and strict antecedent in the
past. The Greek *paideia* included virtually everything known scientifically at that time to the degree that this scientific knowledge was
thought to be relevant to the education of the citizens. In those days
there was no strict opposition between the humanities and the sciences. The classical liberal arts in the Middle Ages included mathematics, astronomy, and musical theory, but not what we now call
history. The *studia humanitatis* of the Renaissance focused on a return to the classical civilizations of the Greeks and the Romans; the
idea of *humanitas* was then closely affiliated with a definite conception of humanism. Today neither one of these conceptions is still
viable. All of this suggests that the concept of *paideia* valid for our
own world cannot simply be derived from the interpretations given
to it in preceding centuries, but in each epoch is to be redefined
repeatedly in light of the actual needs inherent in each historical
situation.

If one tries to specify the educational value of the humanities for our own situation in the twentieth century in the United States, we find that the task is complicated by factors that were not operative in preceding centuries. First of all, we are now confronted with the results of an enormous increase in scientific knowledge. Connected with this are the proliferation of disciplines and the need for specialization. Further, specialization in any given discipline has become so time-consuming that there is often not enough room in a student's curriculum for a humanist education. Finally the distinction between the humanities and some of the behavioral and social sciences has become problematic, as we have mentioned before.

Thus, although it is correct to say that the humanities include concern with languages, literatures, the fine arts, history, rhetoric, and philosophy, one must realize also that *not every* concern with languages is humanistic in character, that a humanist concern with the tradition must be distinguished from a scientific concern with the past, and that philosophy may very well have a function that goes beyond the concern of the humanist. To resolve part of the problem it has been suggested to articulate clearly the distinction between the humanities and the corresponding scientific disciplines, not with reference to subject matters, which in many cases they have in common, but with reference to their respective intentionalities and functions. Once this distinction is made, one can then make a second distinction between the intrinsic intentionality and function of the branches constituting the humanities and the *complex* intentionality of the work that people who are concerned with the humanities actually do. The assumption underlying the latter suggestion is that the work humanists actually engage in often consists of different components, some more scientific in the strict sense of the term, some more educational, some more "philosophical," and some typically humanistic in the limited sense. Once these distinctions have been made, it may then be possible to define what the expression *the humanities* precisely stands for by specifying the guiding idea and function of the humanities unambiguously.

On the basis of these distinctions one could then say that the humanities' primary concern is with the mediation of the tradition. The aim would be to have everyone belonging to a tradition have a genuine experience with that tradition, to help people find an authentic stance in regard to that tradition by means of critical reflection, and to increase the capacity for expression and response. Levi once expressed the same idea succinctly by stating that the aim of the humanities is to help people to think critically, to communicate successfully, and to walk proudly with their tradition. To think critically is the aim of the humanist's concern with philosophy; to communicate successfully is the goal of his concern with languages and literatures; and to walk proudly with one's tradition is the most formidable task of his concern with history.[17] As inheritors of a certain way of thinking, of literary works, and of certain sociopolitical experiences dating in the Western world from somewhere around 700 B.C., people in this world must be able to see their lives in relation to the lives of their forebears; this presupposes accurate knowledge of that tradition, the possiblity of critical reflection, and the capacity for accurate articulation and expression. Thus the problems that the humanities attempt to solve are rooted in the deepest needs and perplexities of the human person who finds himself a member of a long tradition, when he searches in it for his own identity, faces the challenges of communal existence, seeks to ground meaning and value in a world that is much broader than the limits of his own personal horizon, and tries to make a positive contribution to the dialogue between himself and his contemporaries. The humanities respond to each individual's need for orientation in regard to his cultural heritage, reasonableness through critical reflection, and human expression. To this complex end they confront modern man with the great works of the past, literary or otherwise, as well as with the great deeds, actions, and events of which these works bear witness. The task of philosophy is to make certain that everyone familiar with this heritage can find his authentic stance in regard to it, whereas the arts of writing, speaking, and expressing help him to articulate his convictions correctly and to engage in a meaningful dialogue with his peers.

It is assumed here that those who mediate this knowledge and ability do not just tell stories about the tradition and our cultural heritage, but base their explanations and interpretations as well as the grounds for them on scientifically secured data and on careful critical reflection. Yet as teachers of the humanities, their concern is not primarily with this scientific approach to the tradition but rather with facilitating a genuine experience with the tradition. In this way one can explain that the humanities have a concern of their own, which (although in itself not scientific in the limited sense of the term) nonetheless implies engagement in the behavioral and social sciences. A few examples may suffice to clarify this view.

As far as languages are concerned, the humanist is concerned mainly with the art of reading, interpreting, writing, and speaking; yet those who introduce students to this art must make use of insights derived from various linguistic and behavioral sciences. As for literature, the humanists are primarily concerned with the understanding and appreciation of literary works as works of art and of the ideas they suggest; yet most teachers of literary criticism will employ data from various behavioral and social sciences, including history taken as an empirical discipline. History itself has been a cause of great confusion over the past hundred years. In dealing with the tradition the humanist is not concerned with the scientific discovery and explanation of the historical "facts," but with the mediation of the tradition by means of our scientific, historical knowledge of the past. As far as philosophy is concerned, it is not possible here to briefly describe its meaning and function as a humanistic discipline that would be universally acceptable to all those who teach philosophy. Perhaps one could say that, as one of the humanities, philosophy attempts to help people come to a personal and authentic stance in regard to the tradition to which they belong, by introducing them to the great philosophical ideas of the past and to critical reflection.

The grave danger in the demands made upon the humanities still lies in the possible misunderstanding of their role and what this role entails. This misunderstanding is to suppose that the humanities can reach their end by indoctrination concealed as intellectual discipline; this indoctrination will take place when the humanities become separated from the corresponding behavioral and social sciences, as well as in cases in which these sciences are substituted for the humanities. If the humanities are to mold the mind and sensibility of the student and bring an accession of wisdom, it is by virtue of the ideas they present or evoke and the experiences to which they give him entry. And these ideas and experiences achieve their full effect as they are examined critically, evaluated, and made his own by the student.

In order to prevent misunderstanding it is perhaps beneficial to make two assumptions underlying this view somewhat more explicit. First, that the university should produce well-educated human beings, and that a one-sidedly educated scientist is not yet a well-educated person, whether he be specialized in the formal, natural, or social sciences. On the other hand, a one-sidedly educated humanist is not yet a well-educated person either, because today every human being should be able to live a meaningful life in a world which is highly scientific and technological. Today we call a person well-educated if he understands the tradition or the cultural heritage to which he belongs, has some knowledge of other cultures, can express himself clearly and engage in a meaningful dialogue with others, can

understand the works of his tradition and respond to them meaningfully, is familiar with science and technology, has learned to think
critically, and has some field in which he is really well prepared for
either teaching, research, a vocation, or a profession.

The second assumption is that everyone who teaches in one of
the humanities must presuppose and employ a number of insights
made available through one of the sciences. This assumption leads to
many practical difficulties. For although it is true that the distinction
between the humanities and the sciences can be explained by the fact
that in each case the function is quite different, it nonetheless is true
also that most people who teach in the humanities were trained in
departments whose primary concern was scientific and not humanistic. Furthermore, in many universities the humanities are not taught
through a special department, but through programs that depend
for their faculty on members of discipline-oriented departments. In
addition, economy in many institutions dictates that as far as higher-
level courses are concerned, students who take a given course from a
typically humanist and educational concern are placed on a par with
those students who take the same course because it is required for
their major field of study.

This is one of the reasons why teachers who have to teach
courses in the humanities often experience great difficulty in separating the scientific from the humanistic concern. Consequently,
teachers of the humanities often have bored their students to death
with scientific data about Plato, Shakespeare, Newton, or Van
Gogh, instead of helping them to have an experience with their
ideas and works. There also have been teachers of the humanities
who have gone to the other extreme and, disregarding all knowledge made available by the sciences, have engaged in highly questionable forms of interpretation. Those who teach in the arts and
the humanities should be acquainted with insights from the behavioral and social sciences with respect to the people, works, and
materials with which they are primarily concerned as humanists,
and should communicate them to the students. But in so doing the
humanist should not forget his main task, namely, to make certain
that the students are guided to the point where they themselves can
have an authentic experience with their tradition and the great
works it has produced.

I admit that this task will confront the teacher with very specific
problems in each case. In courses of the fine arts the focus should be
on an attempt to help the students come to a genuine understanding
and appreciation of the works of art selected for the courses. Noth-

ing should be added to this, if it does not have a proper place and function within this perspective.

As for history, the humanist is not conerned with making his students professional historians. He too should be concerned with making certain that the students have a genuine experience with the tradition to which they belong. Many historians will have trouble with this suggestion. The scientists among the historians will argue that it is totally unacceptable to use history for the indoctrination of students and the perpetuation or justification of ideologies and false myths. Yet, so the argument goes, this is inevitably the case if the past is mediated in any other way than a scientific one. I am not suggesting that students in the humanities should be indoctrinated, introduced to myths about the past, or steeped in ideologies. The basic concern and aim of the humanities is liberation, not enslavement. But there is a great difference between an attempt to introduce the younger generation to a genuine experience with our tradition through the works of great historians and helping someone develop into a professional historian. The humanist who teaches history should employ the insights made available to him by the science of history.

In dealing with languages, the humanist is concerned first with helping his students to fully master their own language; each student should correctly understand what he hears and reads, be able to express himself clearly in an orderly manner, both orally and in writing. If the humanist introduces his students to a foreign language, be this one of the classical languages or a modern language, his concern is not with making certain that his students can speak these languages. From a humanist point of view it suffices that the students can read the foreign language accurately. The most important task is to help the student to have an experience with the great works of that language. It is clear that no teacher can do so responsibly if he does not know what all the linguistic and historical sciences have to say about that language and its literature. But as a humanist, the language teacher is not concerned primarily with the scientific aspects of a language and its literature but with its proper use and the content of its great works.

Humanists who teach courses in philosophy too should not make the mistake of believing that all students are capable of becoming professional philosophers and philosophy teachers, although they are all capable of learning to think critically about their own experiences. The teacher should explain to his students the great works that the leading philosophers of the past have left us and thus elicit in them the capacity of discovering what is really worth being thought about, as well as the ability to critically reflect upon the experiences that each human being has in light of his tradition.

When the question concerning the relationship between the humanities and interdisciplinarity arises, one should realize that in this case virtually all issues raised are educational and administrative in character. As far as the humanities are concerned the question is not one of whether and how a new "hybrid" branch is to be developed between two existing branches of the humanities. It is rather one of whether or not the humanities should be taught and learned in an interdisciplinary fashion, and if so how this can best be done. Those who are in favor of an interdisciplinary approach to the humanities will have to address the additional problems of where and when this should be done, of the administrative structures that will be necessary, how those who will teach the humanities in this way are to be prepared for this task, and how these teachers are to be recruited. Another question to be addressed by everyone concerned with the humanities is the following: in the process of a student's education taken as a whole, how should exposure to the humanities be combined and integrated with exposure to the formal, natural, and social sciences? A final set of questions that can be asked in this connection is often discussed by interdisciplinarians who are very much concerned about the unity of our worldview, for which the unity of our theoretical knowledge seems to be a necessary condition. It seems to me that one should avoid giving the impression that an all-encompassing, systematic integration of all the branches of knowledge, and particularly of the humanities and the sciences, which would be valid for everyone, could ever take place in an open and pluralistic society. Yet for each individual human being some kind of integration has to take place if he is to live a meaningful life in our world. In my opinion such an integration should not flow from a unitary framework accepted in advance on a priori grounds or, as has often been the case in the past, imposed on either religious, moral, or political grounds. Such an integration is to be brought about through critical reflection, discourse, dialogue, and cooperation. The integration of what we know is not the result of a "system" that someone can hand on to us, but something we all shall have to work towards. It seems to me that the university must prepare its students for this quest toward integration and unity. This can be done by making certain that all students are properly introduced to both the sciences and the humanities. When later, in the real life of society, serious social problems are to be solved, our graduates should be prepared to suggest scientifically feasible and humanistically respectable solutions on the basis of a dialogue in which both scientists and humanists can have a meaningful part.

Summary and Conclusions

In this chapter I have tried to describe briefly the basic contours of the scene in which to a great extent the debate about interdisciplinarity takes place. First, I have argued that the term *discipline* has an educational connotation, and that it thus is to be expected that the discussion about interdisciplinarity (predominantly although not exclusively) is one between people concerned with higher education, either as researchers, teachers, or administrators.

Second, I have suggested making a distinction in the literature between discussions about the formal, natural, and social sciences, and that this distinction is relevant for the debate on interdisciplinary issues. Third, I have argued that in each discipline one should pay attention to its research, educational, and administrative aspects. In the literature some people are concerned with interdisciplinary research projects, others with educational or administrative innovations. Finally I have pointed to the fact that the humanities play a very typical part in our educational system and that for that reason the term *interdisciplinarity* has received a special connotation not found in the natural and social sciences.

In the preceding pages I have purposely stressed the fact that our entire theoretical framework has become enormously complex and that this complexity confronts all those who are concerned with research, education, and administration with problems for which we still do not yet have universally acceptable solutions. These problems range from questions of a purely theoretical nature to questions concerning the political and social implications of science and its practical applications. First there are the problems connected with the enormous increase of available knowledge, which makes it impossible for one man to know everything. Anyone who devotes himself to study and research will have to select carefully what seems necessary to achieve a certain goal, and in most cases such a selection is beset with serious difficulties. Then there are the problems connected with the specialization, professionalization, and departmentalization of the sciences. One of the consequences of this development has been that the relationships among the various provinces of learning have become problematic. Third, there are the grave problems connected with the question of when, how, and to what extent our available knowledge is to be taught from elementary to graduate school. Fourth, there are the problems created by the application of scientific knowledge; these problems pertain to the effect of science and technology upon our own lives and upon our environment. Finally there are the administrative problems connected with the question of how the contemporary university should be structured to effectively meet the most pressing needs of our time.

Given the fact that our entire intellectual framework is affected by these problems, it would be unfair to carry the frustration caused by this over to the work done by those who on good grounds argue in favor of precisely defined forms of interdisciplinary research, interdisciplinary educational innovations, or perhaps even for the need for developing new university structures and units which may be better equipped to effectively deal with the important problems at hand.

Obviously a thorough discussion of interdisciplinary issues will encounter a number of difficulties that flow from quite different sources, such as the methodological problems inherent in all non-disciplinary work, the disciplinary structure of most universities, the complexity of administrative rearrangements connected with any change in higher education, as well as the organizational inertia which has defeated so many innovative ideas. The most important of these problems will be discussed in the chapters to follow.

A number of promising suggestions have been made in the growing literature on interdisciplinarity that relate to the issues discussed in this chapter. The importance of these suggestions can be fully appreciated only if these ideas are evaluated from the perspective of our entire theoretical framework. Only within that perspective is it possible to establish in each case the precise meaning of the theses argued for and the validity of the arguments presented in favor of them, to sharply delineate the field to which the claims made appear to apply, and to judge the value of the ideas suggested within their proper confines. Our theoretical and educational efforts will not be served by vague ideas, platitudes, and unfounded promises; nor will they be served either by criticism that is not to the point.

Notes

1. For what follows here in the first three sections in general cf.: *The Oxford English Dictionary* (Oxford: Oxford University Press, 1971); *Webster's Third New International Dictionary* (Chicago: William Benton, 1966); R. Eisler, *Wörterbuch der philosophischen Begriffe*, 3 vols. (Berlin: S. Mittler & Sohn, 1930); J. Ritter, *Historisches Wörterbuch der Philosophie* (Stuttgart: Schwabe, 1972); F. Selvaggi, "Scienza," in *Enciclopedia Filosofica*, Vol. 5 (Florence, 1967), col. 1151–64; *The Encyclopedia of Philosophy*, 8 vols. (New York: Free Press, 1967); Jerome R. Ravetz, "History of Science," in *Encyclopedia Britannica*, Macropedia, vol. 16 (Chicago, 1974), pp. 366–75; S. E. Toulmin, "Philosophy of Science," ibid., pp. 375–93; E. Schatzman, "Le statut des sciences," in *Encyclopedia Universalis*, vol. 14 (Paris, 1972), pp. 752–74; J. Ladrière, "Sciences et discours rationnel," ibid., pp. 754–67; M. De Diéguez, "Science et philosophie," ibid., pp. 767–72.

2. A. Antweiler, *Der Begriff der Wissenschaft bei Aristoteles* (Bonn: P. Haustein, 1936).

3. Cf. *The Works of Francis Bacon*, ed. J. Spedding, R.L. Ellis, and D.D. Heath, 7 vols. (London: Hurd & Houghton, 1857–1859), 1; *The Works of Descartes*, trans. E.S. Haldane & G.R.T. Ross, 2 vols. (New York: Dover Publications, 1931), 1; Elie Denissoff, "La nature du savoir scientifique selon Descartes, et l'*Histoire de mon esprit*, autobiographie intellectuelle," in *Revue Philosophique de Louvain* 66 (1968): 5–35.

4. Immanuel Kant, *Prolegomena and Metaphysical Foundations of Natural Science*, trans. E. Belfort Bax (London: G. Bell & Sons, 1883), pp. 137–49; cf. *Critique of Pure Reason*, trans. Norman Kemp Smith (New York: St. Martin's Press, 1965), pp. 9, 18, 93–94, 102, 626, 653–65.

5. Kant, *Prolegomena*, pp. 137–38.

6. H.I. Marrou, "Les Arts libéraux dans l'antiquité classique," in *Arts Libéraux et philosophie au moyen âge*. Actes du Quatrième Congrès International de Philosophie Médiévale (Paris: Vrin, 1969), pp. 5–27; Gérard Mathon, "Les formes et la signification des arts libéraux au milieu du IXe siècle (Jean Scot Erigène)," ibid., pp. 47–64; Margaret T. Gibson, "The Arts in the Eleventh Century," ibid., pp. 121–26; Philippe Delhaye, "La place des arts libéraux dans les programmes scolaires du XIIIe siècle," ibid., pp. 161–74; James Weisheipl, "The Place of the Liberal Arts in the University Curriculum during the XIVth and XVth Centuries," ibid., pp. 209–14; H.I. Marrou, " 'Doctrina' et 'Disciplina' dans la langue des pères de l'église," *Arch. Lat. Med. Aev.* 9 (1934): 5–25; cf. Richard McKeon, "Character and the Arts and Disciplines," *Ethics* 16 (1968): 109–23.

7. Jean Ladrière, "Sciences et discours rationnel," in *Encyclopedia Universalis*, vol. 14 (Paris, 1972), pp. 754–67. Cf. Joseph J. Kockelmans, *The World in Science and Philosophy* (Milwaukee: Bruce Publishing Company, 1969); *Philosophy of Science: The Historical Background* (New York: Free Press, 1968); Gerard Radnitzky, *Continental Schools of Metascience* (Göteborg: Akademiförlaget, 1968).

8. H.B. Curry, *Foundations of Mathematical Logic* (New York: McGraw-Hill, 1963); H.B. Curry and R. Feys, *Combinatory Logic* (Amsterdam: North

Holland Publishing Company, 1958); S. Körner, *The Philosophy of Mathematics: An Introductory Essay* (London: Hutchinson University Library, 1960); Jean Ladrière, *Les Limitations Internes des Formalismes* (Louvain: Nauwelaerts, 1957); "Mathematics in a Philosophy of the Sciences," trans. Theodore J. Kisiel, in Joseph J. Kockelmans and Theodore J. Kisiel, *Phenomenology and the Natural Sciences* (Evanston: Northwestern University Press, 1970), pp. 443–65; "Mathematics and Formalism," trans. Theodore J. Kisiel, ibid., pp. 466–99; Jean Cavaillès, *Méthode axiomatique et formalisme: Essay sur le problème du fondement des mathématiques* (Paris: Hermann, 1938); "On Logic and the Theory of Science," trans. Theodore J. Kisiel, in *Phenomenology and the Natural Sciences*, pp. 353–409.

9. Wolfgang Stegmüller, *Probleme und Resultate der wissenschaftliche und analytische Philosophie*, 4 vols. (Berlin: Springer Verlag, 1969–75), particularly vol. 1 (*Wissenschaftliche Erklärung und Begründung*) and vol. 2 (*Theorie und Erfahrung*). To my knowledge these books contain the most comprehensive discussion of the basic ideas developed by Carnap, Braithwaite, Oppenheim, Hempel, Nagel, Campbell, Hanson, Scheffler, Toulmin, Popper, Lakatos, Suppes, Goodman, etc. Cf. Joseph J. Kockelmans, "Stegmüller on the Relationship Between Theory and Experience," in *Philosophy of Science* 39 (1972): 397–420.

10. Wolfgang Stegmüller, *The Structure and Dynamics of Theories*, trans. W. Wohlhueter (New York: Springer Verlag, 1976). This book contains a thorough discussion of the ideas developed by Kuhn, Lakatos, Musgrave, etc.

11. For a discussion of the vast literature on this topic see Leonard I. Krimerman, *The Nature and Scope of Social Science: A Critical Anthology* (New York: Appleton-Century-Crofts, 1969); see the literature quoted there, pp. 759–75.

12. For the various trends distinguished here the publications to follow may perhaps be representative: May Brodbeck, ed., *Readings in the Philosophy of Social Science* (New York: Macmillan, 1968); Olaf Helmer and Nicholas Rescher, "Exact vs. Inexact Sciences: A More Instructive Dichotomy," *Management Science* 6 (1959): 25–52; Stephan Strasser, *Phenomenology and the Human Sciences* (Pittsburgh: Duquesne University Press, 1963); Peter Winch, *The Idea of Social Science* (New York: Humanities Press, 1958); Rudiger Bubner, Konrad Cramer, and Reiner Wiehl, eds., *Hermeneutik und Dialektik*, 2 vols. (Tübingen: Mohr, 1970); Jürgen Habermas, *Zur Logik der Sozialwissenschaften* (Tübingen: Mohr, 1967). Cf. Joseph J. Kockelmans, "Toward an Interpretative or Hermeneutic Social Science," *Graduate Faculty Philosophy Journal* 5 (1975): 73–96.

13. Cf. Karl Popper, "Selbstbefreiung durch das Wissen," in L. Reinisch, ed., *Der Sinn der Geschichte* (Munich: Beck, 1961); *The Open Society and Its Enemies* (London: Routledge & Kegan Paul, 1963); J. Habermas, *Technik und Wissenschaft als "Ideologie"* (Frankfurt: Suhrkamp, 1968); *Strukturwandel der Öffentlichkeit. Untersuchungen zu einer Kategorie der bürgerlichen Gesellschaft* (Neuwied: Luchterhand, 1962); *Theorie und Praxis: Sozialphilosophische Studien* (Neuwied: Luchterhand, 1967); *Erkenntnis und Interesse* (Frankfurt: Suhrkamp, 1968); J.D. Bernal, *The Social Function of Science* (Cambridge, Mass.: MIT Press, 1965); J.R. Ravetz, *Scientific Knowledge and Its Social Problems* (Oxford: Clarendon Press, 1971); J.J. Salomon, *Science and Politics*, trans. N.

Lindsay (Cambridge, Mass.: MIT Press, 1973); E. Schatzman, *Science et société* (Paris: Presses Universitaires de France, 1971); J. Ellul, *La technique ou l'enjeu de siècle* (Paris: Colin, 1954); H. Schelsky, *Auf der Suche nach der Wirklichkeit* (Düsseldorf: Diederichs, 1965); Hans Lenk, *Philosophie im technologischen Zeitalter* (Stuttgart: Kohlhammer, 1971); J. Meynaud, *Technocracy*, trans. P. Barnes (New York: Free Press, 1969); J. Gould, *The Technical Elite* (New York: A. Kelley, 1966); R.E. Lapp, *The New Priesthood: The Scientific Elite and the Uses of Power* (New York: Harper and Row, 1965); K. Baier and N. Rescher, eds., *Values and the Future: The Impact of Technological Change on American Values* (New York: Free Press, 1969); V.C. Ferkiss, *Technological Man* (New York: George Braziller, 1969).

14. Cf. Werner Jaeger, *Paideia: The Ideals of Greek Culture*, trans. Gilbert Highet, 3 vols. (New York: Oxford University Press, 1939–44); H.I. Marrou, *A History of Education in Antiquity*, trans. George Lamb (New York: Sheed and Ward, 1956); Georges Gusdorf, *Introduction aux sciences humaines* (Paris: Les Belles Lettres, 1960); *Les sciences humaines et la pensée occidentale*, 6 vols. (Paris: Payot, 1966–73); Ernst Robert Curtius, *European Literature and the Latin Middle Ages*, trans. William R. Trask (New York: Pantheon Books, 1953); Jacob Burckhardt, *The Civilization of the Renaissance in Italy*, trans. S.G.C. Middlemore (London: Kegan Paul, 1890); Henri Bremond, *Autour de l'humanisme d'Érasme à Pascal* (Paris: Grasset, 1937); R.S. Crane, *The Idea of the Humanities* (Chicago: University of Chicago Press, 1967); W.T. Jones, *The Sciences and the Humanities* (Berkeley: University of California Press, 1965); A.W. Levi, *The Humanities Today* (Bloomington: Indiana University Press, 1970); H.B. Veach, *Two Logics* (Evanston: Northwestern University Press, 1969); W.C. Booth, ed., *Knowledge Most Worth Having* (Chicago: University of Chicago Press, 1967); C.P. Snow, *The Two Cultures and the Scientific Revolution* (New York: Cambridge University Press, 1963); F.R. Leavis, *Two Cultures? The Significance of C.P. Snow* (London: Chatto and Windus, 1962); Aldous Huxley, *Literature and Science* (New York: Harper and Row, 1963); M.E. Prior, *Science and the Humanities* (Evanston: Northwestern University Press, 1963); Th. M. Greene, ed., *The Meaning of the Humanities* (Princeton: Princeton University Press, 1940); Patricia Beesley, *The Revival of the Humanities in American Education* (New York: Columbia University Press, 1940).

15. G.P. Gusdorf, "Humanistic Scholarship," in *Encyclopedia Britannica*, Macropedia, vol. 8 (Chicago, 1974), pp. 1170–79.

16. Otto A. Bird, "Humanities," ibid., pp. 1179–83.

17. A.W. Levi, "Teaching Literature as a Humanity," *Journal of General Education* 28 (1977): 283–87, 283.

Disciplines and Interdisciplinarity

A Historical Perspective

Wolfram W. Swoboda

One of the difficulties persistently plaguing discussions of interdisciplinarity lies in the area of terminology. Amongst proponents of interdisciplinarity, there is little dispute over the need for an alternative to the present organization and transmission of knowledge, which have become grouped, at least during the past century, mainly along disciplinary lines involving the ever-greater fission of knowledge and its increasing specialization. The barriers between fields of knowledge and between disciplines have not only made it increasingly difficult to survey what is known but have also had more immediately felt detrimental consequences. Since disciplinary, specialized knowledge has come to be applied to a growing number of social problems, these attempts at short-term solutions often engender further problems graver than the ones they have "solved."

The matter thus is not purely academic. For example, the use in agriculture of such pesticides as DDT, while having had the immediate beneficial effect of increasing agricultural production, has been proven to endanger the health of consumers. Since then, and under the impact of the energy crisis of the 1970s, the practice of applying fertilizers and substitute pesticides simultaneously to the soil in order to minimize tillage has been found to be linked to the formation of cancer-producing nitrosamines.[1] Similarly, proposals to deal with smog through the addition to the atmosphere of chemical scavengers have been opposed as producing potential mutagenic or toxic agents.[2] The benefits of fire retardants in children's nightwear are offset by the possible mutagenic effects of the retardants themselves.[3]

All of these instances exemplify the dangers that accrue from dealing with problems from too narrow a point of view. The debates about the long-range consequences of the proliferation of nuclear power, about the limits of research in genetic engineering, and about the causes and effects of depletion of the stratosphere's ozone layer are even more dramatic cases in point. But they involve not merely questions of technology or applied science going astray. They are reflections of a much more fundamental problem that is at the base of how knowledge is organized and transmitted to the practitioners. These and numerous other examples demonstrate that theory and practice cannot be delineated in any simple fashion, for if the side effects of technology could simply be attributed to the shortsightedness of technological practitioners, the scientific theoretician with a presumably broader outlook should be able to intervene to correct or anticipate such problems. This he has clearly been unable to do. Thus what seems to be at stake in all of these cases is not so much a lack of available knowledge as the inappropriateness of attempted solutions, brought about by an overly restricted, specialized perspective: a problem of applied knowledge, which, however, is traceable to its theoretical origins.

Supporters of interdisciplinarity (using this term in a very broad sense) agree that an alternative to the exclusivity of specialized knowledge is urgently needed. The discussions break down, however, when various means come to be considered by which the agreed-upon end is to be accomplished. Part of the difficulty lies in a lack of agreement on what the various forms of interdisciplinarity might be. Even given the possibility of agreement on basic conceptual issues, the implementation of any form of interdisciplinarity will almost inevitably encounter serious obstacles. Robert L. Scott, in his contribution to the present volume, has pointed to the most serious of these.[4] The underlying thrust of Scott's argument is that, to be successful, interdisciplinarians will ultimately have to persuade disciplinarians of the necessity, importance, and validity of the interdisciplinary enterprise. Such persuasion, moreover, will have to be able to counter the inertia of various hidden persuaders that exist within the structure and organization of the disciplines themselves. Scott thereby points to an extremely important aspect of disciplinary knowledge, namely, that it rests on an economic, social, institutional framework that has heretofore been almost totally ignored in discussions amongst interdisciplinarians. These discussions, being carried on for the most part by theoretically oriented academicians, have concentrated heavily on the intellectual content of disciplines, to the neglect of their other important features. Yet that content was not developed in isolation but evolved within a social and institutional context. The terminological confusion about interdisciplinarity, therefore, is to some extent due to the artificially constrained definitions of what constitutes a discipline.

To arrive at a clearer view of the strengths (and weaknesses) of disciplinary knowledge, it is of vital importance not to lose sight of the sociological dimensions of disciplines, nor of the implications that these dimensions have for interdisciplinarity. These factors must be considered in addition to the formal and empirical contents of disciplines. Disciplines are clearly more than merely a collection of texts, monographs, and published research results.

One of the few attempts to deal with concepts of *science* and *discipline* on a broader plane is that of Leo Apostel.[5] By defining these concepts as activities, rather than along lines of their epistemic contents, Apostel adds another dimension to the debate. Unfortunately his conclusions are not very useful, since his basic definitions suffer from overformalization. For example, Apostel defines a discipline by the following indicators:

1. P: a group of persons.
2. A: a set of actions performed by these persons.
3. I: a set of interactions or communications among these persons and to other persons.
4. E: a method of regenerating the set of persons by means of certain communications of an educational nature.
5. L: a set of historic learning methods.[6]

Obviously the difficulty with such a definition is that this quintuplet of indicators is not sufficient to distinguish science from many other human social enterprises (such as most trades) precisely because it has failed to include considerations of *content* in these actions, interactions, or communications, and in the historic learning methods. Consequently one would be hard-pressed to explain, using these indicators alone, why astronomy is still considered to be a scientific discipline, whereas astrology is not. Clearly more is needed.

Second, Apostel's approach, while noting the heterogeneity of even a single present scientific community such as physics wherein "cristallography and plasma physics, electromagnetism and astronomy, are well-defined subcommunities of workers,"[7] fails to notice that such heterogeneity is an evolutionary product of disciplines. Such subcommunities were very rare as recently as a century ago. In consequence of this rather static view, Apostel categorizes Helmholtz as "a physiologist as well as a physicist" and Pavlov as "a neurologist as well as a physiologist," and argues for a basic ability on the part of disciplinarians to cross the boundaries of their specialties.[8] But these instances are not so much examples of the inherent complementariness of present disciplines as they are illustrations of the temporal dimension of specialized knowledge. Apostel has failed to notice that there *were* many important relationships between physics and physiology in the mid-nineteenth century in the first case, and the fact that physiology had just become an independent discipline in Pavlov's time.[9] But the connections that may have joined areas of knowledge in the past do not necessarily imply any relationship between them in the present. Surely the best example of a multidisciplinarian along these lines would be Aristotle, but to use such an example would be to argue implicitly that the organization and structure of knowledge has not changed basically since the ancient Greeks. Worst of all, it is not clear, using Apostel's criteria, whether such important figures as Mendel were scientists at all!

Apostel's typology of sciences, superdisciplines, disciplines, subdisciplines, and interdisciplines results from a neglect of the temporal dimension, which tends to confuse distinctions of *time* with distinctions of *kind*. In order to arrive at a more comprehensive understanding of disciplines and interdisciplinarity, the empirical and formal contents of knowledge, its social organization, and its evolution through time must be kept in focus.

The following analysis does not aspire to be an exhaustive account of these factors, but rather to indicate where the important milestones in the development of disciplinarity are to be found, which must not be disregarded if interdisciplinarity is to be something more than a thing devoutly to be wished.

One might begin by tracing the present organization of knowledge in special and separate disciplines backwards in time in order to illuminate the essential features of its development. On this basis it may then be possible to see more clearly a concrete context for modern interdisciplinarity.

Joseph Kiger defines *discipline* as a "recognized branch or segment of knowledge within rational learning," with "certain generally agreed upon canons and standards."[10] He suggests that in contemporary America, the criteria for delineating a discipline include: (1) the number of persons interested in and devoted to its study; (2) the relative importance of those persons; (3) the discipline's generally reputed significance in the academic structure; (4) its age; (5) the existence of a national learned society; and (6) membership of such a society in one of the three national councils—the American Council of Learned Societies, the Social Science Research Council, or the National Academy of Sciences. He estimates that by these criteria there exist currently over sixty disciplines.

This, however, does not indicate the real magnitude of the problem of specialization that interdisciplinarians are attempting to counter. The *Guide to Graduate Study* reflects the problem more accurately. In its "Index to Ph.D Programs," one can find over two hundred area programs (including professional training programs), even when one does not distinguish between subareas such as those of biology.[11] It is questionable, for example, whether the recipient of a Ph.D. in arctic biology from the University of Alaska is really a practitioner of the same discipline as the holder of a degree in mathematical biology from Chicago or of radiation biology from Rochester. On the other hand and in actual practice, having certain researchers describe their research project may not give any clues about what discipline they were trained in. Is the scientist investigating certain molecular structures of DNA a molecular biologist, a geneticist, a biochemist, or a quantum mechanic? The educational and scientific institutions that produce very narrow specialists also seem capable of stimulating hosts of multi-, trans-, and interdisciplinary enterprises. The discipline as training program may therefore diverge sharply from the discipline as research frontier. It should be asked whether any very formal and rigorous definition of discipline is a useful precondition for discussions of interdisciplinarity, or whether attempts at such definition do not actually divert us from investigations of more basic issues.

Although the point may seem obvious, it is important to note that discussions centered on interdisciplinarity relate primarily to the *structure* of knowledge and of education. The dialogue implies that educational reform is necessary, particularly at the level of the university. But to a large extent the dialogue is curiously narrow. It is perhaps reflective of the character of the disputants, who are in the main academic disciplinarians, and raises the question of whether the discussions of interdisciplinarity are themselves interdisciplinary in any meaningful sense. Be that as it may, such restricted proposals for interdisciplinarity will surely remain an isolated phenomenon, as long as considerations of reform do not extend to the *functions* of knowledge and of education.

At the latter level, several important issues appear immediately: How did the separation of disciplines and specialties become the basic organizational feature of knowledge and of education? What functions *do* the disciplines and specialties serve? What functions are they *intended* to serve? For that matter, what is the function of the universities themselves? And in asking this last question, one must ask it also of education generally, of which universities are only a last stage. Education obviously does serve as an institution through which the members of society are trained to perform productive tasks for that society. But it also plays a socializing role by instilling acceptable social behavior and by reinforcing conformity in basic values and attitudes. An educational system also plays an ideological role, even one which enshrines objectivity through professionalization and specialization.[12] If disciplines and specialties are products of universities, universities are in turn products of certain kinds of society, and educational alternatives of interdisciplinarity must keep these essential relationships in focus.

The university is a product of the Middle Ages. There had certainly been learning previously, but it had not been organized into permanent institutions. Neither the Greeks nor the Romans had universities, and what we now know as a university had its beginnings in the twelfth century.[13] What is notable about these early institutions is the direct social stimulus that led to their formation. They were not institutions of abstract learning but rather were intended to serve the direct needs of society. The first of these new schools was probably the medical university in Salerno, known at the time as "the city of Hippocrates," and dated back to the eleventh century, although little is known about it until its regulation by the most prominent member of "the Devil's brood" (as the Hohenstauffens were affectionately known in the Papacy), Frederick II.[14]

Initially the university was a loose association of teachers and students—*"bâtie en hommes,"* in Pasquier's words[15]—who extended the curriculum beyond the constraints of the trivium and quadrivium taught at the cathedral schools. These associations came about with a more general political stabilization in Europe, which led to an expansion of commerce and brought with it the rediscovery of the Graeco-Roman classics via the Arab world. The revival of trade and town life also necessitated a restructuring of law and led to the reintroduction of Roman law. Bologna became the center of this revival. In the early Middle Ages legal studies had declined to training in the drafting of documents—a sort of apprenticeship in applied rhetoric. The tradition in which elements of basic Roman law and of the Teutonic tradition had been combined proved insufficient to deal with the demands and circumstances of a new and changing social, political, and economic order. By the middle of the twelfth century, the new university at Bologna had separated the study of law from that of rhetoric and canon law from theology, and had established legal training as an independent subject for professional study. We have in these examples—Salerno and Bologna—the antecedents of what later became two of the traditional faculties at universities: medicine and law.

In both cases the social importance of these new institutions is immediately evident. In the case of the growth of legal studies, the political and economic implications are of course the most important. Indeed this was clearly recognized at the time, and Frederick II founded a rival university to Bologna at Naples so that students from his kingdom would be able to attend a Ghibelline school. Second, even in the very early instance of a division of subjects—law from rhetoric and theology—this embryonic specialization came about due to demands *from without* the educational institutions. We shall later wish to distinguish such developments from those that lead to a division of fields of learning due to the *internal* accumulation and multiplication of knowledge. But these initial forms of specialized learning were expected to yield a direct benefit to society.

The early organizations themselves reflected the nature of the demand for this new training—a demand for knowledge that, at this stage, was clearly to be applied to the problems and institutions of society. In fact, the university as an organization (rather than just a collection) of teachers and students began with the students. The *universitas* was originally organized to serve the special interests of the students and was patterned along the lines of a medieval guild. At Bologna, which by the middle of the eleventh century was already host to several hundred foreign students, these special interest groups were organized into "nations," which sought to regulate not only prices for lodgings and books but also the form and content of lectures and courses of study, going so far as to place their professors under bond, in order to insure that the students got their money's worth.[16] A very special set of restrictions thus came to be placed on the form and nature of such education.

The professors, on the other hand, excluded from these student "universities" and partially as a counter to them, formed their own guilds (*collegium*) seeking to regulate membership in their profession. This meant that students' choices of teachers became restricted to choosing from a closed shop. Amongst other controls, a certification to teach (*licentia docendi*) was initiated, representing the first form of academic degree as well as a means of excluding certain individuals from the profession. Nevertheless these early universities were relatively fluid (not to say chaotic) organizations in which the students' threat of secession proved to be a decisive bargaining element.

In Paris, on the other hand, the university came to be based on the organization of the masters in four faculties: arts, canon law, medicine, and theology. Each of these was placed under a dean and was connected with colleges that had grown out of boarding houses. With this development the university had become a proprietor of real estate, which now exerted a very different form of control over academic membership than had been the case before. The masters who were in control of the educational facilities were freed of the constraints that students had earlier been able to place upon the educational process and were increasingly able to shape the institution to conform to their own needs and wishes. Indeed the University of Paris became the model for northern Europe. Oxford and Cambridge had very close ties to Paris before separating themselves, and most of the German universities were open imitations of the French prototype.[17]

On this basis there evolved what one might call the era of "faculties." All knowledge was structured in broad categories on the basis of Aristotelian logic, and dialectic, syllogism, and disputation represented not only the form by which knowledge was transmitted but also reflected the manner in which it was organized. Knowledge was strictly related to authority and involved the marshaling of arguments in philosophy, law, and theology, and also in what one now thinks of as an empirical science—medicine. The process of learning became strictly hierarchical; in it the concept of "authority" extended from the content of knowledge to the very institutions of higher learning. What is notable is that very few academicians of this period preceding Renaissance and Reformation were censured for deviations from dogma. Haskins thinks that this indicates the extent to which there existed a freedom of inquiry, of learning, and of teaching.[18] It may, however, only illustrate the conformity that these institutions of learning were able to instill in their membership; potential heretics were simply weeded out at the lower levels of this rigid hierarchy.

These institutions remained primarily centers for practical learning. For, although we regard the Middle Ages as the age of theology, in fact the universities produced very few students of theology. This is not to underestimate the influence of the Church on the universities. But that influence was exerted mainly through canon law, since by the thirteenth century the Church had become a vast administrative mechanism that needed lawyers and administrators. The growth of the university movement itself reflects this demand: in the twelfth century six universities were founded; in the thirteenth, eighteen; in the fourteenth, twenty-one; and in the fifteenth, thirty-six new universities appeared. The university became an important social institution, which to some extent allowed for some social mobility in an otherwise very rigid society. Nonetheless, within their own structures the universities reflected that external rigidity, which partially produced the inertia in the formalized institutionalized knowledge they transmitted. Within this framework there developed the concept of academic discipline.

Disciplina originally referred to the instruction of disciples and was contrasted to *doctrina*, pertaining to the doctor or teacher. The disciples necessarily subordinated themselves to the teacher in a strongly hierarchical setting. Doctrines were considered final and given; this system as a whole (even granting important exceptions) was not conducive to the qualitative growth of learning. In fact, the medieval university was replaced as the main carrier of the European intellectual tradition during the scientific revolution of the sixteenth and seventeenth centuries by a new institution, the scientific academy.

The details of the evolution of scientific societies is too well known to warrant reiteration here. However, several points of contrast between universities and scientific societies may be mentioned, to bring aspects of modern disciplines into sharper focus. First, of course, the university was primarily an educational and training institution, rather than one designed for the active pursuit of research. Insofar as members of the medieval university pursued research activities, they did so as a supplement to and not as an integral part of their educational function. Research activities designed to expand the frontiers of knowledge were extracurricular. The training that students received at universities was designed to be applied directly within the social context. Knowledge was fixed in the nexus of doctrine and discipline. Points of disagreement were settled not by drawing on new knowledge but by placing what was already known onto the scales in a disputation. Knowledge tended to become trivialized, as exemplified by the notorious themes for disputations at the universities of the late Middle Ages. How seriously this process was taken may be illustrated by the fact that the second book of Rabelais's *Gargantua and Pantagruel*, which sharply satirized the disputation, was suppressed immediately upon publication, at the insistence of the theological faculty of the University of Paris.

During the period of Renaissance and Reformation, research activities did increase, but such activities took place largely outside of a university context, even when pursued by members of faculties. The university was a hierarchy by tradition; the new scientific societies became hierarchies by achievement. This distinction is reflected very early by members of the different institutions, in the way they viewed the field of knowledge. For example, whereas Zachary Coke lists theology, law, medicine, and philosophy as "the objective disciplines" in *The Art of Logick* (1654),[19] Robert Boyle, in *A Free Enquiry into the Vulgarly Receiv'd Notion of Nature* (1685), enumerates amongst the physicomathematical disciplines "Opticks, Astronomy, Hydrostaticks, and Mechanicks."[20] The distinction in emphasis between these two sets of institutions thus came to be one between what was already known and what could become known. Further, this distinction was sharpened due to the evolution of these institutions of learning within the context of the Counter-Reformation. The universities played an increasingly ideological role, especially in Catholic Europe where they came to be dominated by Jesuits and Dominicans. The numerous scientific academies that had flourished in Italy in the sixteenth century disappeared and the universities became more rigid.[21] For instance, the physics taught at the University of Vienna well into the eighteenth century was neither the Physics of Descartes nor of Newton, but that of Aristotle.[22] As Galileo had prophesied in his *Dialogue on the Great World Systems* (1630), the center of intellectual advance in Europe shifted from the Mediterranean to Northern Europe, where it was initially carried forward by the academies.

Within the evolving structure of academies there was at work not only a different emphasis on knowledge, but the composition of membership was also radically different from that of the universities. Most of the members of the young Royal Society were distinctive because they could *not* advance through the hierarchical university structures.[23] The divergent backgrounds and interests of the members generally worked against any uniformity of approach or specific subjects to be pursued. Limitations in the availability of facilities often tended to restrict the areas of inquiry to special domains—witness the work of a Fahrenheit or of a Leeuwenhoek. Communications of research results through scientific journals tended to promote the progressive accumulation of knowledge about certain special subjects. On the other hand, the academies lacked the means of recruiting new members to their ranks. The assimilation of the new knowledge into existing structures of transmission had obviously to be accomplished by institutions of education.

A slow integration between academy and university did in fact occur during the eighteenth century, especially through the famous medical faculties at the universities of the Low Countries and at newly founded institutions of Germany. The first of the latter, the University of Halle, founded in 1694, came to be organized along nontraditional lines and became the prototype for other German universities. Halle, led at its early stage by Thomasius and Francke, who were followed by Christian Wolf, tried to limit ecclesiastical authority in its functions, opposed a curriculum based on scholastic learning in philosophy and theology, and attempted to balance the ascendancy that the classics had acquired within the traditional curriculum by the introduction of "modern" topics. Lectures in the vernacular were initiated, Cartesianism and rationalism were stressed, and education became generally more secular.[24]

These initial trends set in motion at Halle were amplified and extended at Göttingen's new university founded in 1737. Here the university became not only an educational institution in the traditional sense but also provided the beginnings of research facilities. By the middle of the eighteenth century, for example, Göttingen's library had grown from 60,000 to 200,000 volumes, and its structure included an anatomical institute, a physical-mathematical institute, a botanical garden, a pharmacy, and—most indicative of the new trend—a scientific society.[25] Moreover, these initially isolated examples of modern educational institutions were suddenly transformed by the virtual abolition of their traditional counterparts in the upheavals of the French Revolution and the Napoleonic Wars. Particularly on the Continent, we notice increasingly fluid boundaries among the savant as educator, researcher, government advisor, and minister. This ability to change roles rather readily enabled the scientific community of the age to exert a very profound influence on the process of educational reform. From France thus came the *École Polytechnique;* from Germany, the modern university. From both institutions stem most of the major influences that have shaped the development of separate disciplines and specialized knowledge.

What we now call disciplines and specialties are a product of the nineteenth century. Their development is closely linked to the evolution of the natural sciences, which in turn (albeit less directly) followed in step with the progress of industrialization. For instance, although biology as an empirical science has its roots in the scientific revolution of the sixteenth and seventeenth centuries and advanced with the growth of medicine and with the extension of geographical knowledge, it remained an almost random collection of heterogeneous information pursued by the very diverse interests and activities of naturalists down to the middle of the nineteenth century.

Modern biology can be said to have its beginnings about 1860 with the convergence of several developments in its various branches: (1) Darwin's theory of evolution; (2) Pasteur's refutation of abiogenesis; (3) Weismann's theory of protoplasm; (4) the discovery of the essential identity of reproduction in animals and plants; (5) the discovery of basic similarities in the means of nutrition and respiration in all organisms; and (6) the reduction of organic processes to the terms of the cell. Although the fields of morphology and taxonomy, of botany, zoology, anatomy, comparative anatomy, and physiology maintained themselves, specialization over and above these began to flourish. Many founders of the "new" biology traveled freely amongst the developing specialties. But they were *predisciplinarians*, rather than multi- or interdisciplinarians in the modern sense. Johannes Müller occupied a joint chair for anatomy *and* physiology at Berlin, and some of his students, such as Ernst Brücke, allowed their interests to stray from subject to subject, making important contributions everywhere. On the other hand, such men as Ludwig, Pasteur, Virchow, Kölliker, and du Bois-Reymond displayed a tendency to work intensively rather than extensively in the area of biology. With the intensification of research there came about a gradual loosening of biology's ties with the fields that had spawned it—medicine and "naturalism." One might say that the place where biology was practiced became relocated from Müller's anatomical theater and the decks of Darwin's *Beagle* to Ludwig's and Pasteur's laboratories. The new institutionalization also promoted specialization through active recruitment. The classic naturalists had virtually no institution available by which to replenish their ranks—the tradition was carried on primarily by men who had an individual interest in nature and had the good fortune to be able to support their work financially. Insofar as medicine provided an institution for new recruits to biology, it was a rather haphazard affair, since many of the most promising acolytes were likely to choose the lucrative benefits of private practice over the uncertain attractions of the laboratory. In some instances there was no choice at all. For example, Brücke, in recommending one of his brightest students for an academic vacancy, wrote: "However, . . . he is a very poor Jew who would only have his salary by which to support himself, which he should be able to do, given the simplicity and regularity of his life-style. . . . I have no doubt that he would be very delighted to be able to realize his wish to be able to dedicate himself to physiology in this manner."[26] Presumably, important aspects of the history of psychology would have developed differently had Freud actually been "able to realize his wish to dedicate himself to physiology."

The evolution of research specialties thus brought with it an alteration in the internal organization and structures of disciplines. There were of course still the texts that served their traditional educational function. But within the disciplines, texts increasingly assumed a secondary role. The treatises of the naturalists had been summations and syntheses of the knowledge of an area—in some senses, "final products." Now, however, they became overviews of what was known, with the purpose of pointing to areas that could further be expanded through additional research. Helmholtz's *Physiological Optics* is clearly a work of this nature, and Darwin's work is as important for the statement of evolutionary theory as it is for the research programs that the theory suggested. Moreover, such frontiers of new knowledge were explored at advanced research institutes.

The institutes became the physical plants in which research in the specialties was carried out. They bridged differences between science, technology, and industry and represented important places of interaction and training for new members of the specialty. It was here that a mentality of belonging to a group was nurtured. The membership of specialties found its identity within and through these institutes. And the very existence and organization of the institutes endowed the specialties with a legitimacy and channeled research efforts within the specialty into particular directions. The acquisition of increasingly complicated and expensive experimental apparatus and of other research tools insured that the primary emphasis in research would proceed along lines in which those tools could be utilized directly. The introduction of increasingly sophisticated equipment thus tended to further define and limit the areas even within a specialty that would be pursued at a particular research laborabory.[27] Such technology acted as a bridge between theoretical and applied scientific work. The technician designing laboratory apparatus had to be well versed in the theoretical problems to be resolved by employing his instruments.

But such apparatus, though initially designed for "pure" research, often had other applications. Notice, for example, that the Siemens-Halske enterprise, which began simply as a workshop for producing instruments for scientific laboratories, grew into one of the giants of the German electrical industry. Similar trends are evident in the development of the German chemical industry, which developed its own research laboratories closely linked to those of the universities. Science was no longer the province of the amateur but became that of the specialist; indeed, it became synonymous with specialization. The opening of an industrial marketplace for the practitioner of a discipline obviously enhanced the attractiveness of the various specialties and facilitated the recruitment for disciplines and specialties. And the existence of societies and journals maintained the solidarity of specialists, even when they were no longer in close physical contact with their colleagues. It allowed the isolated specialist to keep abreast of latest research results and gave him a forum for the publication of his own work.[28] In the pages of the specialized journal, he did not need to compete for an audience with members of other specialties, nor did he need to consider perspectives other than those of his specialty.[29] The growth of vocabularies particular to specialties also favored trends which pointed towards segregation.

Nonetheless, these developments occurred very gradually. The existence of a distinct content in a particular area of knowledge did not always and inevitably cause a new discipline or specialty to blossom. For example, the eleventh edition of the *Encyclopedia Britannica* (1911) has no entries under "biochemistry" or "biophysics," despite the fact that there was a great deal of activity in these areas at that time.[30]

The growth of specialization is also nurtured by a technology that allows for ever-greater diffusion of knowledge, of information, and of technology itself. So, for example, whereas the rate of diffusion of an invention such as pottery making, beginning about 16,000 B.C., was merely 0.25 miles per year, and the rate of diffusion of printing with moveable type, beginning about 1440, was approximately 12.5 miles per year, the diffusion of insulin (1925) occurred at about 12,000 miles per year.[31] This phenomenon alone, though favoring intensive developments in research, is not a sufficient condition for specialization. Certainly an *audience* for a new theory or development in knowledge is needed. The technology for the dissemination of knowledge was the same for Mendel and Darwin; yet the rate of diffusion of Mendel's genetics was for a long time zero, whereas Darwin's first edition of the *Origin* sold out on the day of its appearance. The sociological dimensions of such audiences can reveal important parameters for the development and evolution of knowledge.

Developments of increasing specialization and segregation of disciplines, though most prominent within the natural sciences, were not limited to them. These were more general developments that increasingly affected all of intellectual life. The sciences became the model for other fields of knowledge, and one may even speak of the "scientification" of knowledge in the nineteenth century. Economics, sociology, psychology, and other areas of what had been the arts received support for specialization almost in direct proportion to the extent to which they were able to make an acceptable claim for being social "sciences."

Comte, in his *Cours de la philosophie positive* (1830–42) and his *Système de la philosophie positive* (1851–54), had presented the outlines for a "social science." However, the main stimulus for the development of separate social "sciences" came from sources outside of academic circles. The observational data for the incipient sciences had been gathered by government agencies and offices for some time in the form of census and vital statistics and for the purpose of allowing for more accurate policy formulation and administration. A "science" developed through the application of quantitative analysis to these data by the English "political arithmeticians" and the "moral statisticians" of the Continent. The early stages in the evolution of this science were relatively checkered.[32] In 1856 the Societé Internationale des Études Pratiques d'Économie Sociale was founded, which also published a bulletin. In 1886 a break-away group under Fréderic LePlay founded a journal, *Science sociale,* but since this school was partially reformist in orientation and had no hold within the university system, its activity soon ceased.

The next step came with the foundation of *L'année sociologique* in 1898 by Durkheim, who had argued very strongly in his treatise on method that sociology constituted a discipline separate from other social sciences, and who was one of the few European sociologists to actually hold a chair for sociology; Simmel's appointment was in philosophy, Max Weber's was in economics, as was Pareto's. In Germany the idealist tradition hampered the development of sociology, and Nazism destroyed what little sociological tradition had evolved. Marxist sociology remained everywhere a tradition of itinerant scholars.

As an institutionalized discipline, sociology is really an American product. Although the first sociological society was the Institut International de Sociologie, the publication of its *Annales* in 1895 was paralleled by the simultaneous appearance of the *American Journal of Sociology.* The American Sociological Society was not founded until 1905 by members of the American Historical, Economic, and Political Science Societies, who had become dissatisfied within the confines of those associations.[33] However, these developments had also been anticipated in other ways. For instance, a lecture course in sociology had been offered at Yale as early as 1876, and in 1893 the University of Chicago had established the first academic department of sociology that offered a doctorate. The institutionalization of the discipline disseminated from this base, and by 1967 the United States had the "largest single concentration of professionally trained sociologists."[34]

A similar development may be found in the evolution of economics as a discipline. Here we see the publication of the *Quarterly Journal of Economics,* begun at Cambridge, Massachusetts in 1866, followed by the formation of the American Economic Association in 1885. By way of contrast, although the most prominent early economists were British, the Royal Economic Society was not founded until 1890. The *content* alone of a potential "discipline" is, therefore, insufficient to initiate its independent development unless other conditions are also present. By 1900, of the seven existing journals of economics, three were published in the United States, two in Germany, and one each in Britain and Sweden. The growth characteristic of independent disciplines, mentioned earlier, is very prominent in the field of economics. The *Index of Economic Journals,* which lists articles written in English since 1886, requires 156 pages to list publications for the period 1886–1924; 256 pages for the period 1925–39; 250 pages for the period 1940–49; 210 pages for the period 1950–54; and 290 pages for the period 1954–59.[35] We thus see again the familiar pattern of logarithmic growth in the products as well as the membership of an evolving discipline.

The growth of a discipline does not necessarily bring with it an extension of its field of inquiry. Indeed an inverse relationship seems to hold here, insofar as the realm of any discipline seems to become narrowed by its progressive internal fission into specialties and subspecialties, which attempt to legitimize their activities by emphasizing the differences that *separate* them from each other, rather than the similarities that relate them. One need only reflect on what was included within the discipline of "philosophy" a mere century ago, which is now pursued in separate disciplines, to see the effect of this fission. Economics and sociology have already been mentioned; psychology began to segregate itself beginning in 1879 at the latest, with the foundation of Wundt's experimental laboratory at Leipzig. Similar trends are evident even within evolving specialties that initially may have had an interdisciplinary character. For instance, social psychology, which in its early phase, represented by the work of

Allport, Sherif, Chapman, Volkmann, and others, dealt with problematics that lay between sociology and psychology, has now turned in directions that segregate it from its parent disciplines, thereby legitimizing it as an enterprise independent of them, at least in research and application of results.

As for philosophy, the transition has been essentially one from a faculty to a discipline of philosophy, which means that contemporary academic philosophy is also characterized by disciplinary specialization and segregation. In order to maintain an aura of relevance, the discipline has spawned a series of "philosophies of . . . "—philosophy of science, philosophy of history, and the like. Though by their titles these subspecialties (or metadisciplines, as they are sometimes advertised) would seem to be important communicative bridges between academic areas, they are in fact quite the opposite. The philosophy of science, for instance, can only legitimize itself as an academic institutionalized enterprise by defining itself as an area of study and research *distinct* from the sciences and by doing things that the sciences do *not* do, redundancy being the most cardinal of sins in an enterprise aspiring to efficiency. The curious position is thereby reached, in which philosophers of science address only each other, and in which it would hardly occur to a scientific practitioner who encounters a methodological problem in his work to consult the philosophical literature on scientific methodology. Similarly, there is also a history of science and a sociology of science, both of which specialties tend to foster antagonisms against each other and above all against the philosophy of science.

The worst offender in this regard is possibly the philosopher of history, who is distinguished by having virtually no contact with the field of knowledge he is philosophizing about. The most prominent academic philosophers of history have neither done historical research themselves nor are they even familiar with the more important products of contemporary historiography. The basic premises with which they approach their subject are therefore laughably naive and simplistic. On the basis of such assumptions, however, a formidable logical machinery is set in motion, producing conclusions that cannot fail to reflect the quality of the underlying assumptions.

Left to their own devices, many disciplines tend to develop specialties that are essentially disciplines of disciplines. By the extension of this tendency, there is no reason not to have a history of the philosophy of science or, for that matter, a sociology of the history of the philosophy of science.

Campbell's "fish scale" model of interdisciplinarity, in this perspective, seems an overly optimistic expectation. The historical examples seem to indicate that the growth of disciplinary knowledge along intensive and extensive directions simultaneously is not necessarily conducive to the development of overlapping disciplines or specialties. Quite on the contrary, trends within disciplinary developments point to the growth of increasing gaps between intensively cultivated fields. The existence of such gaps, moreover, is one of the legitimizing factors that argue for the "independence" of a specialty.

Within disciplines themselves, various factors ensure their perpetuity and homogeneity. Although these factors vary in importance from institution to institution, their broad impact may be seen within the development of German institutions of higher learning, which were the first to adopt a disciplinary structure.

In general, German institutions of higher learning grew out of Humboldt's concepts of education, which conceived of an interaction of independent disciplines defined by activities in teaching and research.[36] The University of Berlin, founded at the beginning of the nineteenth century, was organized on Humboldt's standards and became the prototype for other reforms at German universities. Second, the university became closely associated with the Prussian Academy of Sciences, thereby establishing a much closer coordination between teaching and research institutions than had existed theretofore.[37] A similar connection was established in 1826 between the University of Munich and the Bavarian Academy. The growth of research laboratories at other universities, as an integral part of the educational process, imitated the intent of these earlier examples.

Within the hierarchies of developing disciplines, several measures evolved to regulate their growing membership. Insofar as "disciplinary" development initially was centered in the growth of institutionalized natural science, these disciplines assumed two main functions: first, to supply qualified professionals, researchers, and technicians to a growing industrial sector increasingly dependent on technology; second, to secure sufficient recruits for the educational hierarchy of the discipline to ensure the continuity of its academic functions. The first need was met primarily through the *Staatsexamen;* passing it qualified a student for the practice of a profession. In brief, it certified him as being able to apply the knowledge acquired in a discipline. The second need was filled by a series of qualifying procedures leading to the doctorate and beyond, by which academic institutions procured new recruits and extended their membership. In both instances the original intent had been to allow the student to become exposed to a multitude of disciplines and specialties, by a policy that went under the title of *Lernfreiheit*—the freedom to learn. In fact, such broad learning abilities were taken advantage of, as is evidenced by the unusually large number of prominent intellectuals of the first half of the nineteenth century who crossed from discipline to discipline, sometimes even from the sciences to the humanities and vice versa. This policy was complemented by a parallel one—*Lehrfreiheit*—the freedom of teaching, which supposedly assured that the teaching process would remain free from outside interferences. Whatever the initial successes of these policies might have been, the "freedoms" they enshrined slowly and subtly became limited due to the internal development of the disciplines themselves.

The first of these limiting factors was the examination process. The growing number of examinations required of the student of any one discipline or specialty limited the amount of study that he might be able to devote to subjects not directly relevant to those in which he was to be examined. Aspiring professionals tended to channel their studies into the most efficient stream by which to acquire certification. Aspiring academics' activities were also circumscribed by whatever were considered to be pressing problems of the moment. A tradition arose in Germany whereby the professor would choose the candidate's dissertation topic more often than would the candidate. Once the hurdle of the doctorate had been passed, there loomed the *venia docendi,* which was the teaching certificate for institutions of higher learning. Amongst other requirements, the candidate had to demonstrate to the faculty that he was able to pursue useful research in his discipline. Naturally the definition of what is considered useful at any one time is ultimately set by the faculty—those academicians with an existing vested interest in the discipline or specialty. Once an instructor, the young academic was then financially dependent upon student enrollments in his courses, since he had no other salary. This meant that a considerable number of qualified people were effectively barred from pursuing an academic career unless they had another source of income. But even for the latter, their choice of course offerings was strongly influenced by student demands. These demands in turn were generally formulated on the basis of how the courses related to the examination process.

At higher levels, vacant chairs were filled through a process by which the faculty suggested three candidates in order of preference for appointment by the ministry of education. The faculty had to be careful to be certain that the candidates would be acceptable to the ministry, to prevent the ministry choosing an outsider for the vacancy. Criteria for such acceptability could include everything from a candidate's scholarly and teaching activities to his political views. Once installed, the professor was now theoretically free to exercise virtually unlimited *Lehrfreiheit*. But the process of advance through the preceding stages had virtually guaranteed that only social conformists and orthodox disciplinarians reached this last stage.

To these factors which regulated the development of disciplines *within* academic institutions were added forces which exerted themselves from *without*. In fact the main initial stimulus for the increasing segregation of disciplines, specialties, and subspecialties came from sectors of society where such special knowledge could be applied directly and without constant reference to broader related issues. Here industrialization played a key role. The relationship between developments in economies and of applied knowledge can be illustrated clearly by contrasting two cases in which organized knowledge evolved differently: Germany, a latecomer to industrialization, in which, however, technology and education were consciously coordinated; and Britain, birthplace of the industrial revolution, where industry and education had evolved separately and were brought into a relationship only reluctantly.

In Germany in the nineteenth century, industrialization came to be increasingly pursued as a governmental policy, with the state deliberately intervening in the economy. The consequence of such a policy was a rate of expansion in the German economy during the 1870s and '80s, unmatched anywhere previously or since, which propelled Germany to the position of Europe's leading industrial power by World War I.[38]

To a great extent Germany's economic success during this period was linked with the ability of its educational system to supply industry with trained specialists. This is particularly true of industries requiring *new* technical knowledge, in which the degree of specialization is particularly closely correlated to the success of the industry. Industries that do not have the personnel who can make the most efficient use of available resources (remembering that availability of capital in such enterprises is usually severely limited) will inevitably compete at a disadvantage.

For example, in a critique of the state of British chemistry in mid-nineteenth century, Edward Frankland noted:

In the year 1866 there were published 1,273 papers on new discoveries, by 805 chemists, 1.58 paper being thus the average produce of each investigator. Of these, Germany contributed 445 authors and 777 papers, or 1.75 paper to each author; France 170 authors, and 245 papers, or 1.44 paper to each author; whilst the United Kingdom furnished only 97 authors and 127 papers, or 1.31 paper to each author.[39]

Frankland also observed that the total number of British papers on chemistry included those of a rather substantial number of German chemists who had followed Augustus von Hofmann to England. These began to leave England after the death of Prince Albert, who had largely been responsible for recruiting them.[40]

The issue about the respective amounts of chemical research was not a mere academic question at the time. The intensity and extent of research had economic consequences.[41] Britain, which had been the leader in the production of alkali through the middle of the nineteenth century, was quickly surpassed by Germany. The same trends occurred in the production of sulphuric acid. The German dye industry, comprising such newcomers as Badische Analin, Hoechst, AGFA, and others, controlled one-half of the world market by 1870, and its continuing innovations left Britain far behind in the field, Germany's share of the world market growing to 90 percent by the end of the century. In the last third of the century Britain humbly supplied Germany with coal tar for the coal-tar derivatives industry, which virtually became a German monopoly.[42] Parallel developments mark the steel production of the two respective powers, and their output of electrical power; these developments are apparent in the electrical manufacturing industry in which, by 1913, German production ranked second only to the United States but led in exports.[43] The disparities between Britain and Germany were not so much the results of differences in availability of capital as they were of Germany's ability to quickly mobilize trained specialists to develop and exploit new technologies. As David Landes points out, "One should not overemphasize the importance of capital. As in chemical manufacture, scientific knowledge, technical skill, and high standards of performance weighed more heavily in the market place than price."[44] In this context it is important to note that the factors of specialization and technology so important to German industrialization could also propel smaller economies such as that of Switzerland to prominence in certain areas. In the evolution of these new industries, borderlines between "pure" and applied science, technology and engineering often disappeared, since the very creation of such an industry in many cases involved scientific research of the most fundamental sort. The research laboratory became an integral part of such new industries, and the careers of such men as Abbé, Bayer, Duisberg, Siemens, Nernst, Rathenau, Haber, Bosch, and others attest to the symbiotic relationship that evolved between government, industry, education, and research.[45]

The situation in Britain was entirely different. English universities, represented in the first third of the century by Oxford and Cambridge, were antiquated, stagnant, orthodox, and Anglican.[46] The internal dynamics of the educational system moved in a closed circle: Oxbridge students were recruited from the public schools to which they returned as masters. The system proved impervious to attempts at reform. A science curriculum, for instance, was virtually unheard of, so that Charles Lyell could complain:

> After the year 1839, we may consider three-fourths of the Sciences, still nominally taught at Oxford, to have been virtually exiled from the University . . . Chemistry and Botany attracted between the years 1840 and 1844, from three to seven students; Geometry, Astronomy and Experimental Philosophy scarcely more; Mineralogy and Geology, still taught by the same Professor, who, fifteen years before, had attracted crowded audiences, from ten to twelve.[47]

Nor was this gap filled by any other institutions. Before 1820 the Royal Society was notable for the absence of scientists in its councils, and attempts at revising the statutes to remedy this imbalance failed successively in 1823, 1827, and 1830.[48] This was partly due to the position the Royal Society had come to occupy as an integral part of an Anglican establishment whose members considered themselves to be, first and foremost, "gentlemen."[49] The conservative attitude vis-à-vis science, bred by Anglicanism and its institutions, is demonstrated by the fact that of the great English scientists of the first half of the century, only Davy was Anglican and only Thomas Young had studied at an English university. The "experimental scientists in England during this period were usually either Dissenters, or men trained either in the Scottish or Continental universities."[50] The new university founded at Durham at this time was modeled on the Oxbridge pattern. Any developments in the sciences therefore had to take place outside existing institutions and under much more difficult circumstances than was the case elsewhere. English science became organized in provincial societies such as those at Birmingham and Manchester, whose members finally became the patrons of the University of London and of the British Association for the Advancement of Science, which was fashioned after the *Deutsche Naturforscher-Versammlung*.[51] The stimulus for these new organizations was a perceived need on the part of scientists and the informed public for a cadre of trained specialists without which Britain would inevitably fall behind the Continent in economic competition. It was not, however, until a wider recognition of such a threat came about, through the contrast between the Great Exhibition and the 1867 Exhibition of Paris, that reforms began to be considered and to be instituted.[52]

Thus the economic disparities between Germany and Britain, which became ever sharper during the latter part of the century, were preceded by important differences on the educational level.[53] First, whereas elementary education had been compulsory in Prussia since 1763, Britain did not follow suit until 1880. Hence during the technologically important middle of the nineteenth century, Prussia and the other German states could boast of a school attendance of 97 percent of all eligible children, whereas only half of British children attended elementary schools, of which only two-fifths were inspected by the state. But even within the latter schools, only a quarter of their pupils entered their upper classes.[54]

Second, while the first half of the century was marked by the rapid internal development of higher educational institutions in Germany, technical and scientific training in Britain was left haphazardly to private enterprise and initiative, which manifested itself in the "mechanics' institutes" and the embryonic University of London. Foundations such as the Royal College of Chemistry (1845) and the School of Mines (1851) came rather late and were added rather than integral features of the educational system.[55]

Third, although university degrees in the sciences began to be awarded in Britain in the 1850s, professional opportunities for graduates of scientific or technical studies continued to be severely limited. In Germany, on the other hand, the simultaneous growth of education, research, and industry and their increasing integration created a demand for the services of specialists and technicians.[56] Indeed what is most noticeable is the large number of specialists that Germany could support and profitably employ. W.W. Thornton noted at the time that the Kingdom of Württemberg, with two-thirds the population of London, supported, in addition to the elementary schools in all of its towns and parishes, 450 "industrial schools . . . attended chiefly by girls," 523 farming schools, 108 trade schools, 76 industrial academies teaching "science, pure, mixed, and applied," a building-trades college, an agricultural college, and the Polytechnic University at Stuttgart.[57]

In Britain all such developments occurred much later, and only after the economic consequences of the neglect of technical education had made themselves felt. At that stage, specialized training in Britain grew rapidly and assumed an intensity that had no precedent in the German parallel.[58] Owens College, which had been founded in 1851, became the University of Manchester in 1877, and out of its extensions grew the universities at Liverpool (1881), Birmingham (1900), Leeds (1904), and Sheffield (1905). At these new schools, recipients of degrees in the sciences tended to outnumber those of degrees in the arts, indicating a distinct shift in educational emphasis. [59] This shift was also accompanied by an increase in the number of areas of applied science and technology that were made available. The new institutions offered specific certificates in such areas as industrial administration, dyeing, gas engineering, and the like. The British response to German specialization thus was one of an intensity (emphasizing *direct* professional and vocational applicability) greater than even the German model that it imitated.[60] The large-scale evolution of specialized scientific enterprises in Britain during the closing days of the nineteenth century was a response to social demands triggered by the Continental economic challenge.[61]

Forces similar to those evident in Britain shaped developments in America.[62] American colleges, having largely been modeled on their English ancestors at a time when the English university was in decline, remained undistinguished during the first part of the nineteenth century. But shortly after midcentury, and partly under the impact of the Continental European experience, a reform movement began to be felt in American higher education. This trend was also reflected in the growth of other academic and scientific societies. Whereas no such organizations had been founded since the American Philosophical Society (1743) and the American Academy of Arts and Sciences (1780), the establishment of the American Association for the Advancement of Science (1848) was followed in rapid succession by the American Philological Society (1869), the American Chemical Society (1877), the Modern Language Association (1883), the American Historical Association (1884), the American Economic Society (1885), the American Mathematical Society, and the Geological Society of America (both in 1888).[63] From their very titles it is evident that these associations differed from their predecessors of the previous century not only in number but—more important—in kind. They represented the culminations of a reform movement in education that had been initiated by a demand for more practical curricula.[64]

The reformed American university of the second half of the nineteenth century was modeled mainly on a vision of German institutions of higher education, which had been imported by Americans who had studied abroad and by a large immigration of German intellectuals after the the revolutions of 1848–49. This German influence grew stronger as the century advanced, since it had become virtually a tradition for promising young American scholars to study abroad. Princeton and Columbia universities in fact established fellowships for that purpose in the 1870s,[65] and it is estimated that about 10,000 Americans matriculated in German universities between 1850 and 1914.[66] In this way the influences of German trends towards specialization, discussed earlier, made themselves directly felt in American academic institutions during a crucial period in their evolution.

The result was that the reformed American university was largely organized along the lines of a German prototype and was often staffed by academics trained in Germany.[67] This pattern was followed in institutions as diverse and varied as Cornell University, which became the model for the new land-grant colleges,[68] and the Johns Hopkins University graduate school, which tried to copy the German program outright and was later imitated by Harvard, Yale, Columbia, Princeton, and Chicago.[69]

What is most important about these American developments is that they carried the extension and intensification of specialized knowledge far beyond their German model, and that the reforms that set them in motion were initiated deliberately to produce social benefits. Specialized knowledge arranged along disciplinary lines was not intended to serve the purposes of some abstract "truth" or the demands of "pure" knowledge. In every instance the justification for these reforms was expressed in terms of the applicability (however remote) of this knowledge. The problems which led to the general reform of American education in the nineteenth century were seen at the time as social issues rather than as purely pedagogical questions. The social function of education occupied the forefront of debates, and although today's historian of education often seems unaware of these dynamics, his subjects were not. Andrew D. White, the first president of Cornell, harbored no illusion but that the duty of his institution was to train the "captains in the army of industry."[70] Even Daniel Coit Gilman, first president of Johns Hopkins, which he had designed for the pursuit of pure research, openly acknowledged the social function of the university.[71] The fruits of such research were conceded to be indirect and even unpredictable; but that there were to be such fruits was beyond question.

It was primarily the creation of research facilities that transformed the American college into the American university. The research orientation itself furthered the development of separate and independent disciplines and specialties, since demands for appropriate facilities and the associated hardware and software could only be justified by appeals to very specific and clearly defined goals. At Hopkins, where the research movement began (the teaching-oriented-undergraduate studies had been included in the foundation of the university only to appease the populace of Baltimore), investigations proceeded along departmental lines and quickly generated all the trappings appropriate to mature disciplines: The *American Journal of Philology,* the *American Journal of Mathematics,* the *Journal of Experimental Medicine, Studies in History and Political Science,* and *Modern Language Notes* all originated at Hopkins. Insofar as these publications were directly associated with the formation of professional societies, their appearance reflected a growth in the institutionalization and hierocratization of specialized knowledge. The Rockefeller Institute for Medical Research, for instance, was founded and staffed by Hopkins graduates.[72] However, Hopkins's main influence was intraacademic: in 1926, a half century after having opened its doors, about 1,000 of the total of its 1,400 graduates were still active on the faculties of American colleges and universities. This distribution reveals another important feature of the development of disciplines, namely, that at their highest level they remain primarily self-contained and self-regulating enterprises. Despite claims about "benefits which society derives from universities" organized along disciplinary lines, there is seldom any great rush to apply those benefits directly.

Even in a discipline that, at face value, would seem to have many immediate points of application, such as chemistry, there was initially a great imbalance in the areas in which chemists worked. Of the total of 9,000 American chemists at the turn of the century, only 276 were employed in chemical industries. Although some others were employed in other industries and in government and municipal agencies, at least half seem to have been employed in educational institutions.[73] This is not to imply that those working within educational institutions engaged only in pure as against their colleagues' applied research. But in general the academic worked under better conditions, under fewer external constraints, and largely on self-initiated projects. He was justly envied by his colleague in industry who was employed largely for purposes of primitive quality control. Of the two, the academic post was clearly the more attractive.[74] Competition for vacancies therefore became inevitable amongst the junior professionals, the selection process being controlled by senior faculty. A certain orthodoxy was thereby assured to the internal composition of existing disciplines. Similar tendencies spilled over into industry when General Electric, Bell Telephone, DuPont, Westinghouse, Eastman Kodak, and Standard Oil of Indiana established their own research laboratories at the turn of the century.[75] The control of the institution, organization, and composition of disciplines and professions remained largely in academic hands.[76]

This concentration of controls made the university (often by default) the regulative agency for many professions. As a result, the internal dynamics of disciplines within the academic context had effects that reached far beyond the university itself. The development of departments of chemistry may serve as a case in point.

The usefulness of some general chemical knowledge to many professions had been acknowledged in the last quarter of the nineteenth century. The abilities of a chemistry that had before been learned "on the job" in industry fell increasingly farther behind the demands made by a market geared to rapid technical changes. A broader and more formal training program was demanded by some leaders of industry, and the universities were to supply it. But the model on which the program was patterned—the German university—contained an implicit paradox when applied in that specific context: the "social function" of the university in this case was to disseminate new knowledge into society through the teaching of new materials. On the other hand, the structure of the institution of education was geared to a recruitment of researchers rather than of teachers. As William R. Harper, first president of the University of Chicago, had declared: "It is proposed in this institution to make the work of investigation primary, the work of giving instruction secondary."[77] Promotion at Chicago was contingent on publication, which was rewarded by Sisyphuslike sabbaticals that were to be used for further research, resulting in more publication. Specialized research thus became *the* most important variable in the internal dynamics of the university. But pressures were exerted from without the university, with which a research-oriented structure could not readily deal. Ultimately, of course, universities and their disciplinary structures were financed by society. Society thus had special claims on universities. The initial reform movement in education in America had received social support because it had promised practicality and applicability. In this context the various disciplines ultimately had to justify their legitimacy through continued enrollments. Enrollments in turn depended on the degree to which the contents of a discipline were required either for certification in or exercise of a profession. Teachers were implicitly needed by disciplines, but the reward system was not geared to evaluate teaching.[78]

This potential for conflict between the externally directed (teaching) and internally directed (research) roles of disciplines became evident rather quickly. Such tensions grew particularly acute when sources of finance grew more diverse, accompanied by clearer, more immediate, and more heterogeneous demands for demonstrations of the social effectiveness of institutions of education. Such demands can hardly ever be met directly by research projects, and here the American academic was much more vulnerable than his German colleague whom he wished to imitate. His activities were subject to relatively frequent review from the outside; the responses of academic institutions to pressures as varied as the McCarthy hearings of the 1950s, the radicalization of the student body in the 1960s, and Senator Proxmire's "golden fleece" awards of the 1970s are merely extreme examples of such sensitivity. The academic's position was fraught with schizoid potential, since his eventual success as a researcher was dependent on his immediate success as a teacher.[79] American chemists of the 1890s, for example, all had "a common complaint to voice . . . . the demands made upon them as instructors are *alone* culpable for their meager contributions to . . . research. Too many hours of teaching. Too many subjects to be taught."[80] The pressures from within to publish and the pressures from without to teach led to the creation of a host of low-paid posts for assistants and instructors, which relieved the senior faculty from elementary teaching.[81]

The pattern which began to develop within disciplines was as follows: as an independent area of study, a discipline or specialty had to be able to demonstrate the applicability of its contents outside the academic sphere. The basics of a discipline would not only represent its own foundations, but could probably also find application to a number of other disciplines and professions: basic mathematics, physics and chemistry, for instance, were not only the foundations for physicists, chemists, and engineers but also for biologists, physiologists, and physicians. A more advanced level of instruction would be aimed more directly at future practitioners of the discipline itself and of professions derived from or related to it.[82] Graduates of this level often also engaged in applied research. Within the professions particularly, this type of research, when successful, promised the most immediate rewards. From the ranks of these graduates were also recruited new members of the academic discipline who entered the hierarchy at the lowest rank—as teachers of the elementary courses. This meant that the most broadly oriented teaching of the discipline was in the hands of those members who had explored it least through research (remembering that research is virtually the *sine qua non* of academic disciplines). Since the students at the elementary levels demanded information that could be made applicable in various ways, it was the contents appropriate to meeting these demands which were emphasized. The contents of teaching at this level therefore had no necessary connection with the products of advanced research in any one discipline. And since the audience for teachers was largest at this level, instruction could be used not only to convey information but also to function as a public-relations tool aimed at an informed sector of the public that might later play an important part in rallying external support when it was needed.[83] In some ways an illusion of responsiveness could be created at this level. The very fashionable "social conscience" of academia of the 1960s, for example, seldom extended to an advanced level where, on one hand, it would have been less visible and, on the other, might actually have influenced the future orientation of the acolytes.

Teaching activities of disciplines thus played a relatively minor part in the internal dynamics of academic structures. Here research continued to exert the most important influence. By the turn of the century, the doctorate had become *the* ticket of admission to membership in American academic life. The doctorate, of course, certified not teaching ability but the ability to do research—and research of a strictly disciplinary nature at that. The internal structure of the universities quickly came to reflect these internal relationships of disciplines: organization along departmental lines became the standard, regardless of whether or not such organization made any pedagogical sense (and sometimes despite it). For instance, six months after the opening of the University of Chicago, its department of biology reorganized itself into departments of zoology, botany, anatomy, neurology, and physiology.[84] Indeed, whereas in teaching where no specialty is an island, and a multi- or interdisciplinary effort is demanded almost by definition, it is only in research where disciplines can function in splendid isolation.

There was also a second set of forces emanating from the dual functions of teaching and research, which shaped the evolution of disciplinary structures. The population of any discipline or specialty is, in its largest part, a migratory one of students and lower-level instructors and asistants, all of whom move in and out of the discipline. Even graduates to professions having direct ties with any specialty tend to be scattered. Permanent disciplinary structures are therefore, by default, in the hands of the sedentary sector of the discipline's population. For purely demographic reasons, these are the senior academics whose command of space and time in academia allows them to engage in *continuous* research, maintain a running contact with colleagues, convoke meetings with them and with professionals, staff organizations, and control the publication of research results. These potentially powerful means of control came to be vested in senior academics as more of the general teaching load was transferred to the lower echelons.[85]

At the upper levels of disciplines, the teaching function and perspectives of applicability played very small roles. Witness, for example, the founding of the *Journal of Physical Chemistry* in 1896, of the American Electro-Chemical Society in 1902, and of the *Journal of Biological Chemistry* in 1906. None of these developments reflected any contemporary needs of teaching or of the professions, though in this case they were fortunate anticipations of such future needs. They were the results of the research dynamics within academic chemistry. This research emphasis, joined to the symbiosis of disciplines, organizations, a developing "hardware" industry, and an existing publishing industry, spawned quite naturally a massive increase in publications. Universities established their own presses and journals, following the precedent set by Johns Hopkins. By 1904 Columbia University alone issued thirty-five serial publications. By 1909 there even existed an Athletic Research Society in which coaches could display their academic credentials.[86] Rudolph observes that "the consequence of these massive journal performances was to lead many universities to the conclusion that respectability required its own set of journals; this conclusion led to a great deal of publication that was not exactly of high quality."[87] But by assuming that high quality was the motivation for publication, Rudolph has missed an important point. Research was done and results were published not for the benefit of those outside of academe, but to maintain old or establish new hierarchies *within* disciplinary structures and organizations. The institutional structure of scholarly journals serves to reinforce disciplinary hierarchies: at the lowest level, the evaluator, reader, or reviewer is implicitly considered to be qualified to make judgments about a contribution at a level above that of the contributor himself. From there the hierarchy extends to the editorship, and the selection processes for filling the several intervening positions evidently reinforce the hierarchizing and orthodoxy of the discipline in question. Publication outside the prescribed means is to ignore and to circumvent this established disciplinary hierarchy. And in fact no publication is quite as suspect to academics as that by one of their colleagues which has the misfortune to catch the popular fancy. In academic publication, nothing fails like success, for the maxim of American academics became, after all, not "publish and enlighten," but "publish or perish."

The forces that shaped American education during the past century thus are also those that gave it its particular disciplinary nature. The basic impetus had been given by the process of industrialization in mid-nineteenth century. By the end of the century, the division of labor that characterized more and more of the productive process was paralleled by the fission of the educational process into a myriad of specialties.[88] The transition from education by faculties to one by disciplines has already been outlined. But one should also note that the causes of the demise of the old and obsolete multidisciplinary faculties also became obstacles to the development of any future and potentially beneficial a-disciplinary efforts, at least within the academic enterprise.

The rise of disciplines, as we have seen, is inextricably linked with the growth of bureaucracy within academic institutions and outside of them in diverse professions related in varying degrees to particular disciplines. The general characteristics of bureaucracies—self-maintenance, inertia, rule- rather than goal-orientation, and the like—are at work within disciplines as strong counters to any attempt at basic reform.

Society demands of academic institutions, above all, *training*. In an increasingly mobile and specialized society, training becomes the primary tool for economic and social advancement, since a fluid social milieu allows relatively little room for the exercise of static sources of power—inherited wealth and prestige are maintained not so much by virtue of themselves as by their ability to mobilize and manipulate new sources of power. In postindustrial society, power emanates primarily from the ability to manipulate technologies flexibly and efficiently. An imperative for efficiency thereby reaches back from society into academic structures. Disciplines, because of their inherent narrowness, are efficient means for training and for research. Demands for efficient training reach the university primarily through the professions. The orientation towards efficient research (meaning research directed towards narrow goals promising short-term results) arises partly from society and partly from the inner dynamics of existing (and competing) segregated academic structures, as we have seen.[89] The latter dynamics are strong counters against interdisciplinary initiatives within academic institutions, for several reasons:

First, to argue against specialties and disciplines as the *sole* preoccupation in higher education is, after all, to accept in some measure the onus of contending that efficiency is at best a secondary aim in education—that some things are done better inefficiently. Insofar as a great deal of planning within academic institutions is short-term, programs offering immediate results will have an enormous advantage in competing with those which do not make that claim.

Second, academic interdisciplinarians are, like their other colleagues, subject to a constant review by their peers. Their peers, however, are oriented towards a totally different epistemic problematic. Interdisciplinary work will almost inevitably face charges of dilettantism, and interdisciplinarians, in order to maintain themselves in a disciplinary environment, will be pressed to continually prove their credentials as disciplinarians. Their interdisciplinary work therefore can only be pursued part-time, giving even further weight to any criticisms of dilettantism. The problem here is a circular one.

Third, the occasional interdisciplinary program that is funded from without academic institutions proper will have to be justified in terms which apply largely to disciplinary work, and often in competition against disciplinary projects. Eventual reviews of such programs will inevitably be undertaken by administrators who have been educated in a disciplinary framework, often also administer disciplinary projects, and have no criteria of evaluation other than those derived from and applicable to their own disciplinary background. The interdisciplinary project thus may be confronted with a demand to justify itself in terms that apply to disciplines.

Fourth, the continuous extraacademic sponsorship that supports many disciplines is not available to interdisciplinary initiatives. Interdisciplinary efforts have no actual or potential professions from which to draw such support. Even very successful pluri- or multidisciplinary efforts, such as the Apollo Program, are ad hoc enterprises that leave no organizational continuity in their wake, other than results that can be integrated into existing disciplinary structures.

All of these factors represent forces strongly opposed to nondisciplinary developments of an academic nature. Even academic areas that by definition would seem to call for an interdisciplinary approach—such as education—have been recast in a disciplinary mold. This is because the pressures shaping disciplinary research at educational institutions quickly reached back to the pedagogical level.[90] This should hardly be surprising, since the personnel of both areas overlapped, and since the research emphasis dominated the early stages in the evolution of these institutions. Further, the growth of educational institutions also provided a momentum for the accelerating development of an internal bureaucratic structure aiming to streamline the various training programs. These efforts to make the training process more rational and efficient came to depend, quite naturally, on analyses of the educational alternatives available. And also quite naturally, in the context of the scientism that was sweeping education at the time, a preference was expressed for "scientific" analyses. Paul Monroe, for example, one of the early advocates of "scientific" education, argued on the basis of the work of Dewey and James that, assuming laws of human development that could be inductively established, "symbolical or logical" as well as "experimental" and "comparative" analyses of education would transform the field into a scientific discipline.[91] His aim was therefore to provide his discipline with a full research apparatus. Here again a potential new *profession* of education provided a base of support for the appropriate internal reform of the university. These developments were accompanied by the building of institutions in which to train these new professionals. The normal schools were upgraded and transformed into teachers' training colleges, of which forty-six had acquired degree-granting powers by World War I. At universities, departments and colleges of education were established. Specialized means of disseminating the specialized knowledge of the new discipline and profession were found in the form of new journals. In fact, as Bailyn has observed, Monroe, Elwood Cubberly, Henry Suzzallo, W.H. Kilpatrick, and other early missionaries of "scientific" education "became fantastically successful academic entrepreneurs. By World War I they were captains of a vast educational industry."[92]

Education of course had a legitimate need for pursuing investigations of a special kind. But the strict disciplinary emphasis inevitably meant that the new discipline could only justify itself by a clear separation of the process and content of education. Questions of process were declared to lie in the special discipline of education; issues of content were subject to the sovereign laws of other disciplines. Education separate from its contents became an increasingly dogmatic, isolated, and trivial enterprise, until a great deal of its research was a parody of science, the worse for its being an unconscious parody. Amongst the research topics for the doctorate in the mature discipline of education, one finds solutions to "Administrative Problems of the High School Cafeteria," "The Technique of Estimating School Equipment Costs," a survey of "Public School Plumbing Equipment," the intriguing title, "Concerning Our Girls and What They Tell Us," and "Evidences of the Need of Education for Efficient Purchasing."[93] No doubt some of these issues do arise in day-to-day educational situations. But are they really (or were they in the 1920s) *the* crying issues of education? Did education as an area of study really profit from its transformation into a discipline that by definition could only legitimize itself by stressing its distinctiveness with respect to the subject matter of other disciplines?

One would suspect that, given the undercurrent of efficiency and emphasis on "results" within academia, a discipline producing such work as products of its highest levels would have either succumbed of its own dead weight or would have suffered a radical internal transformation. Such an expectation, however, would betray a great underestimation of the inertial momentum of organized disciplines. In the case of education, some reforms were introduced, especially after the discipline had been subjected to massive criticism in the 1940s. More important to its self-perpetuation, however, was the profession that represented the discipline's extraacademic base, and that had assumed monopolistic characteristics through teacher certification, which in turn was in academic hands. Through the exercise of such control mechanisms, the discipline was able to continue to expand: whereas in 1930 (considering only one subarea) American universities had awarded a total of 17 doctorates in primary, preprimary, and exceptional education, this number had grown to 3,193 doctorates by 1970. The expansion of the profession mirrored this trend: in 1930, 44,344 bachelors and 5,641 second-level degrees had been awarded in this educational field; in 1970 the respective totals were 1,191,954 and 190,662.[94]

In summary, the prospects for interdisciplinarity as such, within the context and as a permanent feature of American higher education, do not seem altogether hopeful. There are to be considered the dynamics of institutionalization, which are overwhelmingly disciplinary and which have transformed previous potential interdisciplinarities as diverse as education, philosophy, and social psychology, into disciplines proper. Interdisciplinary efforts grafted onto existing institutions will likely remain temporary or isolated phenomena, most either being terminated or becoming absorbed into disciplinary structures. This is not to say that they do not play very important roles during their lifetimes and even thereafter through the continued work of their initial participants. But given the strength of the social forces within academic institutions, a general turn towards interdisciplinarity as a main academic feature would probably require a thorough revision of the presuppositions and attitudes on which present educational institutions are based. The only model for such reform is the transformation of education in China in the late 1960s, where the introduction of a type of interdisciplinary education included the reeducation of academics.[95] Such changes are not foreseeable elsewhere, although some slow changes in this direction may occur. For the most part, however, interdisciplinary alternatives in education will probably remain confined to small, idiosyncratic, or new institutions.

A possible basis for more general reform could perhaps grow from present multi- and pluridisciplinary projects. Although these are of an ad hoc nature, their number may increase due to continuing and direct social pressures. Efforts along ecological, conservationist, environmentalist lines and the cooperation of various specialties on *both* sides of heated social issues such as the nuclear energy debates may be considered as examples of this trend.[96] Individual specialties on their own, it is now clear, simply do not have the breadth of perspective nor probably the willingness to assume responsibility for offering extensive and intensive solutions to social problems.[97]

One of the supreme ironies of the "scientific" claims of institutionalized disciplinary knowledge is that they rest on an absurdly naive impression of the history of science, namely, that only intensive, sharply contrained, clearly problem-oriented research that promises immediate results is "scientific." *Science News*, in a satirical article on justifications of research grants, pointed to a profound implication of current "grantsmanship" on which so much research depends: that a large number of endeavors that resulted in achievements we would nowadays classify as classics in the natural sciences could not in today's disciplinary context expect to be funded, either because they could not promise immediate results or because they would go beyond the jealously guarded boundaries of existing specialties.[98] Would Darwin get a grant to go on voyage with the

Beagle? Did Freud get any support at all? Do we owe Einstein's special relativity to the support he received from an academic disciplinary institution? And was not Watson's work on DNA constantly threatened because it was not clearly defined as directly integrated into either a specific project or a particular research institution? Similarly, did not such groups as the Vienna Circle, which brought together philosophers, natural and social scientists in a truly interdisciplinary enterprise, exist over and above the academic institutions in which its members were employed?[99] In a very important sense, it seems as though the "scientific" disciplines dedicated to the rational and efficient pursuit of knowledge are quite irrelevant to a whole series of immensely important scientific developments.

The point is that it is not a question of scientific disciplinary knowledge as against unscientific interdisciplinary knowledge. The distinction fails because it is artificial: it makes it too easy for one to be on the side of angels, and here the important issues are often more of a religious than a scientific nature. The problem confronting modern education is simply one of rational, useful, and relevant knowledge, of which science and interdisciplinarity are integral parts. For, as one of the great scientists of our century has pointed out, what can be said of science can be said of interdisciplinarity, and indeed of all knowledge: "Science," he wrote,

> is fundamentally and in the end always an affair of the individual. No possible development can change that. But there are tasks, which stretch beyond a single life; tasks, requiring such prolonged preparation that one person can never really get to them; others so complex, that a division of labor is required. Nay, more, one can even say that, on a close view, all scientific tasks are part of a larger task, and that, as long as they are handled in isolation, progress is impossible. Thus we come upon one of the paradoxes by which our spiritual life is hemmed in: science is an affair of the individual, yet scientific problems can never be solved by an individual. How are we to escape? We cannot leave science exclusively to the study or laboratory of one person, still less can we carry it on in a common workshop. We can at best work in ever widening concentric circles, bring the workers into informal contact and endeavor to reach some sort of systematic progress on the basis of the freedom of the individual . . . . The advancement of knowledge requires specialization and departmentalization as well as free and easy cross-fertilization.[100]

Notes

1. American Chemical Society, *Monthly Science Summaries,* No. 131, October 1976.
2. Thomas H. Maugh, II, "Photochemical Smog: Is It Safe to Treat the Air?" *Science* 193 (1976): 871–73.
3. Michael J. Prival, Elena C. McCoy, Bezalel Gutter, Herbert S. Rosenkranz, "Tris (2,3-Dibromopropyl) Phosphate: Mutagenicity of a Widely Used Flame Retardant," *Science* 195 (1977): 76–78.
4. See Robert Scott, "Personal and Institutional Problems Encountered in Being Interdisciplinary," pp. 306–27 of the present volume.
5. See Léo Apostel, "Conceptual Tools for Interdisciplinarity: An Operational Approach," in *Interdisciplinarity: Problems of Teaching and Research in Universities* (Paris: OECD, 1972), pp. 141–80.
6. Ibid., p. 146.
7. Ibid., p. 148.
8. Ibid, pp. 148–49.
9. See Karl Rothschuh, *Geschichte der Physiologie* (Berlin: Springer Verlag, 1953), pp. 123-27, 157–59.
10. Joseph C. Kiger, "Disciplines," *Encyclopedia of Education* (New York: Philosophical Library, 1971), 3: 99.
11. See "Index to Ph.D. Programs," in *A Guide to Graduate Study: Programs Leading to the Ph.D Degree,* ed. Robert Quick, 4th ed. (Washington: Association of American Colleges, 1969), pp. 625–37.
12. See Burton Bledstein, *The Culture of Professionalism: The Middle Class and the Development of Higher Education in America* (New York: Norton, 1976). Michael B. Katz put the issue as follows: "Education . . . has appeared to be an immediate and effective solution to social problems. There is a surface logic, which remains immensely appealing: Equipping children with appropriate skills and attitudes can cause the problems of unemployment and poverty to disappear. The illnesses of society become diagnosed as simply a lack of education, and the prescription for reform becomes more education. The prescription, for one thing, unleashes a flurry of seemingly purposeful activity and, for another, requires no tampering with basic social structural or economic characteristics, only with the attitudes of poor people, and that has caused hardly a quiver." *Class, Bureaucracy and Schools: The Illusion of Educational Change in America* (New York: Praeger, 1971), p. 109.
13. For a survey of these developments, see Charles H. Haskins, *The Renaissance of the Twelfth Century* (Cambridge, Mass.: Harvard University Press, 1927); *The Rise of the Universities* (Ithaca: Cornell University Press, 1957), by the same author; and Hastings Rashdall, *The Universities of Europe in the Middle Ages,* 2 vols. (Oxford: Clarendon Press, 1895).
14. See P.O. Kirsteller, "The School of Salerno: Its Development and its Contribution to the History of Learning," *Bulletin of the History of Medicine* 17 (1945): 138–94.
15. Quoted in Haskins, *Rise of the Universities,* p.2.
16. See Pearl Kibre, *The Nations in Mediaeval Universities* (Cambridge, Mass.: The Mediaeval Academy, 1948); and Alfred Hessel, *Geschichte der Stadt Bologna von 1116 bis 1280* (Berlin: n.p., 1910).

17. For example, see the sources relating to the foundations of Heidelberg in 1386, in E.F. Henderson, *Select Historical Documents of the Middle Ages* (London: G. Bell & Sons, 1892), pp. 262–66.

18. Haskins, *Rise of the Universities*, pp.51–77.

19. London: Robert White for George Calvert, 1654, p. 4.

20. N.p.: 1685, p. 375.

21. See Martha Ornstein, *The Rise of Scientific Societies in the Seventeenth Century* (Chicago: University of Chicago Press, 1928).

22. See Richard Meister, *Entwicklung und Reformen des österreichischen Studienwesens*, 2 vols. (Vienna: Böhlau, 1963).

23. The sociological aspects of the rise of science in England at this time are analyzed in Robert Merton's classic, *Science, Technology and Society in Seventeenth Century England, Osiris* 4 (1936).

24. Richard du Moulin Eckart, *Geschichte der deutschen Universitäten* (Stuttgart: Verlag von F. Enke, 1929), pp. 299–325.

25. Ibid., p. 324.

26. Unpublished letter from Ernst Brücke to Alexander Rollett, dated 15 November 1879, in possession of the Archiv der Universität Graz.

27. This becomes more true as "big" science becomes even bigger. Such equipment as the Stanford Linear Accelerator, which cost $114 million initially and requires $25 million in annual operating costs, is just one recent example. See further, David S. Greenberg, *The Politics of Pure Science* (New York: New American Library, 1967), p.11.

28. A clear example of the manner in which specialized journals fulfill such needs of a growing profession may be found in the evolution of chemistry in America, where problems of isolation tended to be particularly pronounced. In urging the establishment of an independent journal of chemistry, Frank Clarke asked: " . . . how is all this material published? A little of it in the *American Journal of Science and Arts;* a part in foreign periodicals; another portion in several local transactions . . . . In short the work is widely scattered; and some of it is effectually buried beyond the reach of a majority of our fellow chemists." See his "Address," *Proceedings of the American Association for the Advancement of Science* 27 (1879): 141.

29. For instance, the rather sudden upturn in American chemical research in the 1880s, stimulated by the institution of graduate studies at Johns Hopkins University, led to a rejection of a great deal of that work submitted to the *Journal of Science* by its editor, James D. Dana, who found it "too highly specialized and voluminous for a journal of general science." The work was therefore initially published largely in the *Berichte der deutschen chemischen Gesellschaft* and thereafter in the newly founded *American Chemical Journal*. See Edward H. Beardsley, *The Rise of the American Chemical Profession, 1850–1900* (Gainesville: University of Florida Monographs, 1964), p. 39.

30. A similarly gradual development is evident in the area of cytology, which has come a long way since Bichat's taxonomy of twelve tissues, or for that matter, since Berres's histological atlas, or even the work of Kölliker and his contemporaries. Above that, however, specialties seem to experience exponential growth once they have achieved an independent status. In the case of cytology, the threshold may be placed around 1884 and the initial publication of *Cellule: recueil de cytolgie et d'histologie,* though greatly accelerated growth did not occur until the twentieth century. In 1924 the *Zeitschrift*

für Zellforschung und mikroskopische Anatomie was founded, which now appears in no less than twelve annual volumes. Since that time Virchow's *Archiv* has also found it necessary to establish a separate section for cell pathology. Since 1950 the number of special societies in the area has also grown impressively, so that not only economically advanced countries such as the United States, Japan, and Poland have their cytochemical and histochemical societies, but even Calcutta University has a cytogenetics laboratory. The technological aspects of the specialty are served by institutions such as the Biological Stain Commission. Is cytology a "discipline"? Taxonomically, probably no; sociologically, yes.

31. Hornell Hart, "Acceleration in Social Change," in Francis R. Allen, et al., *Technology and Social Change* (New York: Appleton-Century-Crofts, 1957), p. 51.

32. See Paul F. Lazarsfeld, "Notes on the History of Quantification in Sociology: Trends, Sources and Problems," *Isis* 52 (1961): 277–333.

33. See Albert J. Reiss, Jr., "Sociology," in *International Encyclopedia of the Social Sciences*, ed. David L. Sills (New York: Macmillan, 1968), 15: 12–21.

34. Ibid., p. 17. The number of degree holders in sociology and social psychology grew from 14,609 in 1930 to 261,364 in 1970. Further, the growth rates in professions associated with academic disciplines are illustrated dramatically by the award of 315 degrees at *all* levels of the "social science professions" in 1930 (only 18 of which were doctorates), as compared to the award of 419 doctorates alone in the professions in 1970, the total of degree awards having risen to 26,667! Douglas L. Adkins, *The Great American Degree Machine: An Economic Analysis of the Human Resource Output of Higher Education* (Berkeley: Carnegie Commission on Higher Education, 1975), pp. 97–101.

35. American Economic Association, *Index of Economic Journals*, vols. 1–5 (Homewood, Ill.: R.D. Irwin, 1961–62).

36. See Clemens Menze, "Grundzüge der Bildungsphilosophie Wilhelm Humboldts," in *Bildung und Gesellschaft*, Hans Steffen, Hrsg. (Göttingen: Vandenhoeck & Ruprecht, 1972), pp. 5–22.

37. Berlin's primacy was recognized at the time, and therefore it generally served as a model for other university reform. What contemporaries found most noteworthy about Berlin was the fact that the natural sciences were very strongly represented through such teachers as Ermann, Rose, Mitscherlich, and Rudolphi. Berlin, Halle, and Göttingen all offered courses in experimental physics and chemistry in the 1820s. Berlin also had the largest proportion of faculty to students (1:13) amongst European universities—an area in which Germany generally led: Leipzig, 1:17; Göttingen, 1:17½; Halle, 1:20½; Vienna, 1:22; Paris, 1:27; Cambridge, 1:48½; Edinburgh, 1:102. All these conditions at German institutions were obviously conducive to the development of specialties. See H.F. Kilian, *Die Universitäten Deutschlands in medicinisch-naturwissenschaftlicher Hinsicht* (Heidelberg: n.p., 1828), pp. 27–54.

38. The development of the German railway network is a case in point. By 1871 it was 25 percent larger than that of France, although it does not antedate 1835. The state's role in this growth was a direct one: for, whereas in 1840 92 percent of German railways were still privately operated, the proportion had sunk to 65 percent by 1850 and comprised a mere 5.5

percent in 1860. W.A. Cole and Phyllis Deane, "The Growth of National Incomes," *The Cambridge Economic History of Europe* (Cambridge: The University Press, 1966), 6, part 1: 15–18. See also William O. Henderson, *The Rise of German Industrial Power 1834–1914* (London: Temple Smith, 1975), pp. 207–12.

39. Edward Frankland, "Chemical Research in England," *Nature* 3 (1871): 445.

40. Among these were P.W. Hofmann, Fischer, Fries, Bopp, Caro, Griess, Geyger, Kolbe, and Leibius. See George Haines, IV, *German Influence upon English Education and Science, 1800–1866* (New London: Connecticut College, 1957), pp. 48–50, 55.

41. In each decade between 1873 and 1914, Germany's per capita national product rose 21.6 percent, compared to Britain's 12.5 percent. Germany's share in world output had been 13 percent in 1870, and this grew to 16 percent by 1900, whereas in the same period Britain's share declined from 32 to 18 percent. Henderson, p. 173.

42. See David S. Landes, "Technological Change and Development in Western Europe, 1750–1914," in *Cambridge Economic History of Europe,* pp. 496–504, 559; see also Michael Sanderson, *The Universities and British Industry* (London: Routledge & Kegan Paul, 1972), pp. 16–21; and for a brief survey, Henderson, pp. 186–89.

43. See Landes, pp. 477–96, 516–17, and Henderson, pp. 189–98.

44. Ibid., 517; see also Sanderson, pp. 14–16. The German financial crisis of 1873–96, which was characterized by falling prices, reduced profits and low interest rates, also had the effect of eliminating technologically inefficient industries, while bringing about even closer ties between industry and government.

45. Krupp established a research laboratory in 1862, Zeiss in the 1870s; Siemens and Halske expanded their existing research facilities to include a chemical laboratory in 1872, and Bayer's large laboratory was founded in 1891. For a discussion of the impact of academic training on industry and technology during Germany's industrialization drive, see Jürgen Kocka, *Unternehmer in der deutschen Industrialisierung* (Göttingen: Vandenhoeck & Ruprecht, 1975), pp. 105–10; and for the influence of industry on scientific research, see Lothar Burchardt, *Wissenschaftspolitik im Wilhelminischen Deutschland* (Göttingen: Vandenhoeck & Ruprecht, 1975).

46. See Sanderson, pp. 31–33; and Michelina Vaughan and Margaret Archer, *Social Conflict and Educational Change in England and France, 1789–1848* (Cambridge: The University Press, 1971), pp. 45–59, 93–116.

47. Quoted in Haines, p. 14.

48. Ibid., pp. 25–27.

49. A similarly liberal view of education was expressed as late as 1867 by John Stuart Mill in his "Rector's Inaugural Address Delivered to the University of St. Andrews," in which he argued that professional specialized knowledge was not the proper function of the university.

50. Haines, p. 18.

51. Ibid., pp. 25–27.

52. Whereas at the Great Exhibition of London in 1851, Britain's exhibits excelled in nearly all 100 departments, they received awards in only ten of ninety departments in 1867. Sanderson, p. 9. Arguments for reform,

based on recognition of the threat of competition, were put forward most forcefully by Herbert Spencer and T.H. Huxley. Ibid., pp. 6–8.

53. Ibid., pp. 8–9.

54. All figures are for 1860; see Landes, pp. 568–70.

55. Ibid., p. 571.

56. Ibid., p. 573.

57. See W.W. Thornton, "Technical Education in England," *Cornhill Magazine* 24 (1871): 323–41.

58. Sanderson, pp. 10–12.

59. Abraham Flexner, *Universities: American, English, German* (London: Oxford University Press, 1930), p. 254.

60. Ibid., p. 255. The American tendency to outspecialize the Germans whom they were imitating was even more extreme, so that the German technical schools could finally point to the American example in arguing for their right to grant degrees at the end of the century. See Kocka, p. 106.

61. See, for instance, the alarmed reaction of E.E. Williams, *Made in Germany* (London: W. Heinemann, 1896).

62. For historical sources on the evolution of American colleges and universities, see Richard Hofstadter and William Smith, eds., *American Higher Education: A Documentary History,* 2 vols. (Chicago: University of Chicago Press, 1961).

63. Frederick Rudolph, *The American College and University: A History* (New York: Knopf, 1962), p. 406.

64. For the antecedents to this reform movement, see Richard J. Storr, *The Beginnings of Graduate Education in America* (Chicago: University of Chicago Press, 1953).

65. Rudolph, p.337.

66. Charles F. Thwing, *The American and the German University* (New York: Macmillan, 1928), pp. 140–41.

67. As Rudolph put it (p.334): " . . . the American university was no simple reflection of the German university . . . Yet, because the German example was paramount, almost everywhere in the creation of an American university there was a fundamental attachment to the graduate faculty of arts and sciences, to the idea of a body of scholars and students pushing forward the frontiers of pure knowledge."

68. Ibid., p. 266.

69. Flexner, pp. 73–74.

70. Quoted in Rudolph, p. 266.

71. "If you persist in taking the utilitarian view and ask me what is the good of Mr. Glaisher's determination of the least factors of the missing three out of the first nine million numbers . . . , I shall be forced to say I do not know; and if you press me harder I shall be obliged to express my conviction that nobody knows; but I know, and you know, and everybody may know, who will take the pains to inquire, that the progress of mathematics underlies all progress in exact knowledge." Daniel Coit Gilman, *The Benefits Which Society Derives from Universities* (Baltimore: Johns Hopkins University, 1885), pp. 15–16.

72. Flexner, pp. 80, 86.

73. Beardsley, pp. 61, 43, note 1, and 60, note 59.

74. There is an additional dimension within this framework, which

Greenberg calls the "chauvinism of pure science." He points out that the former editor of *Science,* Philip H. Abelson, noted that "professors have looked dow . on nonuniversity research, have regarded its practitioners as inferiors, and have attempted to curtail their activities . . . Most university science graduates must eventually find employment in nonacademic posts. When they do they accept for themselves what they have been taught is a second-class status." Greenberg, p. 35.

75. Beardsley, pp. 62–66. Here again, research was first introduced as an integral component in industries whose competitiveness was closely correlated with their ability to incorporate technological change.

76. Alvin Weinberg points out that "even the professor of purest intent must be in some measure loyal to the Estate which he represents. As a result, government scientific advisory circles tend to be preoccupied with science at the universities, rather than with science in industry or in government laboratories; the whole structure and cast of thinking is geared to the problem of university science, and the limitations of the university as an instrument of government are overlooked. It would not be a great exaggeration to describe the advisory apparatus . . . as a lobby for the scientific university." Quoted in Greenberg, p. 16.

77. Quoted in Rudolph, p. 352. Cf. Thorstein Veblen, *The Higher Learning in America,* 3d printing (Stanford: Academic Reprints, 1954), pp. 16–17.

78. As Rudolph notes (p. 404): " . . . without research, there would be no departments, no departmental chairmen, no hierarchy—only teachers."

79. The reform movement that initiated the American university had grown out of a Jacksonian democratic view of education and science. William Ellery Channing expressed these views in 1841: "Through the press, discoveries and theories, once the monopoly of philosophers, have become the property of the multitude . . . . The characteristic of our age, then, is not the improvement of science, rapid as that is, so much as its extension to all men." "The Present Age," *Works* (Boston: American Unitarian Association, 1878), p. 160.

80. W.E. Stone, "The Relation of Teaching to Research," *Journal of the American Chemical Society* 15 (1893): 666; the italics are mine.

81. A.G. Mayer, "The Material vs. the Intellectual Development of our Universities," *Science* 20 (1904): 45.

82. Teaching alone is not a sufficient condition for the development of independent disciplines or specialties. Philip M. Morse recollects that in the 1920s, for instance, "MIT had been primarily an engineering school, with the science departments regarded as service departments." *In at the Beginnings: A Physicist's Life* (Cambridge, Mass.: MIT Press, 1977), p. 101.

83. Disciplinarians must sometimes recruit consciously and actively at this level. Morse (p. 134) recollects that "[Karl] Compton and Robert Millikan, the president of Cal Tech, worked to reverse the attitude of American industry [in the 1930s]. What had to be done was to persuade industry that the physicist is a scientific generalist, able to contribute to almost any technological problem. . . . In addition to persuading industrialists that they needed physicists, we also had to persuade more high school and college students that a career in physics would be enjoyable as well as economically viable."

On the other hand, academic institutions tend to be relatively receptive to the formation of specialties stimulated by external markets. As late as 1950, for example, there existed no academic specialty of "Computer and Information Science," so that obviously no degrees were awarded in the field. In 1960, however, eleven bachelors', ten second-level degrees, and one doctorate were awarded, and in 1970 the respective totals had grown to 2,782, 3,791, and 261. Adkins, pp. 98–100.

84. See Rudolph, pp. 396–97, 400.

85. Morse (p. 135) estimates that of those MIT graduates who received Ph.D.s in physics since the 1930s, ½ went on to serve on physics faculties, ⅛ to academic administrative positions, and ⅜ to "nonacademic jobs doing research in governmental or industrial laboratories or guiding scientific policy in high-level administrative positions."

86. Rudolph, pp. 406, 403.

87. Ibid., p. 406.

88. For the effects of management on the development of professions in industry in the early twentieth century, see especially Chapter 10 in Harry Braverman, *Labor and Monopoly Capital: The Degradation of Work in the Twentieth Century* (New York: Monthly Review Press, 1974). The demand by management for specialized training, which the universities sought to fulfill, may have had a secondary effect on the trends towards specialization within academic institutions themselves. However, this issue still needs much more detailed investigation.

89. The claim of being able to produce results, even if very indirect ones, is made—sometimes without any viable justification whatever—even by the "pure" sciences, and constitutes an important part of the rhetoric of grantsmanship. See Greenberg, Chapter 2.

90. Raymond H. Kahn, at the time professor of anatomy at the University of Michigan Medical School, observed in 1966 an odd narrowness in the multidisciplinary premedical training of entering students: "Over 80 percent of our entering students were knowledgeable about the structure of DNA, the triplet coding system as well as many other features of cellular biology. On the other hand, less than 15% had any appreciation of tissue composition and less than 2% were aware of organ structure and function . . . . It is indeed curious that a 'pre-med' student is thoroughly familiar with the esoterics of molecular biology while he has little or no appreciation for tissues and organs and the essential processes involved in their function." Quoted in Greenberg, p. 39.

91. Paul Monroe, "The Opportunity and Need for Research Work in the History of Education," *Pedagogical Seminary* 17 (1910): 55.

92. Bernard Bailyn, "Education as a Discipline: Some Historical Notes," in *The Discipline of Education*, ed. John Walton and James L. Knethe (Madison: University of Wisconsin Press, 1963), pp. 128–30, 126.

93. These titles are listed by Flexner, pp. 102–3.

94. Adkins, pp. 97–101.

95. See *Strive to Build a Socialist University of Science and Engineering* (Peking: Foreign Languages Press, 1972).

96. It is important to note, however, that this kind of broadly interdisciplinary effort tends, as Greenberg has observed in Chapter 2 of his study, to remain isolated on the level of applied sciences. The pure sciences at the top of the academic hierarchy tend to maintain a splendidly isolated disciplinarity.

97. The ability to avoid direct responsibility to the ultimate supporter of disciplinary structures—the public—is an important feature in the development of the modern facade of "neutral" science, which dominates institutions of specialized knowledge and may merit further sociological analysis.

98. See "Grant Titles from History," *Science News* 108 (1975): 266. For the sociology of grantsmanship see Chapter 8 in Pierre van den Berghe, *Academic Gamesmanship* (New York: Abelard-Schuman, 1970).

99. See Victor Kraft, *Der Wiener Kreis. Der Ursprung des Neupositivismus* (Vienna: Springer Verlag, 1950); Otto Neurath, Rudolf Carnap, and Hans Hahn, *Wissenschaftliche Weltauffassung: Der Wiener Kreis* (Vienna: Ernst Mach Verein, 1929); Otto Neurath et al., *Encyclopedia of Unified Science* (Chicago: University of Chicago Press, 1938).

100. Adolf Harnack, "Vom Grossbetrieb der Wissenschaft," *Preussische Jahrbücher,* 1905, pp. 193–94.

The Curriculum, the Disciplines, and Interdisciplinarity in Higher Education

Historical Perspective

Hans Flexner

The history of the curriculum in American higher education has been one of increasing diversification and specialization—from the study of the medieval arts and sciences augmented by the Scriptures, to all that the word *experience* may encompass; from a view of knowledge as absolute and universal, to knowledge as tentative and hypothetical. Organizationally the transition has been from a residential college that consisted of a president who also taught, two or three tutors, and a dozen or so students, to a highly complex multiversity that may consist of literally hundreds of administrators, several thousand faculty and staff, and a student body that is counted in six figures and that may be scattered across the country if not the world. As students have changed—from what was assumed to have been a homogeneous group of youths headed for the ministry or civic leadership, to an incredibly heterogeneous population ranging from high school graduates to adults of all ages with a wide variety of interests, needs, and aspirations—so too have the types, purposes, and programs of postsecondary institutions changed.

The most important change, however, has to do with the faculty. The young, inexperienced, and often impecunious tutors— those who not only taught their youthful charges in the classroom but who were also responsible for maintaining strict discipline and severe moral and ethical standards—bore little resemblance to the old-time college professor and even less to the university professor who has been socialized to professional norms that stress disciplinary research and scholarship and that literally determine the social structure and academic organization of the university.

The main concern of the chapter is with the development and

use of knowledge in its various divisions and in relation to both research and the curriculum. Thus it deals with educational change and reform, at first through the developing disciplines and their impact on the curriculum, but also, and increasingly, through extradisciplinary social, political, and economic forces. Toward the latter part of the chapter the discussion turns to two related notions—general education and interdisciplinarity, the focus of this volume. The former is viewed as a revolt against the fragmentation that had come to characterize liberal education and as a major philosophical and curricular departure; the latter represents, among other things, an attempt to reorganize and integrate knowledge along lines other than those defined by the present disciplines. The intention is not to minimize the contribution of the disciplines in this historical account, but rather it is to consider their value as well as their limitations in a society and in an educational system marked by serious intellectual and social discontinuities. The proliferation of knowledge delineated throughout the chapter is thus seen as both a major source of disintegration and a challenge to the badly needed reassessment and eventual achievement of common goals and values. The extreme importance in all this of the faculty and, in a number of cases, of college and university presidents, receives attention throughout the chapter.

The Emergence of Academic Reform

The most arresting thing about the advertisement that appeared in the *New York Gazette* on June 3, 1754 announcing the opening of King's College (later Columbia) was the description it contained of a curriculum so inclusive in scope that it purported to instruct those who sought to attend the college

> in the learned languages, and in the arts of reasoning exactly, of writing correctly, and speaking eloquently; and in the arts of numbering and measuring, of surveying and navigation, of geography and history, of husbandry, commerce and government, and in the knowledge of all nature in the heavens above us, and in the air, water and earth around us, and in the various kinds of meteors, stones, mines, and minerals, plants and animals, and of everything useful for the comfort, the convenience and elegance of life, [and] in the chief manufactures relating to any of these things . . . [1]

Nor did King's College neglect the religious aim, still paramount in the colonial colleges, particularly among the enthusiasts of the

Great Awakening. But as its first president, the Rev. Dr. Samuel Johnson, advised parents of potential students, "It is to be understood, that as to their religion, there is no intention to impose on the scholars, the peculiar tenets of any particular sect of Christians." Furthermore the announcement failed to include among the purposes of the college the traditional one of training ministers. Instead the emphasis would be on practical and useful studies and on the teaching of "all knowledge." Although Johnson's effort to implement his proposed reforms failed in large measure, it served as an important stimulus to those who followed.

But secular and scientific studies received their greatest impetus several years prior to the founding of King's College, when Benjamin Franklin opened his Academy in Philadelphia. The Latin branch of the Academy eventually came to serve as a college preparatory school, while the English branch was seen by some as a mere trade school and hence of little consequence to collegiate education. However, with Franklin's support, the head of the newly created College of Philadelphia (later the University of Pennsylvania), William Smith, formulated a curriculum comprised in good part of science and practical studies intended to serve students for whom the traditional curriculum had little utility.[2] The Philadelphia program represented a major departure, one that little resembled the trivium and quadrivium from which other programs had been derived. Stated in the most comprehensive, secular terms, the program clearly was not intended to serve a religious purpose.[3]

Both the American Revolution and the Enlightenment hastened the secularization of the curriculum, and nowhere was this more evident than at the College of William and Mary. As governor of Virginia, Thomas Jefferson spent the year 1779 in Williamsburg, where as a member of the board of visitors he attempted to reform the educational program of his alma mater. From the outset Jefferson wanted to make of the college a "genuine university" that would serve as the capstone to his proposed state system of education. Although the changes actually effected fell short of Jefferson's expectations, he was able to abolish two professorships of divinity and one of oriental languages, previously required to serve the Church of England but following the Revolution considered to be incompatible with the freedoms of the new democracy. In their place he substituted a professorship of law and police (later politics), one of anatomy, medicine, and chemistry, and one of modern languages. The responsibility for natural history was added to those of the professor of mathematics and natural philosophy.[4]

By the turn of the century Jefferson's hope of making "a real state university" out of William and Mary had disappeared. Due largely to financial losses and to the removal of the capital from Williamsburg to Richmond, the college declined steadily. But Jefferson's profound commitment to the state university idea as a critical part of his social and political reforms persisted. After years of planning, searching, and preparing, the new state institution in Charlottesville, the University of Virginia, admitted its first group of students in 1825. Its curriculum, expanded by the addition of new subjects, was organized into eight schools or courses of study with a professorship attached to each, in the following manner: ancient languages, modern languages, mathematics, natural philosophy, natural history, anatomy and medicine, moral philosophy, and law.[5] Students at the new university were able to choose which one of the eight schools they wanted to attend. In order to graduate, however, they needed to complete all of the prescribed subjects in that school.

The inclusion, increasingly, of a variety of new subjects eventually led Brown University's innovative president, Francis Wayland, to raise the most fundamental questions yet about the nature and quality of undergraduate education. Wayland was troubled by the thought that the time required for the baccalaureate remained the same, while the amount of knowledge and the number of subjects had increased very substantially. His conclusion—that education had become superficial, that students skimmed rapidly over numerous texts, developing passive receptivity rather than "originating and active power"—has since been reiterated by generations of college teachers, as has his final assessment that "they knew nothing well."[6] It also concerned Wayland that a large and growing segment of midnineteenth-century American society, the sons of merchants, mechanics, and manufacturers, had nowhere to go to further their education, since the traditional curriculum failed to serve them.

As a result of his searching assessment of the American college, Wayland proposed what was one of the most radical curricular reforms of the time. The object of the change, he told the members of the Brown Corporation, would be "to adapt the institution to the wants, not of a class, but of the whole community." And he continued: "It by no means is to be taken for granted, in a country like ours, that every college is to teach the same studies, and to the same extent." It would be far better, he pointed out, if each institution consulted its own community and utilized such facilities as it had to the best interest of that community.[7]

For colleges that chose to adapt their programs to the wants of the whole community, Wayland offered these principles: abandon the fixed four-year term and allow each student to carry, within limits, whatever number of courses he chose; to the extent possible, permit each student to study what he chose, all that he chose, and nothing but what he chose; let the nature of the course itself determine the time allotted to it; in addition to the present courses, new ones should be established on the basis of the requirements of the various classes of the community; students attending any particular course should be at liberty to attend any other; no student should be admitted as a degree candidate unless he has satisfied by examination the studies required for the college; and no student should be obligated to proceed to a degree unless he chose to do so. Wayland's final recommendation seems especially noteworthy in retrospect: every student should be entitled to a certificate of such proficiency as he may have attained in every course attended.

There were of course others, whose opposition to practical and vocational studies was vigorous and extended. Unquestionably the most influential of these was the famed Yale Report of 1828, which argued persuasively in defense of the totally prescribed curriculum as the most effective vehicle for the acquisition of the proper "discipline and furniture of the mind." The discipline in this instance was an approximation of what came to be known as faculty psychology; the furniture was of course the content. For example, "From the pure mathematics he [the student] learns the art of demonstrative reasoning. In attending to the physical sciences, he becomes familiar with facts, with the process of induction, and the varieties of probable evidence. In ancient literature, he finds some of the most finished models of taste."[8]

Among the most influential documents of the first half of the nineteenth century, the Report was widely circulated. Yale had provided a growing number of colleges in the South and the West with the largest number of presidents and faculty supplied by a single institution; understandably, many of them found the orientation of the Report congenial. It was, after all, the clearest and most sophisticated expression of the curricular status quo yet enunciated, and its authors were two of the most respected long-time members of the Yale community.

The continued expansion of the curriculum by the addition of new scientific and practical studies was seriously retarded by the creation of literally hundreds of small local colleges.[9] The major impetus for these institutions, which claimed as their purpose service to their local denominations, was provided by the Dartmouth College decision handed down by the Supreme Court in 1819. Essentially the decision protected private colleges from state interference or control.[10] Although the decision assured their legal right to exist, their survival was another matter. Poorly conceived, often without adequate funds or facilities, and in some cases with only a paper faculty or student body, several hundred of these colleges collapsed on the eve of Civil War—not, however, before they had diverted a number of students from the established institutions, thereby adding to the serious financial problems of the latter.[11]

Yet for all the obstacles, the time was also one of modest reform and innovation. It saw the establishment of a number of scientific schools and institutes, among them Harvard's Lawrence Scientific School, Yale's Scheffield Scientific School, and Rensselaer Polytechnic Institute in Troy. The time had not quite come when the new practical sciences could enter some of the more prestigious colleges and universities by way of the front door. Still, reformers like Presidents Philip Lindsley of the University of Nashville and Eliphalet Nott of Union College, Amherst's President Jacob Abbott, and the University of Vermont's James Marsh were among those who contributed much to the early phases of curricular reform in American higher education.

But given a long and powerful academic tradition that demanded a rigorously prescribed classical curriculum, add a religious tradition concerned primarily with maintaining the orthodoxy, and it is easy to see why major educational reforms were exceedingly difficult to achieve, especially since the greatest opposition generally came from within the institution. Thus the real significance of some of the earlier efforts to reform the curriculum were to be found not so much in actual substantive changes as in the identification and articulation of fundamental problems and possible alternatives for their resolution. While most basic changes had to await another generation, one critic of American collegiate education and a strong advocate of major academic reform, George Ticknor, warrants special attention, even in an abbreviated account such as this. It was through his observations that American college presidents and faculty first came to know the German university.

The Disciplines, the Curriculum, and the Elective Principle

George Ticknor and his friend and fellow Bostonian, Edward Everett, were probably the first Americans to undertake advanced graduate study in a German university.[12] Their experience, and especially the twenty months spent at Göttingen, made a lasting impression on both, but particularly on the brilliant young American scholar and future Harvard language professor. In 1815, the year that Ticknor arrived in the medieval town, Göttingen had an enrollment of some 950 students and a faculty of forty professors and about the same number of lecturers. Since each professor and lecturer usually presented two courses annually, some seventy or eighty courses were being conducted concurrently. The University library contained over 200,000 volumes in a variety of specialized fields of study.

The Harvard of Ticknor's day had an enrollment of about 230 students, many of whom were admitted at the age of thirteen or fourteen, and a faculty of twenty-five or thirty professors, instructors, and tutors. The library of 20,000 volumes was considered adequate for the time.

Shortly after his arrival in Göttingen, Ticknor embarked on a period of study quite unlike any he had ever experienced. He began his studies of Greek, German, Biblical exegesis, fine arts, literary history, and natural history at five in the morning and continued working throughout the day, usually until ten at night. It did not take Ticknor long to discover the "mortifying distance" that existed between a European and an American scholar. In fact, he noted that America did not yet know what a scholar is, much less how to produce one. "Learning," Ticknor wrote as he recognized the important distinction, "is here as much a profession and occupation as merchandise . . . while in America learning is generally an accomplishment and a show—a gala dress but not homely wear."[13]

Ticknor considered the private tutorial the most effective and valuable instrument of university education. So impressed was he, however, by the philosophical seminar, in which students exchanged criticisms of one another's dissertations, that he planned to transplant the idea and practice to the American university. He was especially enthusiastic about "the spirit of pursuing literary studies philosophically." Concerning lectures, Ticknor believed that they were the best vehicle for providing a comprehensive perspective of a broad topic as well as a sense of the significant relationships among the parts.[14]

As a young Bostonian gentleman and Brahmin, Ticknor was as disturbed as were his colleagues by the Biblical scholar Johann Eichhorn, who discounted miracles as natural events or as the delusions of witnesses. A Unitarian, Ticknor fully believed in investigating the very basis of Christianity. But he complained about Eichhorn, "His faith in Christ is, as far as I can understand it, precisely like his faith in Socrates."[15] Yet Ticknor was enormously impressed by the freedom and advanced scholarship that he found in Germany. To Jefferson he wrote,

> The first result of this enthusiasm and learning, which immediately broke through all barriers that opposed it, was an universal toleration in matters of opinion. No matter what a man thinks, he may teach it and print it, not only without molestation from the government but also without molestation from public opinion which is so often more oppressive than the aim of authority. I know not that anything like it exists in any other country . . . . Every day books appear on government and religion which in the rest of Europe would be suppressed by the state and in America would be put into the great *catalogus expurgatorius* of public opinion but which here are read as any other books and judged according to their literary and philosophical merit. They get, perhaps, a severe review or a severe answer, but these are weapons which both parties can use and unfairness is very common . . . . If truth is to be attained by freedom of inquiry, as I doubt not it is, the German professors and literati are certainly in the high road, and have the way quietly open before them.[16]

Greatly as Ticknor admired many features of the German pattern of university education, he soon realized that its unprecedented scholarly achievements would have been impossible without the gymnasium. That institution, far different from the American high school, prepared students for the German university. After visiting two or three gymnasia, which he found in every respect superior to the best American colleges, Ticknor expressed the hope that America might see the wisdom of emulating at least some of their features.[17]

When Ticknor and his colleagues finally returned to Boston in August of 1819, he was appointed Smith Professor of French and Spanish Languages and Professor of Belles Lettres at Harvard University. Ticknor found the college frustrating. Students were divided into recitation sections alphabetically; the prescribed and sequentially ordered curriculum required of all students was the traditional one; recitation, still the most common teaching method, led students to study a given book rather than a subject; and, as one Harvard graduate recalled, teachers were there not to teach but to assign grades.[18]

Ticknor's proposed reforms were comprehensive. His advocacy of more rigorous entrance examinations, of grouping students according to proficiency, of allowing election of certain courses, and of more thorough teaching—all can be traced to his European experiences.[19]

The great expansion of knowledge within the traditional subjects, the emergence of new disciplines, and the demands of the larger community, all, Ticknor believed, necessitated the academic reorganization of Harvard. The division of the college into academic departments would accomplish several desired reforms. Since each department could examine its own students, it would facilitate the process of classifying students on the basis of their proficiency. Such a structure would also focus the students' attention on the study of subjects rather than textbooks. Furthermore, the new structure would provide an efficient means of controlling electives, which had become necessary due to the substantial increase in knowledge, itself a product of the methods Ticknor had observed and admired at Göttingen.[20]

Ticknor urged Harvard to open its doors to students who did not seek a degree but who would benefit from specialized training in one or more subjects. He was quite convinced that Harvard had the resources to do just that. Its responsibilities, Ticknor insisted, needed to go well beyond the provision of a mandarin education for aristocrats, that is, an education designed to perpetuate the power of that class.[21]

Although Ticknor tried for several years to move Harvard closer to his conception of what it should be, his efforts were often frustrated and his success only partial. At one point, in 1823, a student rebellion (of such proportions that over half of the graduating class was expelled just prior to commencement) provided a climate seemingly conducive to reform. While neither the corporation nor the faculty were inclined to adopt Ticknor's total program, they did allow departments to introduce both ability sectioning and a measure of election. But only a few departments experimented on a very limited and tentative basis; in time, Ticknor's department alone continued these reforms. In the end most of the faculty, including those who initially supported moderate changes, decided against Ticknor.

Ticknor's nephew Charles W. Eliot was correct in his assessment of his uncle as "a reformer fifty years in advance of his time."[22] Ticknor was among the first and smallest wave of young American scholars to study in Germany at a time when that country was dominated by Hegelian thought. It was not until the midnineteenth century that the second wave of American students in Germany encountered the concept of research. But the notion was still far from clear in the minds of many who returned, although it generally meant respect for German scholarship and expertise. "Their excellence," wrote Michigan's President Henry Tappan in commenting upon the German universities, "consists in two things: first, they are purely Universities, without any admixture of collegial tuition. Secondly, they are complete as Universities," and this is reflected in their libraries, material resources, programs, and above all in a faculty "so numerous that a proper division of labor takes place, and every subject is thoroughly discussed."[23]

By the 1850s the German university had come to embrace the notion of pure or nonutilitarian learning; it also included the concept of *Wissenschaft,* or investigation that could be historical or philosophical as well as empirical; the overall aim of the German university continued to be expressed in terms of an all-encompassing idealism.[24] After spending four years at Berlin, Geneva, and Göttingen, and somewhat less time at Leipzig, Marburg, and Vienna, James Morgan Hart wrote by far the best and most instructive book on German university life.

> To the German mind [he told American students hopeful of doing their graduate study in Germany] the collective idea of a university implies . . . an object of study [or purpose] . . . and two conditions. The object is *Wissenschaft;* the conditions are *Lehrfreiheit* and *Lernfreiheit.* By *Wissenschaft* the Germans mean knowledge in the most exalted sense of the term, namely, the ardent, methodical, independent search after truth in any and all of its forms, but wholly irrespective of utilitarian application. *Lehrfreiheit* means that one who teaches, the professor or *Privatdocent,* is free to teach what he chooses, as he chooses. *Lernfreiheit* or the freedom of learning, denotes the emancipation of the student from *Schulzwang,* compulsory drill by recitation.[25]

Enthusiastic as Hart and a growing number of American academics were about the new science and the advancement of knowledge, Hart was quick to point out that the German university was decidedly not a place where anyone could study anything. There were art schools, commercial schools, polytechnic institutes, and others for those who needed or wanted them. As Hart perceived it, the German university had only one object—*to train thinkers.* Furthermore, even in the professions themselves theory and practice were carefully distinguished, the former only being considered as legitimately within the sphere of the university.

Hart was among the first to recognize the impact of increasing specialization and faculty intolerance on both the student and the curriculum. With the creation of new professorships in the natural sciences filled by energetic young men often intolerant of students who failed to keep pace with them, and with the same situation prevailing in the older departments, "Our undergraduates have at the present day too many studies, and are hurried through difficult and *disconnected subjects* at too rapid a rate." Urged on by a spirit of rivalry, the new professors in the natural sciences and the new professors in the classics "threaten to tear the youth asunder between them."[26]

Hart's observation is of major importance. It is one of the earliest to recognize the potential effect of increasingly specialized graduate standards on undergraduates, many without graduate pretensions and nearly all totally unprepared for the experience.

In the latter part of the century, Americans studying in German universities could discern a tendency toward painstaking research and minuteness in methods that was as evident in historiography as it was in the laboratory. Importantly, however, while these methods were not perceived by most German professors to have any inherent connection with the much more comprehensive academic purpose of the university, returning Americans spoke of "scientific research," a combination of two words derived from two different contexts within the German university. Thus the German notion of "pure learning" was translated as "pure research," with a narrow methodological connotation that was not a part of the original notion. The broad, contemplative aspect of *Wissenschaft* was overlooked, and almost from the outset the term was narrowly interpreted as "specifically scientific." And the all-encompassing idealism and sense of unity so widespread in Germany was lost altogether on this side of the Atlantic.[27] Unlike the German scientist, many an American scientist viewed this significantly altered and abridged conception of science as the sole purpose of the university.

Nothing so surely symbolized research-oriented Germany, scientific Germany, as the newly founded (1876) university in Baltimore, the Johns Hopkins University. When the trustees asked Presidents Eliot of Harvard, White of Cornell, and Angell of Michigan for their advice regarding the sort of institution that ought to be established in Baltimore, the last thing that would have occurred to the three was a university in the German manner. How, asked Eliot, could one even expect to establish such an institution in Baltimore? What could possibly attract and retain the sort of professors a "true" university must have? And certainly one could not expect the Baltimore schools, or for that matter any other American public schools, to prepare their students for a true university. It would be far better, the trustees were told, to begin with an undergraduate college and to engage only the few professors required during the first year. If successful, similar arrangements could be made for each succeeding year.

On another matter, however, each of the three independently recommended the same person for the Hopkins presidency—Daniel Coit Gilman.[28] It was a happy choice. Gilman left no doubt that he intended to build a graduate university; he saw no advantage in establishing still another four-year college. For several reasons, however, among them the expectations of the trustees and parents and the inadequate preparation provided by most high schools, Gilman noted that it would be a simple matter to mark out prescribed courses, either classical or scientific, lasting four years.[29]

In the graduate university, however, attainment rather than time would be the condition of promotion; the good of the individual rather than that of the classes would be the major factor. By advocating the most liberal promotion of all useful knowledge, especially of departments neglected elsewhere, some election of programs and courses became necessary. Gilman also distinguished between college and university methods. "Liberal advanced instruction for those who want it; distinctive honors for those who win them; appointed courses for those who need them; special courses for those who can take no others."[30]

Nothing, however, could rival in importance the care, time, and effort that Gilman invested in the cultivation and selection of his initial faculty, whom he considered the heart of a great university. Gilman's first selections proved to be remarkable. The oldest of the group, James Sylvester, had already an established reputation as a mathematician both here and in Europe. Ira Remsen, after a distinguished career as a researcher and teacher of chemistry at Hopkins, became its second president. The youngest and perhaps the most talented of the group, physicist Henry Rowland, was engaged by Gilman as an assistant professor. While Gilman continued his two-year search for the best faculty available, young Rowland spent the time in Germany, where his work in spectroscopy won him not only wide recognition and honor but also a full professorship at Hopkins at twice the salary offered him originally.[31] As Gilman later recalled,

In selecting a staff of teachers, the Trustees have determined to consider especially the devotion of the candidate to some particular line of study and the certainty of his eminence in that specialty; the power to pursue independent and original investigation, and to inspire the young with enthusiasm for study and *research;* the willingness to cooperate in building up a new institution; and the freedom from tendencies toward ecclesiastical or sectional controversies.[32]

Gilman's achievements did not stop with the creation of what has often been described as the first true university in America. By placing the medical school and therefore medical instruction under the control of the university, and by utilizing a part of the Hopkins Hospital for clinical and teaching purposes, Gilman and his associates in the medical school created a viable pattern of *scientific* medicine that would be emulated widely in the future.

Both the university and the medical school faculties, both the experienced and eventually the less experienced among them, established and contributed to a number of learned journals, among them the *American Journal of Mathematics,* the *American Journal of Philology,* and the *American Chemical Journal.* Other periodicals were devoted to history and politics, to biology, to modern languages, to experimental medicine, and to anatomy, and appropriations were made to such foreign journals of importance (but that lacked support) as the *English Journal of Physiology* and the *German Journal of Assyriology.* Support was also given to the publication of important treatises such as the studies in logic of Charles Sanders Peirce and his colleagues, the physiological research of Dr. Martin, or the solar spectrum photographs of Professor Rowland.[33] There can be little doubt that Hopkins provided early and continued support for the publication of scholarly and scientific works in the disciplines and in medical research.

The relationship between the Hopkins Hospital and the University would become the prototype during the first decades of the twentieth century. The expansion and use of knowledge from the multiplying disciplines in the new research-oriented universities, together with the practical experience to be gained in the hospital clinics, revolutionized medical training and had a decided influence on other professions. Although Gilman distinguished between undergraduate and graduate methods and procedures, the peculiarly potent scientific and scholarly climate of the university left its mark on many of its undergraduates, particularly those who continued their education to the doctorate.

The organization of knowledge by disciplines had accelerated the pace of specialization and encouraged the establishment of departmental courses. The impact of seventeenth and eighteenth-century science, followed by the industrial revolution, technological advancements, agrarian agitation, and Darwinian science, all had contributed to the rapid increase in specialization. It was, in short, no longer possible to include in a four-year course of study all available subjects. A way had to be found whereby curricular decisions pertaining to the inclusion as well as to the exclusion of subjects could be justified. For Harvard's President Charles W. Eliot the way seemed clear enough—an elective system in which the undergraduate would have considerable freedom in the selection of his subjects or courses.

Eliot's advocacy of the elective system took into account a number of fundamental issues in the development of undergraduate programs. The student, Eliot noted, would have freedom in the choice of studies; he would have the opportunity to win academic distinction in a single subject or in an area of special interest; and the responsibility for developing his own habits and guiding his own conduct would largely be his. There are, furthermore, "natural safeguards" that operate within the elective system. Subjects begun earlier would need to be continued where left off; new subjects would be taken up at the beginning; some university subjects would require prerequisites; finally, Eliot believed, the more able students tended to explore in greater depth subjects congenial to them. "So effective are these natural safeguards against fickleness and inconsecutiveness in choice of studies, that artificial regulation is superfluous."[34]

But the free choice of studies is based on some additional and rather different notions. It implies that no studies are recognized to be of supreme merit. This is so, Eliot maintained, because the materials and methods of university education have always and will always continue to change. Since it is quite impossible for one mind to grasp more than a fraction of the total acquired knowledge, the university should recognize distinguished performance in a single subject. Academic honors bestowed at graduation would encourage more students to pursue special interests and thereby to create new demands for advanced instruction, stimulating teacher and student alike.

Ultimately, the major objective of the elective system, student freedom and responsibility in the choice of studies and in personal behavior, rests on what Eliot perceived to be the moral purpose of a university—i.e., to facilitate the development of self-control and self-reliance through liberty. It is not the business of a university to train men "for those functions in which implicit obedience is of the first importance." On the contrary, "It should train men for those occupations in which self-government, independence, and originating power are preeminently needed."[35]

The elective system provided undergraduates with the opportunity to specialize. It could also have been and in many instances was used to broaden their academic and intellectual horizons. The report of the committee responsible for assessing Harvard's elective system is enlightening. Both faculty and students came to regard certain subjects (the humanities) as designed for "general culture" and others (the sciences) for the training of specialists. In the eyes of the committee, this distinction was an unfortunate one. *Every* department, they urged, should provide courses for students who do not intend to specialize in that department, and such courses should require as much systematic work as other departmental courses. Thus more students should be encouraged to take honors at graduation, but honors should be made to represent something more than "a purely scholastic distinction for young specialists." Students of general culture too should be encouraged to pursue advanced study of subjects to which they do not intend to devote their careers.[36]

It is true that the election of courses designed to provide breadth varied among students, but as Eliot had pointed out, so did their interests, requirements, and aspirations. Furthermore, the term *general culture* was subject to more than one interpretation. It might refer to any part of the curriculum that was neither specifically designated as specialized nor pursued for that purpose by a particular student; or it might be interpreted as a group of courses thought to provide a common viewpoint or a common set of values. In its recognition, and even more in its advocacy of the general, nonspecialized component of the curriculum, the report might well have represented an important reevaluation, perhaps even a turning point, in what had become the history of curricular fragmentation. But the nonspecialized subjects were derived from essentially the same sources and in the same manner as those intended for specialization.

The new departure at Harvard coincided with the return of the third wave of American scientists and their notion of a German "research university," which neither had nor required (recall the gymnasium) an undergraduate college. What it required and had was a faculty of scholars and scientists, of *virtuosi*, whose power in one sense resided in their mastery of knowledge organized into disciplines.

The disciplines became their private arenas. Precisely when the new industrial organization of society seemed to demand a new flexibility in the universities, new combinations of subject matters and new modes of work, a defensive rigidity pervaded the centers of learning. . . . Disciplinary organization, in this setting, was a means for the perpetuation of cultural and academic domination of the *virtuosi.*[37]

The least susceptible to the domination of the *virtuosi,* and hence to the mandarinism of the disciplines, were the nation's land-grant colleges and universities. Their establishment was in fact heavily influenced by agrarian agitation, leading in 1862 to the first Morrill Act. Cornell was funded in part by the Act, and the universities in Wisconsin, Minnesota, Georgia, and Tennessee, among others, were enlarged by Morrill funds. Their initial commitment, and indeed their specific function, was to utilitarian and practical research, and to the preparation of students who could satisfy the technological needs of agriculture and business. In time, however, as these institutions broadened their vocational and technical character, they too fell heir to the disciplinary notions and practices of the older and more prestigious universities.

A growing and increasingly complex society requires expertise in specific fields of study; the disciplinary organization of knowledge proved to be one way of providing experts. But as Norman Birnbaum has observed, trained capacity in one connection "entailed trained incapacity in another respect."[38] Not only had natural philosophy and natural history become physics and botany, but the decomposition went well beyond that level to the creation of subdisciplines and new disciplines. The generalist, the person in possession of generalized knowledge, was rapidly becoming a rarity in the university.

While scientific research and utility were beginning to dominate the university, the proponents of "culture," "liberal culture," or "general culture," (later, liberal education or liberal arts) expressed their dislike and in some cases their hostility toward minuteness and practicality.[39] There were also differences in emphasis within the ranks of the liberal culturalists. Some, like Harvard's Irving Babbitt, were convinced that "the humanities need to be defended today against the encroachments of physical science, as they once needed to be against the encroachments of theology."[40] Babbitt went on to chastise the discipline-oriented classicists themselves for their own "exclusiveness." As Josiah Royce saw it, the traditional curriculum would never lead its graduates to true culture. And for art historian Charles Eliot Norton, "The highest end of the highest education is not anything which can be directly taught, but is the consummation of all studies."[41]

The concept of liberal culture included elements of the aesthetic, the social, and the moral. In their disciplinary roles, the aesthetic and the social were the objects of scholars in the late nineteenth-century American universities, while the moral emphasis received considerable attention in the colleges. At the outset, the liberal culturalist opposed both science and intellect for what was perceived to be their unduly critical approach. Toward the end of the century, however, the intellect gradually became associated with liberal culture itself, to the point at which the basic aim of the liberal arts faculty was precisely to elevate intelligence above all else.

Liberal culture has never achieved a dominant role in the American university; that role has been shared by research and the professions. It was in the liberal arts college that culture would emerge as a major component. The college, however, had developed or assumed the disciplinary approach and departmental structure of the university, a major supplier of its faculty. As it became more common to require a higher degree, usually the Ph.D., the result so far as college instruction was concerned left something to be desired. "Will one pretend for a moment," asked William James, "that the doctor's degree is a guarantee that its possessor will be successful as a teacher?"[42] Buffalo's Chancellor Samuel P. Capen was quite convinced that

> the vast majority of college teachers are not interested in research and they have no special talent for it. Moreover, as colleges are now administered, they have little opportunity for research after appointment to a college staff . . . . The teachers suffer because they are not trained for what they have to do; because the task of leading adolescents to knowledge and wisdom and self-control—the task which they have elected—has slight connection with productive scholarship; because the professional rewards go not to the successful performance of this task but to something quite aside from it.[43]

Here then was the liberal arts college, the curricular and organizational structures of which were determined essentially by its inherited disciplinary approach and by a faculty who for the most part were themselves trained solely in that approach. The elective system, which had reached its peak in the 1880s, was being supplanted in part at least by the major/minor system or some variation of it. But even that system offered the student a choice of programs and courses, or subjects, only. The focus, however expressed, remained on segments of knowledge derived from disciplinary investigations.

General Education and Interdisciplinarity

The emergence of the modern university not only led to the disintegration of the old-time college, but it also imposed upon its own undergraduate college criteria far better suited to university than to collegiate education. No one has yet explained, wrote no less an advocate of rigorous university standards than Abraham Flexner, why the minute investigations of the modern specialist constitute him at the same time the best teacher of young students. The undergraduate and graduate departments possess what is in effect a single faculty. Such an organization is good only, Flexner contended some seventy years ago, if the requirements of a college teacher coincide with those of the graduate school professor, which in his view they do not. The independent importance of research, which Flexner readily acknowledged, is of itself no valid excuse for the partial abandonment by the college of its essential function, teaching. Research sets up its own conditions and these are by no means always or necessarily those that prevail in the college.[44]

But discussions of curricular reforms continued to refer to the number of subjects that could be taught effectively in an age of specialization; essentially the same question, as the reader will recall, asked by Wayland in the midnineteenth century. Subjects, moreover, continued to be defined and developed along disciplinary lines. References to a common body of knowledge for all students became increasingly frequent, and the elective system was charged with destroying the unity that was thought to have characterized the earlier college. Thus, for instance, Columbia's undergraduate curriculum, one-third of which was prescribed in 1918, was one-half prescribed by 1938.

But an increase in prescription was by no means Columbia's most significant contribution. The liberal arts had long been considered appropriate for all educated men. If twentieth-century collegiate education was to remain a liberal one, to what extent could it also be a general education? And more specifically, a general education that could serve students in a twentieth-century world, which in 1917 was profoundly troubled. In its attempt to deal with the question, the Columbia faculty developed a "war aims" course, which in view of its success was followed after the war by a "peace aims" course. The new course appeared in the Columbia catalog for the first time in 1919, and soon thereafter became the core of the now-famous and often imitated Contemporary Civilizations program.[45]

After nearly three decades of general education in one form or another, a University of Chicago faculty committee concluded that "general education is at last in vogue. Its principles bid fair to become the operative educational theory of the remainder of this century."[46] Few reform movements (for it was intended to be just that) have elicited such enthusiastic support, and fewer still have encountered so many obstacles and such severe criticism.

Much of this can be attributed to the confusion that surrounded the idea and practice of general education almost from the outset. The distinction between general education and liberal education was in many respects unclear, although the former was initially advanced *as a means of reforming* the latter. It has even become difficult to determine whether a particular charge is leveled against general or liberal education, since the two are sometimes used interchangeably. Just a year after the publication of the Chicago volume, one observer wrote: "I take it we all agree that general education, if it is worth giving, is also liberal education."[47]

McConnell put it another way: "The adjective 'general' has all but displaced the older 'liberal' in educational discussion."[48] Yet McConnell recognized several important distinctions between liberal and general education—distinctions between content and learning to cope with modern life; between a concern mainly with intellectual development and one that deals with and integrates the student's emotional, social, moral, and intellectual life; between contemplation and action (a difference in methods); between the progressive differentiation of knowledge and restoring order to the curriculum through integration; between increasing specialization and providing a broader, meaningful context for specialization.

The differences cited by McConnell are significant; they are supported by a philosophy and a set of assumptions that differ fundamentally from those upon which conventional or traditional programs and procedures rest. In his treatment of the philosophical foundation of education, Harold Taylor referred to the general education orientation as "instrumentalism" and to the liberal orientation as "rationalism." "Philosophy, education, and society are so closely interrelated," he explained in Deweyan terms, "that to discuss one without reference to the other is to isolate one segment of reality from the other realities which give it meaning."[49]

And there are important differences between the psychological and social foundations of general and liberal education. In contrasting the two, Morse noted that general education

is more concerned with the learner than with the content, which may be organized or reshuffled with less regard to traditional fields. Its goals are individual development in its various aspects, and it places emphasis upon behavior and social usefulness as well as upon intellectual development as an outcome of learning. It is a manifestation of the democratic spirit in higher education, for it admits a wider scope of abilities and a far broader clientele. In its fullest development it is decidedly not merely "old wine in new bottles."[50]

The reference to the "fullest development" of general education points to another source of confusion—the variety of interpretations within the movement itself. Essentially, however, these represent two major orientations with a number of variations on each. The *first* differs little from the liberal education that it sought not to replace but to reform. Its concern is with the academic and the nonvocational, and it deals with a core of courses drawn from the sciences, the humanities, and the social sciences. Its main purpose is to provide a common experience for all educated individuals, but its goals, procedures, and content are substantially those of liberal education.

McGrath distinguished between early general education courses and those developed subsequently.[51] The basic philosophy of the former, according to his analysis, involved the false assumption that an array of information is the hallmark of an educated person. The proper objective of collegiate institutions should be the cultivation of the capacity to use knowledge. General education is, first of all, the unifying element of a culture. It prepares a student for a full and satisfying life as a member of his family, as a worker, and as a citizen—as "an integrated and purposeful human being." It does not, however, ignore differences in purpose, talent, and interest, nor does it attempt to cast everyone in the same mental and spiritual mold. Thus it seeks the maximum development of each student consistent with the general good, and while it puts a high premium on creativity and inventiveness, "it rests on the principle that deviations in thought or in act must be based on understanding rather than ignorance of the purposes, values, and standards of society."[52]

McGrath's conceptualization of general education approaches the *second*, or instrumentalist orientation, and this brings us to the heart of the matter. The rationalist or traditional interpretation of general education ignores or rejects much of what has occurred during the past several decades. The real difference is therefore between *traditional liberal* education and *instrumentalist* programs of *general* education.

With its origin in some of the more venturesome secondary

schools, the instrumentalist position was thought to represent "the best thinking" about general education at the college level.[53] One of the country's distinctive institutions, Bennington College, is a prime example. After a decade of planning, the college opened its doors in the fall of 1932. John Dewey and William Heard Kilpatrick were among its early consultants, and the latter served as board chairman for a number of years.

Bennington has been described as "experimental," "progressive," and, in Philip Jacob's words, "peculiarly potent."[54] Barbara Jones, a member of the early faculty and wife of Bennington's second president, held that

> General education can only be achieved by individuals, and must make sense for them. It should be general in two senses: in that it links the individual with his fellows in some shared knowledge and values; and in that it serves him well in a number of different life situations . . . But his capacity to go on learning, adapting himself to change without losing convictions, is a more important ingredient in his general education than any particular content he may have learned.[55]

The essential features of the program ("The Educational Plan for Bennington College, 1929") are worth noting. The work of the first two years was prescribed, but not in the usual sense of the term. Few if any prescribed programs were alike, for each was the result of numerous conferences between the individual student and her don, and each was established on the basis of that student's background. During the first two years, students were encouraged to join any of several "trial major" conference groups in order to explore curricular alternatives and to prepare for the informal and individual methods of the last two years. Opportunities to pursue secondary interests, as they developed, were provided by individual work rather than by attending additional classes or courses.

In keeping with its emphasis on the encouragement of the affective as well as the cognitive growth of the student, the arts were recognized as one of four major fields, although a remarkably large number of nonmajors availed themselves of the aesthetic experiences provided by the arts faculty. Advancement and graduation requirements were met not by the accumulation of grades (there were none, in the conventional sense), courses, or credits, but rather by ability demonstrated in a variety of activities consistent with particular goals.

Small, self-governing house groups served as centers of social life and of informal student-faculty contacts. Student participation in all aspects of college life was considerable—in governance, program decisions, and student life. The continuous use by faculty and officers of extensive student files facilitated more accurate and thorough diagnosis of the "real needs of modern women." The long winter recess gave students and faculty alike opportunities for travel and field work, and enabled them to take advantage of the educational and work experiences available in such metropolitan areas as Boston and New York. Considering the frequent and informal contacts between faculty and students, interest and competence in teaching and counseling as well as a professional approach to their own activities were high priorities in the selection of faculty.

Admittedly Bennington was and continues to be a selective college. But the experience of the General College of the University of Minnesota, which embraced the assumptions and ideas of the progressive movement, suggested that general education was as appropriate for the less gifted as it was for the superior student. Eckert's assessment, one of several devoted to the Minnesota experiment, revealed that General College students were more disposed than other students to view their experience positively. The General College experiment (in part no doubt because it was a two-year undergraduate program) influenced the more innovative curricula of the numerous community colleges that were to spring up throughout the country.[56]

The functions of a more fully developed instrumentalist program of general education call for a broader and considerably more flexible structure, one that involves a good deal more than the addition of new courses or the revision of old ones. Here the entire college community, and indeed society at large, provide the context for a wide variety of educational experiences. Rather than an end in itself, knowledge serves as a means to a more abundant personal life and a stronger, freer social order.

There is no place in this orientation for the traditional dichotomies, which may be traced to a notion of reality and a system of logic that divides thought into separate and contradictory elements. Taylor's explication of the differences between the instrumentalist and rationalist positions on this point is instructive.

> Reason and emotion, that is, knowing and wanting, are described as parts of an organism at work in ways natural to itself, and the emphasis is placed upon integration and continuity—the integration of the passions and the intellect, of thought and action, of

heredity and environment, of the individual and society, of the past and the present, of knowledge and values, of matter and mind . . . . Liberal education for the rationalist is separated from vocational education, the workers from the intellectual, the artist from the scientist, the past from the present, truth from its context, and education itself is conceived of as a separate term for disciplines and training in the realm of ideas.[57]

The inclusion in recent years of general education and interdisciplinary studies in graduate and professional schools represents a major curricular departure. With the addition of twelve new general education courses, Columbia University, for one, has initiated what is envisioned as a major academic reform, initially affecting the arts and sciences and the schools of medicine, law, and architecture, and ultimately the entire university. General education is confined neither to the undergraduate nor to the graduate level. Starting as a shared undergraduate experience, it "spreads outward from a human center, and the human scholar continues to be concerned with questions of value in the midst of increasingly specialized studies."[58] Thus general education calls for the sort of intellectual breadth, vitality of thinking, and depth of human concern essential to discussions of human issues in their historical and contemporary contexts. Specifically it requires greater utilization of the university's intellectual resources as well as mechanisms to facilitate and integrate contributions from faculty throughout the institution.

In its third year of operation Columbia listed some fifty interdisciplinary general education courses, seminars, and comprehensive areas of study, impressive by any standard. Still the Columbia University Committee on General Education has become increasingly concerned about the state of general education, not only at Columbia but elsewhere as well. While there seems to be little reason to doubt that Columbia is producing competently trained professionals, the Committee is not at all sure whether or not the University has continued in any broad sense to "educate" its graduate students. Indeed,

there are growing complaints that American universities are turning out a new breed of "barbarian" graduates whose degree of specialization is nearly absolute . . . . At the graduate and professional level there are too few courses and programs designed to bring together specialists and advanced students from varying disciplines to explore the larger implications of their research and teaching. Nor has there been sufficient opportunity to confront problems that transcend the traditional boundaries that have long organized and directed advanced study. The organization of graduate education along disciplinary lines is appropriate and necessary. Nevertheless, it has its shortcomings and intellectual and pedagogic initiatives of a trans-departmental and trans-disciplinary nature can strengthen graduate and professional education.[59]

The renewed interest in what appears to be an enlarged conception of general education has not been limited to individual institutions. At a conference devoted to curricular philosophies, members of the University Centers for Rational Alternatives chose to focus on general education. In his address to the group, Nathan Glazer spoke of a "clear mandate" for the social sciences to play a major role in general education. Specifically, Glazer called for the creation of a "sound and valuable general education on *man in society,*" which has in fact been a concern of general education from its inception some forty years ago.[60]

When Morse referred to the "fullest development" of general education, he had in mind the instrumentalist interpretation. But twenty years have passed since then, and during these years a good deal has been written and said about general education.

What does a comparison of instrumentalist programs of general education and current proposals reveal? Both place a high priority on the individual and on his total development; both are concerned with the present social context and with the student's ability to function successfully in that context; both recognize the value of interdisciplinary studies as a means of dealing with contemporary issues and problems; both would provide extrainstitutional experiences; both emphasize the need for restructuring the curriculum to provide greater student inputs and alternatives; both stress the desirability of informal student-faculty rapport; both urge greater faculty commitment to teaching and to the development of the whole student; and consequently both recognize the necessity for reforming the graduate education and training of college teachers. Influential as these factors are, they assume even greater importance when combined in a particular context.[61]

A major emphasis of progressive as well as of general education concerns interdisciplinary studies. Much of our new knowledge and technology have been achieved through specialized research, but the many resulting problems are essentially human problems of interpersonal relations, management, and human values. These are problems that require new forms of integration for their solutions. Brumbaugh and Pace pointed to the increasing interest of researchers themselves in interdisciplinary studies, a recognition that "many basic and important problems cannot be attacked to best advantage by the economist as economist, the psychologist as psychologist, or the physicist as physicist."[62]

Even the knowledge derived from the most highly specialized research frequently requires the mediation of the instructor before it becomes an integral and meaningful part of the student's total education. The manner in which knowledge is obtained is by no means always the most effective way to teach. Morse distinguished between the predominant methods of liberal and general education by designating the former "logical" and the latter "psychological." In the first instance subject matter is acquired in terms of its systematic organization within compartmented fields; the second capitalizes upon the student's motivation, interest, and desire to learn, and hence uses nontraditional patterns of content organization, patterns that frequently cross departmental and divisional lines.

A course or even an entire program, such as the one offered at the University of Wisconsin's Green Bay campus, which focuses on ecological concerns, may be problem oriented. Since the problems encountered by undergraduates can seldom if ever be investigated let alone solved by a single discipline, the interdisciplinary approach constitutes an important element of general education. The approach permits both instructors and students to draw upon one or several disciplines when and as they are pertinent to the solution of a specific problem, however broad or narrow it may be. Often problems require out-of-classroom activities or field studies that not only bring the student into close contact with outside agencies, but that encourage the development of new habits of mind and new procedures.

Interdisciplinary activities also vary according to geography. Data collected by the Center for Educational Research and Innovation (CERI), based on some 132 responses from seventy-two institutions in a dozen countries and categorized according to five fields— General Education, Professional Education, Training Researchers, Basic Research, and Applied Research—reveal that in the United States, General Education is the leading activity utilizing interdisciplinarity. An examination of the responses of those who applied interdisciplinarity to only a single field (rather than to any number of the five fields listed above) is even more significant: General Education was listed twenty-eight times, Professional Training ten times (nine times in the United Kingdom), Applied Research seven times,

Training Researchers three times, and Basic Research once. While such figures must be interpreted with caution, "General Education comes in way ahead of the other categories."[63]

As yet there appear to be few general principles for regrouping disciplines. Thus there is no constant relationship between the idea of regrouping disciplines and of regrouping people accordingly. Practices vary from country to country. The same person may teach several disciplines or he may seek help from his colleagues in other disciplines as the occasion arises, and examples of team teaching are few, except at the research and graduate levels. In short, "Most undergraduates, including those taking courses with interdisciplinary curricula and preparation, only occasionally encounter this interdisciplinarity as a standard feature of teaching itself and usually have to rely on their own ability to unify the courses they study successively."[64]

The tendency has been to regroup disciplines according to fields of study. Engineering, for instance, involves mathematics, physics, and often business administration, among others, while medicine requires a different but equally "standard" configuration. The criteria for regrouping, frequently implicit, vary widely but nonetheless reflect a typology that combines theory-oriented with practice-oriented disciplines, essentially homogeneous disciplines with one another, exact sciences with one or more social sciences, and the so-called "natural regroupings" based on tradition, particularly in the sciences. Strategically, an institution's or an activity's ability to organize on the basis of interdisciplinarity is proportional to how recent it is and to the extent to which it is accepted as a repository of knowledge.

There are, as one might expect, differences regarding the appropriate time for interdisciplinarity. Some believe that it represents the final outcome, the crowning effort, of an educational program that is systematic, uniform, and specific at the outset, so that the concept is considered valuable only at the level of specialization. Others, however, view interdisciplinarity as the key to introductory education and consider disciplinarity superficial and indeed antithetical to the needs of beginning undergraduates. Still others think that interdisciplinarity should be present in any education.

General education in its instrumentalist orientation has been concerned with interdisciplinary studies throughout much of its history. Yet an examination of alternatives to traditional patterns of education has led Ohmer Milton to conclude that the movement from disciplinary instruction toward interdisciplinary integration has not been a strong one. Comparatively few students are currently profiting from interdisciplinary study, least of all those within the "bulwark institution," the large regional and state universities.[65]

While there are a number of reasons for this, James R. Gass, director of the Center for Educational Research and Innovation, probably gets to the heart of the matter when he reminds us that the disciplines serve not only as a convenient and time-honored way of dividing knowledge into its components, but that they also serve as a basis for organizing the institution—and hence the professionals engaged in teaching and research—into autonomous fiefs. "To meddle with the disciplines," Gass cautions, "is to meddle with the social structure of the university in its entirety."[66]

Whether or not most faculty educated in the graduate schools want or even can adapt to new curricular approaches remains to be seen. Surely an adequate reward system and genuine encouragement are essential. Those faculty most thoroughly socialized to graduate-school norms and disciplines have generally not been among the more enthusiastic supporters of curricular reforms and interdisciplinary procedures.[67] The heaviest price for curricular innovation will have to be paid by professors who, in Birnbaum's words, have "encapsulated themselves" in the disciplines as presently defined.[68] Moreover, to create genuinely valuable interdisciplinary alternatives demands skill, insight, and intellectual breadth, often beyond that required in conventional programs. In most cases that task will fall to reform-minded faculty already within the ranks of most universities and colleges, and to similarly oriented and supportive administrative officials. As recent developments in interdisciplinary general education at *all* levels have illustrated, the process is already underway.

Notes

1. Herbert and Carol Schneider, eds., *Samuel Johnson, His Career and Writings* (New York: Columbia University Press, 1929), 4: 222–24.

2. Edward P. Cheyney, *History of the University of Pennsylvania, 1740–1940* (Philadelphia: University of Pennsylvania Press, 1940), pp. 70–81.

3. Frederick Rudolph, *The American College and University* (New York: Random House, 1962), p. 12.

4. Roy C. Honeywell, *The Educational Works of Thomas Jefferson* (Cambridge, Mass.: Harvard University Press, 1931), pp. 54–56.

5. A.A. Lipscomb and A.E. Bergh, eds., *Writings of Thomas Jefferson* (Washington, D.C.: Thomas Jefferson Memorial Association of the U.S., 1903), 19: 433–38.

6. Francis Wayland, *Thoughts on the Present Collegiate System in the United States* (Boston: Gould, Kendall and Lincoln, 1842), pp. 132–60.

7. Francis Wayland, *Report to the Corporation of Brown University, On Changes in the System of Collegiate Education, Read March 28, 1850* (Providence, 1850), pp. 50–52.

8. "Original Papers in Relation to a Course of Liberal Education," *American Journal of Science and Arts* 15 (January 1829): 297–319.

9. Donald G. Tewksbury, *The Founding of American Colleges and Universities Before the Civil War: With Particular Reference to the Religious Influences Bearing Upon the College Movement* (New York: Teachers College, Columbia, 1932).

10. Charles Grove Haines, *The Role of the Supreme Court in American Government and Politics, 1789–1835* (Berkeley: University of California Press, 1944), Chapter 11.

11. Tewksbury, op. cit. Philip Lindsley, acting president of Princeton and later president of Nashville, and a major educator during the first half of the century, saw his own institution decline as a result of the mushrooming colleges, nine of which were established within some fifty miles of the University of Nashville. "Speech About Colleges Delivered in Nashville on Commencement Day, October 4, 1848" (Nashville, 1848), in Richard Hofstadter and Walter P. Metzger, *The Development of Academic Freedom in the United States* (New York: Columbia University Press, 1955), Chapter 5.

12. David Tyack, *George Ticknor and the Boston Brahmins* (Cambridge, Mass.: Harvard University Press, 1967).

13. Ibid., p. 53.

14. Ibid., p. 54.

15. Ibid., p. 61.

16. George Ticknor to Thomas Jefferson, Göttingen, October 14, 1815, Jefferson MSS, vol. 205, Library of Congress.

17. Tyack, p. 55. The German system of education had no "college"; the gymnasium served as the appropriate vehicle for preuniversity education. During this period references to the American college as a "high school" or a "secondary school" were common, partly because it was viewed by returning scholars and students as the counterpart of the gymnasium and in part because it was in fact of secondary quality.

18. Ibid., p. 93.

19. Ibid., pp. 97–98, 109–10.

20. Ibid., pp. 111–12.

21. Ibid., pp. 112–13. For an extended development of the mandarin concept, see Fritz Ringer, *The Decline of the German Mandarins* (Cambridge: Harvard University Press, 1969).

22. Tyack, p. 86.

23. Henry P. Tappan, *University Education* (New York: Putnam, 1851), p. 43.

24. Laurence R. Veysey, *The Emergence of the American University* (Chicago: University of Chicago Press, 1965), p. 126.

25. James Morgan Hart, *German Universities: A Narrative of Personal Experience* (New York: Putnam, 1874), pp. 249–50.

26. Ibid., pp. 344–46. A quarter of a century later, Hopkins President Daniel Coit Gilman also recalled the conflict between the advocates of the classical and scientific studies. Noting the dominance of Latin, Greek, metaphysics, and mathematics during the early part of the century, he observed that "the equal rank claimed by the natural and physical sciences" during the last half of the century was not gained without a struggle. *Johns Hopkins University Celebration of the Twenty-Fifth Anniversary of the Founding* (Baltimore, 1902).

27. Veysey, p. 127.

28. Andrew D. White to Mrs. Gilman, 3 May 1909, in Fabian Franklin, *The Life of Daniel Coit Gilman* (New York: Dodd, Mead, 1910), pp. 324–25.

29. Daniel Coit Gilman, *University Problems in the United States* (New York: Century Company, 1898).

30. Ibid., pp. 9–10.

31. Daniel Coit Gilman, *The Launching of a University* (New York: Dodd, Mead, 1906).

32. Ibid., pp. 41–43. Italics added.

33. *Johns Hopkins University Celebration,* pp. 19–27.

34. Charles W. Eliot, *Educational Reform: Essays and Addresses* (New York: Century Company, 1898), pp. 125–38.

35. Ibid., p. 148.

36. "Report of the Committee on Improving Instruction in Harvard College," *Harvard Graduates Magazine* 12 (June 1904): 616–19.

37. Norman Birnbaum, "The Arbitrary Disciplines," *Change* (July/August 1969): 12.

38. Ibid.

39. Veysey, Chapter 4.

40. Irving Babbit, *Literature and the American College* (Boston: Houghton Mifflin, 1908), p. 31.

41. Charles E. Norton et al. *Four American Universities* (New York: Century Company, 1895), pp. 32–36.

42. William James, "Ph.D. Octopus," *Memories and Studies* (New York: Longmans, Green, 1917), pp. 337–38.

43. Samuel Capen, "Preparation of the College Instructor for His Job," *Proceedings of the Fifty-Ninth Convocation of the University of the State of New York,* 18 and 19 October 1923 (Albany, 1924), p. 13.

44. Abraham Flexner, *The American College* (New York: Century Company, 1908), pp. 182–89.

45. "Contemporary Civilization . . . ," *Columbia College Announcement, 1919–1920* (New York, 1919), p. 34.

46. *The Idea and Practice of General Education: An Account of the College of the University of Chicago* (Chicago: University of Chicago Press, 1950), p. v.

47. Sidney Hook, "General Education: Its Nature and Purposes," in *General Education in Transition,* ed. H.T. Morse (Minneapolis: University of Minnesota Press, 1951), p. 68.

48. T.R. McConnell, "General Education: An Analysis," in *General*

Education. Fifty-First Yearbook, National Society for the Study of Education, Part I (Chicago: University of Chicago Press, 1952), p. 1.

49. Harold Taylor, "The Philosophical Foundations of General Education," *General Education,* ibid., p. 20.

50. Horace T. Morse, "Liberal and General Education: A Problem of Differentiation," *General Education: Current Ideas and Concerns* (Washington: Association for Higher Education, NEA, 1964), p. 11.

51. Earl J. McGrath, "General Education: Theory and Practice," in *General Education: A University Program in Action,* ed. Hugh Stickler, James Stoakes, and Louis Shores (Dubuque: W.C. Brown, 1950), p. 44.

52. Earl J. McGrath et al. *Toward General Education* (New York: Macmillan, 1948), pp. 8–9.

53. Stephen Corey, "Psychological Foundations of General Education," *General Education. Fifty-First Yearbook,* p. 69.

54. Philip Jacob, *Changing Values in College* (New York: Harper, 1957), chapter VI.

55. *Bennington College: The Development of an Educational Idea* (New York: Harper, 1946), p. 115.

56. Malcolm MacLean, *General Education: Its Nature, Scope and Essential Elements* (Chicago: University of Chicago Press, 1934); Ruth Eckert, *Outcomes of General Education* (Minneapolis: University of Minnesota Press, 1943).

57. Taylor, "The Philosophical Foundations of General Education," pp. 36–37.

58. William Theodore deBary, "A Program of General and Continuing Education," *Columbia Reports* 7 (April 1973) no. 4, p. 3.

59. Special Report of the University Committee on General Education, *The Present State and Future Direction of General Education at Columbia,* n.d., p.2. A detailed account of the program may be found in the chapter by Hans Flexner and Gerard Hauser in this volume.

60. *The Chronicle of Higher Education* 8 (5 November 1973) no. 3, p. 7.

61. Hans Flexner, "General Education and Academic Innovation," *Journal of Research and Development in Education* 6, no. 1 (Fall 1972): 55–56.

62. A.J. Brumbaugh and Robert Pace, "Organization and Administration of General Education," *General Education, Fifty-First Yearbook,* p. 283.

63. *Interdisciplinarity: Problems of Teaching and Research in the University.* Center for Educational Research and Innovation (CERI), Organization for Economic Cooperation and Development (OECD) (Paris: CERI, 1972), p. 37.

64. Ibid., p. 39.

65. Ohmer Milton, *Alternatives to the Traditional* (San Francisco: Jossey-Bass, 1972), p. 105.

66. James R. Gass, "Preface," in *Interdisciplinarity,* p. 9.

67. Larry Leslie and Hans Flexner, "Faculty Socialization and Instructional Productivity," *Journal of Research in Higher Education* 7 (1977): 127–43.

68. Birnbaum, p. 20.

Why Interdisciplinarity?

Joseph J. Kockelmans

The literature on interdisciplinary issues is often confusing. One reason is that the authors who concern themselves with interdisciplinarity do not use a uniform terminology. People who have come to the conclusion that in many instances research projects can no longer be defined strictly within the boundaries of one of the "classical" disciplines and for that reason would like to follow a research project wherever it may lead, rather than redefine the project so as to make it fit the requirements stipulated by a given discipline, will often argue in favor of interdisciplinarity. Authors who firmly believe that in an educational setting it is incorrect to expose students to a one-dimensional contact with Western civilization, because this may produce well-trained specialists but certainly not well-educated people, will often argue in favor of interdisciplinarity. And people working in the social sciences who have concluded that one cannot fully understand any social phenomenon if one tries to approach it exclusively from the perspective of one social science alone, and thus are looking for a broader framework in which social phenomena can be more adequately described and explained, will sometimes also favor an interdisciplinary approach.

In order to avoid unnecessary confusion we suggest that one should choose a much more carefully defined terminology, so that a special label can be reserved for each of these legitimate concerns. In so doing it will be easier to examine each one of the proposals made on its own merits. Then if the debate about interdisciplinarity were to end up negatively in one particular area, it would no longer be legitimate to generalize and to declare all forms of interdisciplinarity impossible or meaningless.

For those who are seriously concerned with interdisciplinarity, it is particularly frustrating to have to defend their legitimate concern against the claim that all forms of interdisciplinarity are attempts to solve problems that do not really exist, and that one thus should be glad that this "fad" finally is on the way out. A mistake often made in this connection is the assumption that interdisciplinarity is an attempt to create various kinds of generalists. Once this assumption is made and then interpreted in its most negative form, it is relatively easy to explain that one cannot improve a situation in which there are people who know everything about nothing (Chesterton's definition of the specialist), by urging that we must now move to a situation in which we will have people who know nothing about everything.

Yet one obviously should not make the opposite mistake either. Let us assume that one could make a legitimate point for one particular type of interdisciplinarity; it does not follow from this that everything suggested under the general label of interdisciplinarity will be justified by this fact alone. Yet there continue to be a number of people who, without further specification, defend the view that the solutions for most problems that plague our society and our universities can be found by means of interdisciplinarity. These people have done much damage to all legitimate claims that can be made about interdisciplinary issues.

Thus it is important to make clear distinctions and to examine carefully for each particular form of interdisciplinarity why one should engage in it. This is what I plan to do in this chapter. To that end I shall first make some remarks about the debate on terminology, then I shall discuss the importance of concerning oneself with interdisciplinarity in the limited sense of the term, with crossdisciplinarity, and finally with transdisciplinary efforts. Some critical reflections will conclude this chapter.

Various Forms of Interdisciplinarity; Suggestions for a Uniform Terminology

Need for a Uniform Terminology; Criteria to Be Applied

In the literature the term *interdisciplinarity* is used in both broad and narrow senses. When the term is used in the narrow sense, it refers to efforts geared towards the constitution of a new discipline whose field of study lies between two other disciplines already in existence. A number of these interdisciplines have already been developed over the past decades: social psychology, biophysics, psycholinguistics, etc. In these cases interdisciplinarity is often distinguished from other nondisciplinary approaches to research and education through the use of such expressions as *multidisciplinarity, pluridisciplinarity, crossdisciplinarity, transdisciplinarity,* etc. If the term is used in the broad sense it indicates all nondisciplinary endeavors in research, education, or administration.

There is no unanimity in the literature concerning the terminology itself and particularly concerning the question of how the meanings of the different expressions are to be defined. The differences in the labels and their definitions as proposed by the various authors flow from a number of sources: difference in overall philosophical outlook, difference of opinion concerning what constitutes a discipline, difference of opinion about the sociopolitical function of science and of our entire educational system, about the basic aim to be achieved by nondisciplinary efforts, about whether the debate on interdisciplinary issues is concerned in each case primarily with a research, an educational, or an administrative body of problems, and other questions.

If the debate on interdisciplinarity is to serve a practical purpose, it is important to eliminate unnecessary confusion, while avoiding the mistake of believing that all the relevant issues can be settled by fiat and in a manner which will satisfy everyone. Clarification of the terminology to be employed seems to be a first step in that direction. I will here attempt to define the terminology carefully and to justify the decisions made in such a way that the choices appear to be reasonable but not dogmatic. Yet this principle of tolerance obviously cannot be applied so rigorously that philosophical and scientific discourse and argumentation become impossible. Thus I will attempt to justify the choices without using insights or terminology that will be either incomprehensible or unacceptable to most people. It seems to me that such an effort will succeed to the degree that it relies more on ideas immediately connected with the goal to be achieved than on specific philosophical a prioris.

In selecting and defining the terms to be used here I have been guided by the following principles:

1. The list of terms should not contain anything not immediately relevant to the debate on interdisciplinary issues.

2. The list should be complete in the sense that the labels selected are adequate to characterize the various nondisciplinary efforts in teaching, research, and administration.

3. The terminology should be defined as clearly as possible.

4. Neither the terminology itself nor the definitions given should contain an explicit reference to scientific, methodological, sociopolitical, or philosophical issues about which there is no common agreement.

I am not the first to argue in favor of a clear and universally acceptable terminology. Many authors have already attempted to achieve this goal. Some of these efforts can be found in a book published by the Centre for Educational Research and Innovation,[1] whereas others have been discussed systematically in an unpublished dissertation by Jack L. Mahan, entitled "Toward Transdisciplinary Inquiry in the Humane Sciences."[2] Without the work done by these authors I would not have been able to make the suggestions listed below. However, I wish first to explain my reasons for not fully affiliating myself with any one of the terminological suggestions made by previous authors. These reasons are all connected with the principles just formulated.[3]

Heckhausen's attempt to develop the necessary terminological distinctions has, all of its positive aspects notwithstanding, two weaknesses.[4] First of all the author tries to found his distinctions among six different forms of interdisciplinarity on the assumption that seven criterion levels for defining disciplines should be distinguished. Now in view of the fact that these criterion levels are not universally accepted by scientists and philosophers without modification, it seems very unlikely that those concerned with interdisciplinarity will adopt the terminology that Heckhausen suggests. Furthermore the labels used to distinguish the six forms of interdisciplinarity are developed by the author specifically for this purpose and are notably different from the terms used by most authors.

The reason I prefer not to follow the suggestions made by Piaget, Jantsch, and others is that these authors presuppose either a certain conception of structuralism and genetic epistemology, or a general systems theory on the basis of which they try to clarify and justify the necessary distinctions.[5] Since both structuralism and general systems theory have a limited applicability only, and the philosophical assumptions underlying these positions are not universally accepted, it seems again unlikely that all interdisciplinarians will be comfortable with the suggestions made by these authors.

The proposal by Boisot, which is much more formal in character than those mentioned thus far, is in my opinion a very promising one.[6] I share his position, but prefer to select a slightly different terminology in light of the fact that the one proposed below has already been adopted by many authors working in the field. What Boisot calls "linear interdisciplinarity" is usually labeled by the term *pluridisciplinarity*; for structural interdisciplinarity the term *interdisciplinarity* in the strict and limited sense is commonly used, whereas restrictive interdisciplinarity is known under the label *crossdisciplinarity*.

The suggestions made by Michaud and Abt overlap to a very great extent the terminological suggestions made by Mahan on the basis of the latter's study of the available American literature.[7] The terminology I am proposing is derived from both of these efforts and is the result of combining some ideas suggested by the two European authors and some others made in the American literature as discussed by Mahan. But I find it necessary to change some of the suggestions made by these authors, because the list suggested by Michaud and Abt is incomplete and in addition employs for the description of the term *transdisciplinarity* a formulation that is both too formal and too restrictive. On the other hand, the terminology used by many American authors does not always make clear distinctions about the realms to which the various labels immediately apply.

Suggested Terminology

Discipline: A branch of learning or a field of study characterized by a body of intersubjectively acceptable knowledge, pertaining to a well-defined realm of entities, systematically established on the basis of generally accepted principles with the help of methodical rules or procedures; e.g., mathematics, chemistry, history.

Disciplinary Work: In an educational context we speak of disciplinary work as referring to scientific work (research, teaching, or both) done by one or more scientists within the boundaries of one discipline; e.g., work of a mathematician or a group of mathematicians within the realm of the discipline "mathematics."

Multidisciplinary Education: Education sought by a person who wishes to acquaint himself with more than one discipline, although there may be no connection at all between the disciplines involved; it is often assumed that teaching and research in this instance is done by educators who in each case act as disciplinarians, under whom a person for instance may study simultaneously or successively Greek, French, and mathematics.

Pluridisciplinary Work: Scientific work (teaching, research, learning) done by one or more scientists that implies such juxtaposition or subordination of different disciplines that the competence in one discipline presupposes a rather thorough knowledge of other disciplines, e.g., a biologist who in addition to biology devotes himself to physics, chemistry, and mathematics.

Interdisciplinary Work: Scientific work done by one or more scientists who try to solve a set of problems whose solution can be achieved only by integrating parts of existing disciplines into a new discipline, e.g., psycholinguistics, biophysics. This work does not imply that the original disciplines themselves become totally integrated, although this is not excluded either. The term predominantly refers to research and only secondarily to education.

Crossdisciplinary Work: Scientific work done by one or more scientists who try to solve a problem or a set of problems that no discipline in isolation can adequately deal with, by employing insights and methods or techniques of some related disciplines, without, however, any attempts being made to integrate the disciplines themselves or even parts thereof into a new discipline. It is obviously mandatory to integrate the scientific knowledge that immediately pertains to the problems at hand; however, it is not assumed that the integration achieved in this way and the experience so gained can be used as a paradigm for the solution of other analogous problems, without major modification. The scientists involved in such a project must have some common ground; the work proceeds from such a common ground but does not aim at developing this ground; e.g., economists, social scientists, physicians, and architects trying to find a better solution for the housing problem in a large city. This term is used predominantly to refer to large research projects.

Transdisciplinary Work: Scientific work done by a *group* of scientists, each trained in one or more different disciplines, with the intention of systematically pursuing the problem of how the negative side effects of specialization can be overcome so as to make education (and research) more socially relevant. In transdisciplinary work the discussion between the members of a carefully selected group may also focus on the concrete problems with which society confronts the members of a society or an academic community. The difference between crossdisciplinarity and transdisciplinarity consists in the fact that crossdisciplinary work is primarily concerned with finding a reasonable solution for the problems that are so investigated, whereas transdisciplinary work is concerned primarily with the development of an overarching framework from which the selected problems and other similar problems should be approached. For some authors transdisciplinary investigations should focus primarily on the unification of all sciences concerned with man; in their opinion the aim of transdisciplinary work consists in the development of an all-encompassing theoretical framework that is to be taken as the basis for all empirical research in the behavioral and social sciences. For other authors transdisciplinary efforts are concerned primarily with the unity of our world view; in their view transdisciplinary work presupposes that those who participate in it first try to establish a common ground that implies a conception of our culture, the function of science and education in it, and the basic elements of the entire process of acculturation.

Some Additional Observations

To prevent misunderstanding and to clarify the definitions that have been proposed here, the following observations may be helpful. First of all, today it has become questionable just how the concept of "discipline" should be defined vis-à-vis possible nondisciplinary endeavors. For many classical disciplines of the past have developed to a point where division and subdivision of the realm of study has become mandatory. One could now ask whether or not physics, biology, or psychology can still be called disciplines in the traditional sense of the term, or whether it would not be better to refer to these classical disciplines with expressions such as *superdisciplines* or *federated disciplines,* reserving the term *discipline* for some of the subdisciplines of the classical disciplines of the past. This development has clouded the interdisciplinarity issue to a great extent, because one could wonder whether the relationship between some particular subdiscipline of chemistry and some particular subdiscipline of physics or biology is not much closer than the relationship of the same subdiscipline of chemistry to another subdiscipline of chemistry. If this is the case, then it seems clear that the concept of discipline has to be redefined, so that in turn the term *interdisciplinarity* will receive a totally new meaning.

The distinction between science and discipline can help us to unravel this problem. The term *science* predominantly refers to a complex of related research projects, whereas the term *discipline* has a more educational meaning: one "does" science, but one "studies" a discipline. Once this distinction is made, one can then say that although physics taken as a science may have many subdivisions, educationally it is still possible to select a certain portion of the available knowledge in this realm of investigation that forms a harmonious educational unit, and with which anyone who is educationally introduced to physics ought to become familiar. When we speak of the discipline "physics" we mean that part of the science "physics" which, from an educational point of view, should be taken as its basic unit. This obviously will change over time.

Time and again since the beginning of the twentieth century new sciences have developed between two or more existing sciences.

Although this phenomenon is closely related to the one just dealt with, it originated from a different intention. In the case of the *division* and *subdivision* of existing sciences the development had its origin in a number of factors, all of which were inherent in the science in question. Division and subdivision of existing sciences became necessary either because the realm of phenomena to be dealt with became too large to be treated effectively without some division into smaller fields of research, or because certain phenomena appeared to require special principles and laws, or because it appeared possible to apply principles, laws, and structures developed for one realm of phenomena to other realms of phenomena. In the case of *the development of new sciences* between existing sciences, new sciences were developed, because it appeared that effective treatment of certain phenomena would be impossible without combining and integrating insights originally developed in two or more existing sciences. Examples of this type of development are biochemistry, social psychology, psycholinguistics, etc. According to Donald Campbell, underlying this development was the conviction that one must develop a fish-scale model of omni-science that gradually must take the place of the classical sciences.[8] This phenomenon is now generally referred to by the label *interdisciplinarity,* which in this instance is to be taken in a narrow and limited sense.

The question of whether or not scientists working in the area between two existing sciences should develop a new interscience, and how they should go about materializing such a project, should be answered by these scientists themselves—for they alone are competent in the relevant area—and not by philosophers or educators. Yet once such a new interscience has been developed, there are two new problems: a) is this new interscience of such a nature that as an interdiscipline it should become part of a university's regular curriculum? and b) should there be an administrative unit in the university functioning as a department or institute and being responsible for making available staff, facilities, curricula for students, etc.? It is this partly educational and partly administrative phenomenon which constitutes the subject of the contemporary debate about interdisciplinarity in the narrow and strict senses of the term, and to that debate philosophers, educators, and administrators can, in principle at least, make a positive contribution.

There never has been a time that someone's education was strictly disciplinary. Today too education is in principle never strictly disciplinary, if one looks at it from the perspective of the person who is being educated. In high school, on the undergraduate level, and even on the graduate level, all students are constantly being exposed to more than one discipline at a time, although the doctoral research projects may very well be strictly disciplinary in character. When we talk about interdisciplinarity we usually do not mean to refer to this educational phenomenon, because in the Western world all education is inherently multidisciplinary. It is clear also that as an educational term *multidisciplinarity* should not be used as an expression to be meaningfully applied to possible research projects.

Since the beginning of the universities in the Middle Ages someone who wished to study a certain discipline had first to study certain other auxiliary or propaedeutic disciplines. This is still true today. A physicist must study mathematics before he can turn to mechanics; someone concerned with Old French must study Latin first; a theologian must study philosophy before he can devote himself to theology. When we talk about interdisciplinarity nowadays, we do not mean to refer to this phenomenon either, although it is not exclusively an educational one. In both education and research the subordination and integration of two related disciplines is often essential for the success of the enterprise. We reserve the term *pluridisciplinarity* for this particular phenomenon. The main reason this phenomenon is not treated in the contemporary debate on interdisciplinarity is twofold: first of all, it is not a new phenomenon; pluridisciplinarity is an essential element of our Western idea of science and education; the problems one encounters in this realm have been studied for centuries, and in most cases we know how to handle them. Second, the scholars working in the different sciences will have to decide for themselves if, when, and how combination, subordination, and integration should take place in any given case in both research and education.

In this discussion, therefore, little will be said about multidisciplinarity and pluridisciplinarity. Our focus instead will be on one of the following issues:

1. The question of why the creation of new sciences "between" other existing sciences is necessary or desirable, and of the attitude one should adopt from an educational as well as an administrative point of view in regard to interdisciplinarity in the narrow and strict senses of the term. In other words, the basic question here is, is it correct to continue to develop ever-new educational and administrative units for the ever-increasing number of new sciences developed at the borderlines of the classical sciences? Formulated in another way, is the classical division of the sciences still adequate for the

purpose of defining meaningful educational and administrative units (interdisciplinarity in the strict sense)?

2. What to say about research projects and educational efforts which imply a thorough introduction into different, not closely related disciplines for the purpose of coming to grips with certain socially relevant problems, without the explicit intention, however, of creating new disciplines? One particular problem that is connected with the first and seems of great practical importance is whether these efforts too should eventually lead to the introduction of new educational and administrative units (crossdisciplinarity).

3. How to evaluate the efforts of people who are trying to establish a new type of discourse that would facilitate the exchange of ideas between people trained in different disciplines or interdisciplines? Should one search for several conceptual frameworks valid only for some realms of phenomena, or should one look for an all-encompassing framework? Many people argue that such an exchange of ideas is necessary in order to guarantee the unity of our conception of world (transdisciplinarity).

Why Interdisciplinarity in the Limited Sense of the Term?

In this section I shall present a brief summary of the most important arguments that have been proposed to justify involvement in strictly interdisciplinary research projects, as well as the question of to what kinds of innovations such efforts should lead from an educational and administrative point of view. My primary aim is to provide the reader with information about some of the ideas that various authors have suggested in the past. Where it appears to be meaningful, some critical observations will be added.

All those who have concerned themselves with interdisciplinarity in the strict and limited senses of the term agree that it is necessary in research and teaching to sometimes engage in investigations concerning problems or problem areas that cannot be defined from the viewpoint of the existing classical disciplines but are to be found somewhere between the borderlines of these disciplines. Yet there is little agreement about why one should engage in such investigations or about the practical implications of such efforts. Furthermore there are many reasons that suggest this issue cannot be handled for the natural sciences in exactly the same way as for the behavioral and social sciences. Because two chapters of this book will be concerned with limited interdisciplinarity in the realm of the natural and the social sciences, I shall keep my reflections general here. First I shall describe three different attempts to formulate reasons for engaging in strictly interdisciplinary endeavors; then I shall compare these ideas and add some critical reflections.

A first group of authors share with Donald Campbell the conviction that no individual can achieve genuine competence in one discipline, and thus that multidisciplinary competence is completely impossible for individuals; this is the case in both the natural and the social sciences. What is to be brought about therefore is a comprehensive and integrated multiscience.

Many interdisciplinary programs have tried to combine comprehensiveness with depth. Institutions have tried to train individual, multidisciplinary scholars who have mastered more than one discipline. One should realize, however, that in our modern world there is no longer room for such a Leonardesque aspiration. Where an attempt has been made to institutionalize this aspiration, a system producing shallowness and a lowest-common-denominator breadth has developed. What we need today is not a number of Leonardos, but rather groups of *genuine* interdisciplinarians. Until now people have believed that scientific knowledge and competence can find their locus in single individuals. Now it becomes clear that the locus of scientific knowledge is shifting from individuals to groups. Scientific knowledge has become a collective product that is only very imperfectly represented in isolated individuals. Given this fact, it seems more reasonable to train younger scientists in such a way that they do not have a comprehensive knowledge of one of the institutionalized disciplines, but so that they know whatever they need to know to solve important problems and deal with urgent issues in cooperation with other similarly trained specialists.

Thus one must not think of the multiscience mentioned previously as something that an individual alone could ever master; only the community of scholars can in time bring this ideal closer. Such a collective comprehensiveness of all realms of knowledge should be brought about by means of overlapping patterns resulting from efforts of a unique and deliberate narrowness. Each narrow specialty can be compared to a fish scale on a fish. For every systematically knowable subject matter there should be an adequate scientific approach that leads to a discipline concerning that subject matter or problem area.

The development of this ideal is impeded by the ethnocentrism of the existing disciplines, i.e., by the in-group partisanship in the internal and external relations between academic disciplines, university departments, and scientific organizations and institutions. Most interdisciplinary programs too have impeded the development of this ideal rather than promoting it, in that they tend equally to lead to the organization of ever-new specialties into new departments for decision-making and communication. This ethnocentrism of the institutionalized disciplines and interdisciplines leads to a redundant piling up of highly similar specialties, while leaving great interdisciplinary gaps. Rather than trying to fill these gaps by training scholars who have mastered two or more existing disciplines, one should be making those socioorganizational innovations that will encourage narrow specialization in the areas between these disciplines. One should realize also that the present institutionalized disciplines are just arbitrary composites, and that the present organization by departments is in large part just the product of an historical accident. If the scientists wish to engage in relevant research, they will have to go beyond the existing institutions and work in the direction of a comprehensive, collective multiscience.

A second group of authors shares with the first the conviction that it is indeed impossible for a single person to know the vast accumulation of findings, research techniques, and the different formulations of basic problems across the sciences.[9] Division of labor, specialization, and some form of cooperation are necessary. Given these facts, each scientist and specialist finds himself confronted with the problem of learning where, what, and how to borrow from other disciplines. Such borrowing can be done intelligently only if two major requirements are met. 1) The scientist specialized in one discipline must know what developments in other disciplines have been accumulated in problem areas that relate to his own research interests, so that he will know where to turn when he needs to borrow methods and information. This, the authors argue, can be facilitated by joint seminars, conferences, and readily available literature. 2) The specialist in one science will very seldom find a completely satisfactory solution to his own problem in another discipline, because the units of analysis as well as the levels at which they take place are mostly quite different. In other words the findings made available in one discipline are to be adapted and then incorporated into those of another discipline. These authors feel that if these conditions are met, the methods and findings of two or more disciplines working on related problem areas can serve as a check on the validity of their generalizations to the advantage of each discipline involved.

The authors admit that the results of interdisciplinary endeavors have been rather disappointing until now, for various understandable reasons: many scientists appear to have misunderstood the meaning of interdisciplinary projects; they have often underestimated the difficulties involved in such efforts; administrators are reluctant to change existing institutions; experts in one field can talk to each other relatively easily, whereas the discourse between people who have specialized in different areas seldom leads to a meaningful dialogue. However, the authors argue, much of the discontent and many practical difficulties have arisen through failure to deal adequately with the central and substantive issue, namely, the core problem of why interdisciplinary efforts came into existence at all, and why they are necessary for the development of each of the sciences and not just a matter of individual preference. An examination of this substantive issue, which is at the core of all interdisciplinary relationships, will reveal that each discipline needs the others in a fundamental and basic sense, because each discipline needs the findings of the others as a check on the validity of its own generalizations and theories. When this substantive issue is examined more carefully, many current problems associated with interdisciplinary trends turn out to be minor issues. They merely seem large and even insurmountable as long as the substantive question has not been examined with care. Administrative problems in particular can be solved relatively easily once the basic problem has been clarified.

These authors are thus convinced that the basic considerations that brought problems of interdisciplinary relations to the foreground in an irreversible way will ultimately force the development of continuing interdisciplinary efforts, regardless of the ups and downs to be suffered from the imperialism and self-contained ethnocentrism of the various disciplines or from the blind spots in administrative arrangements.

It is particularly in the realm of the social sciences that one discovers that man does not divide and arrange his individual and social problems neatly along lines laid down by academic disciplines. If the social sciences wish to engage in investigations of genuine human problems, they will have to concern themselves with the real problems human beings actually experience. There is nothing basically wrong with a division of labor in this realm and thus with specialization, as long as one realizes that there is a great deal of overlap in the subject matters or topics considered by the various social disciplines. Which among the social sciences would care to abdicate altogether any reference to human motives, language, the family, the different groups, religious institutions, political and economic life? Thus the different disciplines are actually studying and

theorizing about the same problems or closely related problems of
the human condition. And if this is so, then no social science can
solve its relevant problems in isolation. For those disciplines concerned with man, one of the inherent dangers in working in isolation is the sacrifice of the validity of their generalizations and theories. The best means available for checking the validity of findings
and generalizations in social science today, before any application is
attempted, is to measure them against the findings and generalizations established on the same or related problems by another social
science.

In both the natural and social sciences the core problem of
interdisciplinary relationships for a particular discipline is to determine the findings and concepts it must borrow, and to decide in
which matters it has to be in transaction with other disciplines in
order to stand firmly on its own feet, with all of the supporting
evidence it needs to insure the validity of its formulations. Assessment of what a science needs from other disciplines and with whom
it needs to transact will provide the ingredients for weaving its own
fabric.

As for practical problems connected with interdisciplinary efforts, the authors do not suggest engaging in activities that would
ultimately lead to abolishing the distinction between the existing sciences; neither do they advocate a total reorganization of the structure of the university. What is needed in most cases is a careful
selection of a small number of people of different backgrounds who
are concerned with related problems and are willing to engage in
interdisciplinary efforts, and arrangements that permit sufficient
time and opportunity for joint efforts without making supreme the
physical aspects of the program. For the great problem in interdisciplinary ventures is still the development of coordination and cooperation among people who can pull together, instead of being pulled
asunder by disciplines, schools, and organizational pressures.

There is a third group of authors who, although convinced that
the authors whose views were briefly described in the preceding
pages have made an important contribution to the debate on interdisciplinarity, nonetheless believe that the real issue and its solution
is to be sought for elsewhere.[10] They point out that sometimes we
find ourselves in a position in which we have to admit that we do not
know, or do not yet know, enough about the relevant phenomena.
Sometimes we can legitimately say that we have discovered a number
of insights concerning a given realm of phenomena, but that it
gradually becomes questionable what the precise meaning and value

of our insights really is, due to the fact that conflicting claims are being made in other related fields. In addition, we often find ourselves in a situation in which we begin to realize that all of our findings are questionable in the final analysis, as long as no one is able to indicate how the divergent aspects of the relevant phenomena (which from the viewpoint of the different disciplines appear to be isolated, uncoordinated, and incomparable) constitute some kind of harmonious unity. In the first case we are confronted with a lack of knowledge that the different *disciplines* attempt to overcome; in the second we experience a lack of knowledge that can be overcome through interdisciplinary efforts; the lack of knowledge that confronts us in the third case cannot be conquered by either disciplinary or interdisciplinary efforts, but requires efforts of a *transdisciplinary* nature.

These authors agree with those of the first and the second groups that one should not hold that there is something basically wrong with specialization. In many disciplines specialization has proven to be the road to a solution of a great number of real problems. It may be true that particularly in the realm of social phenomena, specialization is confronted with many and unexpected difficulties not encountered in some branches of the natural sciences; yet it seems unfounded to defend the thesis that specialization has no place in the social sciences. What is needed is not the abolishing of specialization but the development of inter- and transdisciplinary approaches that can deal meaningfully with the negative side effects of one-sided specialization.

For it is indeed true that specialization, institutionalization, and compartmentalization through departmental regulations tend to fragment our knowledge more and more. To obtain a unifying picture of these vast areas of fragmented knowledge, comprehensive analyses seem necessary. Those who engage in these kinds of analyses must go beyond the traditional approaches to scientific inquiry and its techniques of investigation. One such supplementary alternative is the interdisciplinary approach. Yet, although this approach is needed in addition to the disciplinary ones, it appears to be necessary to go even beyond this form of interdisciplinarity. We must develop methods of inquiry that transcend the traditional boundaries and provide integrating and synthesizing frameworks for disciplinary and interdisciplinary investigations. This is to be done by means of transdisciplinary research projects. The weakness of the views presented by the first two groups of authors is that they did not realize that in most cases their suggestions will not work without a transdisciplinary framework.

A careful comparison of these views shows that for the last group of authors it is important to distinguish between interdisciplinary and transdisciplinary efforts and projects and that, as far as limited interdisciplinarity is concerned, the view proposed by the second group of authors appears preferable to that suggested by the first.

As for the first view, no doubt everyone will agree with these authors that the time of Leonardos has past. More and more in our modern world research projects begin to imply groups instead of isolated specialists. Both government and industry often look for teams of well-chosen specialists who can work meaningfully together on large research projects. It seems reasonable to conclude from this that the university should prepare its students for this type of research. Yet it seems that this first group of authors underestimates the complexity of the issues at hand. The basic problem they leave unanswered concerns how narrowly trained specialists can meaningfully communicate with one another and how groups of specialists can successfully cooperate. The authors must presuppose that there is already some general framework, some common ground that all specialists and groups of specialists share and to which they may return when they try to cooperate and communicate.

The second basic problem with this view is that it is difficult to understand how someone could call himself a well-educated person if he were to be ignorant in all fields of learning except in that of his own specialty. Without a rather extensive training in the humanities, mathematics, the sciences, and the arts he would often be totally incapable of correctly perceiving the relevant problems and certainly incapable of adequately dealing with them. This is true particularly for all research projects that directly or indirectly affect society and our environment. The suggestions made by these authors may still be important, but they seem to be relevant only for older graduate students and postdoctoral fellows who can devote themselves to specialization on the basis of a broad education.

Within certain limits I tend to agree with the first group of authors that the ethnocentrism of disciplines, professional organizations, journals, and departments should be criticized. Yet it may very well be that all of these institutions still have an important function, not for the preparation of someone who wishes to engage in meaningful research projects with colleagues trained in other disciplines, but for the balanced education of specialists and teachers.

As for the second and third groups of authors, generally speaking I tend to agree with their ideas and suggestions. The views proposed by the second group of authors does not imply the creation of an encompassing framework. The research projects with which they are predominantly concerned merely presuppose that those engaging in strict interdisciplinary work must have a rather thorough knowledge of the fields and subfields from which they borrow ideas, methods, or results. Yet even these authors admit that in certain areas important interdisciplinary work cannot be done except by groups, the members of which come from different disciplines. In this case too some form of cooperation between specialists with different training is necessary, and the latter again presupposes that some common framework of meaning be developed to make cooperation effective.

These authors could say that the third group of authors is mistaken in searching for such a common ground in advance. Yet I must admit that I cannot envisage a meaningful dialogue or discourse between the representatives of different disciplines except on the basis of a (perhaps limited) realm of meaning that they share or at least are willing to agree upon, and which they do not wish to question, at least for as long as they engage in this kind of dialogue. This in my opinion is a necessary condition for any meaningful exchange of ideas; the question is what this limited frame of reference should be in each case. A second question pertains to the manner in which such a frame of reference can be either discovered or developed. It will not do simply to refer to the life world they all share or to appeal to our ordinary language, because the latter frames of reference are much too unarticulated and thus incapable of directly incorporating any of the specialized frames of reference and languages of the different disciplines involved in each case.

Discovering or developing relevant overall frameworks of meaning seems to be the primary concern of those who write about transdisciplinarity. For this reason I should like to return to this issue in one of the sections to follow.

Strictly interdisciplinary endeavors have led to a number of new interdisciplines. In some instances these interdisciplines developed into regular disciplines with their own departments, professional journals, societies, national and international meetings. In other instances the new interdisciplines became subdisciplines of one of the original disciplines involved. In the literature with which I am familiar I have been unable to find a clear answer to the following three questions: a) Is it in principle correct to continue to develop ever-new disciplines for all the fields of research that are continuously being discovered? b) What conditions must be fulfilled to warrant the development of new educational units, be these departments, institutes, or even colleges? c) In light of the limited resources, what attitude should administrators adopt with respect to this development, and by what standards should they let themselves be guided when choices are to be made?

Prima facie one would be inclined to defend two seemingly contradictory theses: obviously research must go on wherever it is meaningful and feasible; yet on the other hand, it seems unreasonable to argue that new disciplines and new educational and administrative units are to be developed for each new field of research. As far as the latter is concerned, the actual development has perhaps already gone much too far. What ought to happen if the latter were to be correct is not at all clear, in that any reasonable proposal one could make would encounter economic difficulties of astronomical proportions. Some aspects of the problems hinted at here will be discussed in chapters to come.

Why Crossdisciplinarity?[11]

Crossdisciplinarians are people who attempt to tackle problems and issues that cannot be properly defined and solved within the boundaries of any given discipline. These problems and issues may be found in the realm of the natural sciences or the social sciences; many of them, however, seem to involve both the natural and social sciences. People concerned with this type of research usually have no intention of developing a new discipline or interdiscipline; neither do they envisage new educational and administrative units in the university. Most of them will make the claim, though, that our contemporary universities do not live up to all of their obligations, in that they usually do not prepare students for crossdisciplinary work. Yet, so they say, most students who are preparing themselves for a career outside the university (perhaps more than 90 percent of our students) will in their chosen professions, vocations, or careers have to deal continually with problems and issues that no discipline taken in isolation can properly formulate or effectively deal with. Thus these authors argue that every university should prepare its students for crossdisciplinary research.

Although in some instances one individual could engage in crossdisciplinary work, the work can most often be done effectively only by teams. This is due mainly to the complexity of the issues involved and the rather severe limitations placed on the scientific knowledge that one individual can normally master. In those cases in which crossdisciplinary work can be done by one isolated individual, the concern of the crossdisciplinarian runs parallel to that of the interdisciplinarian. One should realize here that crossdisciplinarity and interdisciplinarity overlap to a great extent. The difference between the two consists primarily in the goal the researchers attempt to achieve. Interdisciplinarians attempt to develop new research fields that eventually will lead to new disciplines. Crossdisciplinarians wish to solve important and urgent problems that cannot be defined and solved from the perspective of any one of the existing disciplines. Yet this difference in aim notwithstanding, the actual work in which both types of scientists engage will be very similar. This is the reason that some of the arguments given in favor of interdisciplinarity in the limited sense also apply to crossdisciplinarity.

Many authors who have written on crossdisciplinarity often use the labels inter- or transdisciplinarity to identify this form of nondisciplinary research. Yet in view of the fact that crossdisciplinarians usually have no intention of developing a new discipline, I prefer not to use the term *interdisciplinarity* in this connection. Furthermore, since the primary goal of crossdisciplinarity consists in finding solutions for important and urgent problems, I prefer to avoid the term *transdisciplinarity* here also, although it is true that both cross- and transdisciplinarians have in common their concern with the development of encompassing frames of reference, as will be shown shortly.

Those who are in favor of developing crossdisciplinary research projects share the view that the search for a common ground is the fundamental element of all crossdisciplinary investigation. Without such a common ground there would be no overarching conceptual framework, and thus genuine communication between those who participate in the discussion would be impossible. It is very difficult to discover or establish such a common ground, in that everyone who participates in the discussion brings with him his own discipline's conceptual framework and sensitivity for methods and techniques. Furthermore, when at first agreement sometimes seems to exist among the members of a crossdisciplinary group, often it later becomes clear that the agreement was merely verbal.

Several authors have explicitly addressed the question of how one could facilitate the discovery or development of a common ground necessary for crossdisciplinary discourse. The general consensus is that there cannot be one approach to this problem that would be correct for all types of crossdisciplinary research projects; the solution to the problem depends to a great extent on the kind of investigation that is attempted (Luszki et al.) Those who are familiar with general systems theory, structuralism, or cybernetics have suggested that these approaches, which originally were not developed for crossdisciplinary research projects, might very well contain the core of the answer to the question of how to develop a common ground. Careful reflection, however, shows that each one of these approaches will be valuable only in some but not in all areas of crossdisciplinary research. Furthermore, taken by themselves these approaches provide us only with the formal skeleton of a conceptual framework; to the question of how in each case this formal framework is to be concretized, no universally valid answer is to be expected.[12]

Yet the goal of all crossdisciplinary inquiry is the discovery of overarching conceptual frameworks that will facilitate the unification of the sciences and eventually the solution of important problems with which the existing disciplines acting in isolation are incapable of dealing effectively. Crossdisciplinarians who work exclusively in the realm of the natural sciences usually have no great difficulty in discovering a common framework. In most cases it will consist in the basic principles and methods of physics, chemistry, or biology. On the other hand, crossdisciplinary research projects in the social sciences, and particularly those involving both the natural and the social sciences, confront us with great theoretical and methodological problems. Research projects involve both the natural and social sciences when, in addition to sociopolitical and economic issues, there are technological problems that presuppose a rather sophisticated knowledge of the natural sciences.

Some authors have suggested that the basic problem facing scholars engaged in these types of research projects cannot be solved except by creating specialized generalists, i.e., people competently trained in one discipline who in addition have received a rather thorough training in a number of other disciplines. Most authors feel that this suggestion will usually not work. In their view the members of a given team must in each case discover or develop their own crossdisciplinary frame of reference with its typical theoretical framework and its characteristic methodology, without which it is virtually impossible to integrate the relevant insights already gained in the individual branches of learning represented by the members of the team.

Social scientists who have written about crossdisciplinary research stress that it is not their intention to promote a new school of thought in the realm of the social sciences, a new philosophy or a new ideology. Their efforts flow rather from a sensitivity to problems of human relevance. Their interest thus is in a kind of inquiry that is concerned with social phenomena without compartmentalizing human experiences and depersonalizing man's life because of a too-narrow scope, and without distorting his experiences through the use of scientific frames of reference that are reductionist and reifying. Crossdisciplinary inquiry attempts to examine man and society from a perspective that transcends disciplinary interests and institutional loyalties. It presupposes and takes its point of departure in the insights gained in the various disciplines and interdisciplines; it tries to integrate these insights with the help of a conceptual framework that transcends each one of them and remains much closer to the social phenomena as they are experienced by living human beings in actual societies.

Gordon DiRenzo describes the characteristics typical of crossdisciplinary work as follows. The first is the development of an awareness of what is going on in the different but related disciplines. The second is the development of a sensitivity to convergence; one must learn to recognize where the several disciplines do, and must, come together theoretically and facilitate such a unification; the necessary condition for this is a close focus on the arbitrariness of disciplinary boundaries as well as on their interpenetration. The third is the standardization of scientific concepts and the development of a common scientific language for all behavioral sciences.[13]

Many crossdisciplinary efforts have been disappointing. This has been the result of a number of problems whose force is often too easily underestimated. First of all there is the problem of ethnocentrism: those who play a leading role in the social sciences, either because of their publication record or because of their position in the profession, often explicitly argue that there is no need for crossdisciplinary efforts; all attempts to develop such a crossdisciplinary approach have failed; the work of those who engage in this kind of work is of inferior quality; and most importantly, there never have been generalists and there should not be any now either. Second, it appears to be enormously difficult to engage in crossdisciplinary research in universities where the structure is usually strictly disciplinary. Some people have claimed that this kind of research cannot get off the ground as long as these sciences remain located within specialized departments, because this situation conflicts with the development of the potential of these sciences as contributors to the solution of large-scale problems. Some even wondered whether the traditional relationships between scholars, teachers, and students does not work against large-scale crossdisciplinary research.[14]

Third, crossdisciplinary work is done most effectively by groups of scientists trained in different disciplines. Now it appears that crossdisciplinary collaboration has a number of difficulties of its own that, as was to be expected, are connected with personal idiosyncrasies, difference in philosophical orientation, and differences of opinion concerning the desirability of conceptual frameworks, methods, and techniques; the latter problems have their origin mainly in the affiliation of the various scientists with their "home" disciplines. Luszki has devoted a monograph to these problems: *Interdisciplinary Team Research: Methods and Problems* and has made a number of important suggestions that can facilitate crossdisciplinary team research efforts.[15] However, in view of the fact that team work in this area is relatively new, there are still a number of fundamental problems for which no one as yet has found a reasonable solution.

Yet all of these and other difficulties notwithstanding, the authors maintain that crossdisciplinary research efforts are necessary if research is to be relevant to the real needs of our complex society. Furthermore, they feel, one should not forget that the problems connected with one-sided compartmentalization are even more serious. As for the claim of opponents that it is not desirable and is even wrong to create generalists who know almost nothing about everything, the proponents of crossdisciplinary research projects argue first that there is a great difference between a superficial generalist and a specialist generalist in the sense of a true crossdisciplinarian; for the latter is supposed to have specialized knowledge of at least one of the relevant disciplines and to be willing to engage in efforts geared toward overcoming the limitations of too narrowly defined specialties. Furthermore they agree with those who promote interdisciplinarity in the limited sense, when they defend the view that in our complex society there is need for generalists in the common sense. It may be true that these people should not seek employment at a university; yet the university should prepare some generalists who as "science brokers" can mediate between the specialists and the public at large.

I believe that the authors concerned with the promotion of crossdisciplinary research projects are engaged in an important enterprise. Our complex societies confront us with problems that the sciences in isolation cannot adequately treat. A genuine understanding of these problems and an attempt to suggest solutions presupposes cooperation between those who have specialized knowledge of their relevant aspects. This cooperation in turn presupposes that all of those involved in the discussion try to discover a common ground.

This ground need not always be so encompassing that it could serve as a basis to deal meaningfully with all large-scale problems. It seems reasonable to assume that a limited common ground will be effective, provided it be broad enough to encompass the dimensions that are essential to the problems at hand.

In fact both in government and in industry a number of these crossdisciplinary projects have been and are being developed. It seems to me that the university should prepare younger scientists for crossdisciplinary research. In view of the fact that this type of education conflicts with the departmental structure of the actual university, I share the opinion of the Social Science Research Council that in the larger universities the necessary structure should be developed in which during the last years of their training graduate students could be introduced to crossdisciplinary research projects.[16]

Why Transdisciplinarity?

Those who defend the need for transdisciplinary projects attempt to bring about an all-encompassing framework of meaning, valid either for all sciences or at least for all sciences concerned with man. In their view a transdisciplinary framework is a necessary condition for making integration of insights gained in isolated disciplines and interdisciplines possible, and for restoring a uniform conception of world. Our world has become splintered and fragmented by the fact that each individual discipline and interdiscipline has developed its own general conceptual framework, its own set of theories and methods, all of which in the final analysis rest on implicit philosophical assumptions and ultimately lead to different conceptions of world.

Those who engage in transdisciplinary work are not primarily concerned with improvement of the empirical disciplines in their research aspect; the primary focus of all transdisciplinary work is to be found rather in the educational and philosophical dimensions of the sciences. This is the reason why those who write on transdisciplinary issues are very often educators, philosophers-scientists, and philosophers, and why they place such stress on the idea that transdisciplinary work is absolutely necessary to guarantee that all learning in the university *at all levels* is not just training but also genuine education. Many authors are convinced that genuine transdisciplinary work is impossible without a philosophical reflection on man and society.

There is little unanimity among the authors who have written on transdisciplinarity. Next I shall describe four different views proposed in the literature and conclude this section with some critical reflections of my own.

According to a *first view,* interdisciplinarity has become a fashion; in some cases the interdisciplinary movement has deteriorated into snobbism.[17] Often one does not realize that interdisciplinarity is not progress but rather a symptom of the pathological situation in which man's theoretical knowlege finds itself today. For more than two hundred years specialization has been the predominant trend in research and education; this has led to the dangerous fragmentation of our entire epistemological domain. Our theoretical knowledge has disintegrated, and the human personality has been affected by this lack of integration. Alienation through science is one of the causes of the crisis of our contemporary Western civilization.

A diagnosis of the actual situation does not necessarily give us a solution for the basic problem that confronts us here. Interdisciplinarity, which many people have suggested as the solution for this problem, is counterproductive in that it does not touch on the heart of the matter. The main issue is not one of how to reorganize higher education but one that concerns the meaning of a man's life in a scientific era. The disintegration of the unity of our theoretical knowledge and the corresponding disintegration of our entire intellectual framework has taken place gradually since the time of the Renaissance. It was particularly in the nineteenth century that our knowledge became fragmented due to ever-increasing specialization. The closer our sciences came to a mature state, the more disintegration of the unity of our theoretical knowledge appeared to be an inevitable consequence of the desire to know more and more about minute details. Not only did new disciplines and interdisciplines develop, but in each discipline specialization became necessary. Although much accurate and important knowledge concerning these details has been acquired in this way, the development as a whole has much in common with a cancerous process. This development had particularly ruinous consequences for the university, which is no longer a cultural community. Our universities have become prisons with hermetically sealed cells for inmates with the same record.

People who believe they can counteract this development through interdisciplinary efforts have underestimated the enormous difficulties which prevent genuine *inter*disciplinarity. First of all there are the *epistemological* obstacles: specialization seems to be a necessity; accurate knowledge about details that we need can, as far as we know, not be achieved otherwise; yet specialization makes integration virtually impossible. Then there are *institutional* obstacles: specialization in the disciplines logically led to the departmentalization of the university; it is not easy to see how one could reasonably change this development. Third, there are *psychosociological* obstacles: people educated in our universities are incapable of conceiving of the situation other than it actually has become; neither as individual persons nor as groups can they maintain themselves without this form of institutionalization, professionalization, and bureaucratization. And there are the *cultural* obstacles: development in our epistemological domain is connected with the general conception of our Western culture that one must be able to compete, excel, dominate, and control, and specialization is more conducive to these activities.

In light of these obstacles it is evident that a few conferences or colloquia, some new books and anthologies, or even the development of new interdisciplinary universities will not really contribute much to the solution of the basic problem.

Our theoretical knowledge was originally developed as a function of the humanization of man and nature. Modern science, on the other hand, contributes much to the dehumanization of both man and his environment. Since our specialized disciplines have become disciplines-without-wisdom, they are without direction and without any possibility of human evaluation. This is the reason why a merely formal unification of the sciences is unable to have a positive function in regard to the main problem at hand.

If interdisciplinary efforts are going to bring us to a solution for the problems caused by one-sided specialization and reduction, they must concern themselves first with the origin. Unification that comes after the facts by means of addition is meaningless. Specialization itself must flow from genuine concern for the whole. Thus transdisciplinary efforts that focus on the whole are necessary. Transdisciplinarity can never consist in retroactive measures, whether they be by addition or by formalization. The transdisciplinary concern for the unity of our world must be there first, and from it specialization should flow. It is true that specialization is unavoidable and necessary if we are to survive. Yet specialization without guidance and without concern for the unity of our world is self-destructive. As far as the university is concerned, this suggestion does not mean that the departments and institutes are to be abolished, but that one should stress first that they are the places from which a dialogue concerned with the humanness of man and his world must begin.

In a *second view* transdisciplinary efforts are recommended on the basis of a similar concern for the unity of our theoretical knowledge, with the feeling that the preceding view is much too pessimistic.[18] In this view, instead of acting as a doomsday prophet, one should more carefully reflect on *how* transdisciplinarity could contribute to an effective restoration of the unity of our conception of world. Because the quest for the unity of our scientific knowledge has a history almost as old as the idea of theoretical reason itself, it seems reasonable to suggest that one turn once more to this history in order to see whether a hint can be found there concerning how to deal with the basic problem. In this long history the claim has been made repeatedly that philosophical reflection, which inherently has an integrating function, should play an important part in a search for the unity of our theoretical knowledge. This, however, should not be understood in an imperialist manner, as if only that which philosophy can integrate into an overall perspective can be accepted from all the insights the sciences have to offer us. Just the opposite is to happen: by reflecting critically upon the foundation from which all theoretical efforts flow, philosophy can make a positive contribution to the transdisciplinary unification of the sciences. Philosophy, precisely because it is concerned with beginnings and foundations, should not try to play a role in the integration of the data provided by the sciences; rather philosophical reflection should contribute to the unification of all theoretical knowledge by reflecting on what all sciences presuppose and from which they ultimately flow: the universe, man, and man's world. One should not interpret these statements to imply that the concern for unity is the concern of professional philosophers only. A philosophical dimension is present in all theoretical efforts, and thus the concern for the unity through transdisciplinary efforts is an aspect of all the sciences. It may be true that the scientists often forget that (among many other things) they should be concerned with the whole, precisely because they are so deeply engaged in research concerning details. Yet it cannot be denied that the tendency toward unity is an integral element of all theoretical efforts. It seems that today this concern for unity is served better by cooperation than by efforts of individuals.

A *third group of authors* tries to defend transdisciplinary efforts by an appeal to the social relevance of higher education.[19] As they see it, the basic cause of crisis in the university is its increasing maladjustment to a rapidly changing society. Transdisciplinarity's first objective is to reestablish contact between university and society. The most important problems confronting our society cannot be

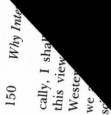

dealt with meaningfully by any given trad
isolation. What is needed is a set of new
effective integration of the existing scien
plines, including the human sciences, dev
long process of specialization. All specializ
edge implies reduction. The consequence
problems that the different disciplines a
longer problems that the members of a s
any given moment in time, but merely re
of these problems. If one is to come to gr
of our modern world, a reorganization of our theoretical knowledge
along transdisciplinary lines is mandatory.

The question of why the university should engage in transdisciplinary research projects and teaching programs has often been
explained with the help of the distinction between training and
teaching.[20] There are authors who think that over the past fifty
years many universities have produced specialists highly trained in
some fragment of knowledge; yet these universities have educated
relatively few people. Transdisciplinarity is thus often offered as a
vehement protest against bits of knowledge that are as alienating
culturally as bits of work are in the production process. Transdisciplinarity should be understood as an attempt to restore the goals of
teaching that were gradually diverted from their declared purposes.

According to these authors neither the sciences nor the various
inter- and crossdisciplinary efforts can help us in this regard. The
reason for this is that disciplinarians are primarily committed to the
careful study of a limited field of phenomena. In so being they apply
methods, follow standards, and try to discover ever-new results. In
all of these efforts they identify with their social position as scholars
who belong to a certain profession and search for recognition from
their peers. Most interdisciplinary and crossdisciplinary efforts are
not very helpful in this connection, in that these efforts often lead to
new disciplines, aim at addition of new knowledge rather than integration, and sometimes lead to subordination of disciplines, which
does not always do justice to the insights presented by all the disciplines involved. Transdisciplinary efforts should therefore be oriented towards the humanities, which are primarily concerned with
man and his environment. History and literature, together with
some kind of philosophical reflection, constitute the framework in
which transdisciplinary work will flourish.[21]

The *fourth view* on transdisciplinarity is in my view the most
intriguing of them all. In attempting to explain this view systemati-

...ll use some ideas suggested by Schwartz.[22] According to
...it is very important to realize that in our contemporary
...n world the sciences have become the actual basis for the lives
...re living. Our contemporary way of living was formed by the
...ences and has adapted itself to the scientific way of thinking,
particularly to that found in the natural sciences and employed in
modern technology. The sciences have become an integral part of
the destiny of contemporary man. For many centuries people have
identified science with progress. In classical antiquity scientific
speculation was a goal and value in itself. In the Middle Ages it was
thought that the sciences retraced the thoughts of the Creator. In
the era of humanism and enlightenment it was believed that the
sciences enhanced the humanity of man (humanism). In the nineteenth century people believed that the sciences helped us to con-
quer and control the earth. Today there are people who believe that
the sciences teach us the "real" truth about things, a task formerly
attributed to either religion or philosophy; for others the sciences
are the most powerful instrument we have to change the world
including the structure of our society.

Most people today believe that as long as people had their religious or philosophical convictions, shared by the greater part of
Western society, the thesis that science can be identified with progress could indeed be justified. However, now that people no longer
universally share either a religious view or a philosophical conception of man and world, the question concerning the real meaning
and function of science has become problematic. Science appears as
a human creation, which, although neutral in itself, can be used both
positively and negatively. The sciences can help us control our environment; yet they also contain the possibility of total self-destruction
for man. Although the sciences have helped to shape our self-
conception, yet they also contain elements that prevent man from
realizing his genuine self.

Those who are concerned with transdisciplinarity basically agree
with this view and suggest that the correct conception of science for
our world can be discovered only through investigations that transcend the boundaries of the individual disciplines. The goal of these
investigations precisely is to ensure that through the sciences man
can provide for himself a position within the cosmos that is at the
same time rational, critical, and humane.

Transdisciplinarians strongly stress the point that there cannot
be any science that does not make some presuppositions and that
does not imply some kind of preunderstanding and some form of

evaluation. No science can be called a genuine science if it objects to these presuppositions being critically examined. The idea of a critique of scientific reason is obviously not new. We are familiar with Kant's *Critique of Pure Reason,* Dilthey's critique of historical reason; and much of our contemporary philosophy of science can be viewed from this perspective, particulary now that logical and methodological reflections on the sciences are complemented by insights from the history of science and sociology of knowledge. Transdisciplinarians have high esteem for these investigations in the realm of philosophy of science and urge the leading scientists to engage in the debate in order to make certain that the perspectives of *all* the sciences are properly represented. It cannot be denied that many people concerned with philosophy of science exclusively or at least predominantly focus on the natural sciences; some others are mainly concerned with the behavioral, social, and humanist disciplines. What is needed, particularly from an educational point of view, is an all-encompassing philosophy of science that concerns itself with all essential aspects of all the sciences and disciplines.

Transdisciplinarians conceive of specialization as a necessity. Until the beginning of the nineteenth century specialization did not lead to grave problems because the unity of the world view as well as the unity of the sciences was then guaranteed either by an all-encompassing religious view, a universally accepted philosophy, or a common ideology. In those days one could speculate about precisely what each individual science was contributing to the conception of the whole. Today we have a great number of highly specialized sciences to which an equally great number of conceptions of world correspond. The question of precisely what each science contributes to our conception of world has become a meaningless question, if it is understood to imply that, independent of the sciences, there is already a uniform conception of world available to all. The unity of the world may no longer be presupposed; it is something to be brought about, and the sciences will have to play some part in the realization of this task.

Yet if one looks at the actual situation it is difficult to understand how the individual sciences could ever make a meaningful contribution to the constitution of the world's unity. For specialization went historically hand in hand with professionalization and compartmentalization. True, some authors have pointed out that specialization need not lead to professionalization and fragmentation. Each science, provided it is learned correctly, is and remains a legitimate perspective on the whole; if conducted properly scientific research leads to a transgression of the borderlines that each science had stipulated for itself originally; if studied in depth every science leads to a center where all sciences converge.

Transdisciplinarians do not deny this, and they admit that one-sided fragmentation is not a necessary consequence of specialization. Yet the real point is still overlooked in these reflections. One continues to presuppose that contemporary man may appeal to a world that already constitutes a harmonious unity in advance. If one looks at the actual facts he will see that each science has tried to develop its own conception of world and then tried to impose that conception on all other sciences. That is why the question of the unity of the sciences must be examined more systematically.

In classical antiquity and throughout the entire Middle Ages it was thought that everything that can be known scientifically constitutes a harmonious unity (*kosmos, creatura*). The sciences were to discover this unity and make it explicit in systematic fashion. The rationality inherent in the unity of the sciences was to reflect the rationality present in the cosmos (order of things = order of ideas). The same conception, but now defended on different grounds, can be found in Descartes's *Système du monde*, Spinoza's *Ethics*, and Leibniz's *Monadology*.

After Kant this conception was given up. For even if God created the cosmos as a rational unity, still we must maintain 1) that we do not know anything about the order of things, except insofar as this order is accessible to us through the scientific study of the way in which the things appear to us (phenomena), and 2) that the realm of phenomena now studied by the sciences is much broader and much more complex than the classical *kosmos*.

Thus, if today the unity of our entire theoretical framework remains to be explained, it must be done on grounds that do not imply any advance knowledge of the order inherent in things. Some people have therefore tried to justify the unity of our theoretical knowledge by appealing to the function of the knowing *ego*; later an attempt was made to explain this unity by positing it as the consequence of man's explicit intention to bring about this unity, or by showing that in his theoretical activities, man is bound by a moral imperative. In our own time most people try to account for the unity of the sciences through reflections of a more formal nature and by appealing to standards dictated by logic and methodology. Others believe that the development of an appropriate metalanguage is a necessary and sufficient condition for the mediation between the different sciences. Some of them are of the opinion that this metalanguage should be derived from our ordinary language in which all transdisciplinary problems are already articulated as life-world issues.

When it became clear that none of these attempts was completely satisfactory, some people thought that perhaps general systems theory, structuralism, or cybernetics could help us account for the unity of the sciences; others have suggested that perhaps the idea that all sciences ultimately flow from the life world could provide us with a clue as to how the basic problem is to be solved. Transdisciplinarians feel that there may be a core of truth in most of these suggestions, but still maintain that we shall not come to an acceptable solution of the basic problem if we cannot find a perspective from which all of these suggestions can be fitted together. In their opinion such an all-encompassing perspective can only be found through philosophical reflection, the latter understood as the critical reflection on man's experiences from the perspective of the *totality of meaning of which we at this moment in time can conceive.*

Be this as it may, all authors agree on one basic point, namely that the unity of the sciences will not follow automatically from the conviction that the order of ideas has to adapt itself to a pregiven order of things. Instead this unity is continually to be brought about and accounted for by those who actually engage in scientific research. These efforts will remain fruitless if we cannot first come to some agreement about the totality of meaning in which, in light of our Western tradition, we would like to live, and about the position that the sciences will have in that totality of meaning in addition to religion, morality, the arts, and our sociopolitical praxis. And this agreement cannot be brought about except by philosophical reflection.

Many scientists will reject these ideas, not realizing that the expression *philosophy* is not used here to refer to the work in which philosophers "of profession" engage but to that dimension in every man's life that critically mediates between what is and what is to come. This suggests that the *entire* community of scholars should continuously reflect critically upon the past in order to prepare the totality of meaning or world in which all of us would like to live.

If the question concerning the unity of the sciences is understood as a philosophical problem in this sense, namely, as a problem intrinsic to man's continuous tending toward meaning, then integration becomes the principle of genuine research, and the questions that lie at the borderlines of each discipline will then appear to be the most fundamental ones. Transdisciplinarity will then be understood as a specific attitude in regard to the sciences, an attitude oriented toward comprehending the contributions of each discipline from the perspective of man's search for meaning, which itself is suprascientific because inherently human.

The individual sciences taken in isolation cannot provide us with such a perspective, except when they become ideologies. There was a time when people believed that the world described by physics could be one in which people can live meaningfully, humanly, and humanely. Today the social sciences often appear as the ideology for our time. Genuine transdisciplinarity implies that one is willing to transcend the limited perspective of one's own discipline, and this implies that transdisciplinarity is possible only in the form of a critical, philosophical reflection in the sense indicated.

Many scientists will object that our transdisciplinarians are being carried away here. They will argue either that all this talk about meaning is nonsense, because it is totally incomprehensible; or they will say that there is no genuine meaning except that for which the sciences themselves can account; or they will perhaps argue that the concern for meaning is the task of philosophy of science. Yet problems of meaning and humane relevance are alien to the sciences, if the term *science* is taken in the strict sense. When the sciences speak about man, they speak about man as an object; some form of abstraction, reduction, and idealization is the price we have to pay in order for them to achieve the greatest possible clarity and certainty. Thus it is understandable why scientists, strictly speaking as scientists, at first have difficulty in seeing the real point transdisciplinarians try to make. Maybe they will begin to see the concern of the transdisciplinarian, when they reflect on those cases in which scientific data were and are being used to promote obviously inhumane causes.

Thus transdisciplinarians suggest that it is important to distinguish between two kinds of reflections scientists may engage in; the first is concerned with the establishment and explanation of the facts and the real state of affairs; the second focuses on the clarification of the meaning of the first in regard to the life we have to live in our world. To these different forms of reflection there correspond two different ways of conceiving of the world and of man himself. When C.P. Snow spoke of two different cultures in Western civilization, he identified the first with the world of the natural and behavioral sciences, and the second with that of the humanities. Perhaps it would have been more important for him to refer here to the two basic ways in which scientific man can and must conceive of the world and of himself. For the real issue to which Snow's distinction points is not one that separates scientists from humanists but one with which *every* scientist has to cope when he realizes that to be scientific and to be human and humane do not necessarily coincide. The question becomes one of how we can make certain that these two indeed will go hand in hand.

The crisis in which modern man finds himself today is connected with the fact that he has lost the unquestionable foundations of the past: religion, a universally accepted morality on the basis of religion, and a universally accepted philosophical world view, in which always a certain ideal conception concerning the humanity of man was implied. Whether religion and a certain conception of morality are inherent dimensions of a man's life or whether they are not, the fact is that both have become powerless in our scientific era as a base upon which all of us can stand. Furthermore it is clear by now that an appeal to traditional forms of humanism cannot save us from nihilism and total alienation. According to transdisciplinarians, neither science nor technology, neither scientism nor technocracy, neither humanism nor nihilist skepticism can lead us away from the crisis in which we find ourselves today, because none of them is capable of transcending the antinomy between a purely scientific conception of world and a human conception of it. If we are to overcome the grave dangers of our era, we shall have to turn to the second form of reflection mentioned above.

No one is saying here that science and technology do not have their positive sides; the point merely is that we shall be confronted with very serious problems if we do not try to mediate the tension between science and life, between a scientific and a livable world. In this process of mediation, both history and literature play an important role along with philosophical reflection.

It will be obvious that the ideas suggested by transdisciplinarians have important implications for the political responsibility of all scientists as well as the educational task of those who teach the sciences at the universities. Over the past 150 years many scientists have based their scientific activities on the following assumptions: 1) science is the only access to the truth; 2) taken as theoretical enterprise science is inherently value free; 3) those who contribute to the advancement of science bear no responsibility for the way the results of scientific research can or are being used; 4) when scientific ideas are to be applied, only scientific and pragmatic criteria are to be taken into consideration. These assumptions create a sphere in which politicians have used or abused scientific findings to further their political ideologies. Obviously on many occasions scientists have objected to their scientific insights being abused; yet even in these cases the ethical principles employed were principles that were determined merely scientifically. Transdisciplinarians are fully aware that transdisciplinary research and reflection are incapable of creating or inventing values and moral standards and of forcing politicians to abide by moral principles. Yet they believe that transdisciplinary reflections could bring about an important change if they were to become an essential part of everyone's education, scientists and politicians alike.

Summary and Conclusion

From the preceding pages it will be clear that the answer to the question of why one should engage in transdisciplinary reflections contains elements that can be set forth in favor of all nondisciplinary efforts in research and education. Of all of these efforts one can say that they have their origin in a dissatisfaction with the compartmentalization of our disciplines and interdisciplines, both as research and educational enterprises. According to many, the administrative structure of our universities has promoted this compartmentalization and thus makes nondisciplinary efforts both necessary and difficult. What is asked for in all of these nondisciplinary efforts is cooperation between the representatives of disciplines and interdisciplines in order to come to a solution for important problems that go beyond the borderlines and the range of competence of our traditional disciplines.

I agree with the authors concerned with interdisciplinarity in the limited sense, that if there are important problems to be found in areas lying between the domains of existing disciplines, which neither of the respective disciplines is capable of adequately formulating and treating, then new research areas are to be opened up and new interdisciplines to be developed. Yet I have been unable to find in the literature a *satisfactory* solution for the problems to which this development leads from an educational and administrative point of view.

As for crossdisciplinary efforts, our complex world confronts us with important and urgent problems that the existing disciplines cannot adequately treat, although in many instances a concern with these problems does not imply the necessity of developing a new discipline or interdiscipline. In these cases an adequate and genuine understanding of these problems and any attempt to find a reasonable solution for them presupposes cooperation between those who have specialized knowledge of the relevant aspects of these complex problems. In the literature I have not found a convincing answer to the question of what steps crossdisciplinarians should take in order to make certain that they have a firm common ground from which they can come to a meaningful exchange of ideas concerning a given problem.

Many authors feel that nondisciplinary efforts are only partly justified by reference to complex problems that the isolated disciplines and interdisciplines are incapable of solving. It seems to be the transdisciplinary efforts in particular that refer to a basic tension between science and society. Specialization in the sciences can regain its value for a man's life only through transdisciplinary efforts, because these contribute immediately to the unification of our overall conception of world. Thus it is not the formal unification of the sciences as promoted by the Vienna Circle that is searched for under the label of transdisciplinarity but rather a uniform framework that is capable of reducing the tension between the world in which we would like to live and the fragmented worlds depicted by the different sciences.

I agree with Gusdorf that transdisciplinary efforts should be concerned primarily with the unity of our entire intellectual framework as well as with the unity of our conception of world, and that all measures to reconstruct this unity out of the fragmented worlds depicted by the sciences are ineffectual. Luyten appears to be correct when he suggests that philosophy and history must play an important part in these efforts. What these authors actually propose seems to imply that all specialization should flow from a very broad education involving both the sciences and the humanities. And this suggestion is in harmony with the idea proposed by other authors to the effect that our universities should not limit their efforts to *training* students, but in addition should focus on an all-around *education* for everyone who enters the university. Schwartz has synthesized these ideas somewhat more harmoniously by asserting that the unity of our conception of world is not to be found or discovered, but that time and again it is *to be brought about,* and that our theoretical justification for such a unity will have to take the form of a transdisciplinary effort.

In order to prevent misunderstanding I would like to make two observations. First, it is generally accepted that far-reaching specialization makes an effective dialogue between scientists of different background very difficult. These difficulties are much greater in the discourse between scientists and social leaders, politicians, and citizens. To facilitate these necessary forms of discourse the university will have to train people who are capable of translating scientific ideas into insights that can be understood by the educated members of the community at large, so that the most important findings of the sciences can be applied to the good for society. Some people believe that transdisciplinary efforts are primarily concerned with the popularization of scientific knowledge. This is obviously not the case, although it is true that our society is in need of such popularization through "science brokers."

Second, people who argue in favor of transdisciplinarity do not suggest that one could educate people to become nothing but transdisciplinarians. Most authors think that the university should educate students to be disciplinarians with a transdisciplinary concern. At any rate, these authors do not intend to suggest that all students should be exposed systematically to all disciplines.

It seems to me that transdisciplinarians tend to get carried away once in a while. Some of them have formulated their basic concern from a conceptual framework and in a language not universally shared by all philosophers, scientists, and educators. Yet I find the basic point stressed by the transdisciplinarians to be a correct one, and a very important one: the tension between the worlds which our sciences describe and the world in which we would actually like to live must be overcome. This cannot be accomplished on the basis of scientific rationality alone; scientific rationality is to be complemented by a form of critical reflection that is of a typically philosophical nature. This reflection will have to become an integral part of all forms of research and education. In other words, the basic thesis of the transdisciplinarians has important implications, which are both educational and political in character. What these implications may be in detail is at this point less important than the willingness to discuss them where they arise. Finally our university students will be prepared for such a discussion to the degree that their specialization has flowed naturally from a broad education in which both the humanities and the sciences have been integral parts.

Notes

1. *Interdisciplinarity: Problems of Teaching and Research in Universities* (Paris: OECD, 1972).

2. Ms., United States International University, San Diego, 1970.

3. To prevent misunderstanding I wish to stress here that it is not my intention to "freeze" a development that is still in progress. My aim thus is not to try to settle the discussion on terminology once and for all, but rather to make a positive contribution to this discussion.

4. Heinz Heckhausen, "Discipline and Interdisciplinarity," in *Interdisciplinarity*, pp. 83–89.

5. Jean Piaget, "The Epistemology of Interdisciplinary Relationships," in *Interdisciplinarity*, pp. 127–39, and *Main Trends in Inter-Disciplinary Research* (New York: Harper and Row, 1973); Erich Jantsch, "Towards Interdisciplinarity and Transdisciplinarity in Education and Innovation," in *Interdisciplinarity*, pp. 97–121; cf. Russell L. Achoff, "Systems, Organizations, and Interdisciplinary Research," *General Systems* 5 (1960): 1–8.

6. M. Boisot, "Discipline and Interdisciplinarity," in *Interdisciplinarity*, pp. 89–97.

7. Cf. *Interdisciplinarity*, pp. 25–26.

8. Donald D. Campbell, "Ethnocentrism of Disciplines and the Fish-Scale Model of Omniscience," in *Interdisciplinary Relationships in the Social Sciences*, ed. Muzafer Sherif and Carolyn W. Sherif (Chicago: Aldine, 1969), pp. 328–48.

9. Muzafer Sherif and Carolyn W. Sherif, "Interdisciplinary Coordination as a Validity Check," in *Interdisciplinary Relationships in the Social Sciences*, pp. 3–20; cf. pp. vii–xii.

10. Mahan, chapters 4–6; Asa Briggs and Guy Michaud, "Problems and Solution," in *Interdisciplinarity*, pp. 185–252; J.R. Gass, "Preface," ibid., pp. 9–10; Guy Michaud, "General Conclusions," ibid., pp. 281–88; H. Holzhey, "Interdisziplinarität (Nachwort)," in H. Holzhey, ed., *Interdisziplinär* (Basel: Schwabe, 1974), pp. 105–29; Reimut Jochemsen, "Zur gesellschaftspolitischen Relevanz interdisziplinärer Zusammenarbeit," ibid., pp. 9–35.

11. Cf. Mahan, pp. 119–96.

12. Cf. Piaget, *Main Trends in Inter-Disciplinary Research;* Anthony J. Wilden, *System and Structure: Essays in Communication and Exchange* (London: Tavistock, 1972); L. von Bertalanffy, *General System Theory: Foundations, Development, Applications* (New York: George Braziller, 1968); E. Laszlo, *Introduction to System Philosophy* (New York: Gordon and Breach, 1972); Mahan, chapter 5. For further bibliography, see the works by Wilden, Laszlo, and Mahan.

13. Gordon J. DiRenzo, "Toward Explanation in the Behavioral Sciences," in Gordon J. DiRenzo, ed., *Concepts, Theory, and Explanation in the Behavioral Sciences* (New York: Random House, 1966), p. 238.

14. Guy Berger, "The Interdisciplinary Archipelago," in *Interdisciplinarity*, pp. 35–74; Briggs and Michaud, "Problems and Solutions," ibid., pp. 185–252; Mahan, chapter 5.

15. Washington, D.C.: National Laboratories, 1958.

160   *Why Interdisciplinarity?*

16. *The Behavioral and Social Sciences: Outlook and Needs* (Englewood Cliffs, N.J.: Prentice-Hall, 1969), pp. 202 ff.

17. Georges Gusdorf, "Interdisciplinaire (Connaissance)," in *Encyclopedia Universalis*, vol. 8 (Paris: 1970), pp. 1086–90. Cf. Gusdorf, *Les sciences humaines et la pensée occidentale*, 6 vols. (Paris: Payot, 1966–73); *Introduction aux sciences humaines* (Paris: Belles Lettres, 1960).

18. Norbert A. Luyten, "Interdisziplinarität und Einheit der Wissenschaft," *Int. J. Interdis. Forschung.* 1 (1974): 132–53.

19. Cf. Briggs and Michaud, "Problems and Solution"; Reimut Jochimsen, "Zur gesellschaftspolitischen"; Helmut Holzhey, "Interdisziplinarität."

20. Cf. Guy Berger, "Opinions and Facts," in *Interdisciplinarity*, pp. 21–74.

21. George W. Morgan, "Disciplinary and Interdisciplinary Research and Human Studies," *Int. J. Interdis. Forschung.* 1 (1974): 263–81.

22. "Interdisziplinarität der Wissenschaften als Problem und Aufgabe heute," *Int. J. Interdis. Forschung.* 1 (1974): 1–131 and the literature quoted there, particularly the publications of W. Dilthey, E. Spranger, E. Cassirer, E. Husserl, M. Heidegger, K. Jaspers, A. Dempf, P. Lorenzen, J. Habermas, W. Pannenberg, H. Albert, K. Popper, H. Schelsky, Fr.-J. von Rintelen, R. Guardini, H.J. Meyer, K.-O. Apel, J. Ritter, H. von Hentig, W. Stegmüller, H.-G. Gadamer, O. Bolnow, E. Fink, etc. Cf. also: E. Becker, *The Structure of Evil: An Essay on the Unification of the Sciences of Man* (New York: George Braziller, 1968); William K. Kapp, *Toward a Science of Man in Society: A Positive Approach to the Integration of Social Knowledge* (The Hague: Nijhoff, 1961); L. Leary, *The Unity of Knowledge* (New York: Doubleday, 1955); Margaret Baron Luszki, *Interdisciplinary Team Research: Methods and Problems* (Washington, D.C.: The National Training Laboratories, 1958); C.F.A. Pantin, *The Relations Between the Sciences* (New York: Cambridge University Press, 1968).

Interdisciplinary Science on Campus

The Elusive Dream

Rustum Roy

The rapid growth of interdisciplinary research organizations on the American university campus is analyzed and traced to the increasing demand from society for universities to be more relevant to its problems. Drawing on extensive experience in initiating interdisciplinary structures, for both teaching and research, principally in the physical sciences and engineering, I will present the potential of and limitations on such units on a campus.

Extensive data on the field of materials research, the largest and prototypic interdisciplinary field in American higher education, are analyzed as a case study to show that very limited success can be claimed for such organizations. Possible courses of university reorganization are presented. Finally I will recommend models for interdisciplinary organizations for the near term as well as the possible long-range future of American higher education.

Origins of Interdisciplinarity on the American Campus

It is in the natural sciences and engineering that, in quantitative terms, much so-called interdisciplinary activity, especially in research, has occurred on American campuses. This paper will draw heavily on data and experience from these fields to make generalizations and draw conclusions* (which will also be restricted to American institutions).

*This paper is based on my experience with interdisciplinarity matters as a faculty member and administrator at a major state university for nearly thirty years, and a parallel involvement with the same interdisciplinary areas through professional societies and the National Academies. My education as

For a hundred years or so that field of humanity's activity that we call science has been fissioning. Natural science became physics and chemistry and biology. Biology subdivided several times to eventually encompass in many universities full-blown departments of botany, zoology, biochemistry, molecular biology, microbiology, and others. Moreover, an organizational pattern that was perhaps necessary for teaching and research soon came to be invested with totally unearned intellectual significance as departments certified themselves as "disciplines."

Till 1950 this fissiparous tendency completely dominated the infrastructure of science, especially on campus, culminating in its part of Clark Kerr's multiuniversity. By 1960 fragmentation and specialization had reached some kind of zenith (or nadir), and the kingdom of knowledge, scientia, was balkanized, nay feudalized, divided into a hundred fiefdoms, each with its army (departmental faculty), local dialect (journals), and religious establishment (professional societies). With budgets expanding, literally hundreds of new colleges and universities being created, and institutional grants being made to putative "centers of excellence," departmentalism (disciplinarity) reigned supreme on the American academic scene. The year 1960 is probably as good a date as any to mark the birth of interdisciplinarity on a major structural scale. American society was heralding a New Frontier, the national psychological climate for attempting new things was good, money for society's affair with education was readily available. Two rather different forces acted in concert over the next fifteen years to shape events.

---

a physical chemist and my principal professional focus in materials science necessarily means that data and models for these fields will be prominent. I write from the vantage point and hard-earned experience and battle scars of having started and directed initially the first major interdisciplinary research laboratory (in materials research) on campus; what is the largest interdisciplinary graduate degree program (Solid State Technology); the undergraduate interdisciplinary program in Science, Technology and Society. My professional career has been intimately connected with the evolution of two interdisciplinary fields—geochemistry and materials sciences—and is currently intricately connected with a third, science, technology and society. Hence I have also experienced the usual range of auxiliary administrative apparatus that surrounds the creation of a discipline: editing one of the first journals in materials, helping to establish a Federation of Materials Science, chairing national meetings without professional society involvement. I have also served as chairman of the National Academies' committee to evaluate United States universities' performance in the prototype field of Materials Science and Engineering.

It was, appropriately enough, a post-World War II phenomenon that the first bases for intellectual "fusion" of the subgroups within science began to appear. C.F. von Weizsäcker traces the fundamental evolution of the new unity in the basic insights of science.[1] The emergence of the grand simplifying conceptualizations of science from the second law, the mass-energy equivalence, to quantum mechanics provided an intellectual pediment strangely at variance with the increasing administrative and pedagogic specialization noted above. Von Weizsäcker traces the removal of the apparent conflicts between biophysical evolution and the second law, and the tentative exploration into somatopsychic interrelations and "sociobiology," perhaps even as far as the biological basis of religion. For the avant-garde of science, synthesis and fusion were the signpost to the future. But these developments in the world of ideas had (and have today) virtually no direct impact on the university community at large. That came from a wholly other source.

Along with the visions of the New Frontier and the Great Society emerged some sobering experience of the problems of society. As far as the general public and its elected representatives were concerned, these problems were brought forcefully into their consciousness not by some concerted social-science research effort but by the writings of perceptive observers; structured poverty and unemployment were illuminated by Michael Harrington, the potential environmental crisis was foretold by Rachel Carson.

The situation can be described by referring to Figure 1. Into the public consciousness formed by its major existing institutions (industry, unions, churches, etc.) had arrived certain identifiable "problem" areas. At the same time the public had started to pour vast amounts into education. The cause for this was not an infatuation with the life of the mind, but, unrecognized by educators, the burden of national salvation was being shifted from religion to education. It was therefore quite reasonable for society to expect that the American university it so munificently supported would address itself to these explicitly identified problems of society. (I digress to establish a point to which I will return. The significance of *naming* the animals in the creation story and elsewhere is well known in religious philosophy. I believe the names or labels that the public can use effectively to describe its major concerns or problems will determine the categories that will one day become standard units on campuses in the United States.)

Many analysts of science policy, including W.O. Baker,[2] have pointed out that President Dwight Eisenhower's reasons for support-

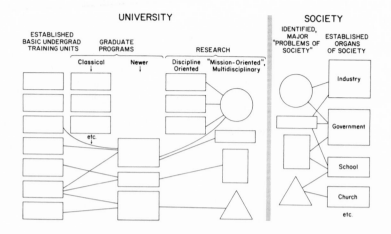

Figure 1.   The relation of university organization to society's needs. Note that it is at the research organization level that the university first responds to and most closely mimics the shape of society's identified problems.

ing the academic community financially in a major way were explicitly connected with its help for two national missions—*defense* and, after Sputnik, *space*. Thus was born the "mission-oriented" financial carrot structure that would determine the course of American higher education. This simplistic quid pro quo axiom of piper paid = time played has since dominated the federal government's efforts to establish mechanisms to attract universities to become involved with the problems of society. And fifteen years experience has proved that this is the *only* mechanism actively tried so far to so involve the universities; whatever is second is far behind. It is regrettable that so few other mechanisms have been tried. For instance, among the hundreds of new institutions created, some could have been built around a problem-oriented division structure.

We have dealt with the demand half of the cycle of Figure 1 and society's explicitly expressed needs. Our interdisciplinary story, of course, is connected with the supply half—the university's response. As the university sector looks through the barrier at the edge of campus toward society, it has one of two archetypal responses. The first one is that of the ivory tower. Why should *we* care about society's other problems? It is our mission to go about teaching and scholarly pursuits. Let them eat cake! The other response, sometimes made by smaller institutions, has been that of the service station. Society brings in its car to have the university check the radiator, fix the tires, or carry out a major overhaul, which is all in a day's work for a university. Of course, it is somewhere in between these two archetypes that the majority of the academic community falls. In fact, the distribution of responses for the same type of academic institution is not very wide. If from here on we consider principally the major research universities, it is quite obvious that they respond to changes in society in a series of sequential steps. At the core are undergraduate teaching programs, which probably respond to change most slowly. Next to that is a layer of the graduate programs, many of them changing substantially faster than the undergraduate programs, in direct response to society's labeled programs. Finally it is in the research areas that the university has its continuing interface with society. Hence the university should first respond to a new societal need in its research organization. And indeed as it has looked toward society, the university has in the last two decades tended to mimic the shape of the named problem in its research organization. As soon as society decided it had an environmental problem, environmental research institutes sprang up in five years. For water problems there are water institutes, for materials problems there are materials-research laboratories, for problems with transportation there is a transportation institute. A critic could conclude that mimicking society at the research level means that the university is being force-fitted by society into an undesirable mold because there is a budget and a federal department and so on. But one could also argue that such corresponding structures are the proper response to training people in research, in educating them with the right mix of courses in order that the students educated by the university may indeed prove effective in societal institutions that help solve society's existing problems.

We may conclude therefore that the appropriate response by the university, if it is going to respond at all, is first to shape new research programs around the needs of society. Very few universities have *led* society in identifying new problems-of-society research areas. Most have been forced to respond. *But I submit that universities have been forced into new interdisciplinary patterns not only by the dollar sign but by the inexorable logic that the real problems of society do not come in discipline-shaped blocks* (see Figure 1). There are no problems in society called "chemistry" or "geology" or "economics." All societal problems are necessarily complex, and a mixture of so-called disciplines is always needed for their study. Mark Twain used to say that "all the easy jobs are filled," and I think that all those discipline-shaped jobs have long since been filled by the academic world. In order to be able to actually study and do research on societal problems, therefore, either an interdisciplinary or multidisciplinary mix is mandated. It is self-evident that such structures are no longer optional, if the university wishes to respond to society's felt needs at the research level.

It is extremely important that this substantive reason for establishing inter- and multidisciplinary groupings on campus be clearly understood and fully accepted. What is at stake here are the academic credentials among their academic colleagues of all interdisciplinary fields and of individuals who work in them. The canard must be laid to rest that problem-oriented research can in some magical way be carried on in traditional (splendid?) isolation. The converse thesis is now held by most, that the quality of such discipline-limited research itself is substantially lowered unless interaction at the multidisciplinary or interdisciplinary level is involved.

Summary Findings: 1. The major force in changing university structures toward interdisciplinarity has not been intellectual; it has been the financial incentive and political demand that the university respond to the perceived and labeled problems of society.

Summary Findings: 2. The ineluctable nature of the problems of society is that they always and necessarily involve many disciplines in their study and solution. Hence the university that does elect to stay in research must create structures for inter- and multidisciplinary research (first) and (subsequently) graduate teaching and undergraduate training. The primary reason for this is that the best research can only be done in the context of the whole problem.

On the walls of the Jefferson Monument are inscribed these words of the first American university president who, as the nation's president, was also deeply concerned with problems of society.

> I am not an advocate for frequent changes in laws and constitutions. But laws and institutions must go hand in hand with the progress of the human mind as that becomes more developed, more enlightened; as new discoveries are made, new truths discovered and manners and opinions change, with the change of circumstances, institutions must advance also to keep pace with the times. We might as well require a man to wear still the coat

which fitted him when a boy as civilized society to remain ever under the regimen of their barbarous ancestors.

For shaping the changes in society that will in turn shape their own future institutions of higher education, the leaders of those institutions can take little credit. No university president, no faculty senate committees have, even after fifteen years, taken any initiative in designing optimum structures for the mission-oriented part of university education. It is almost entirely the result of the interaction of the federal bureaucracy with small groups of research-oriented faculty, working out the best compromise in a generally hostile atmosphere.

The shape of the distant future is not so difficult to discern with respect to disciplines and interdisciplinary units. They are both here to stay and they badly need each other. Intellectually at least, the major disciplines have something to offer in the way people are educated. On the other hand, I am sure most universities realize that from a combined intellectual, political, and economic viewpoint, their mission-oriented interdisciplinary centers are essential to survival. I am afraid that we have had a long history of reductionism in academic organizational structures, which say you've got to be *either* for disciplines *or* for interdisciplinary structures, one or the other. I think that a human being, who is both naked ape and fallen angel, can manage perhaps to organize the university with both an ivory-tower and a service-station character.

Definitions

A serious lack of discipline in the use of terminology has hampered progress in analyzing the sociology of interdisciplinary and multidisciplinary organizations. There is no agreement on what a discipline is, let alone what distinguishes terms such as inter-, multi-, or cross-disciplinary from each other. The approach taken in this chapter is first to identify the empirical realities that describe such units and then to associate specific terms with particular *sets of realities*. Thus whether or not each specific label survives, the same reality syndrome can be identified. I will treat only three terms: discipline, interdisciplinary, and multidisciplinary.

First we note that attempts to define an academic discipline in science prove inordinately difficult. One could start with all human knowledge and attempt to subdivide it on some basis. It immediately becomes obvious that while broad regions on the map of knowledge may be characterized and distinguished from each other, there are no sharp or firm boundaries *between* any contiguous fields. If disciplines represent different areas of knowledge, then lines drawn to separate such areas are inescapably arbitrary. There is simply no principle or measurable property that can separate chemistry from physics at a sharp boundary. Since no fundamental distinction can be made between disciplines, one is forced to turn to an operational one. With what units of a university is the term connected? This immediately yields the result that for all intents and purposes on any one campus, discipline = department. However, in the national consciousness a university department with a strange-sounding name on only *one* campus does not make a discipline. A generally accepted academic discipline seems to come into being when a certain minimum number of departments have been formed at various universities. A discipline implying territorial control over an area of knowledge is constituted when some twelve to twenty universities establish departments. The scope of the discipline is also automatically defined by the activities of these departments.

A personal vignette will illustrate the point. When I was appointed in 1950 to the faculty of The Pennsylvania State University, I who had trained as a chemist and had a Ph.D. in ceramics was among the first faculty members in the United States to be given the title of Assistant Professor of Geochemistry, in a geologically oriented department. Geochemistry as a field of specialization was regarded by the vast majority of colleagues in geology in the nation as an illegitimate invasion of the classical disciplines by "second-rate" interdisciplinary interlopers. By 1970 things were different; geochemistry had arrived as a prestigious member of the discipline club. The required number of geochemistry departments had been created, a full-blown professional society existed, and several professional journals had the word geochemistry in their titles. Ipso facto the discipline of geochemistry now existed, asserting full sovereignty over its territory and in turn making sure that no interdisciplinary interlopers invaded its territory.

If, instead of adopting this pragmatic approach to defining discipline, one attempts to use more classical views of a discipline (such as, the subject-matter range of a group of learned scholars who can carry on together serious intellectual discourse at the frontier of their field) one arrives at instructive contradictions. Thus in 1920 all research chemists could understand what nearly every chemist was reporting at a society meeting; likewise all physicists had had the same courses and read all the same scientific journals.

The disciplines of chemistry and physics were rather clear. In 1970 none of these statements applied any longer. Following a consistent definition set would mean that chemistry and physics have become large federations of "disciplines" so defined. The corresponding departments, and to some extent the professional societies, have to a large extent retained their suzerainty over the same total range of topics, even while the field (as indicated by the research activity number and breadth of topics covered in courses) has been multiplied by more than an order of magnitude and consists of several disciplines. The cause and consequences of the particular course of evolution of our discipline-department structure is discussed in a later section of this chapter.

Hence we present our first definition: A *discipline* is a term used to describe a subject matter area when there are more than approximately a dozen university departments using the same name for roughly the same subject matter.

We turn now to trying to define inter- and multidisciplinary. In this task I am reminded of the story of the definition of an elephant by the nine blind men who went out to touch it. In discussing interdisciplinarity, we have a hundred blind men entering a zoo, with instructions to describe an animal. They all come back with a very precise description of an animal. Of course, having contacted twenty different species at a hundred different points, it very soon becomes impossible to carry on logical discourse about the topic because each person's limited experience is so different from the next. However, taking the approach noted earlier, one can categorize the parameters describing existing institutions and discover commonalities among sets thereof.

Table 1 summarizes the features that are shared by all the discipline-crossing centers (in conception if not always in performance). Mission-orientation is clearly *the* raison d'être for all such

Table 1
Common Features of Multidisciplinary and Interdisciplinary Research

Research done toward a predefined objective (even one as vague as a societal goal) within the rubric of a defined program.

The rubric includes criteria for evaluation and periodic review of programs toward the stated goals.

The research output from the whole program should be more than the sum of the individual components if separately funded.

Its success calls for definite (and unpopular) changes in administration and in reward structure (if longevity is expected) in the typical university.

centers. They also share extraordinarily strict (as compared to disciplinary structures) evaluation and review procedures and, as the fourth item states, are an essentially unpopular and unassimilated incubus in the body academic.

Table 2 provides us with a list of the parameters that distinguish two distinctly different types of activity. I have labeled them multidisciplinary and interdisciplinary, and I believe that in the science and engineering community these descriptors would be widely accepted. However, as previously noted, whatever the titles, the two sets describe separate realities. Let us examine the key differences. The most important of these is that interdisciplinary research (or activity) requires day-to-day interaction between persons from different disciplines. It requires therefore some learning of the other discipline's basic language and the interchange *in interactive mode* of samples, ideas, and results. Naturally this is facilitated greatly by physical propinquity of all team members to each other. Intellectually the diversity of breadth of discipline that can be encompassed in an interdisciplinary team is relatively narrow. For example, while most science and engineering departments can be hybridized, intelligent personal interaction between, say, chemistry and sociology is unlikely because of the language barrier of science.

Table 2
Differences between Multidisciplinary and Interdisciplinary Research

Multidisciplinary	Interdisciplinary
Program management may be by funding agency or internally.	Program management must be local.
Direction and synthesis of subproblems need only occur at manager's level.	Interaction among individual researchers is essential.
The program may be executed at several widely separated institutions.	The program requires some continuous *physical* interaction among personnel from different disciplines.
Individuals can write reports and papers independent of each other.	Two or more individuals often write papers or reports together.
Program integration can be achieved over wide (but finite) spectrum of disciplines.	The interaction bandwidth is typically quite narrow, i.e., the investigators must know each other's basic formalism.

By contrast, in multidisciplinary work the interaction or integration does not need to be carried out at the level of the investigator herself (himself) but rather can be synthesized at a higher level of management. The requirements of geography and bandwidth of disciplines involved are both more relaxed in this set.

We end with two definitions. (1) Interdisciplinary activity on a campus is a day-to-day interactive mode of research or study, in which, in order to do the best work, each researcher's work demands the use of ideas, concepts, materials, or instruments from one or more other disciplines. Such research is usually directed to a specified goal or mission. (2) Multidisciplinary research is mission-oriented work which is so managed as to break down a mission-oriented problem into separate, typically disciplinary components to be carried out by separate investigators with different skills, probably at different sites. The synthesis of the results is not carried out by the primary investigators but at a secondary managerial level.

Overview of the Trends in University Organization

A key question in determining the university's attitude toward problem- or mission-oriented research and education concerns the future trends both external to and within the university. We begin with a summary of some statistical data taken chiefly from the work of Ikenberry and Friedman.[3] (I am indebted to R. Friedman for providing some later unpublished data that are included in the tables shown.)

Table 3
Growth Rates of Institutes and Centers

	1965	1968 (% Growth)		1972 (% Growth)		1975 (% Growth)	
Engineering	125	266	(113)	306	(15)	272	(-11)
Physical Science	355	510	(44)	578	(13)	569	(-2)
Other	2,407	3,603		4,140		4,217	
Total	2,987	4,379	(47)	5,024	(15)	5,058	(1)
phased out		128		476			

Table 3 shows the numbers of supradepartmental organizations which typically go under the name of Center, Institute, or Laboratory at universities in the United States. Two facts stand out. The numbers of institutional units involved, over five thousand altogether, including some nine hundred in the physical sciences and engineering, is very substantial, and hence the problem and the opportunity is a major one. The numbers, while increasing strongly, are clearly approaching some kind of plateau. With the pending relative national deemphasis on education, any rapid growth in interdisciplinary units (IDU) is unlikely. The data of Table 3, however, make it obvious that since five thousand IDU will not vanish and are likely to increase slowly, it behooves the entire academic community to work together to find the optimum role for them within the university structure. One might think that this would be a self-evident and pressing task, given the certain decline in enrollments. It is not, for the universally prevailing atmosphere today remains that of a continuing adversarial stance between departments and IDU, with the administration invariably attempting to function as a neutral referee instead of leader or judge.

Friedman and Ikenberry also attempted to determine the major characteristics of some of the institutes that they grouped into three areas. Some of their data are presented in Tables 4, 5, and 6. Basic parameters describing the IDU include its permanence, whether the faculty's primary tie is with the IDU or the department, and whether there is physical contiguity. On all these scores those institutes within the natural sciences appear to be most highly developed as permanent units within the university. These features correlate strongly with the degree of interdisciplinarity in the same units as shown in Table 5. Thus 60 percent of the projects in the natural sciences institutes have an emphasis or heavy involvement from two or more disciplines in the natural science groups, while in the social science institutes the corresponding figure is 42 percent and in water centers 34 percent. The same trend appears in Table 6 in the *nature* of interdisciplinary involvement, with integrated collaboration appearing in 53 percent of the natural science, 33 percent of social science, and 36 percent of the water centers. If we apply our definitions from the last section it is clear that there is a much higher proportion of *interdisciplinary* management in the natural science units, while presumably in both social science and the water institutes there is a higher proportion operating in the multidisciplinary mode. It is also very important to note that within each class of center, there is a mixture of interdisciplinary and multidisciplinary groups. Comparative studies of their effectiveness could be very instructive.

We are in a position now to paint in the broad outline of interdisciplinarity on American campuses. Over the last fifteen to twenty years there has been an enormous growth of IDUs, so that some five thousand formally designated units now exist. The character of

Table 4 Characteristics of Typical Institutes

	Water	Social Science	Physical-Life Science
Staff housing (Dept./Inst.)	88/12	35/58	25/75
Primary ties (Dept./Inst.)	94/6	54/44	41/56
Temporary/ permanent	54/36	35/65	16/94

Table 5 Extent of Interdisciplinary Involvement

Extent of Involvement	Water Centers		Social Science Institutes		Physical-Life Science Institutes	
Heavy, in nearly all projects	2	(4%)	6	(14%)	8	(25%)
Emphasis in most projects	15	(30%)	12	(18%)	11	(34%)
Some emphasis in selected projects	29	(58%)	16	(37%)	9	(28%)
Work within disciplinary lines	4	(8%)	9	(21%)	4	(13%)
Total	50	(100%)	43	(100%)	32	(100%)

Table 6 Nature of Interdisciplinary Involvement

Nature of collaboration	Water Centers		Social Science Institutes		Physical-Life Science Institutes	
Integrated collaboration	18	(36%)	14	(33%)	17	(53%)
Independent projects	20	(40%)	8	(19%)	7	(22%)
Single-discipline dominance	9	(18%)	10	(23%)	7	(22%)
Little interdisciplinary involvement	3	(6%)	11	(26%)	1	(3%)
Total	50	(100%)	43	(101%)	32	(100%)

these units varies greatly, ranging from multidisciplinary paper organizations serving as fronts for obtaining federal funds to tightly knit interdisciplinary teams drawn out of many departments into shared space, jointly conducting major research projects. The concept and practice of university faculty drawn from several departments working together on a day-to-day basis is very new and of basic significance for higher education. If it is to add something in quality or range of offerings in education or research, university administrators will need to pay a great deal more attention to it than they have in the past.

The generalities in a country-wide survey of all disciplines cannot provide the detailed answers of value to deans and presidents. We turn now to a much more detailed case study, where some of these questions may be answered. By a fortunate coincidence, the field of materials science and engineering, which is the prototype and longest-lived interdisciplinary research activity on campuses in the United States (and by far the largest in terms of dollar funding), has recently been studied by a Committee of the National Academy of Sciences. The so-called COSMAT report is a veritable gold mine of relevant data.

Materials Research and Materials Science as the Paradigm of Interdisciplinary Physical Science and Engineering

History and Definitions

As the organization of science and engineering responds to the changing developments in science policy, in financial support, and indeed in their own epistemology, real models for the actual conduct of interdisciplinary research and teaching are tried. Given the complexity of the problem, by far the best data on interdisciplinary organization at the present time come from case studies of existing examples. Among the fields of science and engineering, where such models exist, materials science and materials research are far ahead of the others in numbers and length of time of development.

It is necessary again to begin with some definitions of terms that are basic to this discussion. *Materials research* is the systematic study of the science or engineering of materials demanding either interdisciplinary or multidisciplinary teams. *Materials science* is an emerging syncretic discipline hybridizing metallurgy, ceramics, solid-state physics, and chemistry. In Figures 2 and 3 the definitions are amplified by showing schematically the relationships of materials science to contiguous disciplines or fields. Materials *science* is a term applied to the first example, in which a new academic discipline is emerging by fusion instead of fission. It is an applied science sitting (often uncomfortably in American academe) between the basic sciences of physics and chemistry and the major engineering degree programs. Figure 3 shows that materials *research* is the research on materials conducted by personnel drawn from many disciplines. Materials *sci-*

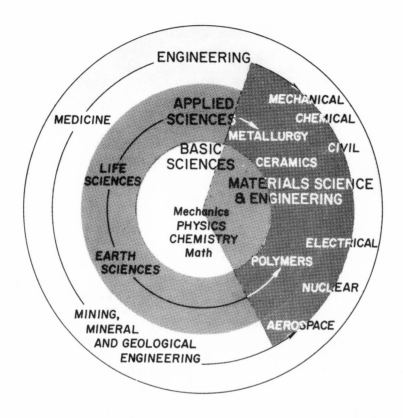

Figure 2. Disciplinary mix in Materials Science and Engineering Subjects within the shaded sector above are considered to be in the field of materials science and engineering. Subjects partly or wholly outside the sector are involved in the field to varying degrees.

ence as an academic discipline has a unique relationship to materials research insofar as *all* of its research is subsumed under materials research. In all other fields the materials research is only a *part* of that discipline's research. It is worth noting that far from being the only pedagogic base for materials research, materials science is not even the largest such base.

Materials research emerged on the national horizon some fifteen or twenty years ago. Its stellar debut was triggered by society's needs, as per Figure 1. Industry had for some time assembled teams

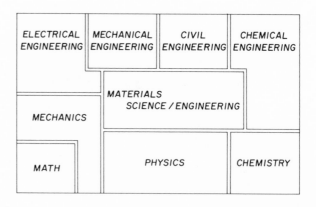

Figure 3.   The scope of materials research. Note that scientists and engineers from a variety of disciplines are involved in research on materials. However, in all these cases, materials research forms only a part of the research activity of the particular discipline: the single exception is the discipline of materials science/engineering. In that case alone does all the research of a practitioner lie wholly within the scope of materials research.

of physicists, metallurgists, and electrical engineers to work on their own "materials problems." Their style, however, had no parallel on the campus. It was Dr. Guy Suits, who was then vice president for research of the General Electric Company together with Dr. W.O. Baker, then vice president of Bell Telephone Laboratories, and several of their colleagues who urged the federal government to a major new intervention on the campuses, as the universities were falling far behind, not only in the amount of training they could do but in the very nature of the research, and training of their students to meet the nation's needs. Physicists were not being adequately trained (within the physics departments) to meet the kind of demand that Bell Telephone or GE envisioned. Neither the nature of the intellectual environment nor the research equipment was adequate. In response to this identified need of society, the federal government, through the Department of Defense (as it happened) injected very large sums of money into a few university laboratories, triggering a major impact on the academic (and government) world.

The sums of money involved—nearly $20 million annually for fifteen years—the all-pervading changes in the naming and restructuring of research groups in universities, industry, and government have been so major that no other interdisciplinary field yet approaches this in size or pervasiveness.

Furthermore it has already been mentioned that by a coincidence, in the last three or four years, this field has received several different concentrated evaluations by various bodies, and a great deal of empirical evaluation data are available. Among these are the National Commission on Materials Policy, commissioned by Congress to do a two to three million dollar study on the whole field.[4] The National Academy of Sciences completed its study of the first interdisciplinary field examined by its usual methodologies. The so-called COSMAT reports are out; the longer report, from which many of the data will be taken, is more valuable for our purposes.[5] Hence we have an excellent laboratory test here, on which detailed comparative data are available, and from which one should be able to draw some useful conclusions about interdisciplinarity.

Materials Research: Its Impact on Education
Let us start with materials *research* and with some data. First the data on the growth in number of university laboratories, and what we may learn from that. There exist now some thirty organizational entities that are officially recognized on thirty different campuses as interdisciplinary *materials research labs.* Distinguish these from *departments* of materials *science.* We note that the word materials did not exist in the label of any department around 1960; it is now in the official titles of some forty-four departments, perhaps as many as fifty; and some seventy-five programs that we know about have the label "materials" on them somewhere. It is these thirty interdisciplinary materials research organized efforts, listed from COSMAT in Table 7, and the fifty or so academic degree programs that provide the data base for our evaluation of interdisciplinary research and teaching in the sciences and engineering on American campuses.

Since the university has three major functions, teaching, research, and continuing education, evaluations of academic programs must study their performance in each of these areas. A good beginning can be made in this direction on the basis of the COSMAT data, since it can be argued that the only possible objective of a major increase in university funding and a radical departure in the

Table 7
Materials Research Laboratories in the United States

Group A: Major Materials Institutions (MMI). Institutions that have a materials-center building providing a physical and intellectual focus for major materials research programs, relatively strong centralization of administration, a major degree program in materials, together with strong materials research in solid-state physics and chemistry.

University of California (Berkeley)[a]	Northwestern University[c]
Case Western Reserve University[e]	University of Pennsylvania[c]
Cornell University[c]	Penn State University[e]
University of Illinois[a,c]	Rensselaer Polytechnic Institute[b]
Lehigh University[d]	Stanford University[c]
Massachusetts Institute of Technology[c]	

Group B: Major Materials Teaching and Research Schools (MTRS). Institutions that have a major or specialized research program in materials science or engineering and an official though small centralized research laboratory.

University of Connecticut[d]	University of Southern California[d]
University of Massachusetts[e]	University of Washington[b]
University of Missouri[d]	

Group C: Materials Research Programs (MRP). Institutions with materials research programs not focused in a centralized laboratory, but often large and typically strong in the basic sciences and run by a committee of senior faculty, with no (or small) materials-designated degree programs. The term "materials research program" (MRP) appears accurately to distinguish the typical characteristics of such centers from the laboratories of the MMI above.

University of Akron[d]	University of North Carolina[c]
Brown University[c]	Purdue University[c]
University of Chicago[c]	Rice University[d]
Harvard University[c]	University of Utah[d]
Iowa State University[a]	University of Wisconsin[d]
University of Maryland[c]	Washington University (St. Louis)[d]

[a]Block-supported by AEC, now ERDA.
[b]Block-supported by NASA.
[c]Block-supported by ARPA for 12 years, now by NSF.
[d]Non block-supported.
[e]These labs have, since the above data were collected, been provided with smaller amounts of block support by NSF, together with one additional institution in the same category: Carnegie-Mellon University.

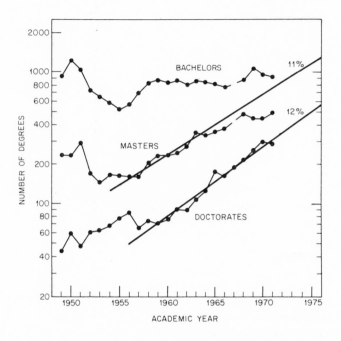

Figure 4. Number of so-labeled materials degrees as a function of time.

mode of funding would include the following. First, to increase the manpower level in the field, i.e., to train more people to the M.S./Ph.D. levels for materials research. Second, to improve that training with respect to mix of subject matter and more relevance to national needs broadly defined. Third, to conduct *interdisciplinary* or other research, which could not be conducted via the traditional funding modes.

A quick overview of the data will help set the stage for our examination. With the special infusion of $20–25 million a year into fifteen major universities superimposed on top of the national 15 percent growth rate across all fields of science, one might expect a substantial impact on the number of degrees. Did the nation get any extra production of degrees in materials broadly defined? Figure 4 shows the data on the growth in the production of M.S. and Ph.D. degrees in the formally designated materials field. (This is a singularly placed department with regard to all of materials research.) We notice that there is a steady increase (11 percent slope) in degrees with time. But we find if we compare this increase with the rest of the engineering

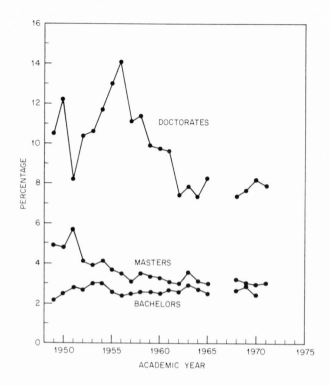

Figure 5.   Number of materials degrees as a percentage of total number of degrees in engineering—note that this percentage has stayed remarkably constant in spite of major injection of funds due to the Materials Research Laboratory program.

fields, in which these materials departments are usually located, that the two slopes are essentially identical. Expressed as a percentage of these materials degrees to all of engineering degrees, the level has stayed remarkably steady (Figure 5). So that although, say, the field of Civil Engineering received the 15 percent increase per year in research funding, while materials science went up 15 percent *plus* its share of the $25 million materials research, there is no evidence that in fact the production of materials-designated degrees increased beyond the normal slope. The same analysis was possible in a roundabout way for physics, which is the other major beneficiary of graduate-degree training in materials research. Again the COS-MAT study found that there is no evidence, strangely enough, of any increase in degree production as a result of this large injection of public money. (If anything there was a negative correlation, i.e., the increase in degree production in physics was higher in universities without materials research laboratories.) One firm conclusion can be reached from the COSMAT data: the IDMRLs had no measurable impact on M.S. or Ph.D. degree production at the favored universities.

If the impact was not in numbers of degrees produced, one might look for innovation in new pedagogic ventures. Here the results are even less understandable. Some thirty institutions have established units for interdisciplinary research (half of them have been continuously block-funded for $20 million per year for nearly fifteen years). This is an enormous advantage and handicap in any competition for teaching and research. Yet the National Academy's Committee could find only a handful of new interdisciplinary materials science or solid-state science Ph.D. programs. Only one of these had attained a substantial production (>10 Ph.D.s per year). And this program together with most of the larger such programs were in the universities *not* receiving block grants. A second category of impact on academic degree programs was a gradual evolution of the traditional metallurgy and ceramics degree programs into materials science or metallurgy and materials science programs. Here again the data have some surprises. One might have expected that the block-funded universities with their financial resources would have been leaders in moving into the newer fields within MSE. Such trends are typified by the emphasis toward ceramics at the expense of metals, and the introduction of the whole area of polymer science and engineering. The data here are again unequivocal. *All* the departments that became the centers of polymer activity (e.g., University of Massachusetts, Case Western Reserve University, Rensselaer Polytechnic, University of Akron) were outside the orbit of the major block-funded institutions. In ceramic materials likewise universities with traditional strengths maintained them, but only nonblock institutions deliberately created new centers of excellence in this field (e.g., Pennsylvania State University, University of Utah); in biomaterials the story was the same, with Clemson, the University of Florida, and others, attempting what the major universities did not.

Research Products and Results

The first result from the data is that block funding of interdisciplinary research did *not* produce innovation in establishing new trends in graduate education—indeed the clear negative correlation is difficult to explain away. Turning now to the data on research activity, we note first that what has been described regarding the emphasis in new degree areas may reflect the emphasis in research at the expense of educational innovations at the same institution.

As we turn to the research *productivity* from such IDMRLs, it is necessary to introduce the concept of the *full-time equivalent in research* (FTER) in faculty effort. (One full-time equivalent in research simply means the hypothetical situation in which a faculty member spends 100 percent of his or her time in funded research.) It is obvious that one cannot compare on equal terms one person spending one summer month and part of his or her time during the year (= 20–25 percent FTER), with a colleague who is a research professor full-time on research except for teaching one graduate seminar a year (= 90 percent FTER). Trying to get data on FTER is extremely difficult, and hence only by direct questioning was COSMAT able to obtain these data. A second caveat is in order. All the productivity-per-dollar or per-person data are derived from salary percentages, and they are used with the *assumption* that universities charge sponsors for all faculty effort devoted to their project. During the sixties this was a substantially uniform policy across the nation, and for everyone that undercharged the federal government for faculty time there were no doubt equal numbers that subsidized teaching from research. However, there is no question that there is some lack of uniformity here. Thus the following data can chiefly be used to establish trends, with the understanding that the "noise" in the data with respect to FTE may be as much as ±50 percent.

How does one evaluate quantitatively the results of research of groups of faculty? The much-maligned use of counting papers, and recently of counting citations, remains virtually the only method available. Science of science students have developed sufficient evidence to show that when *handled with care*, these data are reasonably good and seldom at variance with elaborate subjective evaluations. Research efficiencies and productivity may be more safely compared, since the number of papers and the dollar amount of support are both hard figures. The weakness in these data here comes at the point of deciding what papers to attribute to which financial sources. Thus if one institution gives credit generously to an agency which paid for only 15 percent of its research, while others count only work which is 100 percent supported, there would be substantial distortions in the data. Moreover, these distortions may be deliberate in either direction depending on the track record one wishes to establish. The COSMAT data had the great virtue that they were obtained from a very homogeneous sample, from a detailed and explicitly described questionnaire. However, "noise" in these data even to a factor of two may be unavoidable. Moreover, considering that in most cases five- or ten-year averages are used, and some ten to thirty faculty are involved, *major* trends extracted from the data should be significant.

Table 8
Research Productivity of Materials Centers
(Ranked in order of Papers/Paid Faculty)

Average papers per year	Papers/ Total faculty	Papers/ Paid faculty	Papers/FTE
206	3.62	10.3	17.16
28	1.47	7	28
90	1.45	6.92	6.92
32	1.24	6.4	32
148	4.22	5.28	18.5
124	3.44	4.96	10.33
143	2.97	4.76	46.12
57	2.37	4.38	8.76
137	3.51	4.28	24.9
153	4.22	4.22	15.3
24	.48	4	24
144	3.2	3.69	16.17

For top twelve, average papers/yr = 5, and average papers/yr FTE = 20 per faculty member

Table 8 shows some of the data on the research paper productivity per FTER faculty member in the MRLs. Some of the very high numbers of papers per FTER are undoubtedly due to the "noise" mentioned above. From experience it is not unreasonable to see twenty papers per FTER as the high end of the spectrum. Whether an institution is block-funded or not seems to make little difference.

In Figure 6, in an attempt to normalize the research "products" in terms of support received, there is shown the support per FTER. The figures with medians near $300,000 and $400,000 per year look extremely if not impossibly high at first sight. However, when one considers that a normal single P.I. proposal for $60,000 a year may carry no more than 0.20 to 0.25 of a faculty person's salary (0.25–0.25 FTER), these numbers are seen to be not so shocking. However, such high levels of support on a continuing basis with relatively little proposal writing should result in rather special productivity.

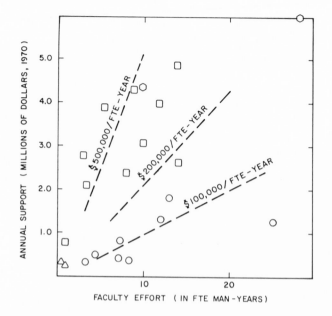

Figure 6. Research support per *full-time-equivalent faculty member in research* (see text for definitions and caveats). Circles are universities without block funds, squares are MRLs originally funded by ARPA; hexagons by AEC, and triangles by NASA.

Data from AEC (now ERDA) statistical reports on research supported show, for example, some individual faculty supported at $200,000 and $350,000 per year on a continuing unreviewed basis, while their colleagues in the same department may have to write and get funded after tedious detailed reviews half a dozen major proposals to generate the same support. What is significant in these figures is not the absolute level, but the fact that there is a range of nearly ten to one across institutes and universities that are generally regarded as comparable.

Figure 7 combining the data costs and publications shows the dollar value associated with each publication from these laboratories by attributing all dollar support to writing papers. Here again we find the surprising range in costs of over five to one. There is no relation to efficiencies of scale, nor is there any correlation with *type* of re-

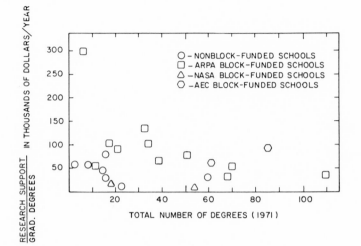

Figure 7. Total research support provided plotted versus research publications from each (see Fig. 6 for code).

search—for example, it could be argued that special facilities (hence higher costs) are needed for something like high-pressure work or radiation-damage research. But this type of correlation did not exist.

Next, Figure 8 associates the same total costs with producing advanced degrees. Again we notice an enormous range from nearly $300,000 per year per Ph.D. produced (i.e., a total of, say, $1.2 million of support to university X per Ph.D. produced in materials research) to $10,000 per year with a median near $75,000. Again a puzzle: What makes one university so much more expensive or less productive than another? The COSMAT committee noted that in seeking to explain these differences no simple solution emerged. High costs were not correlated with quality of universities. Two universities that by general consensus would be regarded as approximately equal in quality and at the very top may differ by a factor of five. The only conclusion that one can come to is that the quality of leadership and management makes a major difference in the *efficiency of research.*

For students of the science of science policy, these data will no doubt provide a gold mine. For the administration and the Congress the science policy question must clearly be faced: Would this money

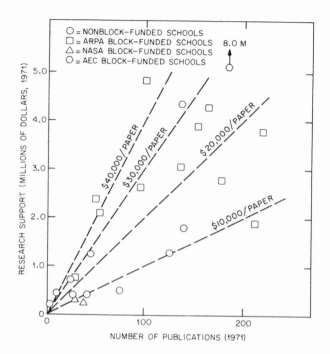

Figure 8. Total research support provided to MRLs plotted versus number of advanced degrees produced (see Fig. 6 for code).

be better spent by restoring it into the normal budget channels? But one now addresses the question most relevant to this chapter: How has the *interdisciplinarity* parameter of the research worked out? Did these MRLs give *evidence* of any marked degree of interdisciplinarity? And did the carrot of the unique advantage of block-funding help? We may attempt to answer this in several ways.

The COSMAT survey attempted to quantify its answers to both these groups of questions by determining the extent to which faculty actually worked together to the extent of having jointly written papers or being jointly responsible for a funded research project, and by comparing block-funded with other universities. Table 9 shows the data obtained. These data indicate that compared to *estimates* for regular science and engineering department faculty, a modest amount of interdisciplinary interaction has in fact been achieved. Here again the spread of values is striking—although clearly some of the data are based on a misunderstanding of the question. Yet in some laboratories, after a dozen years of steady funding for interdisciplinary research, almost no joint papers were being published. In others 20 to 30 percent of the research projects and 10 percent of the papers were interdisciplinary. The COSMAT committee sought a second measure of calibrating the degree of interdisciplinarity achieved. The degree of intra- and interdisciplinary research from the materials group at the Bell Telephone Laboratories was measured by the same parameters; the data are shown in Table 9. Clearly the IDMRLs have not approached what is possible in interdisciplinary cooperation, and what by any generally accepted standards produces the highest quality materials research.

Table 9
Interdisciplinarity Indices (Taken from COSMAT Table 7.38, pp. 7–195)

	Universities in Interdisciplinary Laboratories	Universities in Departments[a]	Industrial Materials Group
Joint contracts	Av. 17%[b]	/5%	
Joint papers *across* discipline	Av. 10%[b]	/5%	40%
Joint papers intradiscipline			Phys. 33% Mat. 26%–56% Chem. 11%
Support from industry (%)	<5% (Avg. of %) <2% (Avg. of $)	18% (Matls.)	

*These data are substantially on the high side, probably due to a misunderstanding of the question, since one lab reported, e.g., 92% joint papers. No actual lists of papers were evaluated by COSMAT itself.
[a]Estimated by deans and department heads.

Another approach to measuring the performance of the MRLs, including the degree of interdisciplinarity, is to make a survey of opinions among the nation's senior research managers in the field in universities, industry, and government. This was done by COSMAT, and the most instructive results are shown in Table 10. The peer evaluation of the performance of the MRLs in general shows that it was with respect to interdisciplinarity that the peers felt that the laboratories—as a whole—had the biggest gap between promise and performance. Finally another kind of interaction measure and a possible value of such IDMRLs was sought in the degree of interinstitutional

Table 10 Expectation and Performance of Materials Centers
(COSMAT Survey of Opinions)

Question	Response	Expectation	Performance
The most important goals that should be achieved by materials centers are: (on a scale of 5—most important—to 1)	Genuinely closely coupled interdisciplinary research	4.0	2.5
	Training M.S.-Ph.D. personnel in materials science	3.3	3.7
	Support of individual faculty projects of excellence	3.3	3.7
	Establishing unique central facilities available to all	3.1	3.4
	Efficient start-up of new work	3.0	3.2
	Mission-oriented multiple investigator research	2.7	2.3
	Effective coupling to industry	2.7	1.5
	Applied research, possibly relevant to industry	2.2	1.7
The general concept of long-range block-funding for support of university materials centers is:	3: Very sound approach 2:Good but not essential 1: Undesirable		2.35
What is the "critical-mass" for a good materials research laboratory concentrating in even a limited area?	In man-years of senior faculty effort (i.e., each m.y. includes necessary postdocs., students, etc.)		10 man-years
If in your view it is a good approach, what median annual level of funding provides the best compromise in the typical major university between the benefit of stability and creativity and the possible loss of outside evaluation and responsiveness to national changes?	$250,000 500,000 1,000,000 other		Avg. $600,000
The materials centers have devoted:	3: Too many resources to science & engineering departments or programs 2: Good balance 1: Too many resources to related fields; physics, chemistry, mech. engineering, etc.		1.5

cooperation. In the early part of this article one of the principal reasons given for starting such institutes on any campus was to respond to society's needs. Since these needs were also being addressed by industry and government, it might be assumed that IDMRLS on campus would couple more and more effectively to their industry and government counterparts. Such coupling would be a double asset since it would be part of the continuing education function of the university.

Table 10 shows that the *subjective* evaluation by peers gives the IDMRLs poor marks on this measure of coupling or interdisciplinarity. The quantitative data in Table 9 for university-industry coupling are even worse, showing that some university MRLs do almost no joint work with industry; only four laboratories had more than 5 percent of their budget from industry. Further examination of these data shows that especially in the new fields of materials science the coupling to industry has been done more effectively by the non-block-funded universities, and indeed by traditional departments.

The Future: The Rationale for Interdisciplinary Units on Campus

In the foregoing I have described the interdisciplinary organizations on the American campus involving science and engineering. The data on the overall pattern of evolution and a case study of one major field provide a backdrop of reality from which we may project reasonable models of future developments.

Before moving to this it is, I believe, necessary to establish a sound rationale for the cultivation of a university structure that fully articulates both disciplinary and interdisciplinary units. In the first section, half of the rationale—the administrative or practical aspect— was detailed. It was argued that the university's relation to society is such that it would be irresponsible if the research and at least graduate education did not reflect in some way the major concerns and problems within society. But there is, I believe, a second reason based entirely on intellectual arguments, which is no less compelling than the first. The argument here can be presented with the help of the simple sketches of Figure 9. We start with the basic datum that the capacity of the human brain changes only at the rate of biological evolution and hence has been essentially constant within the last two or three millennia. In Figure 9 I represent this as a circle of constant

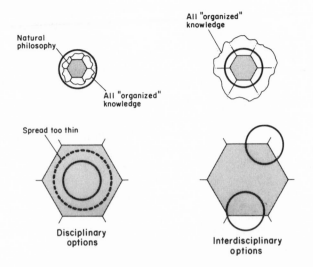

Figure 9.   Steady-state model of department/I.D.-unit relations.

radius corresponding to the fixed median human capacity to organize raw data and information into knowledge, understanding, and wisdom. In the sequence of sketches, estimates of the total volume (= area) of human information and knowledge of a particular time are superimposed on this fixed circle. *This* quantity has changed dramatically in two thousand years. My thesis is that the fundamental change affecting us is in the ratio of the two quantities: the fixed median human capacity, and the exploding sum total of human information. In the "classical" world (prior to the nineteenth century), an educated person could contain within one human brain virtually all codified knowledge, not only knowing the substance of disciplines as disparate as philosophy, theology, and physics—but also being fully aware of the structure of relationships among disciplines, i.e., they could be both disciplinary and interdisciplinary in their education. Examples abound from Aristotle to Pascal to Newton to Thomas Jefferson. A restatement of the education of Renaissance man could be that he had both a disciplinary and an interdisciplinary education.

At the beginning of the twentieth century our qualitative sketches show that the volume of knowledge has expanded so that the knowledge of the natural sciences was now a large fraction of the median human capacity. But there was enough capacity left over that the educated person could see at least the major boundaries of her or his science with other disciplines, thereby retaining the great virtue of being trained to appreciate the relationships among the different sectors of knowledge—retaining depth in a discipline as well as an interdisciplinary outlook.

Our condition *today* is illustrated in the lower two sketches. One option—the one adopted quite unconsciously by the vast majority of the world of higher education—is shown at the left. The volume of knowledge is now seen to be much larger in any science-discipline than the human capacity. The result is the mindless effort of superspecializing, so that students are forced to stay increasingly *within* one discipline "since there is so much to learn." The utter folly of this approach is easy to see. As the volume of knowledge within the discipline becomes larger and larger, where to place the circle increasingly becomes a problem. One response will be to sacrifice depth for breadth (schematically illustrated in the dashed circle) in a futile effort to keep up with the expansion. Indeed this danger of too much breadth, a charge often leveled at interdisciplinary fields, is a much greater danger within well-established but rapidly expanded disciplines. We have mentioned that chemistry and physics are already today federations of disciplines. But they retain sovereign status so that all solid-state physicists (even if they will later work with polymers) will dutifully be forced to take a certain set of nuclear physics courses but none in solid-state chemistry or polymer science. This argument leads to the inescapable conclusion that the attempt to be authentically monodisciplinary is not only poor education but is defeated before it starts. The lower right sketch illustrates the alternative, interdisciplinary model. Here the student is deliberately encouraged to include within her or his finite capacity not only a major disciplinary area but one or two other disciplines. The gain here is not only a different mix—which could in many cases reflect the mix more appropriate to a major problem area of society—but the essential gain of understanding the relationships and interfaces among disciplines. Indeed then the chosen education could reflect both a discipline and a problem orientation—surely an ideal situation. Students of human creativity assert that the introduction of new and different sets of conceptual models in organizing information provides one of the best avenues for innovation. A student exposed to the basic paradigms of a variety of disciplines is therefore much better equipped to look with a new perspective at old problems. Furthermore, in an era of rapidly changing knowledge and job opportunities she or he is also in a better position to change occupations. From the viewpoint of an educator shaping the minds for

the mid-twenty-first century, it would appear almost criminally neg-
ligent to continue with the discipline-limited model, unless the case
sketched out here can be forcefully rebutted. There is no evidence
that narrow specialization makes the best scientists and much
against it. When we consider that some of the greatest names in a
discipline had formal degrees in another (Szilard and Wigner were
trained formally in chemical engineering), the case for insistence on
narrow disciplinary specialization vanishes. Thomas Kuhn has
made the case that changes in science, which may be rationally
obvious, do not occur merely because they are known to be correct.
We must await a basic change in the paradigm of *science-education*
before major changes occur from the lower left to the lower right
models in Figure 9.

Some Workable Models for Interdisciplinary Units

It is my thesis that the structure of all major research universities of
the twenty-first century will include a permanent organizational
framework accommodating both discipline-oriented and mission-
oriented entities. Experiments with various frameworks should have
been completed by now so that some data would have been available
on which the selection of the more suitable styles could have been
based. However, the university world presents the most startlingly
unimaginative picture of uniformity of organization. It would, for
instance, be quite feasible to organize the entire science and engineering activity of a university—especially at the graduate level—*primarily*
around a dozen permanent mission-oriented interdisciplinary laboratories. A *secondary* interlaboratory structure could then focus on each
of the main degree programs or departments. Many of these departments would no doubt coincide with classical disciplines (say, physics
and civil engineering), but the freedom to change the content of
graduate degrees to meet the evolving needs of society would be
vastly improved because the discipline would then be less sacrosanct.
At one stroke the tedium and repetitive dullness of much of the
teaching function would be removed. The deep conservatism of the
academic community is here exposed on its home turf. It may be
argued that it is difficult to reorganize an existing hundred-year-old
structure—although it happens every week in major industrial organizations. But even that excuse vanishes when one thinks of the
several hundred major *new* educational institutions that were created

in the fifties and sixties. Very few of them, and not one of prominence, managed to create a novel structure. Perhaps where affluence failed, adversity will be the mother of invention, and universities will move in this direction when money gets even more scarce.

However, while the experiment with a university structured primarily around interdisciplinary units is highly desirable and would probably serve as a very important model, it is important to provide models for interdisciplinary units that start with the present realities. One *begins* with the axiom that the administration or faculty that chooses this path must interpret fully and consistently its meaning to the entire university community. It must be axiomatic in all dealings of the university that the success of the university depends equally on its discipline-oriented departments and its mission-oriented institutes. The reward structure for department chairmen and institute directors must explicitly recognize their mutual helpfulness as a major contribution.

A "Permanent" Human-Centered Subdivision of Knowledge

Two questions now arise. First, which missions are important enough to be as permanent as the disciplines? I have already made the point that disciplines are far from permanent. Many are new, and the old ones are fissioning. There are certainly some permanent missions that will be with human society far beyond any discipline. They correspond to the basic human needs: it is not difficult to imagine that every major university would have as a fundamental infrastructure not only departments of English and physics and chemistry but permanent units assigned to deal with research and teaching in: food, energy and materials, health, information, transportation and housing, and environment. One can add to this list or subdivide each of the missions. (Just as physics divides into nuclear, theory, solid state, so energy could be split into fossil, nuclear, solar, and so on.) At this stage, however, these half-dozen areas of organized knowledge centered on permanent human concerns should provide the basic structure of the interdisciplinary organization. In Table 11, a corresponding set of disciplines at approximately the same level of aggregation has been set orthogonal to the previous list of IDU. Also shown on the matrix are the relative mutual importances of each mission and each discipline (3 highest, 1 lowest). There will of course normally be much wider interactions when large numbers of faculty are involved in a department or IDU.

The second question often raised is the hardy perennial of all vertical-horizontal organization charts. How does one give direction

How university departments could interact with campus
interdisciplinary units

Departments

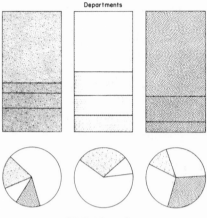

Interdisciplinary units

Figure 10. A model for a steady-state twin organizational structure
for a university, with equivalent department and interdisciplinary units. Each administrative unit has a blend of
faculty affiliated with a few orthogonally related units.

to either a mission group or a discipline if *every* member is spread all
over? The answer here, as in all similar cases where it is asked as
though it were unanswerable, is that it is simple and self-evident.
Each unit whether discipline or mission-oriented needs a physical
and intellectual center of gravity. This means that each unit should
have a critical mass of faculty effort associated with it in terms of
FTE person-years. It also means that perhaps half a department's
faculty should be affiliated with various IDUs, perhaps three or four
different ones. Conversely it means that a major IDU would involve
faculty from four to eight departments, with no one department
contributing more than, say, 40 percent. An IDU also needs to have
perhaps half its faculty holding their principal appointment (and
hence reward structure) within the unit, but it may need only a very
small number of faculty full-time in the unit. These are summarized
in the sketches of Figure 10.

We have already noted that it is essential that deans and department chairmen and laboratory directors be explicitly rewarded for
their performance in *mutual interaction*. For rewarding the faculty a
similar explicit recognition of participation in interdisciplinary work
must be recognized *by statute*. Finally the question of making ap-

Table 11
Rational University Structure (science and engineering only). A model of a university structured around society-oriented interdisciplinary groupings as the basic infrastructure. The present major disciplines contribute to each task-oriented unit to varying extents, indicated for illustrative purposes as high (3), medium (2), and low(1). Faculties offering the disciplinary degree programs would be drawn from different units, giving a richness and societal relevance to teaching often lacking today.

| | "Permanent" Disciplines | | | | | | |
	Math, Computer Science	Physical Science	Life Science	Geological Science	Material Science	Engi- neering	Social Science
Food			3	1		3	2
Energy/ Materials		3		2	3	3	
Health		1	3		1	2	2
Information	3				1	3	2
Environment			3	2		3	3
Transportation	1			1	1	3	3

Permanent Society-Oriented IDU

pointments and granting tenure needs to be radically revised. To be really successful, IDU units must have the power to appoint up to a certain percentage (often small, say, 20 percent) of their faculty without reference to a department (although the latter is always more desirable). The spectrum of institutional arrangements for funding IDUs and departments is so wide that one can complete the model with only a general principle: The permanent IDU needs exactly the same degree of security and tenure capital that a department does—neither more nor less. Any institution concerned with graduate education and research that stays in tune with society's needs will probably make a major contribution by moving in these directions.

Summary

The thesis presented here has been that interdisciplinarity is inherent in the nature of reality, and that a major part of its raison d'être is the university's responsibility for dealing with the problems of society. Over the last two decades attempts, principally by financial inducements, have been made to change the structure of university science and engineering to reflect these societal needs. Principally at the research and secondarily at the graduate-degree program level, universities have responded by creating five thousand institutes. The scarce quantitative data, especially on the major field of materials science and engineering, and anecdotal reports on others, do not offer much evidence of successful incorporation of either the intellectual viewpoint or the administrative responsibilities of interdisciplinarity into university structures. It appears probable that *most* universities will not be able to adapt to serve a useful function in the nation's need for mission-oriented basic research. National planners should therefore start considering the establishment of a national "institute" structure (somewhat like the Max Planck Institute), independent of but alongside universities to conduct such research on the problems of society.

Notes

1. C.F. von Weizsäcker, "The Unit of Physics," in *Quantum Theory and Beyond*, ed. T. Bastin (Cambridge: Cambridge University Press, 1971), pp. 229–63; "Towards a Philosophy of Science," *Proc. Intl. Colloquium on The Meaning and Function of Science in Contemporary Society*, The Pennsylvania State University, September 1971.

2. W.O. Baker—reported in *Chemical & Engineering News*.

3. S. Ikenberry and R. Friedman, *Beyond Academic Departments* (Washington, D.C.: Jossey Bass, 1972).

4. *Material Needs and the Environment Today and Tomorrow*, Report of the National Commission on Materials Policy, U.S. Congress, 1973.

5. *Materials and Man's Needs*, Report of the Committee on the Survey of Materials Science and Engineering. National Association of Science, 1974; Supplementary Reports, especially vol. 3: *The Institutional Framework*, 1975.

Crossdisciplinary Coordination in the Social Sciences*

Muzafer Sherif

The thesis of this chapter is that no single social discipline can claim validity for the formulations developed within its own traditional confines, but must seek valid formulations through crossdisciplinary exchange. Human problems are not arranged or divided neatly along lines coinciding with the divisions between the social disciplines, which have been established through historical developments in universities. On the contrary, the social disciplines study and theorize about many of the same problems, about overlapping problems or closely related problems. Failure to recognize the common and overlapping problems has led each of the social disciplines to preoccupation with minutiae and technicalities within its own boundaries and to the avoidance of validity issues. Their disciplinary ethnocentrisms are encouraged by the structure of universities and professional associations.

Crossdisciplinary efforts at exchange, as well as attempts to deal with practical issues in social life, are bound to fail when overlapping and common problems remain unrecognized by representatives of self-insulated disciplines. Such failures are not merely a result of obstacles to communication, such as differing vocabularies. They reflect fundamental inadequacies in each discipline's development that are traceable, in the larger and longer view, to its insulation.

From the thesis, it follows that each of the social disciplines

*This chapter was prepared by Carolyn Wood Sherif from excerpts of an unpublished manuscript by Muzafer Sherif on "Crossdisciplinary Coordination in the Social Disciplines in Terms of Coordinative Interactionism" and from M. Sherif and C.W. Sherif, "Interdisciplinary Coordination as a Validity Check: Retrospect and Prospects," Chapter 1 in the co-edited book *Interdisciplinary Relationships in the Social Sciences* (Chicago: Aldine, 1969). The longer unpublished manuscript acknowledges the stimulation and assistance provided in informal monthly crossdisciplinary seminars, especially from Charles Craypo, David Westby, Larry Spence, Frank Sim, and George Enteen.

needs the others in a fundamental way, namely, as a means of checking the validity of its own formulations. For example, formulations and research findings about social power, intergroup conflict, or leadership as taught in departments of sociology, psychology, anthropology, political science, and history cannot be totally contradictory or disjunct if any one of those disciplines is to claim validity. Their formulations and research findings need not be identical, nor are they likely to be; however, they must be mutually coherent and supportive. Otherwise some or all of them are either invalid or, as often happens, they concern disparate phenomena that have erroneously acquired the same labels.

On the other hand, when the formulations and findings from several social disciplines on common and overlapping problems begin to cohere and supplement one another, claims and tests for validity can be taken seriously. Then it begins to make sense to attempt their application to contemporary human problems in applied interdisciplinary ventures, where validity issues are necessarily paramount and where correctives to disciplinary insularity are ultimately to be found.

Preparadigm Crises in the Social Disciplines

Debates about crossdisciplinary borrowing among the social disciplines are futile controversies, reflecting the immature ethnocentrism of the social disciplines. The physical and biological sciences have been cross-borrowing throughout their development without too much fuss. Historically, psychology has borrowed from them freely in problem areas bordering their focal concerns (e.g., psychophysics in the study of vision and audition, psychochemistry of stimulus correlates in the study of olfaction and gustation; psychophysiology of the neuromuscular system). In fact, the history of the social disciplines is filled with examples of borrowing, but usually from a more prestigious discipline. Crossdisciplinary exchange becomes debatable when the other disciplines are on a par with, or worse yet, less prestigious than one's own discipline in the academic hierarchy.

The necessity for interdisciplinary coordination among the social disciplines is not diminishing, despite the feverish comings and goings, the research and publication boom of unprecedented proportions within each discipline. In fact, this necessity has become more acute, as unsettling crisis has mounted within the social disciplines. Within the disciplines today, controversies are raging over the fundamentals, without which a discipline can only shoot erratically in all directions. Controversies rage over the very conception of the nature of the human psychological system. There is controversy over what makes humans tick—in other words, about the fundamentals of human motivation. The unsettled fundamentals also include the nature of human social systems. Controversy rages around alternative models of the human social system, particularly those models uncritically adopted from the physical or biological sciences.

It is highly unrealistic to approach the staggering problems of crossdisciplinary coordination *without* sober recognition of the prevailing crisis. The causes of the crisis lie in the world of actualities outside the ivy-covered walls of academia. They lie in the unprecedented changes and upheavals that have been taking place all over the world, including the United States. Therefore the most sensible first step toward crossdisciplinary coordination in the social disciplines is to concentrate on the nature and scope of the crisis. Such an analysis of the crisis situation may even be helpful in developing some practical guidelines to be observed in attempts at coordinating social disciplines. Such attempts at coordination are essential for the shaping of commonly shared paradigms, on whose validated grounds each discipline can develop in depth without the monopolistic claims of the single disciplines and feuding factions therein.

For these reasons, a portion of this chapter is devoted to the crisis in the social disciplines. Since I am a social psychologist, I will use social psychology as an illustrative case. Necessarily, such a discussion entails touching upon the state of things in other social disciplines.

Interdisciplinary Coordination and Levels of Analysis

The term *coordination* is used deliberately to refer to the objective of efforts in interdisciplinary relationships. In particular the terms *integration* and *unification* are avoided. In some circles the latter terms conceal attempts to reduce sociology to psychology, or to extrapolate from psychology to sociology with de facto elimination of the latter, or to reduce both to biology. Such reductionism is both unwarranted and invalid. As many writers have asserted, the whole, the configuration, the system is as much a reality, as a functioning structure, as its parts. The functioning relationships among the parts can and should be studied as structural properties of the system at their own *level* of analysis, with concepts appropriate to that level. Of course research should also focus upon component parts, but not at the expense of denying the structural properties of the system.

The structural level for analyzing human interactions is the sociological *level of analysis,* in which the group, kinship pattern, social organization, or cultural pattern (consisting of norms or social values) is the *unit of analysis.* Both functional pattern (role-status reciprocities) and cultural pattern (norms, social values, etc.) are products of interaction among human individuals who are parts of the social unit (in the past and present), who engage in the vital business of making a living, of striving to *be* somebody, or of improving their role-status relations with others in their particular settings. As products of interaction in the past or present among members, the patterns of human relationships and their culture are subject to change, to transformation with further interaction under the exigencies of new conditions (technological, economic, political, cultural) or under conditions that generate strains between parts and conflicts among normative values. But ultimately the end result of change is not lasting chaos or disorder but trends towards new stabilized patterns. Here, "ultimately" does not imply the millennium but does imply more than a year or two, when substantial changes of larger social units and subunits therein are underway.

The tendency to extrapolation that stretches psychology to "explain" sociology or to take it over is unwarranted and factually invalid. In the social disciplines there has been a special fascination in extrapolating from individual units to construct a model for a group unit; or from small ingroups to an intergroup system, in which these small groups are parties in positive or conflicting relationship to one another. Such extrapolations have been the usual practice of orthodox psychoanalysts, conducted by their own intricate rules. Writers in the camp of logical positivism have also engaged in them, here in the name of unity of the sciences and typically in the direction of some brand of reductionistic physicalism.

Such extrapolation continues in the social disciplines, despite empirical evidence that it is invalid. For example, there is ample evidence, experimental and otherwise, that interaction processes within a human group do not correspond to psychological processes within individuals, nor do groups "behave" like individuals. Likewise it has been experimentally demonstrated, and it should be the common knowledge in the light of historical events, that the attitudes and values usually practiced within the bounds of ingroups need not apply in relation to other groups in an intergroup system.

The conception of levels and units of analysis posits the irreducibility of the sociological to the psychological, or vice versa. However, events at the two levels (psychological and sociological) are in constant traffic, acting and reacting on one another. Interdisciplinary coordination consists of relating the two to one another—studying the interactions between these two levels, discovering their relative weights under varying conditions.[1] Interdisciplinary coordination is a necessity for the social disciplines because neither unit of analysis is self-contained, neither level of analysis represents a closed system. In fact the final test for the *validity* of a theoretical model and of research findings at one level of analysis is their congruence and their mutual support with those at the other level.

Current State of the Social Disciplines Illustrated in Social Psychology

The social disciplines are in a preparadigmatic stage of development, despite a growing literature discussing their alleged paradigms. In a preparadigm stage of its development, a social discipline is in an unsettled, erratic state. This theme will be expanded later through discussing the denotation and connotation of the term *paradigm*. *Connotation* as well as *denotation* will be discussed because psychologically the researcher or the scholar is never value-free in his or her scientific work. Currently the unsettling state of crisis and disarray in the disciplines reflects the lack of common fundamental assumptions, common basic models, and particularly lack of examplar achievements that a discipline can rally around.

The most prominent indicator of the crisis is the low wheat-to-chaff ratio in the glittering piles of research and publication—the harvest. The widely acknowledged crisis in social psychology, in which the ratio of precious wheat to ever-mounting chaff is discouragingly meager, reflects the nature and proportions of the crisis in other social disciplines—representatively because of the strategic position of social psychology, situated as it is between the levels of analysis of sociology and psychology.

Corrective developments that point to ways out of the impasse created by the crisis are underway in social psychology. Such corrective developments include, from within the laboratory itself, the lines of work that came to be known as social psychology of the psychological experiment, experimenter bias in research, and social desirability effects in responding to attitude and questionnaire items.[2] The developments in broader perspective include cultural psychology and environmental or ecological psychology.[3]

In addition to the foregoing, there have also been correctives involving crossdisciplinary and historical comparisons that are particularly helpful in avoiding blatant ethnocentrism. Some of these correctives are indicated by institutionalization of new divisions in the American Psychological Association outside of those divisions traditionally attracting social psychologists. For example, there are new divisions dealing with population issues and the environment and with psychology of women.

All such developments point to the necessity for using multiple levels of analysis in analyzing social-psychological problems and the use of multiple methods for data collection. Conversely, they represent disavowal of rampant "scientifics" that elevate a single data-collection method, such as the laboratory experiment, to the status of orthodox ritual. Such "scientifics" hide behind research technologies, some indiscriminately chosen because they have the appearance of science. These include a proliferation of simulation techniques that often do not simulate anything in real life. Hence what is presented as a simulation model is often nothing more than a game—a universe unto itself, with no counterpart elsewhere. An astounding proportion of the experimental literature is devoted to ever more experiments about other experiments that had no contact with significant problems of social life in the first place.

Preparadigm State of Social Psychology: An Illustration

The unsettling, incoherent state of things in the social disciplines forces questions that must be asked. In social psychology the questions include, what is the shape of our discipline within social science, situated as it is between psychology and sociology? Over forty years ago I started my career with the little book *The Psychology of Social Norms* (1936), which raised this very question. I am even more puzzled now, as social psychology seems caught between rival camps of its own practitioners. What shape are we in? What shape are our parent disciplines in, namely, general psychology and sociology? What shape are our close kins in, for example, culturology, economics, and political science?

Social psychology's fate is inseparably tied to the fate of these parent and kindred disciplines. Piles and piles of research and publication mount. In view of the booming activity and the proliferation of research technologies, a growing number of concerned colleagues are asking the inevitable question: What is the real yield under this mountain of produce that is worthy of preserving and nourishing for younger generations? This is considered an impertinent question by those solidly established in the profession with "all the rights and privileges that pertain thereto." But there is no way of sidestepping this overdue question, for it spreads among the younger generation. It is hard to conceal the stark fact that a discouragingly high proportion of what appears to be a mountain of wheat turns out to be only chaff on closer inspection.

In the confusing air of crisis, we find the rival camps, each a self-contained castle, guarded by cognitivists versus behaviorists, depth versus trait psychologists, sociological versus psychological social psychologists. The partisans are shooting in all directions and, at times at crosspurposes, trying to advance the monopolistic spread of their own wares. In brief, indications are that we have not yet developed beyond our *pre*paradigm stage.[4] A *pre*paradigm stage is signaled by the controversy between rival self-contained castles and by the cartellike use and abuse of communication and instruction outlets.[5] The sure indicator of the preparadigm impasse is the absence of shared fundamental assumptions, basic models, and particularly exemplar achievements recognized as such and therefore shared by all.

When a paradigm shapes up essentials as reflected in exemplar achievements in a given scientific community, certain orientations, certain assumptions, certain models and concepts are no longer matters of serious controversy, and certain others are therefore discarded. Then certain bounds emerge that provide criteria for responsible evaluation of claims and counterclaims of contending theories. In the latter respect, even the sky does not seem to be the limit at present.

Another warning indicator of crisis within a discipline is the emphasis on complete technocratic reliance and on sharpening the techniques and tools of analysis. Such emphasis is analogous to the teacher who finds all of the students failing and decides to tackle the problem by raising standards and giving more difficult examinations. Absence of achievement will be revealed more starkly. Meanwhile the students may rebel or leave.

We need a period of sobering concentration on the unglamorous job of exploring our grounds, testing whether we are working on barren or fertile soil. Such an explanation entails the following:

1. The critical examination of orthodox models, many of them apish imitations of models in more established disciplines.

2. Careful attention to the implications of the corrective developments within our own disciplines that point to the necessity of mending our ways. (For example, emancipating ourselves from our myopic conception of what constitutes the "independent variables" in a social situation—be it an experimental or natural situation.)

3. A greater concern over the validity criterion through giving high priority to efforts to validate generalizations across disciplines (especially across the much-neglected social sciences); across different cultures and across different historical periods within the same cultures; and across different research techniques.

4. A dispassionate sorting out, from the huge pile of chaff, the precious few golden kernels of achievements with a view towards displaying their distinguishing characteristics in theory, instrumentation, and analysis, as object lessons for the professional community.

This period of exploration must include a thorough reexamination of the nature of human social systems *and* the human psychological system, both hitherto conceived, in general, in the image of physical equilibrium or biological homeostatic models. Then social psychology—and general psychology for that matter—can move more effectively toward shaping an appropriate paradigm.

It will be surprising if the concern expressed here over the nature of the human social system in moving towards a paradigm in psychology is not jarring for the traditional psychologist, and even those social psychologists primarily concerned with interpersonal relations. Conversely, emphasis on the nature of the human psychological system may jar a traditional sociologist or economist. Yet the unwitting acceptance of assumptions about the human individual and about the nature of social systems that are not made explicit, or that could not stand the test of empirical study, are at the basis of confusions within both psychology and other social disciplines.

Denotation and Connotation of the Term Paradigm

A pristine supporter of positivism, committed to stripping the scientific enterprise from any value-charged contaminations, will be jarred by reference to the connotation of Kuhn's term *paradigm*. But several readings of Kuhn's use of the term *paradigm*, especially the thirty-four-page Postscript in the 1970 enlarged edition, reveal that the term is used in treating *problems* in the sociology of knowledge. The sociology of knowledge concerns the impact of strong attachment and selective arguments of the partisans to elevate their own model of the human individual or of society for the whole disci-pline—a practice characteristic of the factions within a social dis-cipline in its preparadigm stage.

The label *paradigm* is being used these days to prove anything and everything—especially to advance one's own party's position and to discredit the rival party's position in the theoretical controversies. Here is one illustrative case. In 1976 the Society for Personality and Social Psychology of the American Psychological Association devoted a large proportion of several issues of its official journal (*PSP Bulletin*) to the mounting controversies concerning the present state of social psychology. Some contributors took conflicting stands even on such questions as "Are we in a state of crisis or are we not?" and "If we are, is the sharpening of our research technologies the sure mea-sure to carve our way through the impasse?" They argued over whether social psychology can make better headway as an historical enquiry (Gergen) or as an experimental science or both (Godow). In the Fall 1976 issue of *Personality and Social Psychology Bulletin* alone, there were no less than five contributions that relied on Kuhn's authority on some crucial point to advance their respective stands in the controversy.

It becomes necessary, therefore, to put the essentials into focus from Kuhn's famous book, *The Structure of Scientific Revolution* (1970). In this discussion we need not take sides on two issues on which Kuhn has been widely criticized: (1) whether there are revolu-tionary breakthroughs representing sharp breaks in scientific devel-opments or only cumulative developments at varying rates of prog-ress (the normal science); and (2) whether the Kuhnian core term *paradigm* loses meaning because, as critics pointed out, Kuhn himself did not use the concept in the same fixed sense in different contexts. Kuhn used the term in twenty-two differentiable variations, accord-ing to Masterman's often-cited critical essay. However, as one reads Kuhn's use of the term *paradigm* in different contexts, one cannot help finding a common core. That common core is acknowledged by Masterman in the overall estimate in her critique.[6]

As clearly stated by Kuhn, his conception of the term *paradigm* is built into a closely related pattern on two foundations that are not contradictory:

1. The first is sociological, namely, paradigms as the constella-tion of commitments in the disciplinary community to some definite fundamental assumptions, basic orientations, and operational mod-els. In Kuhn's words: "A paradigm governs, in the first instance, not

a subject matter but rather a group of practitioners. A study of paradigm-directed or a paradigm-shattering research must begin by locating the responsible group or groups."[7]

2. The second and closely related foundation is the substantive one, which sooner or later imposes checks and correctives on the first, namely, the solid exemplar achievements (validated generalizations, theories, and laws) that are incorporated sooner or later as commonly upheld property by the whole discipline. In Kuhn's words, these are "Paradigms as Shared Examples" that set the common tone and orientations in the choice of research models and technologies around which the practitioners in the discipline rally.[8]

With the second part of his conception of paradigm, Kuhn cannot be a comfort to logical positivists. For Kuhn, the operational definitions by consensus of practitioners alone is not sufficient. Intelligence, for example, is not necessarily what the intelligence testers are measuring. The tests, models, and techniques have to be validated to be candidates for inclusion in the shaping of a paradigm. The exemplar achievements in given areas mark the transition from the bickerings of the preparadigm stage (in which rival factions or schools have a heyday) to a postparadigm stage, in which the factions converge on fundamentals.[9]

Contrary to our ingrained expectation and practice in social disciplines, it is too much to expect that Kuhn or any other eminent authority in the physical sciences or in the history of science can write prescriptions for us as to how to shape a paradigm around which we can all rally. We cannot expect him or any other outside authority to sort out for us our exemplar achievements so that we can build our own paradigms. Kuhn's illustrations are all from physics and chemistry, in which he majored in college.

A respectable number of writers in strategic positions in various social disciplines gave their versions of the Kuhnian paradigm and offered their solutions of breakthroughs in their respective disciplines. In some quarters this fashionable term degenerated into calling every bit of research line or every minute theory a paradigm. However, there have appeared also some serious attempts to translate the essence of the Kuhnian paradigms and their implications. Such a serious account, with an informative survey of other such attempts, was put together by John Heyl under the title of "Paradigms in Social Science" (1976). Heyl's translation of the essentials of paradigm is instructive:

The central concept of Kuhn's Structure of Scientific Revolutions is unquestionably that of paradigm, which Kuhn defined variously, but which is (at the very least) the world view—the matrix of theories, models and exemplary achievements through which a scientific community perceives the universe relevant to its particular discipline. Kuhn describes how scientific communities, in a discipline "come to be governed by paradigmatic views"—; what scientists do when under the influence of paradigms ("normal science"); how they came to transfer allegiance from one paradigm to another ("anomaly," "crisis" and "paradigm shift").[10]

This description is plainly sociology of knowledge. The preparadigmatic ethnocentrisms and monopolistic claims of partisan schools to make their own self-contained castle supreme over the others in the whole discipline (preparadigm stage) are followed by their convergence in time on basic orientation, fundamental assumptions, models, and operationalization provided by those who create recognized achievements in their field (the paradigm stage and its stabilization).

If Kuhn had not provided us with the conception of a paradigm, we in social disciplines should have devised such a term by another label. We are in dire need of exploring the unstable grounds for our assumptions, our models, and our methods for the study of particular problems. Concern over moving towards shaping a paradigm will require that we explore our bearings, survey the ground on which we stand, examine whether the traditional models have served us well or have been responsible for our pitifully meager advance, despite the huge expenditure of funds, resources, and toil.

Social Marginality of the Social Disciplines

Every one of the social disciplines is afflicted with a sense of marginality within the wider clan of sciences. Being unsure of itself, bordering on a feeling of inferiority, each social discipline engages in efforts to prove that it has come of age to approach the physical sciences, deservedly established in high places in the clan. Not infrequently the efforts are apish imitations and therefore self-defeating, because the social disciplines go through the motions in form, rather than in substance, imitating their betters. This upward striving is not unlike the case of the upwardly mobile marginal person, frantically trying to go places, but taking the wrong turns on the way because of the ill-advised choice of what "proper things" the "betters" would prefer or approve.

In the eyes of social disciplines the established physical sciences are the rich relatives. We social psychologists frantically aspire to be like them, to be accepted by and integrated with them. The social disciplines, our own kind and kindred (sociology, culturology, history, political science, and the rest), are poor relatives—poor relatives to be kept at a safe distance, lest we are seen in their lowly company by the rich relatives. We are worried that by keeping lowly company, we may lose whatever favorable rating we have scored in the eyes of our rich relatives.

This plainly is a marginality phenomenon that can be readily explained in terms of reference-group theory. That explanation in turn will provide us with effective pointers as to how to get out of the paralyzing state of marginality. Being caught in the state of marginality between two sides of our ties and with strong, almost exclusive fixation on the more distant side of these ties (physical sciences) is the phenomenon of false identity. That is, it is the pretension of claiming to be what we are not, claiming to be in a position that we are not actually in. False identity is not conducive to self-reliance. And without self-reliance one cannot engage in solid theorizing and research. This inference was made the hard way from my long years of concentration on the fate of scientific movements in social sciences, as well as the fate of social movements.

Let me illustrate the specific meaning of the state of marginality, which leads to being off mark, with a lesson I learned from the sound advice of an eminent physicist over twenty years ago. In respect to our uncritical practice of doing science by analogy in the apish imitation of our "betters," the eminent atomic physicist Robert Oppenheimer gave advice worth heeding. In his invited address on "Analogy in Science" to the sixty-third Annual Convention of the American Psychological Association in San Francisco, Oppenheimer stated his concerns for the ways we had been attending to our job and warned psychologists of the danger of falling into the unwarranted trap of reductionism in the following words:

> Between sciences of very different character, the direct formal analogies in their structure are not too likely to be helpful. Certainly what the pseudo-Newtonians did with sociology was a laughing affair; and similar things have been done with mechanical notions of how psychological phenomena are to be explained. I know that when physicists enter biology their first

ideas of how things work are indescribably naive and mechanical; they are how things would work if the physicists were making them work, but not how they work in life. I know that when I hear the word "field" used in physics and in psychology, I have a nervousness that I cannot entirely account for. I think that, especially when we compare subjects in which ideas of coding, of the transfer of information, or ideas of purpose are inherent and natural, that formal analogies have to be taken with very great caution.[11]

Uncritical takeover of models from those who achieved their solid paradigms is no way to build scientific self-reliance in the social disciplines. It is no way to gain respect from our rich relatives. It arouses a whimsical grin, when we parade our uncritically borrowed wares in front of them with solicitous claims for recognition and acceptance. It is more likely that they will accept us if we concentrate first, for a period, on formulating the appropriate problems, raising appropriate questions that require closer examination of the unique properties of the human psychological systems and of human social systems.

In support of the plea for working toward the formulation of appropriate problems and questions, before plunging headlong into the technologies of more mature sciences, an appeal to a scientific authority at the pinnacle is in order. The following quotation affirming the temporal primacy of raising appropriate questions in order to get the right answers or solutions is from the book *Evolution of Physics,* by Einstein and Infeld (1951): "The formulation of a problem is often more essential than its solution, which may be merely a matter of mathematical or experimental skill. To raise new questions, new possibilities, to regard new problems from a new angle, requires creative imagination, and marks real advance in science."[12]

It is to the formulation of its problems that social psychology needs to turn. Similarly a focus on the problem and its clear formulation is the first step toward effective crossdisciplinary coordination.

Reciprocal Interchange Among Social Disciplines as a Necessity

As already noted, social disciplines are quite willing to borrow from the physical and biological sciences and do so avidly. It is the prestigious thing to do. But when it comes to social disciplines, each of the disciplines assumes an "I won't take it from you" attitude. This openness to the physical sciences and supercilious avoidance of the other social disciplines follows from the earlier analysis of marginality.

Therefore it is in order to accentuate the necessity of an ongoing interchange among psychologists, sociologists, economists, and the rest in social disciplines. But a plea for close interchange with sister social disciplines brings the usual objections from the hard-nosed (really bone-nosed) methodologists in our ranks. The usual objections of such purist disciples of positivist bent include: (1) the assertion that "social disciplines are still in a big mess"; then (2) the pat rhetorical question that follows: "What can social disciplines learn from one another except compounding their own mess with the mess of the others?"

The first objection, that we are in a mess, is altogether true. The positivists compounded the mess by imposing their physicalistic models of psychology and sociology without serious concern over their isomorphism with human psychological and sociological systems as they function in real life.

The second objection is altogether false and biased by positivist prejudices. The prevailing mess should be one of the main reasons to reaffirm the necessity of interdisciplinary interchange among the social disciplines. It is no justification for turning our backs on each other so that we can start with a clean slate. Starting anew in a brave new world of technocratic utopia has been tried. B.F. Skinner advocated one such attempt in his novel *Walden Two* (1948) and in his recent entry "Utopianism: The Design of Experimental Communities" in the new *International Encyclopedia of Social Sciences* (1968).[13] The attempt is blissfully unrealistic and myopic in its conception of what constitutes the human environment.

Human beings are inexorably steeped in their history of omissions and commissions. In whatever new moves they have to make, they have to wade through this history, clearing the path of their mess as they proceed. In the crisis in which all the social disciplines are blocked, interchange across disciplines about the wrong turns where they floundered and about the false leads that steered them further from the target can be their most effective activity in the initial stage. Through a series of concerted activities they can mark the dead ends with clear "Out of Bounds" signs, so they will not stumble into them again. The marking of dead ends that have beguiled social disciplines into inappropriate, misleading models can well be one of the corrective developments on the way towards solid grounds of a paradigm. The several disciplines will doubtless discover that they have marked off the same dead ends.

Examples of Advantage from Reciprocal Interchange for Clearing the Ground

A currently popular model both in sociology and psychology is that thriving under the label of exchange theory. (We are not concerned here with internal disputes among exchange theorists.) Its widespread use owes a great deal to its sponsorship by two former presidents of the American Sociological Association[14] and by some influential social psychologists who propagated the theory through experimental studies in prestigious professional journals. The core idea, though adorned with embellishments by the skillful craftsmanship of its partisans, is a reductionistic balance formulation combined with a naive hedonism. The exchangers try to come out on the plus side in the exchange of benefit and cost (or reward and cost) calculations. Their satisfactions increase with a balanced state of cost-benefits as well as individual gains. The sophisticated embellishments and involutions acquired by this core formula in the context of group structures and institutions are admirable craftsmanship, not to speak of fantasy in speculating what costs or benefits are involved.

One wonders whether exchange theory would be flourishing if it were presented now without the trimmings of modern garb and embellishments, if it stood naked as a resurrected version of its original core, namely, the pleasure-pain utilitarianism of nineteenth-century England. Would its hedonistic pleasure-pain calculations be characterized as they were, even at that time, as the typical psychology of the "average English shopkeeper" of that epoch?[15] If there were an ongoing interdisciplinary interchange among the social disciplines, participants versed in and sensitive to the history of such theories would bring to the limelight the commonalities in exchange theory of current decades and in nineteenth-century pleasure-pain utilitarianism. Then they could evaluate how such models have fared in the various social disciplines since then.

Likewise the controversies over cognitive dissonance theory could gain a great deal in perspective and depth if they were conducted through interchange among sociologists, psychiatrists, experimental and social psychologists, all bringing their respective expertise to bear on the problem. For example, sociologists have been dealing for decades with the human consequences of incompatible, contradictory values, which always have cognitive components.[16] Psychiatrists have been dealing with inner conflicts due to the clash of contradictory attachments and identifications that could not possibly be devoid of cognitive components. If all these closely related developments in the same general problem area were coordinated through interchange among the related disciplines, all parties involved would be more likely to move towards a more generalized theory of psychological conflict—which is what dissonance theory was about. What is valid in dissonance theory (which may have been obscured by its label with an auditory metaphor) would be established as part of a more comprehensive formulation.

A final example is concerned with one of the major properties of human groups: that group property known as solidarity among the sociologists and labor people since the nineteenth century, but which became a fashionable topic in some dominant quarters of social psychology under the label of group "cohesiveness." The instructive point that emerges from this example is applicable to other group problems, such as conformity-deviation, discipline, morale, and so on.

The topic of solidarity has received considerable attention in theorizing and research in sociology since the last century. One of its classics is on this topic, E. Durkheim's *The Division of Labor in Society*, first published in 1893. That book elaborated the structural bases of the group property in terms of mechanical solidarity and organic solidarity.

Social psychological research and theorizing took little stock of structural analysis of group properties like solidarity or cohesion. Instead the problems were dealt with primarily in terms of interpersonal attractions or preferences. (See Cartwright's evaluative survey as of 1968.[17]) Interpersonal choices or rejections are of course real; they can be used as meaningful indicators, especially if the structural sociological bounds (like homogeneity-heterogeneity) and limiting factors are duly recognized and explicitly spelled out. But they are not equivalents of the ecological setting, the functional and normative structures within a group, or the states of relationships among groups that affect so compellingly the solidarity or cohesiveness of a group unit. In understanding the need for crossdisciplinary interchange in attaining a proper formulation of the solidarity or cohesiveness problem, I benefited greatly from the paper by Luis Escovar, a psychologist, and Frank Sim, a sociologist.[18]

Perhaps these few illustrations convey the value of interdisciplinary coordination for clearing some of the "messes" in the disciplines.

Crisis in Other Social Disciplines

Not only psychology and sociology but also the other social disciplines (economics, political science or government, culturology, history, and the rest) have had their own images of human nature and of the nature of society or social systems. Their myths and, especially since midnineteenth century, what they supported in the name of a better society, have been shaped by those images, consciously or unconsciously. Thus their courses and strategies in research have also been shaped by images of human psychology and of human social systems, whether these images were based on religious assumptions, philosophical assumptions, or their prior commitments to what they regarded as basic "scientific" models.

The young generation in social disciplines will gain an impressive object lesson through detailed study of the stories of once-powerful schools in the history of the disciplines. Some of the edifices are already wrecks. Examples include Wundtian experimental psychology based on "Mental Chemistry"; the Spencerian-Sumnerian model of human society, which deflected the Darwinian revolution in biology into the jungle of survival-of-the-fittest apologetics; "The End of Ideology" crusade by Daniel Bell (1960), buried postmortem by his own apologetics in his *Cultural Contradictions of Capitalism* (1976)—a work written in a many-splendored style with impressive erudition in social sciences and belles lettres, whose opening lines contain a gloomy forecast from Nietzsche's *The Will to Power*.[19] And study of the history and fate of earlier social Darwinism would surely dampen uncritical enthusiasm for the current fad called sociobiology.

In recent decades the authority of being considered the authentic voice of a social discipline has been enjoyed by no one more than by the school presided over by Talcott Parsons and bearing the label of Structural-Functionalism. (I capitalize the label for this highly influential school of the midcentury to distinguish it from the words. No particular school in this preparadigm stage is entitled to possess the monopoly of the indispensable terms *structure* and *function*.)

In a symposium monograph appraising Parsonian sociology, the editor and coauthor Don Martindale portrayed the state of things well: "So popular did [Functionalism] become in American sociology in the post-World War II period that it was fashionable in the 1950's to treat it [Parsonian School] as coextensive with *sociology*. In his presidential address to the American Sociological Association in 1959, for example, Kingsley Davis denied that there was some special method of functional analysis in sociology. Rather, he insisted that it *was* sociology."[20]

But the near-hegemony of Parsonianism in sociology was drastically crippled within a decade or so. The verdicts of once awe-inspiring pontiffs were being questioned, and second thoughts about their authenticity are still gaining momentum. Alternative ways out of the debris are being sought through increasing corrective developments.

One of the signals for corrective developments was the portrayal of the *Coming Crisis of Western Sociology* by Alvin Gouldner, himself a prominent sociologist. Gouldner took on some of the most influential American sociologists, including Parsons, George Homans, and to a lesser extent Peter Blau, all three one-time presidents of the American Sociological Association, and neosymbolic interactionists like Erving Goffman. He presented lively and informed critiques of their respective basic assumptions or models, whether these assumptions had been left in the background without explicit statement or made an explicit part of the theory for the discipline. These basic assumptions were referred to by Gouldner as "background" and "domain assumptions."[21]

Thus Gouldner contributed to the sociology of knowledge through an assessment also of what kind of group interests these lines of theorizing support, deliberately or unwittingly. The main target for Gouldner's critique was Parsonian sociology and its subsidiaries. Such finger pointing is as it should be: responsibility for the onset of crisis should be proportional to the influence exerted by a school in academia and the powers it wielded in the high positions of the profession.

Years earlier, William James characterized Wilhelm Wundt's prolific writings as a worm with many segments: if some are chopped off, another segment still survives. This metaphor may be even more apt for Parsons's obtruse and convoluted ensemble of writings, amended through the years in the face of the serious criticisms they provoked, especially against his *Social System* (1951), perhaps his major work.[22] I shall confine the discussion to Gouldner's critique of the inability of Parsonian sociology to handle effectively the problem of social change. Social change is perhaps the crucial problem area for rival social theories to prove their mettle. It is crucial because major social, political, and cultural problems the world over are directly or indirectly related to great changes and upheavals. Social change is the order of the day. A glance at the maps of continents and the changed social systems since the 1940s reveals the unprecedented scope of transformations. (On a very concrete and limited scale, just a look at the composition of male-female and minority-group representation among students and daily life-style in the college dormitories suggests the variety and scope of the changes within society.)

It is difficult to take exception to those writers who argue that the unrest and turmoil generated by the black movement, the women's movement, and student political activism and not the nat-ural evolution of social disciplines were responsible for the greatly accelerated polarization within social disciplines today. In this accel-erated polarization, mounting opposition is directed especially by a younger generation of scholars against the orthodoxy of equilibrium models of social systems, as prominently represented by the Parson-ian School.[23] Inability to handle the problem of social change was the focus of criticism by Gouldner and was also the keynote in cri-tiques by Don Martindale and by James Coleman in separate mono-graphs appraising social theory in the 1960s.

Martindale summed up the emerging appraisal in his chapter, "Limits and Alternatives to Functionalism in Sociology":

> The general criticism of the various elementaristic positions in social science of the various forms of holism, including func-tionalism, is that they overestimate *the significance and role of closed systems in social life.* By taking the system as the object of study and treating it as the cause of all else, all other social phenomena are thrust outside the pale of analysis or distorted to fit the *a priori* notion that all social events are system-determined. The realities of social life according to the elemen-tarists are the infinitely varied acts of individuals and plurali-ties. The endless encounters and confrontations of individuals, singly and in concert, runs the criticism, only rarely and tem-porarily approximate a closed system. . . .
>
> However, while sociological functionalists deny that there is a one-sided emphasis in their theories due to *a priori* concep-tualization which arbitrarily excludes some social phenomena from analysis, there has been widespread acknowledgment of the comparative failure of sociological functionalism to handle the problem of social change.[24]

In one of several passages in which Gouldner criticized Func-tionalism for its failure to handle the problem of change, he echoed Parsons's own pessimism. In his *Social System* Parsons wrote about the inability of sociology to formulate a theory of change. In Parsons's words: "A general theory of the processes of change of social systems is not possible in the present state of knowledge. . . . When such a theory is available, the millennium of social science will have arrived. This will not come in our time and most probably never."[25] Gouldner then posed the question: "Why is it that a lack of knowledge should bar development of a theory of the change in social systems, when a similar lack of knowledge provides no impediment to Parsons's theory of social system equilibrium and order?"

Finally, consider the following words of James Coleman, a prominent mathematical sociologist, in an evaluative symposium monograph, *Design for Sociology: Scope, Objectives and Methods*, edited and coauthored by Robert Bierstedt for The American Academy of Political and Social Science:

> The relative absence of studies of social movements by sociologists is particularly distressing because of the frequency of such movements in current society. The neglect of such phenomena could be better understood in periods of social stability than at present, when there are many such movements to study. The current neglect leads one to suspect that the whole discipline of sociology (and not just certain theoretical positions, such as Parsons' and functional analysis, which have often been described as oriented to equilibrium) *has evolved toward the study of social statics, and becomes impotent in the face of change.* Whether this is the case, or whether it is merely that the study of social change, social movements, conflict, collective behavior, and other transient states is simply more difficult, the end result is the same. These are the underdeveloped areas of social research. They are not only backward at present; they are not catching up.[26]

Interdisciplinary Relationships and Problems in Levels of Analysis

For a particular social discipline, a core problem is to discover which of its problems overlap with those of other disciplines or are shared as common problems. Recognition of common problems or overlaps is necessary, in order that the discipline may determine what concepts and what findings it needs to borrow from others and what issues it needs to transact with other disciplines. The need comes with growing recognition of the incompleteness of any one discipline and the urgent search for supporting evidence that permit a discipline to stand on its own feet.

Deliberate assessment by one discipline of what is needed from other disciplines, and who it needs to transact with, will provide a center of gravity during its own development. Such a center of gravity is sorely needed if a discipline is to probe its own domain as deeply and intensively as possible without becoming caught in its own circles. Insulated from related disciplines and lacking a clear notion of its bearings relative to what others have done, intensive study within a single discipline sooner or later leads to floundering into territories already explored by others. The result is confusion and displays of needless ignorance, of the kind typified in the past by psychologists who improvised their own sociology of the family or of culture, or who declared social institutions to be fictions. Similarly, sociologists, economists, and political scientists have been known to psychologize their own brands of perception, motivation, or social judgment, in near-total ignorance of psychology's efforts in these problem areas and typically with disastrous results.

Considerable progress toward the interdisciplinary assessment needed by a discipline in dealing with its core problem can be made through recognition of the different levels of analysis and units of analysis employed in the disciplines.[27] A human eye, a human being, an aggregate of human beings, or an organized human group—each represents a distinctly different unit of analysis, and each is part of a system at a higher level of organization. Each unit of analysis requires concepts appropriate to it. Thus concepts used for studying the individual (e.g., perception, remembering, acting) are not sufficient for analyzing the human group, of which the individual may be a part.

Crossing disciplinary lines that involve different levels of analysis poses greater problems than crossing lines that represent merely historical divisions of labor. For example, a central issue in social psychology is the coordination of analysis at the individual and group levels, whereas politics and the economy are both on the same level of analysis, even though tradition separates their study into two disciplines. The problems are greater in the first instance because the processes underlying events at different levels of analysis cannot be presumed to be similar. For example, the processes producing hunger are closely related to the behavior of the hungry individual, but they are totally inadequate for understanding whether widespread famine will or will not produce riots, social movements, or revolutions. This example may also suffice to show why crossdisciplinary checking is essential for the attainment of valid formulations within each social discipline. The hungry individual behaves quite differently when suffering in isolation or in hopeless fate with others than when joi' ng with others to protest their common deprivation.

Deliberate assessment by one discipline of what is needed from other disciplines must be followed by learning about the units of analysis employed by those other disciplines and the concepts used in dealing with them at their appropriate level of analysis. We should not confuse the difficulties in learning enough about the other disciplines to understand these issues with mere difficulties in communication. Nor should we necessarily expect that representatives of another discipline can do more than clarify the level of organization and analysis on which they are working. It is a simple fact of life that some individuals are content tending their own gardens. It is therefore up to those who keenly experience discontent with the state of their own disciplines to learn what they need to know from others and attempt the difficult task of coordinating conceptual formulations and findings from the differing levels of analysis. The promise is a more rounded understanding of the problems in one's own discipline and, ultimately, valid generalizations about the phenomena of study.

Guidelines for Crossdisciplinary Enterprises toward Closing Validity Gaps

Crossdisciplinary enterprises are sometimes concerned primarily with pushing forward the frontiers of learning in the social disciplines, while at others they are organized to tackle urgent social problems that concern a society. Both kinds of endeavor will doubtless continue, despite the well-known failures and frustrations they engender. They will continue because single-discipline or single-social-agency efforts are increasingly insufficient in a world of growing complexity.

On the other hand, there are genuine obstacles to crossdisciplinary efforts and plenty of examples of multidisciplinary research and multiagency enterprises that die-hard skeptics will continue to cite as glorious failures. The latter have at hand some clever slogans to discourage the uninitiated, for example: "Interdisciplinary cross-fertilization always ends in interdisciplinary cross-sterilization." Readers of this book are unlikely to share such total cynicism. Therefore the following do's and don'ts for crossdisciplinary enterprises are offered with the hope that some of the more obvious pitfalls may be avoided and some of the more important needs may be met.

1. Beware of the notion that the physical proximity or the exchange of notes among scholars, practitioners, policymakers, or administrators from different disciplines and sectors of life defines an interdisciplinary enterprise. The record is already filled with joint conferences, symposiums, books, panel discussions, and task forces that show the error in this notion.

2. While searching for participants in crossdisciplinary enterprises whose centers of gravity are steady in their own discipline, try to avoid participants who present themselves, or are willing to be presented, as *the* representative of psychology, or sociology, or anthropology, or political science. In the absence of common paradigms within the social disciplines, no representative can yet legitimately talk in the name of *the* psychological point of view or *the* sociological perspective. Their first charge should be to clarify for others the mess within their own disciplines and to specify their own premises. If they are staunchly committed to the premises of a school that brooks no challenge, they will also be convinced that they are on the main road with the correct approach, theory, model, and techniques. They will talk *at* each other rather than *with* one another. It follows that fruitful crossdisciplinary interchanges involve persons keenly aware of the problems in their own disciplines and concerned with their limitations in dealing satisfactorily with the problems at hand.

3. The worst possible way to launch an interdisciplinary enterprise is through definitions of what it should be like. In most cases no one knows, since there are relatively few past examples that have met with unqualified success. Abstract discussion in definitional terms brings out the worst in each discipline, as each peddles its own definitions. Premature concern over defining interdisciplinary relations is likely therefore to end in petty power struggles or mutual frustrations over failures to communicate. A far better preparation would be preliminary study of crossdisciplinary enterprises that have proved fruitful in some respect in the past. Such a preparation might also serve the useful function of educating representatives of one discipline about the histories of others.

4. Any crossdisciplinary enterprise should focus on the problems or problem that brings the participants together. Review of how the problem has been formulated in the various disciplines, of where disciplinary problems overlap or are common problems, may

permit its clearer formulation within a broader framework than any one might have achieved alone. The assumptions of the formulations proposed by participants need to be examined in terms of their appropriateness for the problem and for compatibility or incompatibility. If basic assumptions from representatives of different disciplines are contradictory or incompatible, while also firmly held, the enterprise is doomed. A pleasant tea might be more profitable than continued interchange. If they are not incompatible, if they are merely poorly articulated, and if they are not waved like a banner, there is hope for a coordinated attack on the problem.

5. Clarifying the problem through persistent, even painful efforts requires discovering the many-sided actualities of the problem area. Such clarification entails sharing and learning among the participants, including an understanding of the units and levels of analysis that were employed in studying the actualities by the various disciplines. Sufficient concentration at the start upon clarifying the problem(s) in terms of actualities produces benefits, whether the aim is an educational endeavor, a research project, or a plan for action. The premature choice of educational strategies, of research designs, methods, or tactics for action, before the problem is clearly formulated, may be fatal. On the other hand, the formulation of the problem should lead readily to considering feasible alternatives for attacking it.

6. Recognize that the ethnocentrism of disciplinary commitments erects blinders to one's vision, and that fruitful crossdisciplinary exchange requires the removal of such blinders. Such a change is seldom as comfortable as standing pat in one's own backyard. It is not to be expected, therefore, that interdisciplinary enterprises will rapidly become cozy affairs, free of all conflict and contention. Those who succeed in emancipating themselves from the ethnocentrism of a single discipline can contribute to the coordination of lines from several. If and when this occurs, the collaboration is likely to be experienced as exhilarating and adventurous, which indeed it may be.

7. When the time comes for the educational enterprise, research, or plan of action to begin, recall the fatal error of putting all of one's eggs in one basket. The histories of the several social disciplines all point to the necessity of developing and using a combination of varied methods and techniques for investigation. There are no magic educational techniques nor infallible gimmicks for action. Therefore, follow the formulation of the problem with an equally considered choice of methodologies and techniques that are appropriate for the problem. For example, in research, historical methods,

field methods, comparative methods, and experimental methods can be combined with much greater hope for converging validities and greater generality of findings than through excessive refinement of the techniques of any one alone.

These capsule summaries are based on observations through the years of the ups and downs of crossdisciplinary enterprises, including the encouraging yields from research that we and a growing number of others have obtained. While my criticisms of the social disciplines in this chapter have been harsh at times, it is because of my conviction that growing interchange among the social disciplines offers the greatest hope for breaking through the crises and impasse within them. The periods of greatest excitement and of expanded vision in our joint work as social psychologists have been during interdisciplinary efforts—the seven conferences we organized, whose proceedings we published, and the intensive crossdisciplinary study that led to research on social perception and social judgment, group formation and attitude formation, intergroup conflict and cooperation with accompanying attitudinal changes.[28] Thus the prescriptions and proscriptions listed above have been personally tested by experience.

Notes

1. Muzafer Sherif, *Social Interaction* (Chicago: Aldine, 1967), pp. 1–25.

2. There is now a large literature on correctives to the uncritical acceptance of findings in psychological research. Much of it was reviewed conveniently in John G. Adair, *The Human Subject* (Boston: Little, Brown, 1973). For early research on the social psychology of the psychological experiment, see M.T. Orne, "On the Social Psychology of the Psychological Experiment," *American Psychologist* 17 (1962): 776–83; H.W. Riecken, "A Program of Research on Experiments in Social Psychology," in *Decisions, Values and Groups*, ed. N.F. Washburn (New York: Pergamon Press, 1962). For experimenter bias, see R. Rosenthal, *Experimenter Effects in Behavioral Research* (New York: Appleton-Century, 1966). The concept of social desirability was introduced by Allen L. Edwards to explain the finding that responses to tests of personality and attitude correlate highly with normative

expectations. See Edwards, "The Social Desirability Variable," in *Personality Assessment and Research* (New York: Dryden, 1957).

3. The term *cultural psychology* applies most clearly to the pioneering work of Otto Klineberg since the 1930s; see Klineberg, *Social Psychology* (New York: Holt, 1954). See also M. Sherif, *The Psychology of Social Norms* (New York: Harper and Row, 1936); H.C. Triandis, "Social Psychology and Cultural Analysis," *Journal for the Theory of Social Behaviour* 5 (1975): 81–106 and the forthcoming multivolume *Cultural Psychology* under Triandis's editorship.

The very term *environmental psychology* rings strangely in ears accustomed to hearing psychology defined in terms of environmental effects or correlates of behavior. Its use reflects the limited conception of the environment fostered in psychology, especially by behaviorism. See S.B. Sells, ed., *Stimulus Determinants of Behavior* (New York: Ronald Press, 1963); H. Proshansky, W. Ittelson, and L.G. Rivlin, eds., *Environmental Psychology* (New York: Holt, 1969); H. Proshansky, W. Ittelson, L.G. Rivlin, and G. Winkel, eds., *An Introduction to Environmental Psychology* (New York: Holt, 1975); R. Moos, "Conceptualizations of Human Environments," *American Psychologist* 28 (1973): 652–65; and Irwin Altman, *The Environment and Social Behavior* (Monterey, Calif.: Brooks-Cole, 1975).

4. The references to T. Kuhn are to *The Structure of Scientific Revolutions* (Chicago: University of Chicago Press, 1970). M. Masterman's critique is published in I. Lakatos and A. Musgrave, eds., *Criticism and the Growth of Knowledge* (Cambridge: University Press, 1970).

5. See M. Sherif, "Crisis in Social Psychology: Some Remarks Toward Breaking Through the Crisis," *Personality and Social Psychology Bulletin* 3 (1977): 368–82.

6. Cf. also P.F. Secord, "Social Psychology in Search of a Paradigm," *Personality and Social Psychology Bulletin* 3 (1977): 41–50.

7. T. Kuhn, pp. 175 ff., 180.

8. Ibid., p. 187.

9. Ibid., pp. 178, 187 ff.; cf. pp. x, 15 of the 1962 edition.

10. J. Heyl, "Paradigm in Social Science," *Society* 13 (1976): 61.

11. Robert Oppenheimer, "Analogy in Science," *American Psychologist*, 11 (1956): 127–35.

12. A. Einstein and L. Infeld, *The Evolution of Physics* (New York: Simon and Schuster, 1961), p. 95.

13. *Walden Two* (New York: Macmillan, 1948); "Utopianism: The Design of Communities," in *International Encyclopedia of the Social Sciences*, ed. D.E. Sills (New York: Macmillan, 1968), 16: 271–75.

14. G.C. Homans, *Social Behavior: Its Elementary Forms* (New York: Harcourt Brace, 1961); P.M. Blau, *Exchange and Power in Social Life* (New York: Wiley, 1964).

15. W.P. Archibald, "Misplaced Concreteness or Misplaced Abstractness? Some Reflections on the State of Sociological Social Psychology," *American Sociologist* 13 (1977): 8–12.

16. E.V. Stonequist, *The Marginal Man* (Chicago: University of Chicago Press, 1937).

17. D. Cartwright, "Group Cohesiveness," in *Group Dynamics*, ed. D. Cartwright and A. Zander (New York: Harper and Row, 1968).

18. Cf. L. Escovar and F. Sims, "Cohesion of Groups." Paper presented at the meeting of the Canadian Sociology and Anthropology Association, Toronto, August 1974.

19. *The End of Ideology* (New York: Basic Books, 1960); *The Cultural Contradictions of Capitalism* (New York: Basic Books, 1976). While Bell presents the latter book as bearing a dialectical relation to the former, he might better have said that the earlier thesis was in error, since ideology is part of the culture whose contradictions he examines in the later book.

20. *Functionalism in the Social Sciences: The Strengths and Limits of Functionalism in Anthropology, Economics, Political Science, and Sociology* (Philadelphia: American Academy of Political and Social Science, 1965). Kingsley Davis's claim was made in "The Myths of Functional Analysis in Sociology and Anthropology," *American Sociological Review* 24 (1959): 757–73.

21. Alvin W. Gouldner, *The Coming Crisis of Western Sociology* (New York: Basic Books, 1970).

22. Wright Mills, *The Power Elite* (New York: Oxford University Press, 1956); D. Lockwood, "Some Remarks on the 'Social Systems,' " *British Journal of Sociology* 7 (1965): 134–46.

23. Gouldner, pp. 373–78.

24. Martindale, p. 159.

25. Quoted in Gouldner, p. 354.

26. Philadelphia: American Academy of Political and Social Science, 1969, p. 112.

27. T.C. Schneirla, "The 'Levels' Concept in the Study of Social Organization," in *Social Psychology at the Crossroads*, ed. J.H. Rohrer and M. Sherif (New York: Harper and Row, 1951); M. Sherif, "Social Psychology: Problems and Trends in Interdisciplinary Relationships," in *Psychology: A Study of a Science*, ed. S. Koch (New York: McGraw-Hill, 1963), vol. 6.

28. M. Sherif, *Social Interaction*; M. Sherif and C.W. Sherif, *Social Psychology* (New York: Harper and Row, 1969); C.W. Sherif, *Orientation in Social Psychology* (New York: Harper and Row, 1976).

Interdisciplinary Education and Humanistic Aspiration

A Critical Reflection

Vincent C. Kavaloski

"The education I propose includes all that is proper for a man, and is one in which all men who are born into this world should share . . . Our first wish is that all men should be educated fully to full humanity; not only one individual, nor a few, nor even many, but all men together and single, young and old, rich and poor, of high and lowly birth, men and women—in a word all whose fate it is to be born human beings; so that at last the whole of the human race may be educated, men of all ages, all conditions, both sexes and all nations. Our second wish is that every man should be wholly educated, rightly formed not only in one single manner or in a few or even in many, but in all things which perfect human nature."

John Amos Comenius, The Great Didactic (1632)

While specific conceptions of interdisciplinarity[1] and hence of interdisciplinary education vary considerably, the arguments advanced in favor of virtually all of these forms appear to share a common conceptual structure, insofar as they draw upon a common body of general desiderata:

1. *Integration of knowledge.* Interdisciplinary education aims at being an intrinsically integrative learning experience for the student; i.e., it encourages the student to perceive the various components of human knowledge within some larger holistic framework. As Kockelmans puts it in "Why Interdisciplinarity?" interdisciplinarity aims at "contributing to the restoration of the unity of the sciences, and in the long run, of the unity of our world view."

2. *Freedom of inquiry.* Interdisciplinary education stimulates greater freedom of inquiry than conventional disciplinary education, since the student is not confined to a single field in pursuing an idea, theme, or problem, but rather is encouraged to range over several different ones.

3. *Innovation.* Partly because of these two considerations, interdisciplinary education is thought to have a greater chance of getting students to break out of narrow, conventional lines of thinking and to attain something akin to original insights. The assumption underlying this view seems to be the following: since the overwhelming preponderance of intellectual investigation and research is done *within* separate disciplines, with consequently far less effort expended in looking at the intersections of the disciplines, it seems plausible that there is greater opportunity for fresh knowledge to emerge from integrated inquiry and making connections *between* disciplines.[2]

Viewed in the light of these three desiderata, the call for interdisciplinary education in institutions of higher learning appears to constitute a call for educational reform. In particular it appears to demand renewal of the traditional humanistic values of intellectual wholeness, freedom, and creativity, precisely when narrow, specialized education, both academic and vocational, has become the order of the day. Interdisciplinarity resolutely resists the fragmentation of education into a series of separate and isolated fields, each autonomous and presided over by a group of narrow specialists. As Kockelmans's "Why Interdisciplinarity?" makes clear, the majority of interdisciplinary advocates, both in research and in education, do not object to specialization per se— indeed they grant that the complex state of contemporary knowledge requires it; rather they object to the fact that specialization today is divorced from a broad, unifying framework of thought founded on genuine human concerns. The call for interdisciplinary education in our colleges and universities therefore constitutes a call for an authentically humanistic education, one which situates technical expertise and specialization within a broad framework of thought that encourages integration of knowledge, wide-ranging freedom of inquiry, and individual innovation.

In what follows, however, I will argue that this essential humanistic promise, contained within the core of interdisciplinarity, is threatened not only by *extrinsic* barriers (e.g., the institutional, psychosociological, and cultural obstacles discussed by Kockelmans) but also by an *intrinsic* barrier that lies as a hidden presupposition at the conceptual foundation of interdisciplinarity itself. Specifically I will argue that interdisciplinarity, at least as it is conventionally defined and practiced, embodies within itself an *objectivist epistemology* that, ironically, is scarcely distinguishable from that embodied by the very specialized disciplinary forms of education it attempts to replace. This objectivist epistemology furthermore leads almost inevitably to an objectivist *pedagogy* strongly at odds with the humanistic aims of interdisciplinarity articulated above. Interdisciplinarity therefore is floundering upon an internal contradiction between its espoused humanistic goals and its implicit objectivistic epistemology. In what follows, I will criticize the prevailing concept of interdisciplinary education, not to subvert it but rather to provoke it to make good on its radical promise of humanistic learning.

The Epistemological Foundation of Conventional Interdisciplinarity

Scrutiny of the prevailing definitions of interdisciplinarity, pluridisciplinarity, multidisciplinarity, (as given by Michaud, Abt, and Kockelmans[3]) reveals an epistemological presupposition common to them all: knowledge is conceptualized as something residing within or between disciplines or fields. That is, it is conceptualized as an objective (or intersubjectively acceptable) body of information, methods, concepts, and theories. The various forms of interdisciplinarity therefore differ from strict disciplinarity to the extent that they hold (1) that confining people to a single field or discipline in pursuing a problem is often constrictive and fruitless; and hence (2) that marriages, or at least temporary liaisons, between relevant disciplines are necessary for both educational and research purposes. In either case the epistemological assumption is an objectivist one; i.e., knowledge is assumed to be an *object* of human learning and investigation, an object in some vague sense which lies outside ourselves and our lived concerns. Thus we speak of bodies of knowledge and fields of knowledge. As Karl Popper, perhaps the foremost contemporary proponent of this epistemology, puts it, "Knowledge in the objective sense is *knowledge without a knower: it is knowledge without a knowing subject.*"[4]

From an educational point of view, this objectivist epistemology results in an objectivist pedagogy. If knowledge is an object or material lying outside of the student, then learning must consist of some process of assimilation, or internalizing of it. That is, once knowledge is conceptualized as something residing in or between disciplines, *however interrelated they might be,* it immediately follows that the task of the student is to place himself or herself in a position to receive some portion of it. Thus, as I shall argue later, the student too, in a sense, is conceptualized as an object, namely, a potential or actual receptacle of knowledge.

Interdisciplinary education, then, appears to share with even narrowly disciplinary education the following presupposition: the educational process consists wholly (or at least primarily) in the *assimilation* of knowledge that lies within or between bodies of knowledge (i.e., fields) that themselves lie outside the learning subject. Of course this assimilative process might be viewed—as it in fact is by many proponents of interdisciplinarity—as *critical* rather than naive, and as *systematic* rather than sporadic or narrow, but this does not alter the fundamental epistemological character of the presupposition. This becomes clear when one observes that interdisciplinary reform in higher education inevitably takes the form of curriculum change. That is, the content and order of the courses are revised in such a way as to become more integrated or continuous. Once again the emphasis is on knowledge as the object of study, and not on the knowing subjects except incidentally; the focus is on education qua content (namely, curriculum) and not education qua process. The objectivist epistemology, still being present, eventuates in an objectivist pedagogy, but now one in pursuit of a "unified framework." Thus interdisciplinary education, despite its aspirations to go beyond conventional disciplinary education, is still partly in thrall to it. As Morgan states: "The interdisciplinary notion suffers from a fundamental fallacy, namely the presupposition that we necessarily start out with disciplinary approaches as the ultimate modes of knowledge and that we must aim at somehow putting a few of them together."[5]

Three significant and disastrous educational consequences flow from this objectivist epistemology cum objectivist pedagogy, each of them unremittingly inimical to the humanistic values explicitly espoused by interdisciplinarity:

1. Human knowledge is reduced to a body of potential "deposits" or "material" to be consumed.

2. Students function as intellectual consumers of and depositories for knowledge so conceived.

3. Teachers function as agents of the depositing process, agents who, having privileged access to the "bodies" of knowledge, deliver it in measured units to their all-consuming charges.

These three implications will be examined individually in what follows. However, we must realize that they function inextricably together to some extent in most educational institutions of the Western world, constituting thereby a tragic and oppressive denial of genuinely humanistic, liberating education:

> Education thus becomes an act of depositing, in which the students are the depositories and the teacher is the depositor. Instead of communicating, the teacher issues communiqués and makes deposits which the students patiently receive, memorize and repeat. This is the "banking" concept of education, in which the scope of action allowed to the students extends only as far as receiving, filing, and storing the deposits. They do, it is true, have the opportunity to become collectors or cataloguers of the things they store. But in the last analysis, it is men themselves who are filed away through the lack of creativity, transformation, and knowledge in this (at best) misguided system.[6]

Knowledge as an Object of Consumption

What could seem more natural than to think of knowledge as an objective content which exists in fields outside ourselves? As Karl Popper puts it: "Knowledge in the objective sense is totally independent of anybody's claim to know; it is also independent of anybody's belief, or disposition to assent; or to assert, or to act."[7] Yet the first implication of this assumption is precisely the form of a cultural self-deception which Husserl calls objectivism: "What characterizes objectivism is that it moves upon the ground of the world which is pre-given, taken for granted through experience, seeks the "objective truth" of this world, seeks what in this world is unconditionally valid for every rational being, what it is in itself."[8] What objectivism ignores, therefore, is that the objective attitude itself and the scientific knowledge flowing from it are themselves ineluctably grounded upon the pregiven life world (*Lebenswelt*). Objectivism fails to recognize that *objectivity* is necessarily dependent upon the prior *subjectivity* of the knowing subject. Or as Habermas puts it: "This [objectivistic] attitude presumes that the relations between empirical variables represented in theoretical propositions are self-existent. At the same time, it suppresses the transcendental framework that is the precondition of the meaning of the validity of such propositions."[9]

Does this view really come to more than the commonplace notion that there is no knowledge without a knower? Husserl and

Habermas seem to be saying that scientific knowledge of the world exists as knowledge only insofar as it is taken on the ground of a pregiven meaning-structure, and that this meaning-structure is not a product of this knowledge itself but rather of the prior meaning-bestowing acts of a human subjectivity. This meaning-bestowing character of human subjects is thus the necessary condition for the possibility of knowledge as such.

On this view, then, it would be a mistake to conceptualize knowledge as something existing in fields or disciplines independently of or only causally related to human consciousness. To do so would be to embrace a version of the objectivist illusion; it would constitute a reification of knowledge into a thing-in-itself, apart from, or only causally related to, the human knowing process. Yet this is exactly what seems to be involved in the suppressed epistemology underlying conventional interdisciplinary (as well as disciplinary) education. To the extent that interdisciplinary reform is thought to consist solely of manipulating course-content and curriculum toward some objectified "integration," the notion of the student as a creator or recreator of meaning, as a subjectivity capable of an ongoing *process* of inquiry seems entirely absent. Knowledge reduces to a content which must be "covered" and "possessed" by those persons (namely, students) who bear no intrinsic or ontological relationship to it. The "bodies" of knowledge become inert, lifeless—in a word, corpses—with professors authoritatively performing the appropriate mortuary rites. The feeling of deadness that pervades our classrooms is no accident.

The tragedy of the contemporary interdisciplinary movement is that despite its high humanistic aspirations, it has not yet fully extricated itself from the mortuary concept of education as the assimilation of bodies of knowledge—however interrelated—which are realities-in-themselves. It is thus still enmeshed in a lingering objectivist illusion, a philosophical blindness that *conceals* "the subjectivity which ultimately brings about all world-validity"[10] and is indeed the very ground and condition for the possibility of knowledge. Interdisciplinary education is to that extent blocked from taking full account of the meaning of the human being engaged in the active process of intellectual growth. In form, if not in content, it begins to closely resemble disciplinary education and thus leads to identical effects. As Carl Rogers notes: "When we put together in one scheme such elements as a *prescribed curriculum, similar assignments for all students, lecturing* as almost the only mode of instruction, *standard tests* by which all students are externally evaluated, and *instructor-chosen grades* as the measures of learning, then we can almost guarantee that meaningful learning will be at an absolute minimum."[11]

Recent theoreticians of interdisciplinarity can of course reply forcefully to the above analysis by redefining (as some have done) a discipline as a field of *intersubjectively* (rather than *objectively*) acceptable knowledge (see, for example, Kockelmans's "Why Interdisciplinarity?" in this volume). In making this move, its proponents nevertheless hope to avoid committing interdisciplinarity to any specific philosophical doctrine about which today there is not yet common agreement. But is such philosophical neutrality really possible? And if possible, is it even desirable?

If the redefinition is taken in such a way as to exclude objectivism, then it could begin to satisfy my strictures—at least in theory if not in actual practice. It would only remain for me to show how this redefinition overthrows not only the objectivist epistemology delineated above, but also the objectivist pedagogy entailed by it. In so doing I would be demonstrating the necessity for interdisciplinarity to reflect not only on the *content* of education but also on the *process*, as it occurs between teachers and students. This redefinition would therefore be taking sides in an unresolved philosophical debate between proponents of objective knowledge (e.g., Popper, Hempel, Nagel) and critics of this position (e.g., Husserl, Habermas, Gadamer).

On the other hand, if the redefinition is philosophically neutral, as its proponents intend it to be, it would thus mean that interdisciplinarity is at least *consistent* with objectivism (though not necessarily entailing it as earlier definitions did). In that case my argument consitutes a plea for the repudiation of even this tolerance of objectivism by showing that it permits a mortuary approach to education totally incompatible to the avowed humanistic aims of interdisciplinarity. Taking seriously the goals of freedom of inquiry, integration of understanding, and intellectual innovation demands the renunciation of the mortuary conception of learning and the objectivist epistemology underpinning it.

The Crisis of the Teacher-Student Contradiction

A careful analysis of the teacher-student relationship at any level, inside or outside the school, reveals its fundamentally *narrative* character. This relationship involves a narrating Subject (the teacher) and patient, listening Objects (the students). The contents, whether values or empirical dimensions of reality, tend in the process of being narrated to become lifeless and petrified. *Education is suffering from narration sickness.*[12]

What is the epistemological basis of this sickness? Isn't it founded on the supposition that knowledge is a content, an object, which must therefore be conveyed by the narrating subject to the objects of narration? Isn't it in fact the very objectivist epistemological presupposition entailed by the conventional concept of disciplines and even "between disciplines," i.e., interdisciplinarity?

For if we presume knowledge exists as an existent-in-itself, i.e., in bodies of knowledge outside of and ontologically unrelated to the human subjectivity of learners, then how can their educational role consist in anything more than an assimilation, however critical and integrated? In this way the epistemological foundation for the mortuary concept of education is firmly set in place. From this perspective it will be natural to regard students as adaptable, manageable beings: at best, beings which are objects of paternal assistance; at worst, depersonalized receptacles of knowledge. In this conception of education

> Knowledge is a gift bestowed by those who consider themselves knowledgeable upon those whom they consider to know nothing. Projecting an absolute ignorance onto others, a characteristic of the ideology of oppression, negates education and knowledge as processes of inquiry. The teacher presents himself to his students as their necessary opposite; by considering their ignorance absolute, he justifies his own existence. The students, alienated like the slave in the Hegelian dialectic, accept their ignorance as justifying the teacher's existence—but unlike the slave, they never discover that they educate the teacher.[13]

Correlatively, teachers are regarded as managers and directors of the whole process, i.e., as *active* counterpoints to the *reactive* student. Thus the dialectic of learning becomes frozen on the ground of the teacher-student contradiction: the primary interchange is the mechanical interchange between a teacher reified as narrator and students reified as objects of narration. Consequently both students and teachers are denied essential components of their humanity: students are denied not only their role as active inquirers but also their role as facilitators of inquiry for others; teachers, while occasionally aspiring to facilitate inquiry, are rarely allowed within this frozen dialectic to also constitute themselves as co-inquirers with their students.

In this way narrative education becomes fundamentally antidialogical. Neither the depositing of ideas in another nor the simple
exchange of ideas to be consumed constitutes genuine dialogue. Dialogue cannot exist between those who are assumed to know in some
absolute sense and those who are assumed to be devoid of knowing
in an equally absolute sense. And without dialogue, without the authentic communication of co-inquirers, co-intent upon a shared reality, there can be no liberating education.

Indeed antidialogical education is not the practice of liberation
but rather the practice of domination. The more students work at
storing up morsels from the bodies of knowledge that their under-
takers dispense to them, the less able they are to rise above the
mythicized and premanufactured reality deposited in them. The
more completely they accept the passive role imposed upon them,
the more completely they adapt to existence as an inert, static given.
Mortuary education, by denying our essential *historical agency*—our
capacity as historical subjects to collectively transform our social reality—thereby denies us our ontological vocation of becoming more
fully human. Gradually, without even realizing the loss, we relin-
quish our capacity for meaningful choice, for collective action, and
for mutual aid; we are expelled from the orbit of historical praxis
and thereby prepared to take up our adult role as aimless wanderers
across the wastelands of the consumer society. "Everywhere the hidden curriculum of schooling initiates the citizen to the myth that
bureaucracies guided by scientific knowledge are efficient and benevolent. . . . And everywhere it develops the *habit of self-defeating
consumption of services and alienating production,* the tolerance for institutional dependence, and the recognition of institutional rank-
ings."[14] Later, perhaps, even our personal reality—our feelings,
thoughts, and self-identity—will be experienced as a commodity, a
body of recipes, tasks, and needs manufactured by yet another powerful and cadaverous elite.

Of course, as Ivan Illich points out, the educational institution is
not by any means

> the only modern institution which has as its primary purpose
> the shaping of man's vision of reality. The hidden curriculum of
> family life, draft, health care, so-called professionalism, or of
> the media play an important part in the institutional manipula-
> tion of man's world-vision, language, and demands. But school
> enslaves more profoundly and more systematically, since only
> school is credited with the principal function of forming critical

judgment, and paradoxically, tries to do so by making learning about oneself, about others, and about nature depend on a pre-packaged process. School touches us so intimately that none of us can expect to be liberated from it by something else.[15]

Now the question recurs: can the redefinition of interdisciplinarity in terms of intersubjectivity (rather than objectivity) free the interdisciplinary movement from objectivist epistemology and hence from the prevailing mortuary conception of education as indoctrination into a curriculum? The question appears to turn on the precise scope of the subjectivity involved in the notion of intersubjectively acceptable. If, as seems the case, the subjects who legitimate a given body of theory and method as valid are simply the experts and professionals practicing in the area, then knowledge is still something considered to be external to students; *they* are not subjects of intersubjectivity but rather still merely its objects. That is, although an area of knowledge is now thought of not as an absolutely objective body but rather as intrinsically grounded in the intersubjective realm of the thinkers creating (and perhaps teaching) in that area, it still shows forth as an external object relative to the students who are only beginning to learn in the area. They still experience it as an "other," as something outside the transcendental ground of *their* collective consciousness. After all, they do not play a part in planning the content and structure of the course or curriculum; it does not arise organically out of their process of inquiry but rather is grafted onto it as from the outside. No matter how integrated or interdisciplinary it may be, and no matter how "intersubjectively valid," if it is imposed on students as a prepackaged thing-in-itself, it will to that extent constitute a barrier to genuine inquiry that arises and is nourished in the individual's own subjectivity, the sense of wonderment, puzzlement or doubt, the desire to encounter human knowledge only as it relates to the questions he or she is actually asking—and not the ones he or she is feigning. As Paul Goodman notes: "A panoply of integrated courses is the equivalent of one great Text Book written by a wise Educator for 'teachers' who are his mouthpiece. There is no such wisdom. The teachers do not teach it; it does not fit the students. In effect, the ideal curriculum becomes a format restricting the exchange between actual teachers and students in actual classes." Goodman recommends "simply dropping the whole rigmarole of credits and compulsory attendance, and by having free electives and guidance by a staff meeting of the student's actual teachers who know him. John Dewey's principle of an intrinsic organization of the studied, to learn something in such a way that it leads to wanting to learn more, seems to me quite sufficient."[16]

While there might be serious objections raised to the mechanics of Goodman's proposal, his overriding philosophical aim seems incontrovertible: to return to education the essential humanistic *dialogue* between teachers and students, the dialogue of co-inquirers: veterans and initiates co-intent upon common concerns. Only this is consistent with the humanistic idea of education as the bringing-up of young to be, not trainees, not complacent consumers, but rather new centers of initiative for society, beings destined to take over its culture, renewing it and transforming it. In this way, an authentic interdisciplinarity "teaches us that there can be no discontinuity between education and research. By constantly questioning the knowledge acquired and the methods practised, it transforms the University, as Guy Berger puts it, *'from a place where pre-prepared learning is transmitted into a place where new learning is produced collectively'* and that occurs at all levels and stages."[17]

Perhaps then we need to move beyond thinking primarily of interdisciplinary education as an assimilation, however integrated, of a *subject matter,* and begin to think of how it can become an *integrative process* of becoming more human, of realizing our human nature as a nature capable of freedom, integration, and innovation. For as I have tried to show, these humanistic values, the very values that constitute the avowed raison d'être of interdisciplinarity, simply cannot exist, much less flourish, in the prevailing mortuary approach to education.

Can interdisciplinary education move beyond the objectivist epistemology that it unknowingly borrows from disciplinary education? Can it move beyond the conception of human knowledge as a "stuff" existing in or between "fields" that are divorced from the knowing subject? And can it move beyond the deadening mortuary approach to education that springs out of this objectivist epistemology? I believe that it can and must do so, if it is to seriously begin to realize its humanistic aspirations to integration, freedom, and creativity. What would it mean to do this? After all, while I have criticized prevailing educational modes, I have not put forward a clear alternative to them: I have no packaged system, no plan, no concrete prescriptions. But could any such narrow prescription, any preordained recipe, possibly satisfy the requirements of the problem? Wouldn't it in a way just constitute one more content, one more deposit, and thus be implicitly committed to the very objectivism it seeks explicitly to overthrow?

Approaches to Dialogical Education

Nevertheless there are several general approaches to dialogical education that deserve further investigation by interdisciplinarians. These range from the almost entirely nondirected (or self-directed) learning advanced by Carl Rogers to the highly structured case-study method of Robert Hall. Paulo Freire pioneered a successful radical approach to "education as the practice of freedom" in the literacy programs of Chile and Brazil (before the military juntas expelled him), based on the concept of dialogically oriented "culture circles." Neil Postman and Charles Weingartner advance an interdisciplinary inquiry method primarily aimed at secondary schools, but also relevant to higher education. Karl Jaspers, transfixed by the image of perhaps the greatest master of humanistic dialogue, proposes a Socratic education based upon individual freedom and relentless questioning by both teachers and students in order to encourage "a genuine will to know."[18]

At Shimer College, there has been a firm commitment to the centrality of the interdisciplinary discussion class for almost two decades. In our classes, normally composed of six to twelve students, no textbooks are used; rather the students and teachers read and discuss only original, seminal source material. It is understood that, in an important sense, the text is the teacher, and thus the faculty member's role is to facilitate interaction between text and students. Interdisciplinary integration within each course is achieved by arranging the readings according to broad historical and philosophical themes, rather than according to conventional fields. Since historical development and philosophical activity are intrinsically un-disciplined, these themes will necessarily cut across departmental lines.

The present Shimer educational structure owes a great debt to the Great Books curriculum, which Robert Maynard Hutchins (drawing on the earlier honors seminars of John Erskine at Columbia) developed and instituted at the College of the University of Chicago in the 1930s. Shimer, long affiliated with the University, adopted the Hutchins Plan in toto in 1950, complete with Chicago syllabi, comprehensive examinations, and instructors. When the Hutchins Plan began to disintegrate at the parent institution in the late 1950s, Shimer went its own way, modifying the Plan to suit its own needs. The comprehensive examinations were dropped, the social sciences were added to the curriculum, and book lists came and went. Recently Hutchins's original goal of curricular unity has been aided by measures contributing to overall unity of inquiry: (1)

each instructor takes, as a "student," one core course each semester that lies outside his or her area of competence; (2) course papers and exams have been replaced by the single semester paper that aims to integrate the problems and themes of all three ongoing courses. The original Hutchins's emphasis on the small interdisciplinary seminar dedicated to the reasoned discourse in which everyone learns from everyone has, however, been preserved intact.

While lectures are occasionally given in order to supplement the discussion classes, an attempt is made to make them part of the conversation of the course, rather than the mere depositing of information criticized earlier. This might seem paradoxical, for many readers may believe that the lecture is the paradigm case of "narration sickness." However, genuine dialogue, like interdisciplinarity itself, is constituted not so much by any specific activity as by an open, inquiring, caring attitude. As Guy Michaud states: "Interdisciplinarity . . . is basically a mental outlook which combines curiosity with openmindedness and a spirit of adventure and discovery."[19] Thus even lectures can, I believe, be given dialogically, if they are proffered not as deposits of truth to be written down and subsequently dredged up for exams, but rather as personal and provisional findings that must be actively challenged, interpreted, and evaluated by students. Dialogical lectures, unlike conventional ones, are not the last word on a topic, but rather the first word.

If not all dialogue is discussion, conversely not all discussion is genuine dialogue. Indeed one of the recurring problems with discussion classes is the frustration caused by those who refuse to listen carefully to their fellow participants and insist on dogmatically expounding their own views; students too can be guilty of mortuary education. What is needed here is an awareness that such antidialogical narration puts a stop not only to the inquiry of the other students but to that of the narrator as well: by objectivizing ideas he freezes himself or herself in his own initial position.

One of the most interesting and unique aspects of the Shimer program is that the natural sciences as well as the humanities and social sciences are taught via the interdisciplinary discussion class. This of course flies in the face of the most common objection to dialogical education: how can a class have a meaningful conversation about mathematics, biology, or physics when the majority of the members have as yet no substantive knowledge of the subject? Can quantum physics, population genetics, and differential equations really be taught this way?

Surprisingly, yes—at least some of the time. The curricular key to its success rests on the unique historical-philosophical approach, which eschews textbooks in favor of original sources. Thus, for example, Natural Science II, The Evolution of Life, which I am currently teaching, begins with a reading of the easily understood pre-Darwinian creationist theories of Paley, Agassiz, and Cuvier in an attempt to understand the concepts of design, animal "contrivance," divine plan, natural law, and fixity of species, which comprised the Providentialist view of nature. Then Darwin's *Origin of Species* and *Descent of Man* are carefully read by way of contrast. After a series of readings in social Darwinism that connects the course to the concerns of the social sciences, we move on to a discussion of Mendel's original papers. The Darwinian tradition and Mendelian thought finally come together in the twentieth-century work of Julian Huxley, Ernst Mayr, and Gaylord Simpson. The course comes to a close by attempting to situate contemporary ethical, social, and political questions in an evolutionary and ecological framework through a discussion of Lorenz's *On Aggression*, Thoreau's *Walden*, Leopold's *Sand County Almanac*, and Kozlovsky's *An Ecological and Evolutionary Ethic*. Natural Science I, The Atomic Structure of Matter, proceeds in a similar fashion via study of the seminal work of Lucretius, Gassendi, and Boyle, Priestley's phlogiston theory together with Lavoisier's refutation of it, and then the chemical atomism of Gay-Lussac, Clausius, Avogadro, Dulong, and Petit, and ending with the atomic tables of Mendeleef and Cannizzaro. It is important to note that the content of the courses is constantly reviewed and revised by faculty and students acting in concert.

At best, students in these courses learn not only fundamental biological and chemical principles together with the metaphysical, ethical, and political issues historically posed by them but also a method for analyzing original scientific documents. This method can then be drawn on in Natural Science III and IV, in which the more technical works of Galileo, Newton, Mach, Faraday, Maxwell, and Einstein are studied. At worst, students develop a keen facility for talking *about* science in rather vague and high-flown language, while possessing almost no technical mastery or problem-solving competence. Normally the results lie somewhere in between these extremes. Success or failure seems to depend on a number of discrete factors: how carefully students read and prepare for discussions by developing *their own* interpretations of the text; how well the various readings are arranged so as to encourage a sustained thematic development and unified inquiry; and perhaps most importantly, how much mutual trust, respect, and commitment is developed in the discussion group, for this seems to be a necessary condition for an ongoing and genuine community of dialogue.

Of course it can still be objected here that, even at best, what is being taught is not *science* at all, but rather the *history* and *philosophy* of science. This objection is underlain by a narrow conception of science as mere technical intelligence and problem-solving expertise stripped of its philosophical, historical, social, and ethical meaning. Such an interpretation of science, today the prevailing one, is directed toward a blind mastery of the world without questioning ends. It is indeed intimately tied to that dangerous fragmentation of human knowledge that interdisciplinarity seeks to challenge.

Nevertheless the objection does point in the direction of a set of genuine problems that beset the discussion method in science education. First, while the great books of science often present as rich a set of possibilities for interpretation and discussion as the great books of the humanities, there do come moments when there simply is a right answer. Aren't extended discussions about how to solve, for example, a math problem simply a waste of time? Don't such discussions slow down progress in technical mastery of problems, which while not the whole of science is still an absolutely necessary part of it? The Shimer approach to technical mastery stresses working knowledge of a few fundamental problems from each theory on the grounds that these, together with an understanding of basic principles, provides a deeper insight and competence than mere textbook technical proficiency. For example, in the study of the original Euclid, significant discussion centers around the basic theorems: what surpressed premises, if any, are needed in the proof? Which contain inconsistencies and which are trivially true? How does, e.g., a denial of the parallel line postulate lead to non-Euclidian geometry?

Another problem with the discussion method of inquiry is this: since the teacher presumably is a veteran in the subject while the students are novices of one sort or another, the genuine questions of the former will not always be the same as, or at the same level as, the latter. Thus there is always a temptation for the teacher-facilitator, in attempting to spur discussion, to ask questions to which he or she already knows the answers. But if this becomes the rule rather than the exception, it defeats the ideal of co-inquiry upon which the entire pedagogy is based.

My colleague, Michel Nicola, addresses this difficult problem in a recent publication:

What is the teacher's role? Is he there to teach the truth, to guard it jealously from contamination by error, or is he there to develop the critical and analytical faculty of the students, to train *them* in seeking the truth? Of course, the two are not incompatible, and they are both necessary; but at least in general education it is the second that must predominate. To a student (and to every human being) the most trivial truth that he himself discovers is worth more than the deepest wisdom that someone else imparts to him.[20]

On these grounds, Nicola recommends a policy of frequent nonintervention to the teacher:

> The fire must burn on its own terms, not mine. Of course, I have more experience than the students, but this can easily be misused. If I can think at the right moment of the right question that gives the discussion a nudge in the right direction, well and good. Otherwise, it is better to leave it alone in spite of all its shortcomings. If the class would agree on something false (which seldom happens) there is always a chance to return to it later, for if a wrong conclusion has any important consequence these cannot fail to strike people as being strange.[21]

However, one must be willing to accept as the consequences of such an approach that occasionally the discussions leave the students not less but more confused than before. It is hoped that this will be a creative confusion, one that spurs them on to renewed reflection, analysis and dialogue:

> It is a necessary presupposition in any genuine discussion that the *search for answers is more important than the answers*. A discussion teaches by stimulating each participant to think, to seek and create his own personal truth. It cannot do this very well if there is anyone in the group who knows the truth and is in control. Guided discussion, like guided democracy, is not genuine, but at best, an image, a facade.[22]

Such an approach obviously requires a fairly radical redefinition of the teacher-student roles, one that perhaps raises as many problems as it resolves: when must the teacher, as a veteran, intervene to save the discussion from a hopeless muddle? When is it advantageous for him or her to simply state his or her view on the matter? And in general, how does he or she, with an experienced and knowledgeable background in a subject, pursue an authentic co-inquiry with less experienced students whose inquiry will begin at a more elementary level?

The most recent attempt at Shimer to take the ideal of co-inquiry seriously is the faculty decision that part of the responsibilities of each faculty member will include taking, *as a student,* one basic course each year outside the person's area of competence. This proposal makes particularly good sense with respect to the Shimer curriculum, since most faculty members have not experienced the uniquely wide-ranging and interdisciplinary education based upon a discussion of original sources that we espouse for our students. Thus taking these courses is not repeating something we have already learned. Rather the proposal attempts two things: first, to overcome the student-teacher contradiction and envision us all as a community of learners; and second, to provide a broad interdisciplinary base for the faculty as well as for the students. My attempts to link my science courses with the humanities will be augmented by my participation as a student in the ongoing humanities courses. Thus, students and teachers, by all reading the same seminal works in all areas of thought, will possess a broad common basis for discussion. The ideal of interdisciplinarity becomes indissolubly linked with the ideal of co-inquiry.[23]

Interdisciplinary Education and Self-Understanding

While the Shimer method of discussion of original sources as well as other discussion pedagogies needs further exploration by interdisciplinarians, perhaps something more is also in order: a critical reflection of interdisciplinarity upon itself, a self-reflection searching for its own transcendental grounding in the life world of the people involved in it. Such a reflection ought to be pursued not only by professional academic thinkers and teachers with one another, but even more importantly, by teachers *with their students.* Only by some kind of ongoing or recurrent collective self-inquiry in education itself can we really confront the student-teacher contradiction and all the encrusted levels of alienation surrounding it. Only through a dialogue of self-examination can we begin to find our authentic relationship to one another not as teacher versus student, but rather as co-inquirers: teacher-learners *together with* learner-teachers. We need to dialogically confront critical questions, perhaps not even to answer them in any conventional sense but rather to dwell within them together, in order to sense our relatedness to one another and to the process of humanization. In what sense and to what extent are we learners and teachers implicated in what is learned and taught? Can we understand the intellectual tradition we are working with in our mutual educating process except by the communication and working through of our own prior belief systems and our own situation? What is the nature and value of the integration we seek in interdisciplinary studies? And most important perhaps, what is the meaning of our being-together, learning from and teaching one another, a being-together that lies at the living heart of education as inquiry?

Such questions, if pursued honestly and relentlessly by those involved in interdisciplinary education, must necessarily constitute the end of mortuary education and the beginning of what Paulo Freire calls co-intentional education: "Teachers and students (leadership and people), *co-intent on reality, are both Subjects*, not only in the task of *unveiling that reality*, and thereby coming to know it critically, but in the *task of re-creating that knowledge*. As they attain this knowledge of reality through common reflection and action, *they discover themselves as its permanent re-creators*."[24] In this way interdisciplinary education might begin to practice the humanistic values which it espouses. It would be an educational process that involves both the receptivity and the activity of all, the *freedom* to be free together, the *integration* of the person and not just of the content, and the creativity springing from authentic wonderment. It would be an education that is person-centered and process-centered, and not just content-centered; it would take full account of human knowing as an activity grounded in human consciousness and yet moving outward to the world through praxis. Through the dialogical I-Thou relationship the human being melds together learning and growth: "Man becomes an I only through a You."

Yet in an important sense this type of education is still largely to be created. For liberating, humanistic education can never be one more content, one more deposit, one more premanufactured thing, but rather must constitute itself as a collective historical task, a task to be confronted through radical dialogue. And such dialogue cannot be in any sense pregiven, but must forever spring anew from the mutual commitment and trust of people engaging in an enterprise they believe in: "Only by virtue of faith does dialogue have power and meaning: by faith in man and his possibilities, by the faith that I can only become truely myself when others also become themselves."[25] So that the understanding we seek in interdisciplinary education, the understanding that sees the world whole, is nothing like an object or commodity, though as Marx foresaw, the cultural forces of industrial capitalism might thus seek to reduce and distort it. Rather it is something far deeper, and at the same time closer at hand, a state attained through transformation and self-transformation. This understanding, if it emerges at all, emerges only through invention and reinvention, through the restless, caring, hopeful, impatient inquiry that we humans pursue in the world, through the world, and—most of all— *with* and *for* one another.

Notes

1. I am, of course, using the term in its generic rather than specific sense. However, when I speak of "interdisciplinary education" I mean to contrast it to conventional "disciplinary education," which normally involves several fields but does so with little or no attempt to connect them. See especially the various definitions of *discipline, multidisciplinary, pluridisciplinary,* etc., by Guy Michaud and C.C. Abt in *Interdisciplinarity* (Paris: OECD-CERI, 1972), pp. 25–26. Contrast with the redefinitions of these terms by Joseph Kockelmans in "Why Interdisciplinarity?" in this volume.
2. For a good discussion of at least two of these three desiderata, see Guy Michaud, "General Conclusions," in *Interdisciplinarity,* pp. 281–88.
3. See references in Note 1 above.
4. *Objective Knowledge: An Evolutionary Approach* (Oxford: Clarendon Press, 1972), p. 109.
5. George W. Morgan, "Disciplinary and Interdisciplinary Research and Human Studies," *Int. Jahrb. Interdis. Forschung.* 1 (1974): 273.
6. Paulo Freire, *Pedagogy of the Oppressed* (New York: Seabury Press, 1973), p. 58.
7. Popper, p. 109.
8. Edmund Husserl, *The Crisis of the European Sciences and Transcendental Phenomenology* (Evanston: Northwestern University Press, 1970), p. 68.
9. Jürgen Habermas, *Knowledge and Human Interests* (Boston: Beacon Press, 1968), p. 307.
10. Husserl, p. 68.
11. *Freedom to Learn* (Columbus, Ohio: Charles Merrill, 1969), p. 5.
12. Freire, p. 57.
13. Ibid., p. 58–59.
14. Ivan Illich, *Deschooling Society* (New York: Harper and Row, 1970), p. 74.
15. Ibid., p. 68.
16. *The Community of Scholars* (New York: Vintage Books, 1964), pp. 312–13.

17. Michaud, p. 285.

18. Rogers, op cit.; Robert T. Hall and John U. Davis, *Moral Education in Practice and Theory* (Buffalo: Prometheus Books, 1975); Freire, op. cit., and *Education for Critical Consciousness* (New York: Seabury Press, 1973); Neil Postman and Charles Weingartner, *Teaching as a Subversive Activity* (New York: Dell, 1969); Karl Jaspers, *The Idea of the University* (Boston: Beacon Press, 1959), p. 52.

19. Michaud, p. 285.

20. Michel Nicola, "Teaching Science from Original Sources by a Discussion Method," *American Journal of Physics* 44: no. 10 (1976): 984–85.

21. Ibid., p. 985.

22. Ibid.

23. A further manifestation of the dialogical emphasis at Shimer is the cooperative self-governance structure of the College. Students and faculty, elected by the community at large, comprise all administrative structures including the Board of Trustees. All the top-down bureacracy of traditional colleges and universities has been replaced by participatory democracy committed to dialogue. See Robert Richardson and Vincent Kavaloski, "Cooperative Self-Governance for Higher Education: The Shimer Experiment," unpublished manuscript, Shimer College files.

24. *Pedagogy of the Oppressed*, p. 56. Different yet complementary ways into the ground of humanism via some form of interdisciplinarity have been suggested by George Morgan in "Disciplinary and Interdisciplinary Research and Human Studies" and proponents of transdisciplinarity discussed in Kockelmans, "Why Interdisciplinarity?"

25. Karl Jaspers, *The Origin and Goal of History* (New Haven, 1953), p. 221.

Interdisciplinarity

Reflections on Methodology

Jonathan Broido

Preliminary Methodological Questions

Any glance at the literature on interdisciplinarity will show that there is very little in it that can be unequivocally described as clear-cut methodology. There are indeed attitudes that prescribe more carefully what we ought to be looking for, and there are approaches that narrow down the possibilities and suggest definite patterns—whether by recommendation or by way of illustration and paradigm. But none of these amounts to a methodology in the narrow and well-understood sense of the term: an assortment of well-defined methods that can ensure that by following them one will be able to accomplish some significant interdisciplinary task.

It may be that this situation in itself is enough to engender considerable skepticism about the legitimacy of our more pretentious interdisciplinary aspirations, even when these are adequately defined from a conceptual point of view. This, however, is not an extraordinary state of affairs, when we compare it with the methodological problems of most of the significant human enterprises—be they scholastic, social, or educational. It is invariably easier to formulate problems than to offer solutions, and most of those tasks that seem to us sufficiently important are not operationally definable in any conceivable sense.

But many of the tasks offered by any serious contender to the title of "interdisciplinarity" will not and cannot admit of clear-cut methodologies, and such tasks will therefore have to be accomplished with heuristic prescriptions, partially successful paradigms, and halfway hunches. In other words, the problems of essential interdisciplinarity will always require increasing ingenuity and creativity.

It may seem odd that I hasten to make declarations about solutions before clearly stating the problems. But the point in putting the cart before the horse is exactly that of avoiding at the outset the confusion between the conceptual understanding of tasks and knowledge of methods of accomplishing them. I believe that some of our interdisciplinary tasks and how they should be performed can be clarified, but this in no way mandates that we should be able to provide algorithmic prescriptions that would guarantee the desired returns. And I believe that it is important to show why this state of affairs is unavoidable when it comes to interdisciplinarity, so as to be able to concentrate our efforts on what is both feasible and instrumental.

Conceptual versus Methodological Transparency
A task is *conceptually transparent* when we understand clearly enough what its aim consists in, i.e., when we have a set of traits that conceptually characterizes what is to be accomplished. A task is *methodologically transparent* when we have a clear enough understanding of methods whereby it will be successfully accomplished. The task of playing chess optimally is conceptually transparent, but it is far from being methodologically so (at present): it takes a very short while to explain the rules of the game and what would constitute an admissible victory, but no one has yet come up with a practical method to *guarantee* the best possible performance. On the other hand, the task of solving a system of linear (algebraic) equations or that of formulating a standard business-reply letter are both conceptually and methodologically transparent.

What is striking, perhaps, is the fact that there exist conceptually transparent tasks that, for purely logical reasons, could never become methodologically transparent. This is one of the major lessons of modern logic.[1] Nor are such tasks extravagant or unusual when we come to deal with disciplines, sciences, and theories. We have, for example, a perfect understanding of what constitutes a transformational grammar for a certain school of linguists, and we may be highly interested in the well-understood task of determining whether a certain (finite) stock of linguistic strings agrees with (or is explained by) such a grammar, but on strict logical grounds there can be no general methodology for settling such questions.[2] Similar observations may apply to the question of whether structures that are used integrally by one discipline are explicable in terms of those that typically occur in another discipline. And since this kind of question places us immediately and squarely in the interdisciplinary domain, it is not difficult to see how the foregoing logical hints may reflect on our methodological premonitions.

The Problem of Explication

Other authors generally characterized various types of interdisciplinarity and the grounds on which they are conceived and advocated. In dealing with methodology we have to be more specific about types of interdisciplinarity qua tasks. Thus the idea of interaction between disciplines is admittedly a vague and complex one, involving many different tasks on many different human and categorical levels. Bringing two different disciplinarians to deal with a common, predisciplinary, human problem does not necessarily presuppose or even suggest that the theoretical considerations of one disciplinary activity will have any bearing on those of the others. The task of providing a common axiomatic basis to two sciences need not require that there be a great commonality in the structures employed by the disciplines associated with such sciences. Yet such disparate types of tasks could all be conceivably subsumed under the aegis of interaction.

Moreover, the accepted common terminology for different sorts of interdisciplinarity is not automatically specific enough for setting up particular tasks in every case. A crossdisciplinary application of economics, psychology, and sociology to a problem of human well-being may correspond to significantly different tasks conceptually, depending on how one chooses to conceive of human well-being. If it is defined as a multidimensional concept in which different aspects are combined by artificial weighting, no significant interdisciplinary integration need be presupposed, and the only metadisciplinary vehicle to be used may be that of decision theory. On the other hand, if the different disciplinary aspects of human well-being are not regarded as independent, a completely different set of interdisciplinary tasks will arise.[3]

A further difficulty is that even when we have a sufficiently clear demarcation of the differences between types of interdisciplinarity, the significance of tasks associated with a particular type will seem to hinge crucially on what we mean by terms such as *discipline, subject matter, methods, observable entities, structures.* Depending on how we interpret such terms with respect to both external references and inner meaning relations, the corresponding tasks will differ significantly. Thus the tasks of creating hybrid disciplines and of integrating disciplines to a greater or lesser extent must change radically according to whether we regard naively conceived subject matters as adequate differentiae of different disciplines, and according to whether we choose to conceive of subject matters in an ontological or an epistemological mode. (This is discussed further in the sections on the substantial view of disciplines.)

Similarly, if the task offered (or required) is that of eliciting such "common structures" as underlie different disciplines, we may be in doubt as to the type or the hierarchical level on which we should seek the structures or compare them. Different interpretations of structuralistic interdisciplinarity result here in tasks that are in entirely different categories. The structures alluded to can be part of the theoretical object-language of a given science (e.g., lattice structures in crystallography), or they can prescribe the way we are to interpret the significance of a discipline (e.g., political science interpreted as dealing with *systems*), and they can even allude to features of analytical tools of disciplines, which are characterized by commonality of certain mathematical structures on purely metalinguistic levels. Here we have at least three levels of discourse, which may be labeled *object-linguistic, metalinguistic,* and *mixed object-metalinguistic.* Separation between these levels is not so clear-cut, but it is nonetheless presupposed by many interdisciplinary attitudes. For instance, the structures of probability theory, as presupposed in all applications of statistics, are not going to satisfy the structuralist's quest after fundamental common structures of certain sciences or disciplines that make a heavy use of statistics. Here the emphasis is not on mere commonality (on whatever level) but on "underlying." Thus the structuralist will often make a claim about the "essence" of a certain discipline, in which the "subject matter" is not merely abstracted away or simply neglected but is claimed to be *explicated* in structural terms.

Before we proceed to some discussion of key terms of interdisciplinarity, and the impact their explication would have on prospective tasks, we want to eliminate certain interdisciplinary areas or aspects from our present consideration of methodology. We are referring primarily here to the curricular, administrative, and behavioral-science aspects of implementing interdisciplinary programs of various kinds. One or another of these aspects will be important to the implementation of any type of interdisciplinarity. But we can distinguish at the outset between these approaches in which the curricular, administrative, or psychosocial aspects are the main methodological consideration, and those in which such features do not constitute the first essential methodological problem, even when they have to be considered.

Consequently we will not discuss any approach to interdisciplinarity in which different disciplines are allowed to remain *immune,* scholastically and theoretically, to impacts of other disciplines. Instituting a multidisciplinary program, in which different disciplines contribute independent portions of the information that is to be imparted educationally, or that is to be considered administratively in decision-making, would be an example of such an approach.

One methodological question that multidisciplinary approaches raise seems to merit attention, even if we aim at higher levels of interdisciplinary interaction and integration. It is a common criticism of multidisciplinary approaches that they achieve breadth and extent at the expense of depth and understanding of intent, and that a "smorgasbord education" could hardly bring about any meaningful discourse between the different disciplines. Similarly, when the onus is on the decision maker, it is felt that such approaches provide no way of fitting together and gauging against each other such claims and pieces of information as are supplied by different disciplines.

This type of criticism has to be met, we believe, in the practical implementation of *any* type of interdisciplinarity. In no case do we want interdisciplinary education to detract from the specialized understanding and competence one might achieve. Prima facie this seems to pose a practical problem of the time and effort that individuals can invest in study or appreciation of different disciplines. Yet this practical problem has a theoretical ramification, which is that interdisciplinary approaches *on any level* should also be evaluated on an information theoretical basis. More explicitly, we may require that interdisciplinary approaches should "save" specific disciplinary information by eliminating theoretical redundancy and by integrating similar insights of different disciplines, and in addition that interdisciplinary approaches should increase specific competence and understanding in different disciplines.

This desideratum seems to be a corollary of more fundamental interdisciplinary approaches. Yet here, as for other desiderata, one has to distinguish between what is theoretically promised, mostly on conceptual grounds, and the psychosocial problems of implementing those approaches that carry such promises, potentially. Implementing a certain interdisciplinary approach may require that each discipline, even by itself, should now be taught and discussed very differently than formerly. Similarly, one may discover that at certain stages it is well worth *accentuating* differences and clashes between different disciplines, rather than immediately trying to mitigate and reconcile them. Yet such practical corollaries raise a host of psychosocial and political methodological questions that we are in no position to solve at present—although our own suggested approach to interdisciplinarity (instrumental interdisciplinarity) makes it incumbent upon us to address these very questions.

Disciplines: Subject Matters and Structures Revisited

At this point we reconsider the notion of a discipline (with an eye to the methodological instrumentalities in any further explication). Almost any analysis here starts with a crude notion of a distinction between subject matter and structural elements. The structural elements, which are of different type-levels, are applied either to the subject matter itself or to what can be said about it. At first approximation one can separate the structural elements into those that are typical of the very disciplinary description of its subject matter—which we call here *object-language structures*—and those elements, on the other hand, used in manipulating the object-language structures themselves—which we may call the *metalinguistic structures*. For the sake of clarity it ought to be said immediately that the term *object-language structures* does not refer merely to the *use* of the so-called *observation language* of a discipline, nor is it meant to be restricted solely to those theories that are presently upheld by a given disciplinary community. It is meant to include any structures that can serve as an integral part of any theory that could conceptually be admitted by a disciplinary community as pertinent to its subject matter. Such structural elements may include any *entities* and *relations* which are admissible by the standards of the discipline at hand, however theoretical or nonobservable they might be. Thus group structures of interaction properties in nuclear physics, or lattice structures in stages of logical-cognitive development in Piagetian psychology, will be equally considered object-language structures, no matter how theoretical or occult they may seem from the vantage point of other disciplines. On the other hand, mathematical truths about such groups and lattices will involve structures that are metalinguistic, even when these themselves can be studied in terms of groups and lattices. The distinction between object-language and metalanguage structures is therefore necessarily semantical and depends essentially on the particular discipline we wish to consider, since the metastructures of one discipline can be the object-structures for another. The notion of a structure in itself, of course, cuts across various logical levels.[4]

With the crude distinction between subject matter and structures, one may observe at this stage that specific disciplinary communities have their typical behavioral practices and norms. These can be characterized and studied in their turn from the vantage point of particular historical, sociological, economical, and anthropological disciplines. We may refer to such aspects as the *general pragmatic aspects* of a discipline (inasmuch as they are not subsumable under subject matter and structures).

The crudity of this distinction, from an instrumental point of view, seems to be due to the fact that it tells us so little about how to pick a subject matter in different cases, or at least how we should distinguish between different disciplines in terms of subject matters. It becomes quite obvious, in looking at the actual practices of different disciplines, that subject matters can never be conceived independently of some typical object-language structures; that such structures are in fact part and parcel of the way the subject matter is selected, as well as the manner in which it is handled. The trouble with the crude distinction between the matter and the form of a discipline—as inevitable as it may be for analysis—is that it suggests that the subject matter is externally given, so to speak, independently of the epistemological *modus operandi* of what we consider a discipline "directed at it."

Thus, although any two different behavioral disciplines can be construed as belonging to the science of man, it would be of no informative value to describe their subject matter as "human beings" or "human phenomena," nor will a simple subdivision into subclasses of phenomena help us here, as long as it is purely *extensional;* for such a subdivision would be tantamount to a purely conventional naming scheme, without any clues to what the names stand for, *intentionally.* This becomes especially apparent in the case of disciplines with a strong sense of rivalry. Freudian psychology and behavioristic psychology are different disciplines, although they often claim to be dealing (in some sense) with the same "subject matter." This is because they endorse different object and metalinguistic structures. But crudely, the attempt has often been made to construe the difference as one between two subject matters—"behavior" versus "personality."

It is obvious, however, that this prima facie difference in subject matter is of no use in interdisciplinary methodology. From the point of view of behavioristic psychology, for instance, *personality* is explicable only in terms of behavior patterns, or else it is purely mythical. So inasmuch as personality is meaningful to a behaviorist, it is part of his or her subject matter and can even constitute his or her subject matter proper, in a generalized behavioristic sense. To say that the use of the different labels explains anything about the difference between disciplines is logically a case of *equivocation,* in which we use the same terms in radically different senses and yet assume that they can be used comparatively. We do not have here a third fixed sense of *personality* whose reference the behaviorist chooses not to study while the Freudian does. The sense in which the bona-fide behaviorist chooses not to deal with "Freudian" personality is not referential but conceptual.[5]

The same kind of trite observation can be made by considering disciplines that seem to have an exclusive right to a specific subject matter. The science of crystallography gives rise to several disciplines at various stages, but inasmuch as these can be distinguished and particularized, they must involve specific object-language structures whose specific disciplinary significance can be brought out only on the background of some more general discipline—of chemistry, physics, or even of common-sense observation. In either case crystallography focuses on the relationship between elements of broader subject matters and certain solid geometrical structures and lattices. It would be patently misleading to identify the subject-matter of crystallography as nothing but that of certain chemical compounds, or that of certain atoms or molecules. Such a claim would not explain why crystallography, as a discipline, is essentially committed to use, in investigating crystals, solid, modular, geometrical structures and their combinations.

This feature of the crystallographer's discipline cannot be regarded by us as a mere historical accident about the reference of the word *crystals* and its study. As a discipline crystallography is henceforth committed to the use of certain types of geometry in studying this "reference." In all such cases the meaning of the subject-matter label and its reference become inexorably intertwined (notwithstanding the conceptual distinction between *reference* and *meaning*).

The example of crystallography is useful also in considering the impact of a radical swing in the opposite direction—that of trying to express the notion of a discipline only in terms of the formal structures it employs. At first sight, at least, it seems conceivable that a certain type of crystallography, a certain subdiscipline of sociology, and a number-theoretic geometry may all use the same formal structures. Although we shall have much more to say about this in connection with certain interpretations of structuralism, it seems to us a plainly bad move to identify disciplines just on the basis of (formal) isomorphism of their object-linguistic structures. This eliminates completely the referential, empirical ingredient of any substantive discipline and reduces it, in the final analysis, to a mathematical activity. Quite apart from metaphysical considerations, such a "Pythagorean" outlook will not be very hopeful to interdisciplinary methodology, beyond engendering some mutual

respect among those disciplinarians who face similar formal methodological challenges.

The element of truth in the claim that whatever can be explicated clearly about a discipline can be explicated structurally may
occlude the perception of other elements in what we customarily call
a discipline. No matter how perspicuously we manage to exhibit the
formal structures used by a discipline, this can never tell us exactly
how they will evolve, or how they will be refined or even be super-
seded by other structures. An indication of an empirical discipline's
unique substantial concern will require, in addition, some relatively
independent means of pointing to the referential application of
those formal structures that are typical of the discipline. Such osten-
sive means will be invariably rooted in background disciplines and
praxes that go beyond the specific discipline at hand. If this seems to
beg the question as to the subject matter of such background disciplines and praxes, or their own referential application, so be it. I see
no way of avoiding this infinite regress, while retaining some measure of commitment to empiricism.

The Substantial View of Disciplines

The first fact to emerge from the preceding discussion is that the
subject matter of a discipline cannot be specified independently of
its object-language structures. These are an essential ingredient of
what the subject matter is for a given discipline, at any stage of its
development. But on the other hand, an *empirical discipline* cannot be
characterized or distinguished only by a formal specification of the
structures it employs. The particular significance of using certain
structures, within a *particular* empirical discipline, must have to do as
well with the existence of a "referential residue" (i.e., the given or
phenomenal aspect of the discipline and its science). This referential
ingredient can further be pinned down, or specified—beyond what
is provided by the disciplines' structural characterization—only by
using other scientific or everyday disciplines and practices. (This
does not mean that we think there is a way to pinpoint completely
the referential ingredient. See the statement at the end of the previous section.)

The first of these observations, which we might call "the structural point," holds for nonempirical disciplines as well. It is completely futile, for instance, to describe a certain geometry as dealing
with *points, straight lines, incidence, being on, distances,* etc., as its subject

matter, without automatically presupposing that we know already something about the *valid* relations, for that geometry, between these elements. The formalistic school in the philosophy of mathematics (Hilbert et al.) expressed this by saying that the basic elements of geometry are only implicitly defined. The *structural point* is demonstrated here not only by the fact that possibilities of structural relations between the different types of elements are an essential ingredient of what they are as the subject matter of geometry, but also by the fact that these fundamental structural possibilities include relationships between things of the same fundamental type: there is no way of explaining what a particular straight line is without referring to other straight lines (as, say, in the "postulate of parallels" in Euclidean geometry). But this last observation applies to nonmathematical disciplines as well: what is the proper characterization of a sociologist's subject matter? Is it society, human beings, or relations between human beings? We can say that a sociologist studies human beings in the same structural sense that a geometer studies points and straight lines. For the sociologist, a human being is essentially a relational being, essentially capable of standing in various relations to other such beings. But we may equally well say that he or she studies society, just as we can characterize the geometer as studying a certain kind of space. Ultimately it is a moot point, structurally, what aspect of the subject matter we stress in labeling it.

The case of mathematical disciplines, however, is singular in the following respect: a formal specification of the relevant object-language structures (or the "meaning postulates" of the elements thereof) is conceivably all we need to do in specifying the relevant subject matter (this is exactly the contention of the formalistic school). And furthermore, if we grant that this is so to a great extent, we must also admit that we have to regard the notion of a mathematical discipline as much more restricted than that of an empirical one. Inasmuch as the fundamental structures that an empirical discipline uses change with a sufficient degree of continuity, we can still speak of it as being the "same discipline." But in contrast, there is a sense in which a specific mathematical discipline is completely determined by its fundamental object-language structures (even though it may split into more specialized subdisciplines and increase the stock of its derivative structural insights). In the case of empirical disciplines we would be ignoring the *referential point* if we were to retain the same degree of rigidity. We cannot divest the *structural point,* as applied to empirical disciplines, of its temporal connotations; and the sameness of an empirical discipline is a matter

of relative stability, in which certain structures play a more fundamental role than others.

Although this may be regarded as a semantical issue, it is not a
trivial one. What we would be willing to regard as the same or
different disciplines will have a bearing on how we conceive of interdisciplinarity and its appropriate tasks. In this context we wish to
maintain a middle path between the extremes of a rigidly structural
interpretation of a discipline (which would do only for mathematics,
if at all) and an interpretation in which it is only the referential
residue (or even the label of the *subject matter*) that counts, as would
be the case if we maintained that Aristotelian physics and twentieth-
century quantum mechanics are instances of the same discipline.

The *referential point* (as we may describe our second point) is the
hallmark of any empirical science. It can be appreciated on the background of our previous remarks, by comparing the case of pure
geometry with that of applied geometry, e.g., in physics or geodesics.
If *straight lines* are made to refer to (roughly) or correlate with paths
of light rays, then whatever the appropriate geometry for dealing
with such interpretation, it will always require an extrageometrical
ingredient. This is expressed in the fact that we are in need of
independent *rules of evidence* (*coordinating definitions, operational definitions,* etc.) for identifying the above paths or parts of them, for
measuring angles of incidence, etc. Such rules would have to make
use of practices and theories borrowed from other disciplines and, in
the limiting case, they might presuppose everyday practices of direct
observational corroboration, whose underlying structures we may be
unwilling or find it hard to unravel. The referential residue of a
certain applied geometry (or any other empirical discipline) is therefore evinced in the fact that neither the identification of its subject
matter nor the structural possibilities inherent in its object are ex-
hausted by a formal specification of its present object-language
structures, i.e., of the particular pure geometry it happens to conform to.

The Substantial View

The substantial view of disciplines is one that regards certain disciplines (i.e., those to be called *empirical*) as inseparable unions of
content and form, when neither content nor form is specifiable to
more than a relative degree of perspicuity. This view would apply
whether we regard disciplines as *ritualized projects of inquiry* (stressing the disciplinary and the knower's side) or as studies of certain
objects of *inquiry* (stressing the elements of "science of" and ontol-

ogy). The substantial view takes all such dichotomies—content/ form, subject-matter/structure, object of inquiry/inquiry of objects, ontology/epistemology—to be both partial and inexhaustively complementary. Each side of the dichotomy is partially reflected in the other, but the combined efforts of separate specification cannot capture an empirical discipline in its entirety. What a discipline will refer to has a direct bearing on the evolution of its structures, even when this is less noticeable than the opposite effect. The identity of the discipline is maintained only by the continuity of the feedback process between these abstract polarities of matter and form. (Compare this with the subsection "Ignoring Structural Uniqueness" in "Naive Reductionism," below. The statement is primarily applicable to empirical disciplines.)

In dealing with the methodological problems of interdisciplinarity it is advantageous to endorse such a view. This is not because of its venerable philosophical anchorings (Aristotelian, Kantian, and Hegelian, among others) but because some other major views of disciplinarity seem to exclude arbitrarily some important interdisciplinary tasks almost to the point of abolishing them, while they accord other tasks an exclusive status. The practical problem of establishing a significant interdisciplinary interaction between members of different disciplines often hinges on accomplishing tasks that are removed from consideration by those major views. And this presumably may be attributed to the fact that, tacitly at least, different people (even members of the same discipline) have different conceptions about what constitutes a discipline. The substantial view is in this respect the more liberal, in allowing for a wider range of prospective interdisciplinary tasks.

Two of the major approaches to disciplinarity (and hence interdisciplinarity) are those connected with the structuralistic movement, on one hand, and with the movement for the unity of science, on the other. Characteristically each of these movements overstresses one or another side of the dichotomies discussed above. From the substantial point of view, then, each of them has its typical sins of omission. Even before we discuss more explicitly these movements and their methodological problems, it may be noted that structuralism overstresses the structural, epistemological, manipulable and "innate" aspects of discipline, whereas the unity-of-science-school and its like overstress the subject matter, the ontological and "outer" elements, in an attempt to reduce all subject matters to a few or a single subject matter. Correspondingly, for structuralism, the fundamental interdisciplinary task is that of specifying the relationships between structures in different disciplines, in particular the relationship of sharing a common structure. The unity of science, on the other hand, seeks to *reduce* the fundamental objects of inquiry of one discipline to those of the other (say, those of biology to those of physics). But although many of the methodological problems of these interdisciplinary tasks are common, when judged from a metalinguistic point of view, the typical sins of omission and the dispositions toward them are different. The common structural element of structuralism may fail to elicit the unique referential concern of each discipline, whereas the reductive enterprise of the unity of science may gloss over the structural particularity of a discipline and its subject matter.

In turning to the actual methodological problems of interdisciplinarity, we shall first deal with the tasks and the problems faced by proponents of these approaches, as paradigmatic of the methodological issues faced by any approach to interdisciplinarity that overstresses one or another side of the dichotomies we try to synthesize. These issues contribute to and reflect on the problems of any other intermediate approach, such as that of the substantial view. I shall then try to show how the substantial view should give rise to a methodological conception that is richer than the *sum* of the methodologies of structuralism and the unity of science.

Structuralistic Attitudes to Interdisciplinarity

From an interdisciplinary point of view, the salient insights of various structuralistic movements can be characterized as follows:[6]

1. The essential ingredient in disciplines and their subject matters can be brought out by uncovering their basic or underlying structures. These structures cut across conventional intra- and interdisciplinary lines of division. Within disciplines certain structures are *invariants* of the different ways in which a discipline may describe, or relate to, its subject matter, and therefore they capture its essence. Across disciplines, such structures allow us to relate disciplines to one another and create structuralistic metadisciplines. The hierarchical organization of structures and their commonality, across disciplines, is interpreted as having deeper epistemological, ontological, or genetic-evolutionary significance. (See 4 below.)

2. The fundamental notion of a structure should be *independent of* alternative *modes of describing* particular structures.

3. Structures can be conceived both *statically* and *dynamically:*

statically, as relational systems of elements with determinate relational laws or regularities; dynamically, as systems of transformations of elements within relational systems, with invariant regularities, or constraints imposed on composition (or combination) of such transformations. Consequently, in describing and using structures, one may choose to stress the conceptual aspect (as in mathematics) of constituting an integrated set of laws, or the transformational dimensions (as in Piagetian psychology and Chomskyan linguistics), or the element of self-regulation or control (as in cybernetics and system theory).

4. Structures can be arranged hierarchically in terms of *containment* (embedding, homomorphisms) and *refinement* (expansion, reiteration, composition). This leads to the discovery of invariant developmental sequences and of master structures, which represent the totality of structural possibilities inherent in cognitive disciplines, and in structured human activities in general (e.g., as in the work of Piaget, Chomsky, Lévi-Strauss). This in turn is interpreted philosophically as having an ultimate epistemological, ontological, or genetic-evolutionary significance (depending on the philosophical or scientific predilections of the individual structuralist). The epistemological significance of master structures is that they correspond to innate structures (mental or cognitive) in terms of which phenomena have to be organized. Ontologically such structures convey deeper truths about the structure of reality. The combined epistemo-ontological insight, in a Kantian mode, is that these structures are a necessary constituent of objectifiable phenomena. Genetically these structures may correspond to fundamental genetic structures and the evolutionary and developmental possibilities inherent in them (from an information-theoretic point of view).

5. The hierarchical organization of structures and masterstructures, implicit in various disciplines and across disciplines, does and will enable us (eventually at least) to reorganize human disciplines among similar hierarchical lines, leading to the creation of masterdisciplines that would reflect the significance of innate structures.

6. The notion of structure likewise cuts across logical type-levels. This means that the same structures occur both on the level of object-language and on the metalinguistic level. And this means that structures essential to metadisciplines (such as logic or mathematics) could reflect and be reflected by structures of certain disciplines (such as cognitive psychology, linguistics, and anthropology) that deal with symbolically manifest activities, and alternatively with other disciplines (other psychologies, sociology, genetics, economics, physics)

that uncover the regularities behind human and nonhuman activities that are not symbolically manifest. This again points to the innateness of fundamental structures and their developmental sequences.

7. It is presupposed by structuralists that human beings as bearers and imposers of their innate structures, with their developmental potential, are capable of discovering these structures. This relates to 6 above, in the sense that the fundamental structures and their developmental-combinatorial potential provide an adequate machinery, on metalinguistic levels, for explication of these very same structures on other ("lower") levels.

Methodological Issues and Questions

Even the awkwardly compact summary above cannot fail to convey the fundamental impetus of structuralistic attitudes—the feeling, common to structuralists of different philosophical and scientific persuasions, that those structures that underlie a great multiplicity of human activities and disciplines, and which remain invariant under their myriad transformations and modes of application, have a deeper significance than any particular manifestation of such activities or disciplines. Yet in the final analysis, no particular philosophical understanding of the "deep" significance should be taken as ultimate, if we apply the fundamental impetus to its utmost. For each and every such understanding will be anchored in a philosophical regimentation (e.g., specific demarcations between ontology, epistemology, and logical-combinatorial machinery), which is itself *not invariant* structurally (when compared with other philosophical regimentations). It becomes apparent, then, why the fundamental impetus of structuralism has to be considered from so many angles and be given to many interpretations.

Although we sympathize with the fundamental impetus, it is clear that its elaboration gives rise to a host of philosophical and methodological questions. These have to do in particular with the notion of a structure and with the methods for discerning underlying structures and structural commonalities behind different descriptions. For example, what do we mean by a "structure," and how does one establish structural equivalence of what is depicted by two different linguistic or symbolic descriptions? And how do we go about uncovering the deep structure (or at least the underlying structures) behind a set of structured surface phenomena? We will refer to these questions as the *inner methodological questions* (of structuralism).

A different type of question has to do with what structuralism seems to leave out of focus, in assessing its own significance: If the fundamental innate structures of different systems (disciplines, transformational stages, languages, cultures) are the same or equivalent in logical potential, how do we assess their seeming or contingent difference? Is it purely conventional, or does it have a deeper significance?

Strictly speaking this is not a methodological question; but it has a bearing on interdisciplinary methodology. If it turns out that contingent features are crucial to members of different disciplines, how will we overcome this by structuralistic methodology? We shall leave this question of *contingent specificity* to the last part of our chapter (but compare with the final question in this section).

Still another question has to do with the interpretation of underlying structures as fundamentally innate (particularly in connection with the seventh point of our summary exposition in the preceding section): How do we know when the application of a given set of structures (or structural tools) is sufficient metalinguistically to account for, or bring about, the discovery of structures of the very same kind? We call this the *question of self-discovery*.

A final question has a direct practical bearing on interdisciplinarity: If disciplinary specificities can be explicated after all in terms of (structural) differences between dynamic systems that have the feature of structural self-regulation and control, as in point 3 in our exposition, how can we overcome the disciplinary entrenchment that must result from the tendencies of such systems to preserve their own structure (or invariant features)? We refer to this as the *question of structural* (disciplinary) *entrenchment*.

Structures and Equivalence of Structural Descriptions
The most important methodological problem for the structuralist, in answering the inner questions, is that of recognizing the structural equivalence of (what is referred to by) different descriptions. This is especially true because of the variety of ways the structuralist uses to describe structures, and because the notion of a structure should, in principle, transcend the particularity of description. It is not always recognized that this is not a trivial question, and that in some cases it is not even methodologically transparent. We start with a few illustrations.

Simple isomorphisms. A certain structure ("a group") is described (statically or conceptually) as consisting of four elements (A, B, C, D) and an operation, $\otimes$, between them. The structure is completely specified by one "multiplication table":

Table 1

$\otimes$	A	B	C	D
A	A	B	C	D
B	B	A	D	C
C	C	D	B	A
D	D	C	A	B

Another structure is described dynamically as a set of four transformations on four types of objects or "places," as depicted by Figure 1. Figure 1 may be taken to represent the transformational rules for the structure depicted in Table 1, when we interpret I as multiplication by A, J as multiplication by B, etc., but the interpretation of the transformational system could be conceivably quite unrelated (referentially) to that of the first table. Whereas, say, Table 1 can have an arithmetical significance (multiplication between 1, -1, $+\sqrt{-1}$, and $-\sqrt{-1}$), the transformational system can represent those rotations of a square around its center which leave its "place" in space unchanged.

The transformational description can always be replaced by a relational description. Transformations can be combined: this means that we can define (or look in our system for) a transformation whose result would be identical to that of applying successively two transformations. Thus for any two transformations, σ, τ, define

$\sigma \circ \tau$ = that transformation whose result is the same as the net effect of applying σ first and then τ

When we compile a table of transformation-multiplication for the system described in Figure 1, we get Table 2. Looking at Tables 1 and 2 allows us to see that the two structures described are the same, whatever their particular interpretation. This is because there is an obvious way of matching the symbols of operands and operations in the two descriptions that preserves (or matches) all the relationships depicted in the tables. We refer to this as a case of *simple isomorphism* (between structural descriptions!). Mathematically this means here that there exists a one-to-one mapping (or translation device), ψ, of the fundamental symbols in one structural description (A, B, C, D, and $\otimes$) onto symbols playing similar logical roles in the other (I, J, K, L, and $\circ$, respectively), so that whenever a relationship obtains by the first description (say, $Z = X \otimes Y$), then the translated relationship obtains in the second, ($\psi Z = \psi X \circ \psi Y$), and vice versa. Another way of expressing the idea of simple isomorphism is to say

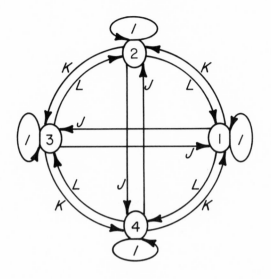

Figure 1

that our descriptions are the same except for notational difference (*I* for *A*, *J* for *B*, *K* for *C*, *L* for *D*, and o for ⊗, in the above).

Table 2

o	*I*	*J*	*K*	*L*
I	*I*	*J*	*K*	*L*
J	*J*	*I*	*L*	*K*
K	*K*	*L*	*J*	*I*
L	*L*	*K*	*I*	*J*

Examples of simple isomorphisms abound in structuralistic literature. In fact we can safely say that this is the main device used in establishing the equivalence of structural descriptions.[7]

But unfortunately this is far too simple to answer the needs of structuralistic interdisciplinarity, or even that of structuralistic disciplinarity. This is primarily because the availability of simple isomorphisms hinges on having at our disposal the appropriate structural descriptions, in which the basic symbols can be matched in a one-to-one manner on the basis of their logical type. But there are good substantive, psychological, and methodological reasons why

caste *A*

Figure 2   caste *B*   caste *C*

caste *D*

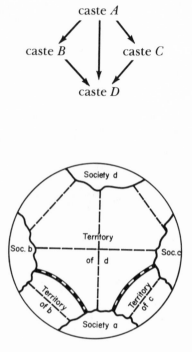

Figure 3.   The children of a marriage between Society X and Society Y ($X \neq Y$), belong to that Society Z whose territory is crossed by the straight path between X and Y. If $X = Y$, the children remain within the same society.

this is not bound to happen generally, why it is not worth doing in some cases, and why it cannot be done in others.

Logical Equipotentiality of Structural Descriptions
Two anthropologists may be interested in describing two different cultures in terms of two different institutions, which are relationally of a different logical order. The first anthropologist, say, describes the order of dominance between castes in civilization α. It is a transitive, antisymmetric, two-place relation, depicted in Figure 2. The second anthropologist describes the outcomes of marriages between members of different societies in tribe β, as seen in Figure 3. The relationship depicted there is three-place (between X, Y, and Z), and the diagram shows it is functional (i.e., for each X and Y there is exactly one Z satisfying it).

These descriptions do not offer us an immediate simple isomorphism—if only for the fact that before we can show such a structural equivalence, the matchable relationships must be of the same logical kind (especially, if one is two-place, so must be the other).

Nonetheless Figures 2 and 3 provide exactly the same structural information; they are structurally equivalent, or logically equipotential. This is because there is a way of representing each structural description, with all its pertinent features, within the other. In other words, given the dominance relation between castes, we can logically define a triadic relation between castes that may even have a direct anthropological correlate and that is isomorphic to the marriage-outcome relationship for societies in β, and vice versa; for the tribal societies we can logically define a binary relationship, in terms of marriage outcomes, that will be isomorphic to the dominance relation between castes in α. For the tribe, for instance, we can define:

Society X is *inferior* to Society Y if and only if the children of the marriage between them will belong to X, and $X \neq Y$.

A picture depicting this "inferiority relation" can be made simply isomorphic to Figure 2 for dominance. All we have to do is replace the word *caste* by the word *society* and replace A, B, C, D by the lower-case tokens, a, b, c, d.

Similarly for the caste system, we can define a concept of immediate joint responsibility as follows:

Castes X and Y are *immediately responsible* for Z (when $X \neq Y$) if and only if Z is dominated by or equal to both X and Y, and if any other caste (apart from Z) that is dominated by both X and Y is dominated by Z as well.

The total information about immediate joint responsibility can be then captured by Figure 3, when we replace the word *society* by *caste* and when we replace *the children of marriage between* by *the immediate joint responsibility of* and *belong to* by *is* (and when we change lower case to capital letters). By this we obtain of course a simple isomorphism.

The importance of this last example is greater than its contrived appearance may suggest. The claim of Chomskyan linguistics, for instance, is not that there exists a simple isomorphism between deep structures as represented by generative-transformational grammars for different languages, but that such structures are logically equipotential in the sense that they are intertranslatable into one another, as in the example above. The same kind of notion, and its limitations, is crucial to the understanding of the philosophy and methodology of science both from structural and historical perspectives.

Relativity theory, for instance, has often been described as having changed our fundamental Euclidean structural notions of space and time. It has been said that Einstein showed that space (or spacetime) is not Euclidean. Yet when we consider this from the point of view of the logical equipotentiality of structural descriptions, we may claim that Einstein did no such thing. This is because the type of non-Euclidean geometry used by Einstein is structurally equivalent (or logically equipotential) to a Euclidean geometry of the same dimensionality. The structures of each non-Euclidean geometry can be represented as substructures of those of Euclidean geometry of the same dimensionality, and vice versa. This was known to Einstein and to his predecessors by the late nineteenth century. The structural equivalence, however, is not and cannot be a matter of simple isomorphism. But more importantly, the fundamental difference between the structural geometrical tools of relativity theory and those of Newtonian physics lies in the enormous difference between their utility (insights provided) in describing a selected portion of our reality and in commensurately solving a cluster of problems surrounding it. Similar observations apply to the differences between natural languages or those between any two equipotential structural descriptions that are not trivially isomorphic.

How to Decide about Structural Translatability
We are thus led to a fundamental methodological problem of any approach to interdisciplinarity that entertains the possibility of essential interaction between disciplines. Given two structural descriptions, can we systematically decide when one of them is interpretable as a substructure of the other? Several other "inner" methodological questions of structuralism would be solved if we could answer this question satisfactorily. For instance, we may ask whether two given structural descriptions contain a common substructure. The only methodological tool we would have to add, in order to decide this issue, would be one instructing us about the classifications of all substructures of a given structure.

The problem of interpretability or embeddability in general, however, is not methodologically transparent. This means that there is no a priori mechanical method which would enable us to solve any such problem effectively in a finite number of operations. This is true if we do not limit the complexity of interpretation. Here we have to distinguish between cases. In some cases the structures are specified *determinately*, in their entirety, as *finite structures.* In some other cases structures are specified *generatively* and *transformationally* as *potentially infinite structures.* Our anthropological examples above belong to the first category, whereas the structures used in Chomskyan linguistics are of the latter. Only for determinately finite structures can one come up with a decision procedure for interpretability, within specified limits of complexity, provided that there is an agreement on what constitutes our interstructural logical language.[8] But when one of the structures (the interpreting one) is potentially infinite this cannot be done, although the infinite structure too is generated from finite structures. This methodological observation is related to two different ways in which structures are used by structuralists. In one we describe a certain finite set of a structured set of phenomena (or symbolic data) in terms of a specific finite structure, which for our purposes exhausts the relevant information. In the second, we describe a potentially infinite number of such phenomena or data as being explained or covered by a potential infinitude of structures that can be generated by combinations, reiterations, and composition of a given (finite) stock of finite structures. We can refer to the latter as a *recursively generated system.* If we ask whether a given structure (finite) can be interpreted within, or explained by, a given recursively generated system, the answer is that there is no general methodology of doing this and there could not be one, as was proved mathematically.[9] Thus, in a sense, we have no methodology for deciding on the innateness of a proposed recursively generated system. The question of self-discovery that we raised before, as well, is roughly of the same order of hopelessness. If one wants to know whether a recursively generated system is such that it could generate an adequate structural description of itself or its basic program, the answer is that there could be no general method for deciding such issues. Thus there is no way in which we could be sure that we could, in principle, come up with a proper description of our innate mental, linguistic, or genetic structures, even if such structures exist and are specifiable in a symbolic recursively generated language. We may even be creatures whose innate structures preclude them from discovering these structures.

Finite Determinate Structures
The question of interpretability of one such structure *within* the other can be solved methodologically and mathematically, but it is not elementary from a nonmathematical point of view. I shall outline here the main features of one such methodology:[10]

1. It is assumed that both structural descriptions can have the form of a *relational diagram*. This means that for each of these descriptions we have a finite list of symbolic elements, which may have different logical and ontological significance. Some of these elements are specified as relations between other elements, and the diagram will provide a complete description of the type-level of each element and to what other elements it could apply meaningfully, as well as the complete information about which elements stand or do not stand in which relations. As an example of such a description we take Figure 2, in the anthropological example above. This reduces the following relational diagram:

Symbolic elements: A, B, C, D, **R.**

Type and order specifications: **R** applies to ordered pairs of elements in *A, B, C, D.*

Relational information: **R** holds for the pairs $\langle A, B \rangle$, $\langle A, C \rangle$, $\langle A, D \rangle$, $\langle B, D \rangle$, $\langle C, D \rangle$ and none other.

2. For simplicity consider the case of *first-order structures*. These are described by diagrams in which there are two type-levels, a set of individuals, such as the castes or societies in our examples, and a set of relations and predicates of such individuals. It should be understood that the word *individual* is used technically here. It applies only to (the reference of) such symbols as are not applied in the diagram, affirmatively or negatively, to anything else.

3. For purposes of illustration let us suppose further that the two structures we describe diagrammatically have each a single relation between individuals. Let one structure, Σ_1, have S_1 as its set of individuals, and $\mathbf{R}_1^{(2)}$ as its relation (for illustration, assume $\mathbf{R}_1^{(2)}$ to be a binary relation). Let S_2, $\mathbf{R}_2^{(3)}$ be the set of individuals and the relation between them for a second structure, Σ_2. To make the example instructive let us assume that $\mathbf{R}_2^{(3)}$ is a ternary relation (as in "The children of marriage between X and Y belong to Z."). We want to know whether Σ_2 is interpretable in Σ_1 (when "interpretable" means here the same as "weak, type-preserving interpretation" in the Appendix.)

4. Assuming that the size of S_1 is not less than that of S_2, there will generally be many ways to match elements of S_1 with those of S_2. Let ψ be any map that chooses for each element in S_2 a different element in S_1. This constitutes simply a renaming of objects in S_2 by names from S_1. The map ψ allows us to define in $\psi(S_2)$—the set of elements corresponding to S_2 by ψ— a relation $\mathbf{R}_{2,\psi}^{(3)}$, between triads of its elements, which behaves just like $\mathbf{R}_2^{(3)}$ for S_2. This establishes a

simple isomorphism between Σ_2 and the diagram $\langle \psi(S_2), \mathbf{R}_{2,\psi}^{(3)} \rangle$, but we still do not know whether this diagram is interpretable in Σ_1.

5. To decide whether $\langle \psi(s_2), \mathbf{R}_{2,\psi}^{(3)} \rangle$ is interpretable in Σ_1, however, we have to consider all the *automorphisms* of Σ_1 (the interpreting structure). An automorphism of a structure is, in this context, any permutation of its individuals that preserves all its relations. For instance, in the structure described by the diagram in paragraph 1 above, or by Diagram 1, there are only two such automorphisms: the identity permutation, which leaves each element unchanged, and the permutation that leaves *A* and *D* unchanged but moves *B* into *C* and *C* into *B*. (When we replace every *B* by *C* and every *C* by *B* we find that the diagrammatic description of the structural relation remains unchanged.)

6. Given any set of ordered sequences of individuals in Σ_1—call it **T**—we can say that **T** is *invariant relative to* Σ_1 when (and only when) **T** remains unchanged by any automorphism of Σ_1: this means, for instance, that if α is such an automorphism and $\langle X, Y, Z \rangle$ is an element of **T,** then $\langle \alpha X, \alpha Y, \alpha Z \rangle$ is an element of **T** too. This concept of invariance applies, of course, to any set of ordered sequences—or even to a single individual (i.e., an individual is an invariant if every automorphism leaves it unchanged).

7. We need only one mathematical theorem:

Theorem. If **T** is the set of all ordered sequences for which a relation (or a predicate) among, between, or of the individuals of Σ_1 holds, then that relation is interpretable in the language of Σ_1 if and only if **T** is invariant relative to Σ_1.

We will not prove this here.[11] For illustration purposes, suppose Σ_1 is the structure defined in the diagram in paragraph 1 above. And suppose we have a triadic relation **R***—among its individuals—which holds for the following triplets and for none other: $\langle A, B, B \rangle$, $\langle A, C, C \rangle$, $\langle A, D, D \rangle$, $\langle B, A, B \rangle$, $\langle C, A, C \rangle$, $\langle D, A, D \rangle$, $\langle B, C, D \rangle$, $\langle C, B, D \rangle$, $\langle B, D, D \rangle$, $\langle D, B, D \rangle$, $\langle C, D, D \rangle$, $\langle D, C, D \rangle$. Then this set of triplets is invariant because the only nontrivial automorphism of Σ_1 (switching *B* and *C* around) leaves it unchanged. It follows then that **R*** must be interpretable logically in terms of **R** $(= \mathbf{R}_1^{(2)})$ (the fundamental relation) of Σ_1. And indeed **R*** holds for $\langle X, Y, Z \rangle$ if and only if $X \neq Y$ and **R** does not hold for $\langle Z, X \rangle$ and does not hold for $\langle Z, Y \rangle$. And for every $U \neq Z$ if **R** holds for both $\langle X, U \rangle$ and $\langle Y, U \rangle$ then it holds for $\langle Z, U \rangle$ as well. An example of a noninterpretable predicate in Σ_1 would be that of "being anything but *C*." This is so because the set $\{A, B, D\}$ is not invariant in Σ_1 (there is an automorphism of

Σ_1 that moves B out of this set). Consequently this property is not logically interpretable in Σ_1 and neither is the property of "being C."

8. The complete methodology for determining whether Σ_2 is interpretable *in* Σ_1 consists, then, in combining all the above techniques. Make a list of all one-to-one mappings of S_2 into S_1 (this can be done because of the finitude). For each such mapping, ψ, check whether the relations between the individuals of Σ_1 that correspond, by ψ, to those of Σ_2 are interpretable in Σ_1—using the theorem above. If there is such a mapping, then Σ_2 is interpretable. Otherwise it is not. (A stronger notion of interpretation would require that ψS_2 be interpretable as well.)

9. This methodology can be extended to structures of greater logical complexity (more type levels), as long as the structures are determinate and finite (see Appendix).

10. We can also use these methods to decide what are the finite structures that are interpretable in two different structures. This provides a measure of the structural commonality between them.

Interdisciplinarity and Potentially Infinite Structures

Unfortunately, when we conceive of disciplines structurally, the problems of interdisciplinarity cannot be reduced to the case of finite determinate structures, because structurally a discipline is more akin to a language with an infinite potential. To ask whether the structures of one discipline are interpretable within those of another is usually tantamount to the question of whether every finite structure that can be generated by one (recursively generated system) is interpretable within some structure generable by the other. The answer to such questions has to be worked out separately for different cases and demands ingenuity, creativity, and imagination. The only thing a methodology can supply here, for the general case, is a description of various heuristics—rules of thumb that have proved useful in discovering interpretations. Some such heuristics are suggested by studies in "artificial intelligence," but limitations of space do not allow us to venture here into this field, despite its extreme usefulness and suggestiveness for interdisciplinarity (see the last note for the chapter).

Discovering Underlying Structures

Because many structuralists tend to think of certain types of structures as more fundamental than others, or even innate, the problem arises as to how to decide about the underlying structure behind a given set of structured surface phenomena. We label certain structured phenomena or data as *surface phenomena* when their "naive" or prima facie structural description, as suggested by our culture or by features of the phenomena themselves, does not conform to the structuralist's expectations of the kind of structures these phenomena "ought to be about" (i.e., to the innate structures). Thus the use of terms such as *surface structure* and *deep structure* weaves together a genuine methodological problem and a philosophical bias. The genuine methodological problem is again the problem of interpreting certain structures (called here surface structures) within a generative system of other structures (called here underlying or deep structures). The philosophical bias is that particular structures called deep are considered both innate and exhaustive, if by "exhaustiveness" we mean that the structures at our disposal will be sufficient to generate systems within which we could interpret any phenomena we can attend to, structurally. It seems rather that the philosophical bias in favor of certain structural systems is due mainly to their scientific success in explaining a great variety of phenomena, in different disciplines, that at the outset seem to differ greatly. From an interdisciplinary point of view, however, the success is measured not merely in terms of the ability to provide some common structures shared by different disciplines, but more importantly by the degree to which those separate surface structures that are explained by a structural underlying commonality are initially felt, by members of the disciplines themselves, to be vitally important in considering their subject matter. Furthermore the structuralist's contribution to interdisciplinarity also depends on the degree to which the common underlying structure he or she will provide is instrumental in facilitating the solution of those problems felt to be most important or crucial to each discipline, as judged by its members. This may explain both the successes and the limits on possible future success of some favored structuralistic tools, such as system theory and cybernetics.

System Theory
By the same token, we can approach claims to universal applicability of any given structural mode of analysis and explanation, such as system theory. The early successes of this tool have led some people to regard it as a panacea to all the problems of interdisciplinarity. But a brief inspection ought to convince us that this mode of explanation must fail in some interdisciplinary tasks. If we are justified in the remarks made in the preceding section, it will become obvious that system theory cannot succeed with any discipline whose main concerns do not meet the conditions for applying system-theoretic no-

tions. In its classical form, the system theory of von Bertalanffy sought to describe dynamic systems in terms of the rates of change in their elements or parts—when such rates were expressed in terms of functions of all the elements of the system. Thus a description of a system of three elements could take the form of a set of three differential equations $\{dx_i/dt = f_i\,(x_1, x_2, x_3): i = 1,2,3\}$. It is clear that in this exact mathematical form, system theory may not apply to structures whose developmental stages are discrete. But this is not the main obstacle: in general we may characterize a system-theoretic specification in terms of the relations between the dynamic aspects of a system and some of its static features. Specifically, we can talk of a *transformational basis* for a system as a set of transformations whose compositions will allow us to calculate any transformation that preserves the system. What system theory tries to do, then, can be described as the attempt to specify the transformational basis of a (dynamic) structure in terms of *functional relations* between the elements of the system. And we can characterize various types of systems, system theoretically, by various overall features of these functions. (For instance, when the basic transformations are all functions only of the element they transform, we have a degenerate system in which the parts "develop" independently of each other.) Conceivably we could describe any structure in this way. A serious obstacle to this program, methodologically, is that the basic transformations of the system may be undefinable, or uninterpretable, in terms of the relational language of the structure. Using theorems such as those in the section on finite determinate structures, above, one can easily show that a structure-preserving transformation α is structurally definable if and only if it "commutes" with every other such transformation (i.e., when $\alpha \circ \beta = \beta \circ \alpha$, for any automorphism β). This is not always satisfied for the basic transformations of a structure. It is not true, for example, for three-dimensional rigidity and place-preserving transformations of solids. This may not seem an obstacle, when it is confined to this mathematical example, but we have to remember that our main concern here is in applying system theory to problems of interdisciplinarity, and that the structuralist's notion of a discipline insists that everything relevant should be elucidated structurally. It follows, then, that single elements of a system can have no referential residue unless this can be captured in terms of specific structural roles, such as that of the top caste in the dominance lattice. Hence the system-theoretic description of a structure will be justified only if the basic transformations can be characterized by purely relational means and by the variable that stands in place of the transformed element. Any totality of elements or parts that enters into the description, then, must be definable within the structure itself. When this is not available logically, the system-theoretic description of what interests one discipline must be done from the vantage point of another background discipline. Any universal application of system theory to interdisciplinarity, however, must overcome the disciplinary entrenchment of those disciplines in which important structures cannot be conceived as systems, within the discipline.

The Multiplicity of Underlying Structures: Reverse Semantics

It shoud be clear from the previous discussion of structuralism that we view the methodological problem of innateness as unsolvable, in the absolute sense. The problem of uncovering the most fundamental structures is similar in this respect to the problem of providing the best scientific explanation for an array of phenomena, or to that of finding the best solution to a mathematical or a conceptual problem. We do not know what constitutes "best"; we know only when one explanation or solution is better than one other. We can methodologically compare the merits of two explanations, but this requires paying attention to the gestalt features of an explanation. When we say that "X is a good explanation of Y"—when Y is a particular *explanandum*—we are saying much more than "X accounts (in some sense) for Y." Not only does X have to satisfy one minimal requirement for accounting, but it has to fit somehow into a larger scheme of accounting, in a way that significantly goes beyond Y. And this means very often that explanations *sufficiently similar* (structurally) to X will account for items of information that are prima facie *sufficiently different* from Y. Information theoretically, this can be expressed in the following way: let $I(Y)$ denote a measure of the information contained in Y (a linguistic description), which combines measures of statistical, syntactical, and semantical information relative to what we take for granted. If Y has no factual content, the information will be purely structural. Let $I(Y/X)$ denote the amount of information that would have to be added to X (and background assumptions) in order to complete the information contained in Y. If Y follows logically from X, for instance, the only thing in $I(Y/X)$ would be the structural information about the minimal derivation of Y from X. [We notice that this notion differs considerably from standard accounts of statistical or logical information measures in which, when Y follows from X, $I(Y/X) = 0$.] If X were all we knew, above and beyond our background assumptions, the value of the information contained in "X accounts for Y" would be $I(Y) - I(Y/X)$, which measures how much information we save by introducing the explanation. But if we want to consider the gestalt effect of our explanations, we have to evaluate rather the *maximum* of $I(Y^1) - I(Y^1/X^1)$ when Y^1 *contains* Y and X^1 is *structurally similar* to X. Now it is obvious that we cannot evaluate an absolute maximum of this kind, simply because it involves the total amount of knowledge that might be available to humanity. This means that the relative value of explanations may change as we learn more about the world and our activities within it. A structural account that looks to us fundamental now may be demoted from this position and be regarded later only as part of a *more* fundamental structural explanation.

We thus have to contend with the specter of a multiplicity of "underlying structures," and we must be cautious in imposing our favorite structure on surface phenomena. The methodological problem here is that we often start our investigation with a tentative assumption about the type of underlying structures, but what we can gather by observation cannot decide the issue between competing deep structures. One may investigate a language in which apparently there are no tenses, or words like *before* and *after,* yet one may be convinced that the speakers of the language do in fact deal with temporal structures. To substantiate such a hypothesis one may look for use of ad-sentential phrases (like "I hope that"), whose underlying semantics may be based on a linear relation—reflecting our linear preconception of temporality. We call this kind of investigation reverse semantics, because it consists in looking for surface phenomena that match and are perfectly explained by our preconceived standard deep structures. However, in many cases this enterprise of reverse semantics cannot be conclusive. There are cases in which along with the standard underlying structures there will exist, perforce, other *nonstandard* deep structures, which could generate the surface phenomena just as well. And this will be true even when in principle the standard depth structures are sufficient to explain every surface phenomenon. Thus in the final analysis we have to resort to comparing measures of *simplicity* and *information-saving* between our hypothetical underlying structures. As far as interdisciplinarity is concerned, however, this may pose another problem to overcoming disciplinary entrenchment, as in the case of system theory: the way in which members of a discipline conceive of the broader significance of their discipline may not agree with our standard deep structures; it may be biased toward some nonstandard explanation.[12]

Naive Reductionism: The Unity of Science

Since we devoted so much space to structuralism, we are obliged to restrict our discussion of those movements that seem to reduce sciences (not necessarily disciplines) to one another and establish interdisciplinary interaction by such means.

The naive reductionist stance is that given two disciplines, we may be able to reduce the science associated with one to the science associated with the other and ultimately, it is hoped, come closer to a hierarchical unification of science. The sense of reduction implicit here is not that of interpreting one structure within the other, but that of reducing the fundamental objects of one science to those of the other. The fundamental objects of the most fundamental science in these reductions (say, nuclear physics or phenomenalistic psychology) could not be reduced further. Consequently the most fundamental objects of a master science are not conceived structurally but as ontological or epistemological units: they are "atoms" of scientific cognition. One attempted beginning of such a venture is represented, for instance, by R. Carnap's *Logische Aufbau der Welt*.[13] Another attempted beginning may be found in N. Goodman's *Structure of Appearance;* generally naive reductionist sentiments seemed to flourish in the nineteenth century and the beginning of the twentieth, along with the positivistic movements (especially among philosophers of science who were scientists themselves).

Some Methodological Issues

Generally speaking there could not be a purely mathematical methodology for naive reduction of empirical sciences, as contrasted with the problem of reducing finite determinate structures. This is obviously because each such tentative reduction must have empirical import: it is subject to revisions and even refutations, according to our findings in both the science to be reduced and the science to which it is to be reduced. If someone, say, attempted to define the simplest living organism in terms of a certain type of configurations of atoms and molecules, this would have to be understood as a theory that should be cross-evaluated by both biology and physics. If we found one such tentative configuration that fails to satisfy the *meaning postulates* of the biologist about *living organisms,* we would have to amend the definition or reject it (one such postulate may be that a living organism must be capable of assimilation and procreation in one sense or another). Thus the methodology of naive reductionism must involve a reliance on the empirical sciences: it must constitute a dialectical project of self-undermining. This is not necessarily an objection, since it is to a great extent an essential feature of any scientific and conceptual revolution. It shows, nonetheless, that such reduction of sciences is bound to be an extremely lengthy and painstaking process.

Ignoring Structural Uniqueness
The greatest fault of naive reductionism, from the point of view of interdisciplinary aims, lies in the tendency to misinterpret the significance of the very reductions it may succeed in effecting.

Suppose that a particular naive reduction had been successful, that living organisms had been shown (empirically and conceptually) to be identifiable with certain structured agglomerates of molecules, or that the theoretical constructs of motivation theory had been shown to be reflected exactly in complex relationships of long sequences of stimuli and reactions. To describe such complex configurations and structures one would need various mathematical and logical tools. The naive reductionist tends to view such tools as having no essential significance as far as subject matters go, since the most common motivation of naive reductions is to show that "so and so is nothing but so and so." If one could say that living organisms = physics + specialized structural notions, one might be tempted to say that biology is nothing but a specialized branch of physics.

The trouble here is in the notion that one could retrieve all the meaningful information about biology, *as a discipline*, by knowing physics and by knowing which pure structures would be needed in order to reconstruct biology. The problem with this view was discerned even by Plato in his *Theaetetus*.[14] The example he gives there could serve our purpose. If one considers the word *Socrates* as being made up of the letters *s, o, e, r, a, c,* and *t,* can one say then that knowing the letters is tantamount to knowing the name, or how it is spelled? The answer is of course negative. But the naive reductionist does not make such a claim. His or her position is more likely to be this: That knowing, or knowing how to spell, the word *Socrates* is tantamount to knowing the letters that make it and, in addition, the *structure* by which the word is made. But even this is incorrect—inasmuch as we understand by structure a pure conceptual tool and not a substantial ingredient (in the Aristotelian sense). What can we say here of the structure of *Socrates* relative to the letter stuff of which it is made? If we think of a structure as something divorced of substance, then the structure of *Socrates* is that of a linear sequence of the type $x_1x_2x_3x_4x_5x_6x_7x_1$, in which different variables stand for different symbols, and such a structure could be represented by a relational diagram just as others we have depicted. This structural description exhausts the pure structural information we can perceive in the way *Socrates* is made of its letters. But of course it is still completely wrong to insist that if we are given the letters that make up some name and are given the information that these letters are to be arranged in conformity with the above structure, then we will know the name. Thus we conclude that the substance or object of inquiry is more than the mere sum of both its stuff and the *pure* structure by which it is made of this stuff. Yet no one who actually tried his or her hand at a naive reduction does this, in fact. The naive reductionist who takes his or her venture seriously, like Carnap in the *Aufbau,* will try to depict exactly how it is that a particular structure applies to the building blocks, and this presumably is what Aristotle meant by *essence.* Our quarrel is only with those who misrepresent this venture, or with those who merely claim it can be done without showing exactly how.

We will have more to say about this in the discussion of "instrumental interdisciplinarity." We end this philosophical digression by noting that, even apart from the substantial point raised above, the particularity and the complexity of the *pure structures,* which would have to be used in reducing one subject matter to another, can fully justify the existence of relatively separate disciplines. The structures involved may be so complex that, for the purposes of relating them to one another, it will become impractical and instrumentally grotesque to go via the underlying science. The success of a naive-reductionist enterprise would then be not in reducing one discipline to another but in showing what particularity of structure can account for the need for one discipline when we take the perspective of another discipline and its subject matter.

The Unity of Science

It goes without saying that we have no a priori reasons to expect that all sciences could be arranged hierarchically, in a tree structure, by naive reduction. This seems to apply especially to the social and behavioral sciences. At present we fail to see, for example, any way by which sociological and psychological sciences could be reduced to a particular sociological or psychological science, or to any third science—unless we incorporate in such a science a simple *sum* of existing sciences. But this last device, of throwing everything into one bag, cannot solve the problem of interdisciplinary discourse and cooperation. It would just confer on it a new title: "Intradisciplinarity."

Ultimately the question of possible naive reductions hinges on what we are willing to take as our logical and our conceptual machinery. This will be discussed further in the following sections.

Instrumental Interdisciplinarity

What can be gathered from our previous methodological discussion, in a theoretical manner, can be reached practically as well. Because the structural and conceptual framework of a discipline is inseparable from its unique concern, any attempt to reach interdisciplinary communication is blocked at the outset by the existence of separate frameworks. A purely structural comparison will not do either, because the unique concern of empirical disciplines contains a referential residue—so that even if we were to elucidate the structural games of one discipline to members of another, the latter may fail to see why such games are relevant to their particular subject matter.

The practical methodological problem is compounded because it has psychological and sociological dimensions. Even if we could theoretically elucidate successfully the concerns of one discipline from the vantage point presupposed by another, such vantage points are not always held consciously. Practicing, bona fide members of a discipline may not be aware even of what their discipline presupposes naively. Yet they will tend to interpret much of the world beyond their discipline from the vantage point of such naive presuppositions.

Practically, then, an essential interdisciplinarity cannot be successful if it is perceived as an immediate threat to the separate existence of disciplines, or to their *raison d'être*. But if the psychological and conceptual disciplinary entrenchment is common among members of disciplines, or disciplinary experts, then almost any attempt to create an essential interdisciplinarity may be taken as such a threat, since we require that any such interdisciplinarity may make some essential features of one discipline relevant to those of others.

A Dialectical Approach

The only answer to such a seemingly insurmountable obstacle is dialectical: *it is practically crucial that we should use that which we are trying to destroy.* Thus the first practical methodological heuristic must be that if we try to overcome *disciplinary entrenchment*, we should make use of it in the process.[15]

More particularly, when we deal with the way of establishing relationships between two disciplines, A and B, this has two corollaries:

I. If we want to make B *relevant* to A, we must interpret the relevant features of B in terms of the *minimal conceptual framework* that is presupposed (tacitly or explicitly) by A.

II. If we want to defend the *autonomy* of B, relative to A, we have to carry out our demonstration of B's relevancy to A in a manner that justifies the unique concerns of B.

The first corollary has several theoretical and practical presuppositions:

Ia. We have to be able to explicate consciously what is the minimal conceptual framework presupposed by a discipline, if by a conceptual framework we understand something like the "naive philosophy of the discipline."

Ib. We should be capable of interpreting some essential features of other disciplines within this explicated "naive philosophy."

Ic. But because the "naive philosophy" of a discipline is in fact explicated without special regard to the interpretability within it of the widest range of features of other disciplines, it follows that the only way in which a wide interpretability will be available is by extension of our logico-structural machinery.

Before we discuss further these presuppositions, we note that in general they show that the first corollary requires inevitably that we develop interpretative schemes—whether they are taken to have a structural or referential significance. But this of course seems to make the second corollary unrealizable. If we interpret relevant features of B in terms of what is necessarily presupposed by A, how can we defend the autonomy of B?

The only answer to this dilemma that we can provide is that a defense of the autonomy of a discipline B to another discipline A, in which it can be significantly interpreted, must take the form of an *instrumental, problem-oriented,* defense. In other words, in such a case (when sufficient interpretability is available), one must show that the discipline B is instrumentally superior to A in solving some problems (which can be construed as problems for A as well). Corollary II has therefore a further presupposition:

IIa. A defense of the autonomy of one discipline B to another A can take several forms: either not enough relevant features of B can be interpreted in the minimal framework of A, or else one has to show the instrumental superiority of B over A in solving some problems that are interpretable as problems for A.

We notice that in the first case, when not enough interpretability is available, purely structuralistic relations may constitute the main ground of interdisciplinarity (and may still allow for what we call *metaphorical interdisciplinary heuristics*). In the second case, when enough interpretability is available, purely structural comparisons may be insufficient, if they do not involve substantive considerations, such as those of naive reductionism.

These considerations lead us to a developmental conception of interdisciplinarity that evolves in three successive stages, which we label here naive honesty, radical egocentricity, and instrumental sublation, respectively. Although these stages overlap in many ways, each of them presupposes the previous stages. We shall first characterize briefly their methodological intentions and significance. A fuller elaboration and illustration of the interdisciplinary challenges, uses, and benefits that accrue to this approach will follow.

Naive Honesty. At this stage one attempts to explicate and elucidate the minimal framework presuppositions behind each discipline (its "naive philosophy"). It may be argued that success in naive honesty means that one is no longer naive, since full awareness of one's naive philosophy implies the possibility of recognizing alternatives. While this may be true, we stress that the import of the word *naive*, as we use it here, is primarily not in the connotation of unreflectiveness, but in the assumption of *minimality*. In other words, naive honesty amounts to answering honestly the question, what would be the minimum we would have to presuppose if we took the language of our discipline as a part of a way of talking about things in general?

Radical Egocentricity. This stage is to some extent implicit in the previous one. It represents the attempt to apply the minimal framework of a discipline to the widest range of problems, and in particular to problems outside what members of a discipline may regard as its proper domain. As we shall see, there is an important distinction between the *effective domain of applicability* of a discipline, in each stage of its development, and its *theoretical range of commitment*. The latter represents the range of all problems that could be interpreted as problems for a discipline, given its minimal general framework—even if it has no way of solving them elegantly or effectively. The effective domain of applicability refers to the range of problems that could be solved effectively, within its present state of art. One of the major difficulties in interdisciplinarity is that members of a discipline often take its effective domain to represent its range of commitment.

How radical "radical egocentricity" is will turn out to depend on what we, or members of a particular discipline, can be made to accept as logical-combinatorial machinery. The more we load onto logic and the more we extend our logics, beyond standard logic, the more radical we can be in applying the disciplinary egocentricity.

The complexity of the constructive machinery accepted will likewise affect the outcome of our egocentric exercises. We assume, however, that a radical stance allows us to consider any theoretical construction that is potentially possible from the standpoint of the minimal framework and its own minimal logic. The actual reluctance to use theories that are based on such constructs has to be ascribed again to the gap between the present domain of effectiveness and the theoretical range of commitment. But such theories are clearly within the latter range.

Instrumental Sublation. This stage consists primarily in instrumental, problem-oriented comparisons of different disciplines, which is based on exercises in radical egocentricity (even when such exercises are futile!). What we mean by instrumental comparison is the comparing of disciplinary formulations and solutions of problems, in terms of notions such as inner complexity, explanatory utility, and predictive power, and in general in terms of information-theoretic measures that combine syntactic, semantic, and statistical features.

Exercises of instrumental comparison can lead to different types of outcome:

1. A particular substantial problem of discipline B is not interpretable as, or has no correlative in, a problem of another discipline A—whatever the logical-constructive machinary we use. In such a case we will have shown the (partial) essential independence of B from A. (This relation is not symmetrical, of course, for many instances.) If this case applies to all the "substantial" problems of B, the only interdisciplinary import it might have for A will consist in using purely structural metaphors (borrowed from B). In other words, this relationship could be interpreted as a relationship between metalinguistic features of the disciplines.

2. Some substantial problem of B is interpretable as a problem for A (in its range of commitment), but B is shown to be more effective in solving it. This breaks down to two (not necessarily mutually exclusive) subcases, depending on how we interpret the term *more effective:*

2.1 B's greater effectiveness is a matter of lesser intradisciplinary (or inner) logical or structural complexity in specific problem solving.

2.2 B's solution has a greater explanatory utility, mainly because it can be connected to the solution of a greater or finer range of problems. If this last subcase obtains, we can say that B is *instrumentally substantiated* for A, vis-à-vis a certain class of problems. If *only* the first subcase obtains, for the specific problem, we can say that, relative to that problem, B is *instrumentally permissible* for A.

It is perhaps worth dealing separately with the following:

Every substantial problem of B that cannot be construed naturally as purely metalinguistic or methodological is interpretable as a problem for A, and A is more effective in solving it. We can talk of a *complete* reduction of B to A.

We notice that in this case it practically never happens that A's solutions have a lesser syntactic complexity, when considered in isolation, *for every problem* of B. It is primarily in overall explanatory utility that A will have some advantages. And in case this applies to every problem of B, we can talk of complete substantial reduction.

As an example of this case we can consider the reduction of classical thermodynamics to statistical (quantum) mechanics. Although every problem of the first can be construed as a problem for the latter, and although the latter will have a greater overall explanatory utility in solving such problems, including the availability of solutions to problems that are not solvable in classical thermodynamics, it is equally obvious that there exist many problems that are logically less complex to solve in classical thermodynamics. Thus statistical mechanics is *instrumentally substantiated* for classical thermodynamics, but the latter is only *instrumentally permissible* from the former point of view.

It is perhaps misleading to contrast overall explanatory utility with the internal logical or structural complexity of particular solutions: the latter enters as an ingredient in the former. We allow ourselves this simplification because explanatory utility is much more of a gestalt measure and is never restricted to a consideration of one disciplinary problem. Thus the internal logical simplicity of a solution is usually but a small factor in its explanatory utility.

The hard cases of essential interdisciplinarity are those in which only certain problems of one discipline are readily interpretable in terms of another discipline, while others are not thus interpretable, or are interpretable only by extension of our logical and constructive tools.

It should be stressed that the meaningfulness of such distinctions, among cases and subcases, rests on our understanding that "can be interpreted in A" be read as "can be interpreted in the *minimal* conceptual framework presupposed by A." If we were to allow, in interpreting in A, only the use of such issues as are actually considered proper by practitioners of A, we would be too restrictive (as per naive reductionism). But if, on the other hand, we were to allow in such interpretation *more* than the minimal *Weltanschauung* of A, many of the above distinctions would collapse altogether (as per reckless structuralism!).

The envisioned contribution of instrumental sublation is that using the methods of interpretative interdisciplinarity, relative to sufficient logical machinery, will allow us to compare the instrumentalities of different disciplines vis-à-vis different problems and map the types of instrumental dependence and independence between them. This extends even to the case where the interpretative exercise is futile, no matter what logical tools we allow ourselves; for then the moral of demonstrated futility will be the demonstration of disciplinary independence.

In such ways we believe that instrumental sublation (and the previous stages) provides one key for transcending various interdisciplinary misunderstandings, animosities, and competitions. This is not because it tries to gloss over them, or mitigate them by diplomacy, but because it takes them seriously enough and attempts to spell out what such differences mean and what would be their consequences. If someone said "that is reducible to this," the instrumental approach would ask "How much did you pay (in terms of instrumental utilities)?" If someone said "this cannot be reduced to that, and therefore may not be scientifically legitimate," the same approach would ask "suppose it were; would you pay the (instrumental) price?" And even in the case in which it can be argued, on logical or other grounds, that "that is not reducible to this, at any price," such an argument is interdisciplinarily valuable, simply because it shows that the minimal conceptual framework of one discipline is not strong enough to handle every concept that might arise in another discipline.

We note that in practice instrumental sublation has an additional benefit. Beyond justifying the unique concern of one discipline and not threatening the ontological presuppositions of others, it allows in fact for the exportation and importation of methods and terminology from one discipline to another, when this is instrumentally justifiable, at least on a purely metaphorical level. But this remains to be shown.

Methodological Elaboration and Illustration

Naive Honesty

At this stage we limit ourselves mostly to the methodological confines of philosophical analysis, including dialectical analysis. (This sense of *dialectical* is Platonistic, i.e., searching for the grand presuppositions behind our usage of concepts and behind our conventional meaning relationships.) More particularly, we may restrict ourselves to philosophy of science (including logic) and analytical philosophy. From the point of view of philosophy of science, the major notions used have to do with the distinctions between the ontology and theoretical constructs in the object language, and between these and pure metalinguistic structures. The use of logic cuts across the "object" and "meta"-language: Considering what logic will be proper (in spelling out what is the theoretical range of commitment), or mention of logical and mathematical theorems, belong to the metalinguistic levels. But a theoretical construct of the object-language may be defined logically and mathematically relative to its basic ontology.

As noted in the section on structuralism, the ontology and the structures of the *object*-language of a discipline are not entirely separable. Nonetheless, as far as the naivete goes, practitioners of different disciplines will tend to think of certain elements as primitive, not reducible, and of others as mere constructs. The notion of "the average white Anglo-Saxon male," for example, will not be thought of in the ontological mode (except perhaps in some literary or rhetorical discipline). It will have to be regarded as an indirect device of talking about a whole population and will therefore presuppose the existence of *individual* white Anglo-Saxon males and the existence of a *population* of all such individuals, as well as the additive measurability of some features of such individuals.

The point of "honesty" is that we should incorporate neither more nor less than is presuppositionally required for the purpose of a minimal general framework. If a certain economic analysis proceeds by explaining economic behavior solely in terms of maximization of utility functions, then the minimal general framework will have to contain the presupposition that human and institutional choices in general are to be explained by maximization of utility functions. This may be at odds with the extradisciplinary beliefs of a particular practitioner of the discipline, who does not think this scheme applies to ethical choices. But nonetheless it would represent part of the minimal framework he or she is committed to, as far as the particular disciplinary practice goes.

Likewise it is important methodologically that we do not omit anything that is minimally presupposed. If someone is committed in a discipline to the existence of certain objects, certain observable traits of those objects, and to correlations between such traits, one is committed also to concepts that are definable as correlations of such correlations, and so on, to any logical level. Furthermore, if the identifiability and reidentifiability of traits presuppose the existence of a proper spatiotemporal framework, then this too needs to be included in the framework. Hence the conceptual framework that will emerge in such a case is committed as well to the viability of all concepts that are defined, say, by complex mathematical functions of long temporal sequences of events that are specifiable in terms of the presupposed objects, traits, and spatial matrix. And this must be so, even if the practitioner of the discipline at hand is not at all disposed to using such constructs.

The use of analytic philosophy and its methods figures mostly in the exploration of inner-meaning relations, or structures that necessarily connect certain concepts in the minimal framework (sometimes called *meaning postulates*). For instance, in the case of a certain nominalistic or behavioristic psychology, we may have to inquire about the relationship between the notion of human being and those of certain observable traits of such beings (the latter may presuppose a spatio-temporal matrix). We would then have to ask whether for such a psychology human beings are merely the bundle of all their observable traits or not. If there is such a bundle, we will have to ask further, what typology of bundles distinguishes human beings from other bundles—as a matter of conceptual presupposition, or necessity. By such questions we tease out the minimal framework presuppositions.

It is obvious, practically, that there is a limit to the thoroughness of such a venture, and that excessive zeal here may lead us straight into intractable philosophical controversy. It is possible, however, to avoid much of the controversy and open-endedness by sticking to a common core of philosophical and semantical analysis, and by limiting the elucidation of the framework to those features that will be needed in the next stages of instrumental interdisciplinarity, as applied in particular exercises. Philosophers may disagree about the demarcation between mental and physical events and "entities," but in analyzing the presuppositions behind a certain disciplinary practice we can often reach a decision about its naive philosophy, in this regard. Suppose a historian is willing to state that a certain king was in constant pain, much of his life, without anyone suspecting it, on the sole testimony of recently discovered secret memoirs. This of course presu*µ*poses that the memoirs were not designed to deceive future historians. But even if we grant this methodological assumption, we still have to add that the historian's naive philosophy uses a "mental" notion of pain, according to which believing in one's own pain entails being in pain.[16]

As a final remark on the methodology of naive honesty, we note that the technique of uncovering necessary presuppositions may make use of notions of depth structures, in the process of separating *logical* from *surface grammatical* structures. This may become susceptible to all our earlier admonitions against the presupposed innateness and uniqueness or exclusivity of depth structures. Here again we have to resort to the insufficient excuse of minimality. We consider only as much semantical analysis as necessary to bring out those features of the minimal framework that we may need, but we admit that this leaves the door open to alternative minimal frameworks. For our purposes it would suffice if we used one of them.

Radical Egocentricity
Since this stage consists primarily in specific exercises, some of its salient points are demonstrated by using simple examples. These should serve us as well in illustrating the feasibility and significance of instrumental sublation.

Example 1.   An economist E, who specializes in explaining economic behavior in terms of optimization of utility functions, meets a psychologist P, who describes in a psychological study the following reliably consistent behavior of a subject S: When faced with a choice between two types of alternatives A and B, he chose B; when faced with a choice between B and C, he chose C; but when faced with a choice between A and C alone, he chose A! Could this kind of behavior be explained in terms of the minimal framework assumptions of E?

If E is not egocentric, he may leave the problem to the psychologists, since it seems to deal with certain situations and not with commodities. But any thorough analysis (naively honest) will reveal that for E commodities are implicitly understood in terms of choice situations and values, the structural point. If E is egocentric but not radical enough, he will face a problem that his discipline, or its present state of art, cannot resolve, since a necessary presupposition about utility functions is that they should induce transitivity of choice [if $f(B) \geq f(A)$ and $f(C) \geq f(B)$, then $f(C) \geq f(A)$].

The exercise of radical egocentricity begins with the recognition that there is nothing about E's discipline—apart from past habits of association—that in principle limits the notion of commodity to a particular ontological or logical level. The question then becomes, what possible change in the notion of a commodity will allow E to explain P's findings, within his own conceptual framework?

The direction we have to take is one in which a new notion of commodity will be *constructed* logically out of elements that are ontologically accepted by E's minimal framework. (Hence we have to rule out "psychological states" and their like.) This leads us to considering compounds that are made up of "old" commodities and sets of such commodities. If the old commodities are represented by *A, B, C* (or their outcomes), then the "new" commodities would be symbolized by *X/S* where *X* ∈ {*A,B,C*} and *S* is a subset of {*A,B,C*}. In such a compound *X* represents the old commodity and *S* represents the *range* of commodities available at each trial. Thus in the choice between *A* and *B*, when only these are available, the new commodities will be *A/*{*A,B*} and *B/*{*A,B*}. The value of each choice will consequently be a function of these new objects. So, although for our subject, $f(B/\{A,B\}) > f(A/\{A,B\})$ and $f(C/\{B,C\}) > f(B/\{B,C\})$, we could still have $f(A/\{A,C\}) > f(C/\{A,C\})$. There is no logical contradiction.

We shall discuss this example further when we elaborate on its instrumental interdisciplinary ramifications.

Example 2. A behaviorist B is confronted with a theory (in motivation theory)—proposed by a nonbehaviorist K[17]—that the intensity of a specific kind of reaction is a function of both *specific stimulus strength* and an internal quantity known as "level of specific energy accumulation" (a measure of specific motivation). This was initially designed to explain the findings that, when a subject is deprived for a sufficient amount of time of the typically strong or full stimulus that would elicit a certain response, it will react in a similar way to much weaker or partial stimuli; and after even longer periods of deprivation, the subject may even seem to "explode *in vacuo*."[18]

Mathematically K's model may be expressed in a pair of equations:

$$I(t) = \text{Const} \cdot t - \int_{t_0}^{t-\epsilon} f(R,S)\, dt \tag{1}$$

$$R(t) = g(I,S) \tag{2}$$

where *f* and *g* are suitable (monotone) functions, and where *R, S,* and I represent, respectively, the strength of specific response, the fullness and intrinsic strength of specific type of stimulus, and the strength of specific internal motivation.

The first thing B has to recognize (as some behaviorists did), in facing this model, is that the original phenomena it purports to explain constitute an issue for his discipline as well. This is a direct consequence of naive honesty, since B's minimal framework allows for the variables R and S, as defined, as functions of time, and since the phenomena can be described without recourse to nonobservable variables (the identity of the subject is presupposed by B, as well, but can be made operational).

Furthermore B is committed to considering any purely behavioral consequence of K's theory. In particular, by eliminating I from K's equations, we get

$$R(t) = g[C \cdot t - \int_{t_0}^{t-\epsilon} f(R,S)\, dt,\ S(t)] \tag{3}$$

which is a purely behavioral consequence.

It may well be that B has never employed such a mathematically complex relationship, and he may be reluctant to do so now because he has no clear-cut experimental-statistical methodology for acceptance/rejection of theories of such complexity, but he cannot deny the feasibility, or even the possible instrumentality, of Eq. 3 and what it represents.

The next move in this exercise would be for B to try to explain what is expressed by (3) above in terms of his more conventional models of reinforcement. Here the problem resembles that of the first example. As long as B insists on restricting *his* notions of stimulus and response to relatively short episodes (in which their intensity and structure have a determinant or even constant form, as functions of time), he will not succeed in accounting for K's findings. This insistence is not a corollary of B's naive philosophy, but is more a conditioned habit that arises from attending to particular phenomena in the past. In removing the inessential restrictions (even by his own ontological presuppositions), B will have to generalize the notion of a stimulus. The outcome may be that now the notion will be made to apply to whole (subject) *histories* of short ("old") specific stimuli and responses. In terms of such notions, which are still within his naive philosophy, B may be able to account for the phenomena at hand, but he will inevitably have to pay the price in greater mathematical complexity of theory, which is to be suspected, if Eq. 3 is correct.

Instrumental Sublation Through the Preceding Examples
Before concluding this chapter with some general reflections on the methodology of instrumental interdisciplinarity, I want to pursue the above examples further under the umbrella of instrumental sublation and its stated intentions.

First note that in neither of these examples did we violate the fundamental ontological presuppositions of any of the disciplines involved. What is changed is the extent to which logical and combinatorial tools are used. The question is, how are we to evaluate the significance of such moves from a disciplinary and interdisciplinary point of view?

In the first example a general notion of commodity combines the old commodity with the horizon of choices in which it is presented. From the psychologist's point of view this is natural enough. The subject's response should be a function of the total setting of the trial, or a gestalt function. Objects of choice are not merely things in themselves but acquire their meaningfulness from the background contrast. And if such a psychologist wants to adjust, methodologically or structurally, to the economist's way of thinking, he or she might claim that those psychological dimensions of the objects, whose measures may be used in describing the subject's choices, are not really separable but are integrated within the setting of choice— so that the dimension used implicitly in making choices varies from case to case. From the psychologist's point of view, then, there may be definite ontological-psychological correlates of our new commodities (such as $A/\{A,B\}$). But for the economist these new commodities will remain on a higher theoretical level, as constructs relative to his or her ontology.

This already explains one feature of the interdisciplinary relations that might emerge: E and P may go on mistrusting each other's ontology, for different reasons, but they may agree on the same structural features of explanation, vis-à-vis a particular class of problems. This is not without its risks, for, as pointed out earlier, mere structural analogy cannot gloss over differences in substantial concerns. And such differences ultimately will be reflected in overall instrumental differences.

Consider the economist again: is it enough to point out that the new objects are mere constructs (from his or her point of view), and that they resolve the apparent dilemma of intransitive choices within the general framework of utility functions? Would this induce E overnight to change the specific meaning and reference of *commod-*

ity? The answer depends on the instrumental utility of such a move, beyond the avoidance of the initial "contradictions." One consideration will have to do with the computability and measurability of the new utility functions. To determine the proper argument of such a function, we will have to make sure that in economics in general we can determine the range of possible choices as it appears to potential customers. Furthermore, if originally we had N commodities, we will now have $N \times 2^{N-1}$ possible commodities. This threatens to make economic computations extremely difficult unless we can introduce new meaning postulates that will introduce connections between values of structurally related commodities. [For example, we might have $V(X/S) \geq V(X/S')$ when $S \subseteq S'$.]

These considerations do not mean that our proposals will be rejected by E. On the contrary, they or their like may bring about a meaningful revolution in economics, if we manage to pay with new explanatory successes for complicating the initial machinery that it uses. If this is the case, our economist might even be induced to use hybrid expressions that would have some psychological connotations, e.g., "market awareness" or "market gestalt perception."

Some of these considerations apply to Example 2 as well. The major difference between the examples may depend on the difference between the instrumental value of the envisioned reductions (and the machinery expansion) in economics and behavioral psychology, respectively. Whereas, say, the initial computational difficulties of the new commodity and utility function may pay off eventually, the generalization of *stimulus* to cover complicated sequences of stimuli and responses may not be worth the computational troubles, even if it works in principle. A simple elimination of internal variables may eliminate many insights as well, and this is a psychological factor we cannot ignore. The particular way we describe a structure has a deep effect on our ability to read from it various structural features.

What the examples show, in any case, is that we can engage in instrumental sublation, and that it may in certain cases exceed its targets of relative justifiability. It may lead to cross-fertilization, and to borrowing of metaphors at least, which can be done when the *literal meanings* and *literal references* in the metaphor do not threaten the framework in which it is applied. In the most interesting cases of interdisciplinarity, the relative intractability of different disciplinary points of view can be interpreted in terms of the outcomes in prospective exercises of instrumental sublation and its preceding stages.

We may discover that the price of relative interpretability is ridiculously high or even infinite (when such reductions are logically impossible) from an instrumental point of view.

Why Is Such an Approach Different?

The foregoing examples exhibit some of the features of what we call instrumental interdisciplinarity, but they are insufficient in themselves to demonstrate either the radicality or the innovativeness of such an approach. Nor do they provide us with a definite methodology of radical egocentricity, or of instrumental sublation.

The common methodological element in both structuralistic and naive-reductionist approaches is that they seem to interpret, translate, and reduce, in one sense or another. But this has a different significance for the two types of approach. Whereas the structuralist tends to regard the fundamental structural logical tools as invariant, or seeks those that would be invariant across the disciplinary board, the naive reductionist allows in principle for an open-ended horizon of logical and structural tools, but tends to ignore the specific substantive significance of the particular tools and their specific mode of application, as required in different reductions.

The significance of instrumental interdisciplinarity in this context lies in the fact that whereas, like naive reductionism, it allows for an open-ended range of logical and constructive tools, it takes the specificity of each construction to have a substantive disciplinary significance. Not only might it explain the specificity of one discipline from the vantage point of another, but the instrumental benefits of treating structures *as if* they were unanalyzable often can be shown to correspond to the "hang-ups" (or unique concerns) of an otherwise reducible discipline. In viewing specific structures as essential substantive ingredients, our approach comes closer to some structuralistic approaches. What instrumental interdisciplinarity eschews in either of the above approaches is their fundamentalism— "atomistic" in one case and "Platonistic" in another.[19]

The Question of Logical Machinery

One reason why it is difficult to convey here the full impact of instrumental interdisciplinarity is that only a large number of successful paradigms of radical egocentricity, requiring a wide array of different logical tools, would give us an insight into the significance of the open-endedness of the logical-structural tools and their choice.

Example 3. Suppose we are examining, again, the dominance lattice:

Σ_1:

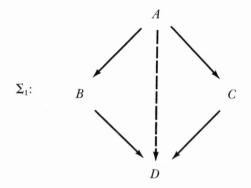

where arrows are understood transitively, so that A is dominant over D as well. We now inquire whether a *linear* structure Σ_2:$X{\to}Y{\to}Z$ can be interpreted within this structure. The basic theorem of the section on finite determinate structures gives us one kind of answer: *it cannot be done*. But this answer of course assumes that *each "individual" of Σ_2 has to be interpreted as an "individual" of Σ_1*. Intuitively the answer looks wrong (if we look at the above arrow-diagrams), since A, B, D seem to be related to one another as X, Y, Z, respectively. The trouble, however, is that B by itself (or "being B") cannot be defined in purely structural terms in Σ_1. (Any attempt to do so will bring C into the picture and destroy the linearity.)

But this answer is *not* definitive. If we chose stronger logical tools of interpretation, we would be able, after all, to interpret Σ_2 within Σ_1:[20] Consider all the structurally *definable sets* of "individuals" in Σ_1. These would be exactly all the subsets of $\{A,B,C,D\}$ with the property that they contain B if and only if they contain C. In particular choose the subsets $S_1 = \{A\}$, $S_2 = \{B,C\}$, and $S_3 = \{D\}$. Define a relation $\rangle$ between subsets by

$S_i > S_j$ if and only if *every element of S_i is dominant*
over every element of S_j

It is clear that the derivative structure $\langle \{S_1, S_2, S_3\}, > \rangle$ is *simply isomorphic* to Σ_2.

This example is enough to show one possible effect of the open-endedness of logical tools on the interpretative potential of any given structure. We notice further that it is perfectly within the specification of radical egocentricity, since the subsets S_1, S_2, S_3 and the relation $>$ between them are *definable within the minimal framework presupposed by* Σ_1.[21]

Injective versus Expansion Interpretability

The above example is about interpreting within a structure, when the word *within* is understood broadly enough as referring to those *set-theoretic* structures, of any *type level* (e.g., sets of individuals, sets of such sets, sets of these different sets, etc.), which can be regarded as *contained* in the fundamental interpreting structure itself. We call such questions *questions of injective interpretability.*

Ultimately, however, what we regard as contained depends on our logical conventions. In the above example, it was possible to regard Σ_2 as contained in Σ_1, partly because the sets matching the individuals of Σ_2 were on a type level not above that used in specifying Σ_1 itself (as was apparent from the pictorial representation), and because these sets and the desired relation between them were definable in Σ_1. The situation looks quite different, if we consider human insight and ingenuity, when we try to interpret one structure relative to a structure that seems to be *poorer,* prima facie. We then need logical tools that will allow us to construct sets and structures that are *significantly richer* than those that immediately appear to be contained in the interpreting structure. We call such questions *questions of expansive interpretability.* It is these questions in particular that call for stronger logical tools—whether by using set-theoretic constructions of higher type and order levels, or by using nonstandard logics (e.g., intensional logics).[22]

Example 4. Suppose we *reverse* the question of Example 3 and ask whether we can interpret Σ_1 from the standpoint of $\Sigma_2:(X\rightarrow Y\rightarrow Z)$. The latter, linear, structure of three elements looks "poorer" than the four-element lattice Σ_1. But if we consider what sets of ordered pairs and relations between such ordered pairs we can define relative to Σ_2, we get a positive answer to this question of expansive interpretability. We could, for example, choose the set S of ordered pairs $\{\langle X,X \rangle, \langle X,Z \rangle, \langle Z,X \rangle, \langle Z,Z \rangle\}$ as a basis. These are all the pairs whose elements are nonintermediate in the *linear* structure of Σ_2, and therefore are set-theoretically definable with respect to Σ_2 (since we can define there the notions of "first" and "last"). Next we can define a relationship $\mathbf{R}^*$, between ordered pairs, say, $\langle u,v \rangle$, $\langle u', v' \rangle$, which says that *u is not before u' and v is not before v'* in the linear order of Σ_2. $\mathbf{R}^*$ again is perfectly definable relative to Σ_2.

The resulting structure $\langle S, \mathbf{R}* \rangle$ is depicted by

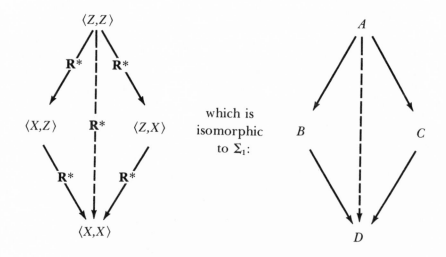

which is
isomorphic
to Σ_1:

Example 5 (nonstandard logics). There are many cases, in interdisciplinary relations, in which the best strategy in explaining the meaning of concepts and structures involved in one discipline from the point of view of another (its minimal framework) is to use logical locutions that are not standard from the point of view of ordinary logic. (see Note 22). We may, for instance, use a *counterfactual subjunctive conditional,* "if ... were ... , then ... ," in explaining the meaning of the term *dangerous* as applying to some past historical circumstance. The historian may insist that such and such a situation "was dangerous, although no grave consequences resulted from it," and what he or she means could be explained further by the statement that "if the situation were to include an external military attack, then the empire would have fallen." Now a behavioristic social scientist may insist that this is completely speculative, unscientific, etc., because it is not confirmable by any correlation between observable circumstances (because, say, the combination of the above situation and an external attack never occurred in history). The methodology of expansive interpretability can demonstrate how a concept that is counterfactually explicated can be interpreted relative to a structure involving no such concept; furthermore, an exact semantical representation of the counterfactual conditional would also reveal that one could provide "scientific methods" for confirming such counterfactual subjunctive clauses.

One semantical analysis of "if p were the case, then q would be the case" interprets it as meaning, roughly, "In all possible cases in which p is true and which are *sufficiently similar* to the actual case, under this constraint (truth of p), q is true." This account can become exact if and when we can provide an exact explication of the notions of "possible case" and "sufficient similarity" between such cases.

In the historian's case, for instance, we might interpret "actual case" to refer to the "dangerous situation" he or she is dealing with, whereas a general "possible case" would be any momentary situation of any civilization in history that would be described in the same categories used to describe the actual case. Inasmuch as the historian is willing to provide us with a sense of sufficient similarity between such situations, which semantically seems to underlie his or her use of a counterfactual conditional, past and future observations can be used to confirm or disconfirm the characterization of the actual case as one of a dangerous situation. It is clear that this can make sense to the behaviorist, if the similarity relation is in principle possible between observable and unobservable situations.

Since similarities can usually be traced back to, or can be explicated in terms of, structural commonalities, the logic of (counterfactual) conditionals can be used in various expansive structural interpretations, when different structures are taken to constitute our possible cases.

Typically, as with the historian above, the actual case involves a certain structure, with a certain number of elements and relations between them. The *antecedent* of the subjunctive conditional involves some additional elements and relations that do not exist in the actual case. If we try to add these elements to the actual case, we may have to disrupt some of its features. The counterfactual conditional will tell us to look at those augmented structures in which the original structural features were least disrupted. If we can decide on a *measure* (or degrees) of similarity between structures, we shall be able to determine what those least-modified structures are, and consequently we shall be able to test the conditional by checking whether its *consequent* holds in all of them.

To pursue our example further, suppose that a society is described in terms of a (causal-like) relation of *immediate modifying effect* between its elements, a relation that need not be transitive. A *feedback* is then described as a *cycle* of such relationships $x_1 R x_2, x_2 R x_3, \ldots,$ $x_{n-1} R x_n, x_n R x_1,$ $(n > 1)$, (when $x_1, \ldots, x_n$ are *different* elements). The *strength* of the feedback cycle is defined as 1/(its length). Our historian's pet theory maintains that society is stable as long as:

1. Every immediate modifying effect is part of some feedback;
2. Every element modifies some element and is modified by some element; and
3. The sum of strengths of all feedbacks passing through any given element (to be called the stress on the element) lies between two numbers (say, $^{1}/_{5}$ and $^{4}/_{5}$).

The similarity between two structures, in this context, will then be measured by the difference between the sum of three numbers characterizing each structure: the number of elements, the number of feedback cycles, and the average stress per element (the latter equals [number of cycles]/[number of elements]).

Thus the following structures are stable:

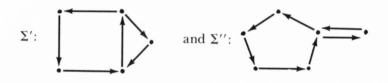

Σ':   and Σ'':

And the difference between them equals $1 + 0 + ^{1}/_{15} = {}^{16}/_{15}$.

Assume now that our actual case (the "dangerous situation") is represented by the structure Σ^*: $X_1 \to X_2 \to X_3 \to X_4$. What would be the most similar stable case containing an additional element? We have to minimize the number of additional cycles and then minimize the difference in average stress. It is not hard to see that under these constraints, the best choice would be a single cycle with five elements. (The difference would be $^{21}/_{20}$.) If we took the five-element cycle obtained and asked the same question, the answer would not be the same, because a single six-element cycle would have an average stress of 1/6 (too low). So if we were to add two elements to Σ^* and retain the stability, the minimally different stable structure would have to be a two-cycled one (with a difference measure of 3 $^{1}/_{12}$).

Now assume further that an *external attack* is understood as the introduction of a new element that will have an immediate modifying effect on (at least) two elements that already stand in such a relation. Thus an external attack on Σ* must result in a structure that *contains* the diagram (as a proper *sub*diagram):

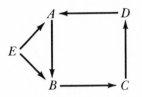

where ⟨*A,B,C,D*⟩ is some cyclical permutation on X_1, X_2, X_3, X_4 above. The historian's claim about the dangerous situation Σ* can now be understood as meaning that no stable structure *sufficiently similar* to Σ* can contain the above diagram. This can be verified fairly easily: for instance, if we try to do this with the elements, *A,B,C,D,E* alone, then we would have to draw an arrow to *E* from one of the other elements. In either case the stress on one of the points would be too great (> $^4/_5$). (On the other hand, if we adjusted the stresses, by adding new elements we would have to introduce *seven* new elements at least, which would make the new structure too different.)

The value of this example to the behaviorist is that now he or she could understand the term *dangerous* as an "operationalizable" term, if he or she so wishes. The rules of evidence for confirming the danger of a structure like Σ* would be simply those of confirming the historian's pet theory about the stability of social structures in general. One could also test whether external attacks that ended in the collapse of an existent structure really did operate on dangerous structures, etc. The important point logically is that when we use nonstandard logics, we are conveying extremely complex structural information about actual cases—and sometimes doing so in a much less cumbersome manner than by using standard logical constructions.

This only hints at the interdisciplinary future of various intensional logics. The use of various *modal, temporal, epistemic, doxastic,* and *conditional* intensional logics will move many issues from the domain of seeming substantive disputes to the domain of *instrumental disputes.* These at least could be made relative for different human purposes and could be handled methodologically, on an interdisciplinary basis.

Conclusion

We have attempted in this chapter to consider some of the ramifications of essential interdisciplinarity—the attempt to establish meaningful relations between different disciplines—which can contribute to relative understanding from different vantage points, to cooperation and cross-fertilization in the solution of common predisciplinary problems, and to structural and substantive unification at times. We have not considered many metadisciplines that have a direct bearing on such enterprises. In particular it must be obvious that various aspects of (so-called) artificial intelligence are directly relevant to the type of interdisciplinary tasks we have considered. Heuristics for greater ingenuity in problem-solving stress, among others, two important elements for instrumental interdisciplinarity. First, logical or linguistic elements that are logically unnecessary to formulate a problem make an enormous difference when it comes to solving it. This is a feature of the majority of the ingenious solutions in mathematics and in science. Second, and relatedly, metaphors borrowed from apparently irrelevant disciplines and practices, substantively, prove to be extremely useful methodologically in problem solving.[23] Similarly, the mathematics of pattern-recognition, which is already highly developed, ought to play a major role in further development of similarity-measures for structures and their utilization in expansive interpretation, using nonstandard logics.

It is equally obvious that a further development of (nonstatistical) information theory ought to play a major role in instrumental interdisciplinarity. In this connection one of the most promising notions is that of (nonstatistical) randomness of sequences. Basically the idea is to measure the randomness (negative information) of a sequence by the relative efficiency or simplicity with which we can describe it. We can apply this notion for the purpose of instrumental evaluation of explanations and in particular assess the value of unifying interdisciplinary explanations of various types. From this instrumental point of view, for instance, embedding two different disciplines in one framework will be valuable *only* if it saves specific disciplinary information. Put otherwise, the information measure of the unified description of the disciplines should be less than that of the sum of their separate descriptions.

If we consider in particular the questions raised and the answers provided in this chapter, we must admit that the treatment is sketchy and quite fragmentary. Many questions have been left open and others have been treated by way of example and illustration. This is not only because some of these questions are not and could not be methodologically transparent, but it is also due to my view that a useful interdisciplinarity of the essential kind must often be specific–problem-oriented. We support this view by the logical truism that there cannot be an overall measure of instrumental comparison that is suitable for all disciplinary purposes, and by observing that different disciplines will be of different instrumental value vis-à-vis different problems.

Nevertheless we can summarize the main insights suggested in this chapter under the following two headings.

Essential Interdisciplinary Practice
In following the insights of the substantial view, it is necessary to develop an approach that makes the unique concerns of different disciplines meaningful from an interdisciplinary point of view. Practically, this means that interdisciplinarity should start on the level of *disciplinarity*. Exercises of naive honesty and radical egocentricity should be incorporated into separate disciplinary teaching. This presupposes some *metadisciplinarity* in the form of training in logic, mathematics, structural elaboration, philosophy of science, and semantics. The impact of the substantial view extends, as we suggested, to developing measures of instrumental comparison that are made relative to specific predisciplinary problem clusters. Trying to achieve too much, in this respect, will result in such general insights, as in the case of structuralism, as would often become restricted to the metalinguistic level, or as might end in the quagmire of universal naive reduction.

Instrumental Interdisciplinary Theory
Here we can summarize our main results as follows. Instrumental comparisons (proceeding to instrumental sublation through radical egocentricity) pose different kinds of tasks of injective and expansive interpretations. When these can be carried out on the level of the object-language structures, they are preferable to those that are restricted to metalinguistic structures on either disciplinary side. In the latter case the interdisciplinary relations take the form of metaphorical interpretations whose utility can be judged on a heuristic basis, as in problem-solving theory.

The meaningfulness of the distinction between *injective* and *expansive* ventures rests primarily on limiting the structures and the tools involved to logical levels and types that are close enough to those used in specifying the specific disciplinary basis of the interpretation (in the injective case) or in allowing these structures and tools to range far beyond (in the expansive case).

Whatever the interpretative enterprise involved, there is only one type of methodological problem for which we can offer a definitive solution. *Given two (set-theoretical) descriptions of finite structures, and given an upper limit to the set-theoretic type level we may employ in interpretation, we can decide whether it is possible to interpret one structure in terms of the other structure, within the specified set-theoretic limits on the complexity of the construction.*

Other types of interpretive ventures, which involve an interpretation within (potentially infinite) recursively generated systems, do not admit to a general algorithm for resolution.

Although the definitive result above may seem to fall short of many expectations, we note that it is extremely useful for the purposes of instrumental interdisciplinarity. The instrumental value of interpretations, as well as the instrumental value of treating the interpreted disciplinary structures as autonomous, depends on our capability to limit the complexity of the interpretation, when an interpretation can be carried out. A mathematical elucidation of this, and some related results, is provided in the Appendix. (A further development leads to a fuller mathematical theory of structural interpretation, which blends together features of elementary model-theory and Galois theory of algebraic extensions, but extends the scope of the latter to dealing with structures in general. A rigorous deductive presentation of this theory, as well as the proofs of the theorems of the Appendix, will have to be relegated to another forum.)

Appendix: The Logic of Structural Description and Interpretation

The fundamental feature of this chapter is that notions of *structure* and *structural interpretation* are explicated by relations between structural descriptions (or, more precisely, descriptions of structure). Any specific concept of structure will be determined, accordingly, by the presupposed convention about equivalence and nonequivalence ("synonymity" and "heteronymity") of such descriptions. Different conventions may give rise to different concepts of structure.

Our strategy will therefore amount to the following: select a well understood sense of "structure"—such as is used in mathematical logic—and apply it to the *level of descriptions* in explicating those equivalence relations between descriptions which might underlie different senses of "structure." We restrict ourselves further to those conventions of structural description whereby, for any description, there will be some equivalent description set in a standard type of formal language (a *standard extensional description*). It will be assumed that such a standard description will be based on a determinable list of symbols, will presuppose a *type* assigned to each symbol, and will logically determine which truth-value assignments to *atomic sentences* in the language of the description itself fall under the description (in analogy to the way a *theory* is said to determine its *models* in mathematical logic).

Consider the following example of defining *types* and *atomic sentences* by rules:

1. o is a type.
2. If $\tau_1, \ldots, \tau_n$ are types, so are $[\tau_1, \ldots, \tau_n]$ and $\langle \tau_1, \ldots, \tau_n \rangle$.
3. Only what can be shown to be so by 1 and 2 is a type.

An *atomic sentence* is either a string of symbols (of the description) $SS_1 \ldots S_n$, where type $S = [\text{type } S_1, \ldots, \text{type } S_n]$ or is of the kind $S = \langle S_1, \ldots, S_n \rangle$, where type $S = \langle \text{type } S_1, \ldots, \text{type } S_n \rangle$. The typing of symbols will be *description-relative*, so that we can assume that some symbol is of type o (even when its intended meaning assigns it a different type in a broader logical hierarchy). A structural description will be consistent and complete when it allows for one and only one truth-value assignment to the corresponding atomic sentences. Such a structural description, Δ, can be given a *set-theoretic interpretation*, denoted by $\sigma(\Delta)$, as follows: if type $S = 0$, then $\sigma(S) = S$; if S has a square bracket type $[\tau_1, \ldots, \tau_n]$, then $\sigma(S) = \{\langle \sigma(S_1), \ldots, \sigma(S_n) \rangle \mid \ulcorner SS_1 \ldots S_n \urcorner \}$ is true by Δ, where $\{ - \mid - - - \}$ means "the set of all—such that $- - -$"; if type $S = \langle \tau_1, \ldots, \tau_n \rangle$, then $\sigma(S) = \langle \sigma(S_1), \ldots, \sigma(S_n) \rangle$, where $\ulcorner S = \langle S_1, \ldots, S_n \rangle \urcorner$ is true by Δ. ($\langle -, -, \ldots, - \rangle$ denotes the ordered sequence of $-, -, \ldots, -$.)

The *constructible* (finite) *objects relative to* Δ are those which can be obtained by the following rules:

1. Any o-type symbol is such an object.
2. Any finite set of such objects is such an object.
3. A finite ordered sequence of such objects is such an object (for interdisciplinary purposes it is better not to define such sequences in terms of set-forming, as is done in set-theory).

Notice that these "objects" are linguistic, *par-excellence*, and need not be confused with whatever they are meant to depict. The o-type objects will be called *individuals*. In the following we shall assume (unless stated otherwise) that the number of symbols is finite, and we shall present results for complete and consistent descriptions.

Automorphisms.   Let ψ be any permutation of the elements of Δ° – –the set of individual symbols of Δ. (In the mathematician's language ψ is *a 1-1 mapping of Δ° unto itself.*) Extend ψ to the constructible objects of Δ by stipulating that when S is a set, $\psi S = \{\psi x \mid x \in S\}$, and when $S = \langle A_1, \ldots, A_n \rangle$, $\psi s = \langle \psi A_1, \ldots, \psi A_n \rangle$. A constructible object is *invariant* under ψ when $\psi A = A$, set-theoretically. ψ is called *ground automorphism* (automorphism, symmetry) of Δ, when for any symbol S of Δ, of a *square-bracket type* (e.g., [o], or [o, $\langle$o,o$\rangle$]) the object σ (S) (the set-theoretic interpretation of S above) is invariant under it. This means the same as requiring that applying the permutation ψ of the individuals to the atomic sentences of the (complete and consistent) description does not change true sentences into false ones or vice versa. The ground automorphisms of Δ under the operation of *transformational composition* constitute a *group* (cf. any textbook on group theory), denoted by G_0 (Δ). For any subset S of Δ° ($S \subseteq \Delta^\circ$), G_0 (Δ/S) denotes the subgroup of those automorphisms under which every member of S is invariant, or fixed. The objects invariant under all automorphisms of G_0 (Δ/S) will be called *invariants of Δ, relative to S.* Those objects invariant under all automorphisms of $G_0(\Delta)$ will be called invariants of Δ.

Definable Objects.   As a final preamble consider the following: Let $\mathscr{L}_{set}$ (Δ) be a standard language for basic set theory, enriched by adding the individuals of Δ as *atoms* (nonset symbols). This language will contain the constructible objects relative to Δ (along with other, infinite, objects, if we add enough postulates of set theory). Any such object, A, will be called *definable in Δ, relative to S*—where $S \subseteq \Delta^\circ$— when there is a *predicate* $P(X)$ of $\mathscr{L}_{set}$ (Δ), containing no extralogical symbols apart from members of S, for which Δ [or $\sigma(\Delta)$, more precisely] *entails* that $P(C)$, if and only if $C = A$, set-theoretically. When A is a *set* this can be seen to be equivalent to the existence of such a predicate $Q(X)$, for which $\sigma(\Delta)$ entails $Q(B)$, if and only if $B \in A$. When S is empty, we say that A is *definable in Δ.*

The Basic Theorem of Definability.   For finite complete and consistent descriptions Δ, this is the statement

A constructible object relative to Δ is definable in Δ relative to S if and only if it is invariant in Δ, relative to S.

Although this result is not automatically true for descriptions with infinitely many individuals, there are many ways in which it can be generalized to such cases. For instance, if every individual of Δ is a member of some *finite definable* set of individuals, then the theorem still holds true (for *finite* constructible objects!). For those familiar with *model theory*, it may be noted that the theorem can be generalized for any complete description by replacing "invariance in Δ" by "invariance in any elementary extension of Δ." The theorem can be extended to infinite set-theoretic objects of $\mathscr{L}_{\text{set}}$ (Δ) by amending our notion of definability to allow for infinite conjunctions and disjunctions of ordinary predicates.

Interpretability and Corollaries. Suppose we have two complete and consistent descriptions Δ_1 and Δ_2. In general we shall assume that any notion of *interpretation* of Δ_2 relative to Δ_1 can be represented mathematically by a 1-1 mapping, ζ, of the symbols of Δ_2 into objects of $\mathscr{L}_{\text{set}}$ (Δ_1), satisfying:

1. For any symbol, S, of Δ_2, with a square-bracket type (a predicate or relation symbol), ζS is a set and is *definable* in Δ_1 relative to $\zeta\Delta_2{}^0 = \{\zeta x \mid x \in \Delta_2{}^0\}$.
2. $\ulcorner SS_1 \ldots S_n \urcorner$ is true in Δ_2 if and only if $\langle \zeta S_1, \ldots, \zeta S_n \rangle \in \zeta S$.
3. $\ulcorner S = \langle S_1, \ldots, S_n \rangle \urcorner$ is true in Δ_2 if and only if $\zeta S = \langle \zeta S_1, \ldots, \zeta S_n \rangle$.

Various notions of interpretation are obtained by imposing further restrictions. The following are important in *interdisciplinary applications:* A *regular* interpretation ζ: Add the requirement that $\zeta\Delta_2{}^0$ is definable in Δ_1. A *strict* interpretation ζ: Add the requirement that ζ_c is definable in Δ_1 for any individual c of Δ_2. A *type-preserving* interpretation: For any symbol S of Δ_2, ζS is of the same set-theoretical type in $\mathscr{L}_{\text{set}}$ (Δ_1) as $\sigma(S)$ is in $\mathscr{L}_{\text{set}}$ (Δ_2). An *embedding* is a type-preserving interpretation, ζ, for which $\zeta(S)$, for any individual, predicate or relational symbol S in Δ_2 is equal to $\sigma(S')$ where S' is a like symbol of Δ_1. An *isomorphism* is an embedding of Δ_2 onto the whole of Δ_1.

Finally, and most important, we can say that an interpretation is of a *limited-type complexity* when an a priori upper bound can be set on the "difference" between the type-complexity of interpreted symbols and their corresponding interpreting objects. I shall not describe here how to rank the complexity of types of symbols and objects, although this can be done naturally in terms of the numbers of different brackets and the lengths of ordered sequences used in constructing these types.

An immediate consequence of the basic definability theorem is the following:

There is a universal decision procedure (a mechanical algorithm) for settling questions of the type: Is there an interpretation (of any specific kind) of type complexity $\leq N$, of one finite complete description relative to another such description?

For instrumental interdisciplinarity, the limitation on the complexity is essential. For several purposes the underlying relations of descriptive equivalence depend on the availability of co-interpretability within limited complexity, as well as on other constraints. This is particularly pertinent when two descriptions which are nonequivalent mathematically have nonetheless the same overall interpretative potential. If we treat explanations and metaphors as structural interpretations between descriptions, then the utility of such explanations will often hinge on the relationship between the complexity of interpretation, the amount of *structural information* transferred (see below) and the relative simplification affected by the interpretation. Interpretations which do not have sufficient explanatory utility, from this point of view, will be more often than not rejected.

This appendix concludes with two further introductory notes.

Structural Information Measures.   Given the notion of invariance and definability in a structured description, one can introduce a measure of the *structural information* which a description Δ gives about any particular constructible object, A, in its language. This measure will be a function of the minimal set of like objects (of the same type), which contains A, and which is invariant in Δ: The larger this set, the less information is provided. One such convenient measure is $I_{\Delta}(A) \underset{\mathrm{df}}{=} -\log(m/N)$, where m is the size of this minimal set and N is the number of objects of the same type as A. It is then possible to give measures of the average information provided per object of a (finite) type τ. These measures are related to the potential of the description to serve as an *interpreting host* for other descriptions (under a given complexity of interpretation). On the other hand, the potential of a structural description to be interpreted in other descriptions, as well as the potential for *theoretical simplifications*, is related to its degree of symmetry [size and structure of $G_0(\Delta)$]. It can be easily seen that this amount of symmetry increases as the average information per object decreases. Since the utility of an explanatory interpretation depends on both kinds of consideration, the central structural features of important types of explanation will often display a careful balance between "symmetricity" and "internal informability."

Galois Theory. We finally note that by using various concepts of elementary group theory one can provide various necessary and sufficient conditions for the availability of interpretations of several kinds, in terms of relations between groups of automorphisms. For example, there is a regular type-preserving interpretation of Δ_2 in Δ_1 only if $G_0(\Delta_2)$ is (mathematically) isomorphic to a *normal* subgroup of $G_0(\Delta_1)$. Likewise, a sufficient condition for *regular* embeddability of Δ_2 in Δ_1 is that there exists a subdescription Δ_2' of Δ_1, which is isomorphic to Δ_2, for which $G_0(\Delta_1/\Delta_2'^0)$ is a normal subgroup and for which any element of $\Delta_1^0 - \Delta_2'^0$ is moved by some automorphism of this subgroup. (G_2 is a normal subgroup of G_1 when for any $g_1 \in G_1$ and $g_2 \in G_2$, $g_1^{-1} g_2 g_1 \in G_2$.) Such theorems apply to a wide variety of descriptions with finitely many symmetries and can be developed in analogy to classical Galois Theory in Algebra. The applications to general questions of interpretability lie in the possibility of interpreting any interpretation of Δ_2 relative to Δ_1 in terms of embeddings of Δ_2 in structural descriptions derived set-theoretically from Δ_1. For finite descriptions and limited complexity interpretations, this does not add anything new, but makes some problems easier to solve computationally. For certain descriptions with infinitely many individuals, however, it extends the range of decision procedures.

Notes

1. Thus, by Gödel's Theorem (1931) and related theorems, the task of deciding whether a given formula is provable in a formal system could not *in general* be methodologically transparent. This reflects on many other tasks; see, for instance, S.C. Kleene, *Introduction to Metamathematics* (Princeton: Van Nostrand, 1952), pp. 204–13; and M. Davis, *Computability and Unsolvability* (New York: McGraw-Hill, 1958), especially pp. 66–101.

2. This too is an offshoot of Gödel's theorem: there are transformational grammars for which the question of grammaticalness would be undecidable (this corresponds to the so-called "Printing problem" for computer

programs [cf. Davis, p. 71]); and furthermore we cannot decide in general whether a proposed grammar gives rise to a decidable predicate of grammaticalness. This corresponds to the undecidability of the question whether a given computer program will always come to a stop (cf. Davis, p. 78).

3. For example, one might want to provide a psychological correlate of socioeconomic status or treat some psychological states as limited supply commodities.

4. By "structure in itself" or "pure structure" we will be referring throughout this chapter to formal (uninterpreted) structures. In this sense it is obvious that it is even possible that a given structure (on one level) and a structure used in studying some of its properties (logically, a metalevel) will be identical (or isomorphic).

5. In the sense that a biologist "chooses" not to study *unicorns*. The ordinary sense of "choosing to deal with A rather than with B" conceptually presupposes that both A and B have a (different) reference.

6. This is based mostly on what is upheld in the works of J. Piaget, N. Chomsky, and C. Lévi-Strauss. See for instance, J. Piaget, *Structuralism* (New York: Harper & Row, 1970).

7. A good example is Lévi-Strauss's book *The Savage Mind*. Chomsky, however, must have had a more sophisticated version of equivalence, since the typical depth structures invoked are not necessarily simply isomorphic to each other but are claimed to be of the same potential (see equipotentiality below).

8. See the subsection on *finite determinate structures*, as well as the Appendix: The interstructural logical language was taken to be in the first case a first-order predicate calculus containing as nonlogical symbols only the symbols of the structural descriptions; in the latter case it was a set theoretical extension thereof.

9. This follows essentially from the same result that leads to the undecidability of grammaticalness in general. See Note 2.

10. As described below, the methodology is appropriate only for a notion of interpretation that takes each symbol of a basic individual in one structural description (zero-type symbol) to be interpreted by such a symbol of the other. This can be generalized, however, for various kinds of interpretation, provided that the type-complexity of the interpretation is restricted (see the Appendix).

11. This theorem bears a strong resemblance to several theorems in model theory and in particular to *Beth's Definability Theorem*. See J.R. Shoenfield, *Mathematical Logic* (Reading, Mass.: Addison-Wesley, 1967), p. 81. It is generalized in the definability theorem of the Appendix.

12. It can be shown, for instance, that no "ad-sentential" phrase can be used in such a way that it would reflect only underlying *linear* structures (which may be our conception of temporal deep-structures). The usage of a phrase like "it was always" could also be interpreted as reflecting certain nonlinear structures, and similarly with "I hope that."

13. In English translation: R. Carnap, *The Logical Structure of the World* (Berkeley: University of California Press, 1969).

14. Plato, *Theaetetus*, 203a to 208c. Compare Plato's *Theory of Knowledge: The Theaetetus and the Sophist*, trans. and comment, F.M. Cornford (London: Kegan Paul, Trench, Trubner, 1935).

15. This does not mean that overcoming disciplinary entrenchment is a necessary condition for doing instrumental interdisciplinarity. But it is addressed in particular to those who think it should be overcome. The contention of instrumental interdisciplinarity, however, is that one can and is practically obliged to use this entrenchment.

16. The case in which believing in having X entails having X is taken by some philosophers to constitute a criterion of demarcation between the mental and the physical, i.e., when this case obtains, X must correspond to a mental entity or state. The example is admittedly trivial.

17. K. Lorenz, "An Energy Model of Instinctive Actions," in *Motivation,* ed. D. Bindra and J. Stewart (New York: Penguin, 1966), pp. 23–27.

18. Ibid., p. 23.

19. This is not to suggest that every or even most structuralists are full-fledged Platonists. The label *Platonistic* here suggests only the belief that all structures can be generated by a fundamental logic of primary structures, and that this represents a higher and more fundamental form of knowledge. Piaget and Lévi-Strauss avoid the Platonic extreme version of such views, but nonetheless maintain, with other structuralists, the above principles.

20. One could, in addition to the interpretative strategy adopted below, use a notion of (injective) interpretation when the interpreted relations of the structure to be interpreted would be definable in the interpreting structure only *relative* to the interpreted individuals (see Appendix A).

21. The relation $>$ can be defined by $S_i > S_j$ if and only if every element of S_i is dominant over every element of S_j and no two elements of S_i or of S_j stand in dominance relation.

22. By *intensional logic* we understand a logic in which the referential value of a compound (e.g., the truth-value of a sentence) is not a *function* of the referential-values of its atomic referential components (e.g., smaller sentences of which it is made by logical operators). Thus the logic of counter-to-fact conditionals is *intensional* because one cannot always determine the truth-value of such a conditional strictly on the basis of the truth-value of its antecedent and consequent.

23. These two elements are equally important to interdisciplinarity. The first provides a perfect *heuristic* rationale for radical egocentricity; the second explains why even borrowing metaphors, from a discipline that cannot be viewed as embeddable in a logical extension of one's own discipline, may prove extremely useful. Neither of these tasks is methodologically transparent, since one cannot program a heuristic that would guarantee ingenious solutions in every case. Properly speaking, the present usage of *heuristic* is restricted to procedures that increase the likelihood of finding a good solution to a problem, but do not guarantee such discoveries.

Personal and Institutional Problems Encountered in Being Interdisciplinary

Robert L. Scott

What we call problems of course do not exist as clearly recognized entities, begging for discrete labels. Ironically, their existence is problematic and depends on the circumstances in which persons find themselves and the point of view from which they are working. What constitutes for one person in a particular situation a clear problem may for another person be altogether benign, or in another situation be quite conducive to what many people find perfectly normal activities.

That paragraph should strike most readers as being too truistic to bear mentioning. Too often, however, when our own interests are involved, we take whatever troubles us as *real* problems and treat those who seem untroubled or recalcitrant as out-of-touch, biased, wrong, or just plain stupid. In short, we are apt to take ourselves as being in touch with some special Truth that, if only understood by others, would obviate any opposition except perhaps that springing out of bad faith.

Unfortunately it seems to me that a rather frequent strain of what I call "millennial interdisciplinarity" is too often easily discernible in much of the writing on this important matter. Politics and persuasion mark the discourse and relationships of those who have not experienced the proper insight, so the millennial attitude runs; especially in the academic world these features, so typical of the rough-and-tumble of other social spheres, have no place in the higher pursuit of knowledge. The attitude that informs this chapter is quite the contrary.

The previously outlined history and the previously projected goals of interdisciplinarity have suggested but not directly addressed certain specific problems and dilemmas that are inevitable within academic structures. It is the purpose of this chapter to set forth those problems and dilemmas. Although what follows will be assertive, the assertions should be read in the spirit of probes toward rather than definitions of problems. The specific circumstances in which persons find themselves will give content to their own problems. My reduction to six dilemmas is transparently an attempt to simplify arbitrarily what must always be quite complex.

One further preliminary: as the early chapters of this book sought to demonstrate, interdisciplinarity is plagued with misunderstandings about terminology. Terms that may seem at first blush to be transparent are frequently used with differences that prove to be substantial, as they deviate from an inchoate but strong core of beliefs concerning the state of higher education.

No one can hope to fix with certainty what are after all parts of a living language long in use in hundreds of colleges and universities. I give here a glossary only as a rough guide to my use of the terms in this chapter. My description of these terms is basically in harmony with the one proposed in Kockelmans's "Why Interdisciplinarity?"

Interdisciplinary. The mingling of several disciplines traditionally distinct in such a way as to create a unified product: a course, a paper, or even a curriculum. If the result is substantial and gains wide acceptance, a fresh discipline may be established.

The term *interdisciplinary* is frequently used as a genus for which such other terms as those mentioned below stand as species. I occasionally use the word in a generic sense, as I trust the context will make clear.

Multidisciplinary. The mingling of several disciplines traditionally distinct in such a way as to maintain their separateness, even though they may be associated. A familiar example is the requiring of a student to take a group of courses in diverse disciplines, e.g., music, mathematics, and sociology. Generally the only unity sought is the product that may be taken as a person's education.

Pluridisciplinary. The mingling of several disciplines traditionally taken to be closely related, e.g., mathematics and physics, or Latin and Greek. Such mingling may be curricular convenience or the sense of a natural reinforcing of or service to a unified product.

Crossdisciplinary. Seeking to draw, even expeditiously, upon various distinct disciplines in such a way as to solve particular problems individuals face in research, writing, or pedagogy, or to solve social problems. The term may be distinguished from *pluridisciplinary* in that the disciplines are not necessarily those traditionally associated, and from *interdisciplinary* in that the final product will be unique to a particular situation. But admittedly, *crossdisciplinary* and *interdisciplinary* are often taken as synonyms. For that matter, *crossdisciplinary* is often used as I use *pluridisciplinary*.

Problem 1. Everyone (Nearly) Already Believes in Interdisciplinary Education

Especially in the United States, where colleges and universities have a long tradition of elective education and requirements for widespread distribution of courses, especially for undergraduate degrees, calls for interdisciplinary efforts may be greeted with some combination of "What's all the fuss about?" or "Yes, of course; that's what everyone believes in."

What everyone believes in usually turns out to be rather indiscriminate mixtures of offerings by currently recognized disciplines determined more by tradition and convenience than by any other rationale. Most undergraduate education in America is thoroughly multidisciplinary. The ease with which most faculty members accept the broaching of the subject of interdisciplinarity is born of this multidisciplinary environment and a fair degree of satisfaction with their own education, which each probably views as having blended various but related disciplines, in a quite sensible pluridisciplinarity.

Too often, then, proposals seem to take on characteristics that faculty members are used to seeing in themselves and their surroundings, with two somewhat different results, both fundamentally complacent:

The larger portion of faculties are likely to listen with varying degrees of patience, but with increasing conviction that what is being talked about already exists, and therefore that nothing much needs to be done differently. The familiar phenomenon of assimilation operates in higher education as well as in other well-established social environments. Seldom are college faculties conservative, let alone reactionary, in any well-considered way. But the complacency that easily assimilates suggestions for change to what already exists has made more than one innovator welcome as the greatest boon a clear-eyed, earnest enemy.

A smaller portion of faculties are likely to become ready adherents of any proposal for joint research or educational innovation, for innovation has a high value among persons who view themselves as a creative minority. Perhaps only the extreme pressure of ongoing responsibilities keeps this portion from being the larger.

Adherents easily won are as easily lost in most causes. In the cause of interdisciplinarity, early adherents are lost for reasons just suggested: misunderstandings about what is involved, and the pre-emptive press of ongoing business. I will return to this latter point in developing Problem 2 and Problem 5. Briefly put: it will be simple for early adherents to decide what innovative efforts are more likely to be sustained and perfection more progressively approached working along familiar, well-established disciplinary lines than along interdisciplinary ones. Further, tangible rewards will be more certain, and this reason alone makes the loyalty of younger faculty members a bitter sacrifice in the last instance. Yet adherents must be sought, and they are likely to be found only among that smaller portion of any faculty, who are in their own ways nonetheless complacent.

My assertion of the double problem of complacency may strike some readers as foolish and easily refuted by the obvious presence on every faculty of a small number of persons who are anything but complacent. These are persons who eagerly seek causes to espouse; these are the misfits. Some of these will be persons of the highest ability, but more are apt to be misfits for good reasons and are likely to remain misfits regardless of the disciplinary or interdisciplinary auspices under which they work. Perhaps the distinction upon which I am insisting had best be left tacit, since little tangible action can be taken on the basis of it anyway. As Mendoza tells Tanner and Straker early in the third act of Bernard Shaw's *Man and Superman,* "Sir: I will be frank with you. Brigandage is abnormal. Abnormal professions attract two classes: those who are not good enough for ordinary bourgeois life and those who are too good for it. We are the dregs and scum, sir: the dregs very filthy, the scum very superior. *Straker.* Take care! some of the dregs'll hear you. *Mendoza.* It does not matter: each brigand thinks himself scum, and likes to hear the others called dregs."

In the face of undoubted complacency, it is an error not to assume that a great deal of interdisciplinary research and education is being done, and especially to label the efforts one finds as ersatz. Regardless of what one wishes to accomplish, good sense dictates surveying the particular ground one occupies and ascertaining to what degree one may build on foundations already settled. A good portion of this book has addressed itself to just such prospects.

The First Dilemma: Timing

One must neither move too fast nor too slowly. That is one of those simple truths, always available and easily stated, but never resolved in any formulary way. In the present setting, it means that acting too quickly will invite strong assimilative responses from the complacent, who, although vaguely uneasy, will act impulsively but firmly, only to find that no action is necessary. To act too slowly is to miss opportunities for building bridges for some smaller portion to cross from complacency to more clearly understood action. But if crossings are to occur frequently, those who cross must take some part in building the bridges. Other persons may be encouraged and lightly goaded; circumstances may be manipulated to make cooperation attractive or at least palatable; but the only bridge across an intellectual chasm is of one's own making.

Problem 2. Everyone (Nearly) Believes in Specialization

No matter how often one indulges the threadbare crack about specialization being "learning more and more about less and less until one knows practically everything about nothing much," the obvious power of specialization is affirmed by the very tempting forth of the crack. In spite of the existence of the elective system, distribution requirements, and a plethora of special programs designed to mix into various stews the substance of the many disciplinary endeavors, specialization, and its administrative concomitant, departmentalization, remains supreme.

The process of fission, not fusion, has created the modern academy. As a contemporary institution, the university is rooted in the first distinction of natural philosophy from philosophy. The ground was prepared when *science* became not simply a Latin word for a kind of practical knowing but a knowing of reality itself; specialization increased, as Malthus held population would, geometrically (even though some critics might claim that its output is less than arithmetic in spite of the seeming profusion of publication).

The dramatic success of twentieth-century physics has overpowered the imaginations of the great body of college and university faculty members, setting a model in most minds for what a discipline should be. Indeed the model is so persuasive that physics today is less a discipline than a family of disciplines, and from one point of view, the very existence of departments of physics might be taken as the most concrete example of interdisciplinary activity.

The process of fission is so powerful that many university departments now claim subdisciplines so distinct and so important to the whole that in graduate schools in which the requirement of minor fields for graduate degrees still exists at all, it commonly is waived, so that students who seek doctorates in economics or anthropology often are offered programs that purport to specialize within their fields and to buttress the whole with only several important subspecialties, also within their fields.

Psychology, perhaps the most successful of the behavioral sciences, is also generally the most clearly subdivided, even though the labels for the subdivisions are scarcely stable. Often social psychology is taken as a prime example of interdisciplinary development; psycholinguistics may be another example. If so, the conditions that made these combinations possible may well have been the strong, continuing tendency toward specialization. And this tendency must be held in mind by anyone interested in interdisciplinarity. Often interdisciplinarity is presented as if it were some sort of antidote for a dreaded poison called specialization. The good sense of such auspices should be carefully weighed.

Almost all faculty members view themselves as members of certain disciplinary fields. As such, they probably know better, both personally and professionally, persons like themselves working in the same fields at other colleges and universities than they know their nondepartmental colleagues in the institutions that employ them. This phenomenon has been widely documented and commented upon. It is especially true in large universities with extensive graduate programs, and in the sciences. No expert in spectral physics takes the accomplishments of his or her chosen specialty lightly, nor can afford to, even though he or she may be acutely aware of its shortcomings; for him or her the solutions to these very failings are both the property and the future of his or her field. In spite of the waxing and waning of success and popularity, not necessarily synonymous, and occasional realignments, the thrust of specialization remains a strong article of faith. It is strong because for most faculty members its efficacy is well demonstrated.

Nor must the accoutrements of specialization be taken lightly, such as the scholarly journals and articles on which to a very large degree the promotion and prestige of individual faculty members depend. The good opinion of their disciplinary colleagues on other campuses has long been of more immediate moment to most faculty members than that of their immediate collegiate fellows in other disciplines. The validation of their own worth rests with the symbols jointly controlled by the cross-collegiate fraternity. In the situation of tightening budgets on the campuses of the mid-1970s the lines of disciplinary control are being strengthened as more and more tenure and promotion committees, compelled by straitened means, become exceedingly careful in making their decisions. Increasingly these decisions are more heavily influenced than ever by the response of "outside evaluators"; only specialists detached from the immediate departmental corporality within which individuals work can render fairly the requisite opinions.

In short, there is a distinctly political face to the circumstances in which interdisciplinary efforts must thrive, or not. Most faculty members dislike the idea that their activities may be governed in any part by considerations labeled "political" and consequently reserve the label for the activities of others. Thus a firmly committed disciplinarian is apt to see his or her own activities as properly guided by the demands of science and those of professed interdisciplinarians to be opportunistic, that is, political as he or she sees it. These sorts of problems will be examined further below.

The tendency just mentioned is reinforced by an often firm and sincere conviction that interdisciplinarity is apt to be sheer dabbling. Given the assumptions of the efficacy of specialization, what else can it be? Of course multidisciplinary efforts toward pluridisciplinary-educated undergraduates may be the most immediate concrete referent for such convictions. Even those who teach introductory courses in well-established disciplines, courses that often require a survey of the subspecialties of the discipline, are apt to be the least respected persons in their own departments and are often the youngest. For persons who have made solid contributions are those who have developed a limited aspect of the discipline in such a way that they have transcended the elementary level necessary for introductory teaching and have earned the right to concentrate on the limited aspects in which they have demonstrated their superiority.

If the attitude mentioned occurs within disciplines, certainly its dynamics will extend into enterprises that seek to mix disciplines, especially for the benefit of students who are themselves tyros. So strong is the argument, that many faculty members find such teaching or even such research threatening and will undertake it only as a member of a team on which they can serve as experts in limited aspects of the whole.

The Second Dilemma: The Part and the Whole
Into this discussion of problems growing from the strong commitment to specialization, introducing the notion of a team highlights a

particular reticence. Most recognize the claim that the whole is greater than the sum of its parts, but few wish to take responsibility for the whole, whatever it may be in respect to any particular parts. Most will accept some whole; indeed the very notion of "discipline" is such. The very idea of interdisciplinarity may for many persons represent a claim so extensive that they shrink in becoming modesty. It is as if someone whispered to them, "Then shall you be as gods knowing good from evil."

The dilemma then is to realign part-whole relations in such a way as to countenance and even to encourage continued specialization. The picture of interdisciplinary efforts as leading to fresh specialties is for many faculty members much more attractive than the idea that specialties as such are simple no longer germane to serious problem-solving. In saying this I wish to emphasize the importance of considering the strong attachment college and university faculty members have to disciplines and the sort of resulting perplexities that might arise for interdisciplinarity. I do not mean to suggest that there is a particular pattern for resolving these difficulties that will in all cases prove the most desirable.

Problem 3. Interdisciplinarity May Occur on Various Levels of Higher Education and Consequently Involves Choices of Level for Concentration

That interdisciplinary efforts may occur on the undergraduate, graduate, or postgraduate level seems too apparent to bear mentioning. But at times even obvious choices carry with them complicating elements.

Part of the difficulty is the continued use of the term *interdisciplinary* as a genus to refer to a number of distinguishable activities. At this general level, everyone (nearly) believes in interdisciplinarity and thinks first of undergraduate education, which proceeds in the United States in a multidisciplinary fashion toward a more-or-less clearly recognized pluridisciplinary goal. For some interested in interdisciplinarity, the status quo of undergraduate education will simply be confounding; for others, it will offer opportunity for making that education more rationally pluridisciplinary.

For innovators most concerned with the undergraduate level, crossdisciplinary efforts seem to be most promising. The advance of specialization has rendered many disciplines simply too complex for undergraduates to master, even at elementary levels of the disciplines and especially on the lower levels of a college career. Further, the immediate world into which most college students will graduate is offering fewer and fewer parallels for the application of the most successfully specialized disciplines and, even in the immediate context of the college classroom, offering fewer clear instances to use illustratively.

If one were discussing these issues in the metaphor of the stockbrokers, one might offer crossdisciplinary studies, in which sequences of courses or learning experiences are organized so as to focus on some current social-political-economic problem, as a growth issue. Some such undergraduate programs are discussed elsewhere in this book.

These efforts are interdisciplinary in that they bring to bear several lines of disciplinary inquiry in some common context for some particular purpose. Sometimes teams of teachers are involved; sometimes individuals seek to discuss with undergraduates or to arrange field problems in such a way that several disciplines must be mingled in order to make even initial analyses possible. These means of interdisciplinarity raise, and often beg, the question of just where integration will occur. In various courses? In a whole sequence that a student goes through? In several such sequences? In the solving, at least tentatively, of the problems set for particular students or groups of students? Or in the minds of the individuals, hopefully, but no place else?

In general the aims of crossdisciplinarity seem to be to create persons whose first allegiance is to responding to immediate, socially relevant problems, and for whom the various disciplines are existing resources to be tapped when they promise to yield applicable tools, insights, or evidence, and never learned simply for their own sakes. The latter stipulation flies directly in the teeth of the prima facie claims to the extrinsic disinterest the most sharply defined disciplines profess on behalf of pure science.

In a very real sense crossdisciplinary education is but a contemporary claimant to the role of a liberal education as it has been expressed for generations in American education. Throughout the nineteenth century a traditional, classical curriculum was assumed essential to the formation of the socially responsible, flexible person. With the rise of the elective system in the early twentieth century, such a person was held to be best formed by individual choice, with of course some judiciously general guidelines. This system was well adapted to the growth of strong disciplinary specialties. But crossdisciplinarity holds that neither tradition or individual preference will suffice in a rapidly changing, troubled world. Two apparent facts govern educational strategy: the impossibility of mastering a significant body of knowledge that will not become obsolete nearly immediately, and the press of problems that threaten to engulf not only the foundations of what we have come to consider civilized culture but humankind itself. Thus problem-orientation and adaptability need to be stressed directly.

A few would argue that the work of undergraduate students in problem-centered, crossdisciplinary education potentially is useful directly in solving these problems. Such claims in the United States were popular in the late 1960s, when students worked in political campaigns, in volunteer social agencies, and in projects designed to educate some groups of persons outside the colleges or universities. These sorts of activities, of course, fly directly in the face of the assumptions of formal education as only preparation and often in the face of well-established interests in business and government.

Even if no such claims are made for direct efficacy of undergraduate education organized around problems in such a way as to encourage students to learn selectively and applicatively the lessons of various disciplines, the interaction between the college undergraduate student and the everyday stream of social, economic, and political life will be deepened. Those interested in any manifestation of interdisciplinary education must be prepared to deal with the issues growing out of the sharpened awareness of education as ongoing social activity rather than separated reflective activity.

One might conclude quickly that, while graduate education remains strongly disciplinary, undergraduate education is moving and should move more strongly toward interdisciplinarity, in its crossdisciplinary sense, building on the traditions of the elective system and required distributions of courses offered for liberal arts degrees, especially since contemporary disciplines have become much too complex for undergraduates to cope with anyway. But one will uncover immediately a number of difficulties with such a tidy solution to selecting levels.

In universities with extensive graduate programs, undergraduate work in a discipline is usually deemed mandatory for advanced work that will become even more specialized. If these programs are to continue, at least portions of undergraduate preparation must be allowed to remain as training and proving grounds. In some disciplines, especially the natural and physical sciences, for an undergraduate student to undertake crossdisciplinary study may constitute a decision not to enter graduate school. The degree to which such thinking may permeate other disciplines is more difficult to conclude, but in the United States the model of the physical sciences especially is so powerful as to encourage general emulation.

Again, many persons who pursue graduate degrees are teaching undergraduate students, either as departmental assistants or part-time instructors or as members of faculties of two-year or four-year colleges. These persons are often motivated to find materials immediately applicable to their pedagogical tasks. The pressure on all teachers in institutions of higher education in the United States to hold or at least to be working toward graduate degrees, preferably doctorates, does not seem to be abating in spite of Jacques Barzun's brilliant essay, "The Ph.D. Octopus," written nearly forty years ago, and all the similar voices since.

The difficult tensions between the roles many graduate students assume as students of a discipline and as teachers, or future teachers, of undergraduate students is a force that will work to keep graduate education in America resembling undergraduate, or vice versa more likely. These tensions resulted in an apparently strong move toward the development a decade ago of Doctor of Arts degrees, degrees designed to be less specialized and more pedagogically oriented. The movement seems to have very quickly abated, however, probably because most graduate faculties had little interest in the fundamental problems involved and strong interest in continuing what they were already doing. These conditions were intensified by the apparent inevitability that a Doctor of Arts degree would be considered, in spite of any official proclamations to the contrary, to be a second-class degree pursued for second-class purposes by second-class persons.

Further, ironically enough, many existing graduate degrees are interdisciplinary, at least in the multi- and pluridisciplinary senses. On the master's level many programs developed since World War II were designed to apply to particular problems or sets of circumstances the methods and materials of several disciplines. Thus departments or schools of public administration, some with only programs for the master's degree, exist to bring to bear the disciplines of economics, sociology, psychology, political science, and others on the sorts of problems suggested by the title. Master's degrees in family studies, ethnic studies, museum management, and even hotel and restaurant management are common, and similar programs may become even more common. In short, the master's degree generally is becoming more and more like the successful model of the Master's of Business Administration.

The trend suggested is made evident in a peculiar way that is not often commented upon: some of the most successful disciplines no longer give master's degrees, that is, these disciplines accept students only to work toward the doctorate and retain the master's degree, if they retain it at all, only to confer on unsuccessful candidates for the doctorate.

In working out concerns with interdisciplinarity, one cannot ignore the strong interaction between the undergraduate and the graduate levels, nor can one ignore the apparently strong societal pressure for advanced degrees or certificates that will be awarded to persons especially prepared with, hopefully, the sort of flexibility necessary to work in business, governmental, and cultural institutions.

The analysis up to this point may suggest a dual system: cross-disciplinary education at both the undergraduate and master's degree levels, and continued disciplinary education for very specialized graduate work leading to the doctoral degree. But that answer, if it is one, scarcely strikes me as pat. I intend it mainly to emphasize the complexity that must be dealt with. In any decision about interdisciplinary education, the levels and interactions must be considered carefully.

One may arrive at another initially simple conclusion. Since interdisciplinarity, in the strong or specific sense, depends on the mastery of at least one specialty, the postdoctoral level may be the most appropriate for intensive development of the necessary skills and research. One advantage that postdoctoral education has for the purposes of interdisciplinarity is that it is much less formalized, simply because it has not been extensive enough to encourage educational administrators to formalize it.

One can argue, of course, that postdoctoral education is quite extensive and strong simply because it is not formalized; it is the natural, ongoing activity of every dedicated scholar. If so, then the question for those interested in interdisciplinarity is, how can the sorts of interactions that will lead to research and personal development be encouraged in both formal and informal ways?

If interdisciplinary research depends on one person developing sufficient skill to move freely in two or more disciplines, then more fellowships will have to be granted for such purposes. If interdisciplinary research depends on the cooperative effort of several persons from different disciplines working as teams, then institutes funded for such special work may be necessary. In either case, or both, such efforts will compete directly with similar efforts along strictly disciplinary lines. And at this point we have circled back to what I have called the second problem with its attendant dilemma.

The Third Dilemma: One Cannot Start Anywhere but Must Start Somewhere
Inevitably a person will concentrate his or her interdisciplinary efforts on some academic level or another. But the effects of doing so will have strong implications for his or her activities, and the activities of others, on other levels.

Problem 4. Interdisciplinarians Must Persuade Others to Cooperate with Them

In general academicians do not much care for the idea of persuasion, especially when that notion is applied to what they consider to be the decisions they may make about their academic lives. If this judgment is correct, then the necessity of interdisciplinarians to persuade others to change their established patterns of activity, and the strong inclinations that go with their disciplinary allegiances, in itself constitutes a serious problem.

Of course interdisciplinarians may well share the attitude common to academicians generally, that is, that politics corrupts science and is to be shunned as far as possible. How then may cooperation be attained? As the result of the detached marshaling of facts in such a manner that claims may be verified as true. Presumably when the truth is demonstrated, persons of good will must act consistently with it.

This pristine view of human behavior of course will not stand a clear-eyed examination of the conduct of most departmental or college faculty meetings, but nonetheless exerts a powerful pull, especially when arguments may turn from the settings in which the participants are so familiar with the topics and the terms that they can overlook the influence of prestige, uncertainty, and sheer guesswork that commonly occurs in making curricular decisions and even in setting priorities for research programs. Stubbornness and sheer fatigue are apt to assume as important roles in departmental meetings as in labor negotiations.

Facts do not speak for themselves (and are not abundant in comparing disciplinarity with interdisciplinarity), nor do demonstrations often obtain a clarity and finality that obviate interpretations. To believe that one can proceed to build toward change, especially change that takes concerted cooperation from others, without persuading, is either to be at best naive or at worst hypocritical. The hypocrite holds that others are politically motivated and attempt to persuade, while he or she, possessed simply by pure motives, only demonstrates.

Much of the current literature setting forth the case for interdisciplinarity has a decidedly millennial flavor. The vision is simple and the drama that enacts it old and familiar, when its thematic content is brought into relief.

The first theme: higher education, as it is now constituted, has entered its last days. Its external connections with the society that sustains it have been allowed to atrophy by a self-indulgence that has increasingly made the production of knowledge esoteric rather than relevant to the very real problems besetting society. In the late 1960s, when college enrollments were burgeoning and the students exceedingly restless, these observations were fueled with arguments born of intense concern by students for the larger problems of society; in the mid-1970s, with students increasingly worried about employment and, in the United States at least, with curves of population that predict slackening enrollments soon to be followed by sharp drops in what has long been considered the normal age range of students, these observations are being fueled with arguments that academicians have been living in a fool's paradise of expansion and can no longer seem to prosper in spite of unconcern for social relevancy.

The second theme: higher education must be reborn, and the rebirth necessitates capturing again what has been lost sight of, that is, truth is single; what is true must be a whole. In discipline after discipline, the argument goes, specialization has run its course. The challenge of the future is creating new disciplines, most readily available in concerns neglected because they fall between existing disciplines. Or, in a slightly different variation, interdisciplinary efforts will bring insights that may transform existing fields, bringing theories that will unify what is now valid but discrete.

Obviously I have exaggerated these arguments for the sake of clarity and emphasis, even at the risk of giving offense to some serious, systematic, and complex thinkers. Because of this risk, I have not illustrated the analysis with a specific critique of particular pieces of literature but have merely invited those interested in interdisciplinarity to be alert to see if a millennial vision does often lurk, at least faintly, in arguments for that interest. Enthusiasm must be generated or interest will not be sustained. Inevitably interest in change must take present circumstances as seriously ill-constituted and hold out the prospect of a better future. Enthusiasm, especially when cooperation is needed from a larger body of fellows, can scarcely keep silent.

The Fourth Dilemma: What Attracts, Repels

Any movement, even a localized effort on behalf of interdisciplinary education and research in a single college or university, needs to be initiated and maintained. To maintain the movement, the loyalty of early adherents must be continued, new adherents must be recruited, and the cooperation, or at least the acquiescence of the larger community within which the group exists, must be encouraged. Unfortunately, the sorts of persuasion conducive to these various ends are not often compatible. Arguments that help maintain the loyalty of an ingroup may irritate and even enrage those not closely allied. For example, the most readily available strategy for group solidarity is to populate the setting with vicious enemies or at least with boobs whose opinions do not count.

In arguing for interdisciplinarity, a strong case for the aridity of existing specialties may win early adherents. Once won, these will probably continue to scorn the esoteric and irrelevant, and yet the larger community within which the group must mature and flourish will remain for some time composed of hard-working, dedicated specialists. The ranks of most college administrations are apt to contain many persons who have long since rested the case for their own academic merit on the accomplishments of disciplinary work.

To be a scorned, prophetic minority may be the quickest way to gain the attention of potential adherents and to fix the solidarity of an initial group, but no "saving remnant" hopes to remain a remnant.

Of all the dilemmas that face interdisciplinarians, this one seems to me the most serious and difficult. Interdisciplinarity can be presented as part of the normal, evolving academic whole. It may claim to strengthen disciplinarity, not supplant it. But on such a basis it will probably engender little animosity and little enthusiastic support from a core group who will dedicate extreme efforts, take serious personal risks in foregoing work more certainly designed to achieve professional advancement; in short, the sort of group necessary to establish a thoroughgoing, imaginative program. But a more militant approach is apt to leave enthusiasts cut off from institutional support.

Problem 5. Interdisciplinary Research and Education Must Be Administered

There are two sets of administrative problems, doubled. Interdisciplinary research and education must be administered and must function in a larger administrative setting of the college or university. In addition programs must be established, and once established, maintained administratively.

Leadership that accomplishes the tasks necessary to establish a program is not always best for maintaining an established program. The problems alluded to are much like those discussed in the preceding section. But leadership, once established, tends to perpetuate itself, even though it may not be well adapted to shifting circumstances. One advantage of a participative group in which hierarchical relations are not clearly fixed is that leadership functions are more easily distributed and rotated.

In many ways, difficulties that may beset interdisciplinarians are of the same sort that face any program being established and maintained in colleges and universities. These difficulties are often exacerbated by professors who tend to disparage administrative functions and those who perform them; that tendency, which is common enough to be frequently observed by anyone with collegiate experience, is especially apt to find expression from those who are attracted to interdisciplinary programs because they are to some degree rebellious and lack adherence to established enterprises and to the administrators, on departmental, college, or university levels, who symbolize them.

Many administrative problems will be eased if early in interdisciplinary enterprises an existing administrator or two are recruited as a part of the program. Since administrators are from one point of view at least marginal persons, persons often disparaged for lack of insight, foresight, or courage, they may be more easily made a part of new programs, including interdisciplinary programs, than one might think initially. In fact administrators might be especially apt to support interdisciplinarity, since they have by becoming administrators probably ceased to function as specialists in the various disciplines, but retain some convictions of the usefulness of their disciplines and, forced to deal with representatives of varied interests, to see the relationships of their disciplines to others.

Government in colleges and universities tends to depend on both benevolent despotism and committee-centered democracy. The interactions of these are ordinarily perplexing, but the higher in the administrative hierarchies one goes, the more the former dominates.

Internally, participatory forms build enthusiasm and potentially are more innovative and critical, but they are also slow; and often decisions, rather than being the best critical choices, become vague compromises. On the other hand, responsibility for final decisions resting in a single person gains the advantage of quicker and bolder action, but may well sacrifice loyalty or may found loyalty on personal authority and continued success. When either erodes, the group tends to founder and often to disintegrate. Participatory forms, however, may also founder and disintegrate simply because of indecisiveness.

Externally, administrators and other outsiders respect solid, participatory groups, but like to deal with the stability and clarity more often represented by a single spokesperson. A group that appears to put forward continually differing requests by different spokespersons is not apt to be taken seriously for long.

The fundamental question may be reduced to this: how much efficiency does the group need or can it afford to sacrifice in favor of building loyalty, loyalty that may serve well in repeated attempts to find viable forms of interdisciplinary cooperation? I assume that such forms will not be quickly and easily found, and that repeated failure is apt to occur and needs to be tolerated.

The basic function of college and university administration is to get and distribute money. Inevitably decisions about research and education will be made, sometimes quite consciously and sometimes haphazardly. But in terms of educational and research policy, the function of higher administrative offices is to maintain and serve as a filtering system for innovation. The latter word, even though often written large these days as a motto, refers in practice to slowly developing pressure that may deflect slightly the evolutionary stream in the major parts of the structure of a college or university.

The task of keeping nourished the existing programs in any institution of higher education is so enormous that administrators have very little discretionary money. A worthy institutional goal, quite apart from any thought of change in interdisciplinary directions, would be to refuse to allocate the complete resources to the sheer maintaining of existing functions, but this goal is exceedingly difficult to achieve under any circumstances and will be even more difficult to achieve in the future, considering what public and private funding of educational institutions seems to hold.

Departmental administrators in traditional disciplines know that funds for new programs are difficult to find. Their knowledge makes them competitors for new funds and suspicious of new programs as future competitors. This suspicion will be intensified if the advocates of the new programs seem to be making claims that would obviate what they consider to be their traditional functions. If those claims are allowed to stand, then their own competitive positions are weakened.

In short, advocates of interdisciplinary research and education should think very carefully about the advantages and disadvantages of striking poses that may be viewed as threatening to established interests. Of course one may always view oneself as a wolf, ecologically valuable in weeding out the winter-weakened and diseased from the herd of deer. Some of the herd, however, may turn out to be old bucks with sharp hooves and the wolf but a pup.

Most wolves were probably puppies first, and all puppies are adorable, or seem so especially to those outside the family. Funding agencies, governmental and private, frequently see themselves as being primarily adapted to encouraging new growth rather than maintaining well-established research or educational functions. Often such agencies announce special goals to be achieved and listen gladly to proposals to meet these goals in fresh ways. In either case interdisciplinarians probably have special advantages if arguments made elsewhere in this book are valid. These advantages of course should be pressed in seeking outside funds. But in all cases the active cooperation of the administration of one's own institution is vital. Outside agencies simply are not interested in supporting enterprises that cannot count on active support from within their own immediate environment.

Money in an institutional setting transmutes into various forms: space, released time, and clerical aid, for example, all important to fledgling programs. With administrative cooperation, rather extensive enterprises can be founded without large outlays of new funds, if some existing resources of the sorts mentioned can be diverted, even temporarily. Space has a high symbolic as well as pragmatic value, but is so scarce and highly prized in most institutions that it is often difficult to divert.

Although "a man's reach must exceed his grasp, or what's a heaven for?" in the immediate context, programs should nonetheless be carefully matched to resources. Risking is important, but some risks are better than others, and some are so destined to fail that clear analysis will show them not to be risks at all. In such cases one may decide that the experience will somehow yield useful results even though the larger program will be short-lived. For example, I once witnessed a highly innovative teaching program founded at a college with what its sponsors considered very generous support. The support was generous if looked at simply as a total figure or as a portion of the ability of the relevant administrators to commit funds in the particular circumstances. Yet the funding for this very intensive, highly individualized teaching program was just a little more than one-half the average credit-hour cost in that particular college. In short, the program operated for several years on voluntary faculty overload, but there came an end to the simple energy on which that resource depended, and also an end to the program.

Perhaps one of the most serious administrative problems stems from the adaptation of the system of evaluating and rewarding faculty members within the structure of disciplinary departments. The difficulties may prove preemptive for younger, untenured faculty members with low rank and relatively low salaries. Interdisciplinary teaching and research are apt to be highly time-consuming and productive of ends that are not as readily assessed as those of more traditional programs. The primary responsibility for breaking through this impasse lies with interdisciplinarians. Departmental chairpersons, deans, and vice-presidents may be understandably cool if they are simply asked to exempt from ordinary evaluation persons who are active interdisciplinarily, but may well accept, at least tentatively, concrete proposals for alternatives that will enable negative as well as positive judgments to be made.

The Fifth Dilemma: The Pragmatic
Power does corrupt, but without power little can be accomplished.

Power corrupts because it must be used. If used, choices will be made that obviate, for the moment at least, the alternatives *not* chosen, with whatever degrees of virtue these possess; and power creates circumstances in which projects must be judged and can never be judged completely fairly.

College and university faculty members often talk as if they would like to live in a set of institutional circumstances in which all conditions for success or failure would be in each instance present and all points of view considered equally in assessing programs. Who would not? But very few will.

Problem 6. Higher Education Involves Students and Students Must Be Involved

One of the lamest jokes on a college campus, but not so lame as to fail to hobble forth consistently to gather its quota of feeble smiles, is the professor's weary lament: we could run this place well if there just were no students around. Seemingly with that spirit, this chapter has been composed. Students may be in the background of any mention of education, but only discreetly, tacitly.

Such an attitude misrepresents not only what should be but what actually is. The impact of student opinion and activity has always been substantial and seemed especially intense in the late 1960s and early 1970s. It will continue to be so.

In the expansionist atmosphere of education in North America and Europe of the 1960s, intensified by obvious student unrest, often generated by social-economic-political circumstances, new programs, new schools, new colleges, and even new universities were founded with what now seems to be amazing rapidity. Some of these changes are discussed elsewhere in this book. But in Europe a great deal of the energy of change was directed against elitism in higher education, and elitism was identified with an aloof disciplinarianism, that is, aloof from the needs of the greater portion of a society's people. In the United States elitism was also a focal point, but much less clearly so, and the elitism was identified with a close link between the availability of university education and especially research to restricted portions of the economic community. The reaction was often in the interest of making the power attributed to research more widely available and even to judge that some interests, for example the protection of the environment, were legitimate and others, for example exploitation of natural resources, were not legitimate and hence should not be supported at all. Regardless, the impact was to cause higher education at least nominally to be more conscious of its social responsibilities. If being more socially responsible means applying knowledge to problems of the larger society, one should observe that applied fields have always tended to be crossdisciplinary and its practitioners pluridisciplined; engineering curricula and practices generally are premier examples.

One may readily assume, with the winding-down of the war in Vietnam and the increasing economic unrest compounded of inflation and unemployment, that the drive of the student revolt of the late 1960s has waned. And so it has. But one should not conclude that the forces unleashed have disappeared or may not be reinforced by rather different student interests.

Two factors, at least in the United States, must be considered: first, the expected sharp decline in that portion of the population traditionally considered college aged, i.e., eighteen to twenty-four years old; and second, the increasing anxiety of students to be employed—simply holding a college degree is no longer the assurance of employment it was a half-dozen years ago.

A great many changes in higher education responsive to expected—and in many instances actual—enrollment declines can already be observed. Most obvious are the burgeoning programs designed to widen the appeal of and availability of college-level programs to groups not traditionally expected to populate student bodies in large numbers. Attracting older students by expanding the campus into the larger business and social environment is apt to turn educational programs sharply toward more immediately applicable learning. Professional education has long tended to be crossdisciplinary—journalism, social work, and medicine are good examples. Even nonprofessional programs are becoming much more interested in proving that they are relevant to persons deeply engaged in the day-to-day life of the society and the economy. The assumption being pressed in many instances is that a well-educated person is not so much one who is prepared specifically to fill a job niche as one who has a multidisciplinary education in situations, which has caused him or her to organize a variety of tools and materials to focus on a number of discrete problems. In short, the motto taking shape is "adaptability" for a rapidly changing future. Many of these claims will be tested in the near future, and the claims are per se open to interpretation as demands for some form or another of interdisciplinary research and education.

The Sixth Dilemma: New Lamps and Old
Interdisciplinarity presupposes disciplinarity, and if one truly wants new lamps that person should want to retain the old. Although the trick may be akin to having one's cake and eating it too, precisely that may be mandatory. The traditional separation of the pure and applied sciences will no longer quite do. Both will have to be keenly attentive to the other if either is to prosper.

If much of the student protest of the last decade has been aimed in one way or another at elitism, we must be conscious of the likelihood of creating a new elitism, one born of an attitude that sees the pragmatic necessity of expanding the market for higher education and meeting the interest in socially and economically relevant learning, but considers these things the price of the quiet survival of "real" education and research, which will go on quite independently in the true academy that must, unfortunately, coexist with the more raucous, younger, less worthy sibling, who of course will lack the rights of primogeniture.

Interdisciplinarians must consider carefully whether their programs will flourish if they progress apart from the traditional disciplines. Further, as good disciplinarians also, persons attracted to various forms of interdisciplinarity will want to consider the contrary question: can the traditional disciplines flourish without the sorts of innovation that interdisciplinarity promises? Of course if no such promises seem imminent, perhaps the goals of interdisciplinarity in those particular cases need to be reexamined.

Students and younger faculty members are often the most innovative members of academic communities simply because they do not know enough to keep immediate needs and feelings subordinated to well-established, ongoing tasks. Their expressions of needs may seldom result in patterns from which perfect products may be cut immediately; but if these products are perfectible, surely new patterns must be evolved.

Conclusion

The discussion of problems in this chapter has scarcely been definitive. Although at times one might find prescriptive tendencies here, these are more in the spirit of probing to raise responses that might help readers see problems in the concrete terms that they will have to deal with, than of offering ready solutions. In some version or another, however, I am strongly convinced that the six problems presented here must be addressed by anyone projecting an interdisciplinary program within the modern college or university.

Interdisciplinary Programs in the United States

Some Paradigms*

Hans Flexner and Gerard A. Hauser

The contexts for interdisciplinary programs and studies are many. They include freshman and senior seminars, interdepartmental majors, core curricula, interdisciplinary clusters, and interdisciplinary colleges.[1] There is, furthermore, a corresponding diversity of institutional types—Hampshire, Green Bay, Bowling Green State, Redlands, Santa Cruz, Evergreen, Brockport (SUNY), Michigan State, and many others—that support in varying degrees such interdisciplinary arrangements.

Another distinction pertains to the relationship between the disciplines and the curriculum. In one major orientation the disciplines are considered *the* source of the curriculum. "If learning time is to be economized," writes Philip Phenix, "*all* material should come from the disciplines, and *none* from other sources."[2] For Phenix, the authentic disciplines are approximations of "the given orders of reality," and reveal as well the paths by which one may come to realize truth, "which is simply to say that the disciplines are the sole proper source of the curriculum."[3]

There are others, however, who contend that while the disciplines may be a source for the potential content of the curriculum, it is the individual human being who is the primary referent in curriculum development. For proponents of this view, the main purpose of a general education is not to provide training and methodological expertise in the disciplines, but to lead the individual to a "discovery and appreciation . . . of himself and others and the world about him."[4] In

---

*The introductory section and the analysis of the first two paradigms is written by Hans Flexner, the analysis of the third paradigm by Gerard A. Hauser.

this context the basic questions are not, What knowledge is necessary to get by in a technological society? but instead, What does it mean to be a human being? What does it mean to know? How do human beings live together? What does freedom mean? Evolution? Peace? Death? War? The essential referent both in raising such questions and in interpreting the answers is the individual.[5]

The distinction is of primary importance. So long as the curriculum is designed and taught by instructors who are not after all subject to it, and so long as the students who are expected to experience the curriculum have no voice in its development, it remains something imposed upon them from the outside. Although this can be as true of interdisciplinary as of disciplinary courses, the former are generally considered innovative and consequently perceived as a more viable context for interaction.

In addition to differences in contexts, institutional types, and curricular/disciplinary relationships, interdisciplinary programs and courses vary in their objectives, curricular emphases and arrangements, faculty/administrative strategies, and evaluative procedures. Among the more commonly encountered objectives are the following: to prepare humane generalists and cultural "comprehensivists"; to encourage value-centeredness; to promote individualized, self-directed, active learning; to infuse the spirit of the humanities throughout the college; to strengthen the commitment to liberal education; to develop the aesthetic capabilities of students; to integrate knowledge in the lower-division humanities and science courses; to combine the humanistic with the social-science approaches in the investigation of international relations; to educate a "new type" of engineer who will be competent in design and who will build his career on a union of technology and the humanities.

Joint student/teacher preparation of syllabi and reading lists; joint discussions of teaching procedures and evaluation; development of a multidisciplinary study center for the humanities, utilizing a theme-centered, interinstitutional approach—these represent a few curricular arrangements. Others include small group-learning sessions involving interdisciplinary topics; summer seminars for training teachers and potential teachers in interdisciplinary approaches; freshman preceptorials; the elimination of distribution requirements, GPAs, and credits; joint student/teacher development of a series of interdisciplinary seminars for general studies programs; cooperative effort among three colleges to link their academic resources to the resources of their region in an attempt to deal with regional problems in an interdisciplinary manner.

Evaluation is at best a difficult task. It becomes even more so when attempts are made to compare interdisciplinary and control groups on conventional forms of achievement, since the former are frequently concerned about and deal with emphases, knowledge, and skills that are beyond the scope of a single discipline. Although interdisciplinary programs and courses often rely on methods and instruments used in more conventional situations, their evaluative procedures are characterized by a high degree of faculty and student input, by greater utilization of consultants and off-campus visitors, and by attempts to integrate evaluative criteria and methods in the early stages of program planning.

As in all curricular departures and innovations, it is finally the faculty—their attitudes, philosophical preferences, and truth strategems—upon whom the burden of success or failure falls. However, their task and their attitude toward that task are influenced greatly by the nature and extent of administrative support. Here are some faculty/administrative practices and strategies identified in a number of interdisciplinary contexts: faculty development specifically for interdisciplinary teaching; released time and reduced loads for faculty to prepare, individually and cooperatively, for interdisciplinary teaching; financial support, when required, for interdisciplinary study; faculty and student workshops, seminars, and conferences that utilize university-wide facilities; increased exposure of faculty to interdisciplinary problem-oriented education on a number of different campuses; faculty-development summer workshops, retreats, and training sessions; the establishment of integrative studies committees; opportunities to teach new courses dealing with interdisciplinary aspects within areas of expertise; random grouping of faculty offices to reduce departmental competition and jealousy and to facilitate open and friendly exchange of ideas and interdisciplinary efforts.

The foregoing account of the diversity of interdisciplinary purposes, contexts, and practices is not of course intended to be in any way complete; the Appendix, "A Selective Listing of Interdisciplinary Programs," and the literature quoted there will provide the interested reader with numerous sources. The purpose of that account is to provide the reader with some idea of the distinctions and variety of interpretations, as well as the range of operations, that are associated with the notion and practice of interdisciplinarity. Some of these will be recognized in the models or paradigms that follow.

The three paradigms included in this chapter were selected for several reasons. The first, because it represents one of a very few programs that seriously involves faculty, students, and administrators from many of the graduate and professional units of a major university known for its long-time commitment to disciplinary as well as interdisciplinary research. The second paradigm represents one of the most radical and comprehensive curricular, instructional, and organizational innovations undertaken by any college in recent years. The third paradigm represents one of the comprehensive programs conducted exclusively at the graduate level and designed to integrate the humanities into problem-oriented study and research of a transdisciplinary nature.

Paradigm A

Columbia University has long been known for its undergraduate general education program, which has been described, lauded or criticized, and emulated in one fashion or another. But the present formulation is, partly for that reason, not directly concerned with the undergraduate program; its focus is on general education, interdisciplinary developments at the graduate and professional levels.

The University Committee on General Education serves as the main advisory body of the program and includes among its members representatives from the major academic departments, the various professional schools, the chairmen of the Humanities and Contemporary Civilization programs, and the University administration.[6] The Committee deals with all general-education programs at the University. At the undergraduate level this consists of Humanities A and B, Contemporary Civilization A, and an optional course in the upper division, Oriental Civilizations and Humanities. The program also offers University courses in general education open to advanced undergraduate, graduate, and professional school students. Important for the present volume are the interdisciplinary seminars in the graduate and professional schools.

The expanded program comprised twelve pilot courses in 1973–74, thirty-one in 1974–75, forty-six in 1975–76, and fifty-three in 1976–77, with 42 percent of all general-education enrollments being at the graduate level. Nonetheless the Committee believes that there are still too few courses and programs at the graduate and professional levels designed to bring together specialists and advanced graduate students from a variety of disciplines to explore interdisciplinary relationships and their larger implications for teaching and research.[7]

Based in part on experience accumulated in some sixty years of undergraduate general education, the program has established a number of criteria applicable to its graduate and professional courses. Areas of knowledge should be generally relevant and useful and should have a "perennial human significance"; they should not be the initial step in the development of research competence in a particular discipline; they should be interdisciplinary and bring the insights and skills of one discipline to bear on problems important to another; they should "seek to elicit the value questions or human options implicit in various fields; they may very well provide an historical or cross-cultural perspective on contemporary problems."[8] Some of these courses are new and have been created especially for the program; others have been given since the inception of the program; and still others were existing departmental courses that satisfy some of the criteria of general education.

Essentially the graduate and professional programs are comprised of and organized according to the following activities: the Thursday General Education Seminars; the Seminars in the Professions and the Humanities; the Special Lectures, Programs and Conferences in the Humanities; the Society of Fellows in the Humanities.[9]

Thursday General Education Seminars
During the past few years these seminars have examined educational activities and policies. The 1973–74 seminars concentrated on the place of general education in the University and in society, while the following year was devoted to an examination of practical examples as the base for a clearer definition. "Professionalism and Humane Values" was the focus of the fall 1975 seminars, which were succeeded in the spring of 1976 by seminars concerned with "Science and Human Values." The eleven sessions devoted to these seminars were very effective in attracting faculty from both the professional schools and the arts and sciences. The fall 1976 seminars, which considered "Liberalism and Liberal Education," dealt with the relations between the two traditions and their historical and philosophical foundations.

The proceedings of these seminars are printed in *Seminar Reports,* the demand for and publication of which has more than doubled over the year. The utility of these reports is unquestioned, especially for use as texts in classes and seminars that deal with the professions. From the beginning these seminars have been supported by a grant from the Carnegie Corporation, which has also assumed some of the cost of publication.

Seminars in the Professions and the Humanities
Among the most successful experiments, each of these seminars is based in a professional school and hence addresses itself both to the curricula concerns of that school and to the larger social and intellectual issues that characterize these interdisciplinary seminars. Thus profession-school faculty and arts and sciences faculty join in interdisciplinary efforts to investigate problems of mutual interest. Such seminars have been held in the School of International Affairs, the Graduate School of Journalism, the Graduate School of Architecture and Planning, and the College of Physicians and Surgeons. A new seminar was added this year by the Graduate School of Engineering and Applied Science. In view of its scope and its enrollment (in excess of fifty people, including Columbia faculty and students as well as faculty from other institutions and community residents), the seminar has been divided into four working task forces, each of which is responsible for investigating questions of values and ethics in these four areas: Death and Survival, Reproductive Medicine, Behavior Modification, and Neonatology.

As a result of these activities and others, plans are being formulated for the establishment of a new Center for the Study of Health Care and Human Values, which will serve as a regional or possibly a national resource. Since the Center is expected to encompass the Health Services General Education Seminar, the seminar may be able to continue on a permanent basis.

Funded by a grant from the Rockefeller Foundation, these seminars have been unusually effective and indeed of considerable utility to a variety of individuals and groups. A case in point is the new seminar on Professional Ethics in Engineering, housed in the Graduate School of Engineering and Applied Science. An interdisciplinary group of faculty and students will examine case histories and, drawing upon extensive available material, will formulate a new code of ethics for the professional engineer.[10]

Special Lectures, Programs, and Conferences in the Humanities
This year for the first time the General Education Program cooperated with the Departments of Music, of Art History and Archaeology, of English and Comparative Literature, and with the Casa Italiana in sponsoring the first of a possible series of conferences devoted to specific interdisciplinary topics. Of particular interest is the "first, modest effort," the "Piers Plowman Festival," which dealt ostensibly with a fourteenth century text. But,

in actuality, the lectures, seminars, exhibits of art and manuscripts, a medieval cooking class, and a concert of fourteenth century and modern music, turned out to be an interdisciplinary celebration of fourteenth century life and culture. A large number of students, faculty, and curious New Yorkers attended the various events, and the *New York Times* featured the festival in an article carried on the front page of the paper's second section. . . . It was put together primarily by interested graduate students with the help of faculty and members of the General Education Program's staff.[11]

A number of other conferences, symposia, and festivals are already planned for the coming year, including one conference on the topic "Science and Imagination." These conferences are not only relatively inexpensive but they serve as useful vehicles to explore areas of broad interest in an interdisciplinary manner.

Society of Fellows in the Humanities
Among the early plans of the Committee on General Education was one for a program of "Teaching Fellows in the Humanities." In 1975 the Mellon Foundation and the Kenan Trust provided funds for the creation of such a program. The following year the first postdoctoral Teaching Fellows in the Humanities joined the senior faculty and together formed the Columbia Society of Fellows in the Humanities. In an effort to enhance the role of the humanities, the group is exploring and clarifying the relationship of the humanities to the natural and social sciences and to the several professions. The program is also designed to strengthen both the intellectual and academic qualifications of the Fellows, "first, by associating them individually and collectively with some of the finest teaching scholars in the University; second, by involving them in *interdisciplinary programs of their own design;* and third, by affording time and resources to develop independent scholarship within a broadening educational and professional context."[12]

Student Response to the Program
For this survey only those courses and seminars directly encouraged or financially supported by the Committee on General Education are included. While the survey is limited and the information less than exhaustive, the returns are revealing. In a numerical scale of 1 to 5, 1 is very negative and 5 is very positive.

Quality of Instruction:

$1 = 1\%$
$2 = 2\%$
$3 = 8\%$
$4 = 30\%$
$5 = 59\%$

Value of Subject Matter:

$1 = 0$
$2 = 2\%$
$3 = 6\%$
$4 = 25\%$
$5 = 67\%$

Levels of Study:

Freshmen: 4%
Sophomores: 13%
Juniors: 25%
Seniors: 25%
Graduate students, all levels: 33%

Relation of Course to Majors or
  Areas of Concentration:

Integral part: 26%
Directly related: 29%
Indirectly related: 38%
Unrelated: 7%

Comments

Although the General Education program is extensive and involves a growing number of faculty, students, and administrators as well as some faculty from other institutions, its broad goals and specific operations are not at all incompatible with those of the University. The *Seminar Reports,* for example, are the work of a variety of scholars from units throughout the University augmented by a few invited participants of recognized competence. Their quality and utility, both within the University and in a number of other contexts, seems to be assured. While the participants represent a rather remarkable variety of specialties and orientations, their real concern about and interest in a common problem or issue, and their growing understanding of and even commitment to the values of an interdisciplinary approach, has apparently had a salutary effect in both teaching and research. The approach, or some variation of it, may have merit for other institutions, as it does not require any fundamental changes in the organizational structure of the institution.

Paradigm B

The Newark State College experiment, "Individualized General Education" (hereafter IGE), is unique. It involved a major curricular change as well as a new procedure or method; it occupied the students' entire time for a period of two years; it comprised not a selected group but an arbitrary cross-section of entering freshmen.[13]

A major hypothesis of the IGE program asserted that students could better attain their goals if they were sought consciously and directly rather than "as incidental by-products of required courses in the usual subjects." One of the goals sought to develop "an awareness of the *interdependence of all living things and of fields of learning.*"[14]

At the outset two sections of sixteen students each were randomly selected from the entering freshman class majoring in general elementary education. These were matched with thirty-two other entering freshmen in the same major and with identical or similar aptitude scores. Each of the two experimental sections was taught by one professor as his sole teaching responsibility. Since the student/faculty ratio in the college was 16:1, faculty time available for the experimental sections was the same as for most freshmen. Each of the IGE sections was assigned a meeting room where it arranged its own schedule.

At midterm and at the end of each semester each student rated herself on the objectives of the College. The instructor also rated each student, after which the two ratings were compared and discussed in a private conference, which culminated in an agreed-upon grade for the semester.

Rationale for the Program

"The thinking behind the IGE experiment is more important than the detailed activities of particular students or sections."[15] With this statement, not an uncommon position for originators or early innovators, the rationale of the program is introduced. The instructors of the IGE sections differed from others in the College in academic background, temperament, and teaching style; they shared a dedication to the investigation of better ways to stimulate and to guide student growth toward the objectives of a general education. The IGE program differed fundamentally from traditional freshmen/ sophomore courses "in at least" the eight respects listed below.

1. Individualized rather than regimented. In the IGE program each student is treated as a unique individual. Hence his abilities and his readiness to learn are appraised so that he may be guided in a series of learning experiences appropriate to *his* needs and potential.

2. General rather than specialized. The IGE program, consistent with the objectives for a general education endorsed by the College faculty, offers a broad range of activities. Thus it *starts* with the recognized interests of the students, but it does not stop there. Instructors continue to call attention to other kinds of reading, to visits, to group experiences, and to individual projects of genuine interest to the student. Students read in fields new to them, and in such sources as the *New York Times,* the *Saturday Review, Scientific American,* and various journals of art, music, drama, and other sources that reveal new facets of contemporary life.

3. Integral rather than piecemeal. The program does not subscribe to education that is parceled out in specific unrelated courses and offered by separate departments. The program is a response to the need for integral rather than piecemeal reform. As Winslow Hatch, a long-time member of the United States Office of Education, charged: "Experimentation in higher education is piecemeal, inadequate in scope, design and pace, whereas problems in higher education are massive, multifaceted and interdependent."[16]

4. Active and involved students rather than passively receptive. "No characteristic has been more evident in most of the students at Newark than their docility." (It is useful to recall that this was just prior to the advent of visible student dissatisfaction and discontent.) The IGE program challenged the apathy and conformity. Students were bewildered by their new-found freedom, as they had no experience or guides of scholarship to refer to. Most actually sought the security of some authoritative direction. It required several months for most students to take the opportunities, deliberately provided, *to create their own curriculum* in light of their personal values, their intellectual curiosity, and their responsibilities as citizens of the contemporary world. In responding to the student demands for greater participation in decisions that primarily concerned them, the report states, "We believe that the IGE program anticipated this coming wave of student initiative and provided better channels for its wise development."[17]

5. Universal rather than provincial. Non-IGE freshmen and sophomores have had little or no encouragement to explore the world around them—or even the world close to them. They had been occupied with assigned book chapters and required themes so that, they said, they had not felt free even to hear renowned speakers who appeared on campus from time to time. Thus the IGE schedule was deliberately designed to be flexible in order to permit some off-campus visits and a wide range of reading.

6. "True disciplines" rather than subject-matter content. This is one of the most important and fundamental distinctions in the program. The curriculum should *not* be organized around the so-called "disciplines" of traditional subject-matter, but around distinct procedures which are "disciplines of mind and spirit" in a more genuine sense. Among these "true" disciplines are Problem-solving, Creativity, Valuing, and Deciding.[18] In short, these represent activities basic to personal growth and social progress. "The great limitation of required courses of the kind offered at most colleges is that while they require students occasionally to practice good intellectual skills these seldom become conscious principles or virtues." Objectives of the IGE program refer to open-mindedness, scientific method (problem-solving), critical thinking, personal integrity, aesthetic appreciation, ability to communicate, and responsible citizenship. These can all be seen as true "disciplines."

7. Functional in life rather than solely verbal and academic. One of the goals of the IGE program calls for students to "participate actively as informed and responsible citizens." This goal, according to the report, is not attained by mastering textbooks. Because of their flexible schedule and considerable input into their individual curricula, students are able to attend meetings, legislative sessions, demonstrations—all of which enable them to be more in touch with dynamic social forces beyond the college.

8. Finally the program was planned to be exciting rather than dull. "We were," the report states, "disappointed in the initial inertia of our students; encouraged by their growth in the ability to propose interesting and worthwhile projects; further confirmed in part by their boredom when they re-entered the conventional junior year; but never satisfied that we had succeeded fully."[19]

A Sample Program

Each section developed its own program week by week. Shortly after the beginning of the term, one section reported the following decisions:

a. Each student would read one book a week and his written reactions would be distributed to all.

b. The *New York Times* or the *Herald Tribune* would be read daily by each student.

c. All students would read the Sunday edition of the *Times* and bring to class the various sections of the paper as a basis of discussion.

d. All students would buy and read: Smith, *Learning to Learn;* Barzun and Graff, *The Modern Researcher;* Orwell, *1984;* Twain, *Huckleberry Finn;* Levin, *The Question of Socrates.*

e. All students would watch the Ibsen play on TV Friday evening.

Another section listened to records of Renaissance music; provided individual piano lessons for some students; engaged half the section in a T-Group session; arranged to participate in physical education activities in the gym; attended an exhibit of Renaissance paintings; and a group who had been learning conversational French, planned a summer trip to France.

Subgroups were formed to work on a wide variety of projects. All lectures and other activities of the regular College program were considered possible resources for the IGE program. The number and variety of places visited, books read, and papers written was truly impressive, as were the projects pursued.

In spite of appearances created by more than the customary degree of flexibility, the program was in no way chaotic. The activities and educational experiences of each student had the organizing principle of personal growth. Each student kept a daily log of his activities, so that one thing led to another. Whether one activity was a continuation of another, or whether it was chosen precisely because it was different, contrasting, or complementing, "the project fitted a readiness in the learner at the particular time." But the organizing role of the faculty has not been sufficiently emphasized. For it was the instructor who clearly became the most vital factor in the program. In at least three instances, IGE instructors assumed a fairly directive role, proposing projects, making assignments, setting limits, and the like. *"In every case the activities of the students reflected the values, interests and knowledge of the principal instructor."*[20] This, even though these instructors were chosen because they were themselves liberally educated, with a broad range of knowledge and various interests and aptitudes.

Control by instructors of more limited interests would have narrowed the range of student growth. Indeed, several competent specialists declined to accept leadership of an IGE section because they were afraid their preparation had been limited to too narrow a field. . . . The more a teacher thought of himself as limited to a particular discipline, the less likely was he to wish to undertake IGE instruction.[21]

Student Reactions

When seniors (who were asked to look back upon their lower-division IGE experience) were asked to cite the best features of their program, the following were mentioned most often: freedom to choose areas of study that crossed departmental (disciplinary) boundaries; independent study; being treated as adults; visits to other colleges and schools; our professors; opportunities and cultural advantages; and friendships with "real persons."

In sum, the objective evidence (questionnaire data) revealed relatively few and smaller differences between the IGE and the control groups, despite widely different programs during the first two college years. Significantly, however, the data clearly refuted any hypothesis to the effect that the IGE group was less adequately prepared for their upper-division years. They did not, however, show a marked superiority over the other group. The data did reveal that more IGE than control students completed their studies; fewer IGE students failed or received poor grades; IGE students reported better study habits; IGE students gained more in critical and consistent thinking and in knowledge of both the natural and social sciences even though taking *no courses in these subjects.*

Comments

Unlike the Columbia model, the IGE experiment represented a fundamental reform. For that reason, as the history of higher education has revealed, it may be difficult to emulate, although the cost factor seems to be less formidable than in other departures of similar scope. Some of the obstacles, though serious, are neither insurmountable nor unexpected. There are ways to reduce the time seemingly required for many of the new students to learn how best to avail themselves of their newfound freedom, although time devoted to that process may be among the best educational investments. Unquestionably the heavy demand upon faculty time and effort could well be a major problem. This would be particularly irritating if the individual faculty member chose to pursue his own research and thereby take advantage of the institution's reward system. The problem of motivation, common to all forms of education, is a continuing source of annoyance to IGE faculty.

But the model has its advantages. The individualized procedures; the emphasis on general education; the focus on the integration of experience, both educational and social; the close and informal contacts between faculty and students; the emphasis on problem-solving—all heighten the sense of interdisciplinarity and contribute to interdisciplinary practices. The model's conception of "true disciplines" (Creativity, Valuing, etc.) in fact calls for an inter-disciplinary approach, as does the absence of either a departmental or divisional structure.

Paradigm C

In 1970 a group of faculty members at The Pennsylvania State University began to study the question of whether or not the University should prepare its students to conduct interdisciplinary research and discourse, and if so, how this might best be accomplished in the humanities and social sciences. Their discussions considered whether contemporary problems profitably lent themselves to interdisciplinary discourse, what relevance the humanities might have in such discourse, whether training within traditional disciplinary boundaries was sufficient to meet complex contemporary problems satisfactorily, and whether such interdisciplinary education was feasible within the constraints of time, budget, and prospective employment presently facing education and students. Colloquia on the topic were held to gather widespread and divergent expert opinion, and recognized experts on interdisciplinary study were sought for consultation. After two years of careful deliberation, a proposal was submitted to and funded by the National Endowment for the Humanities. It awarded the University a developmental grant lasting four years to help in establishing the Interdisciplinary Graduate Program in the Humanities (IGPH).

The founders of IGPH shared the conviction that contemporary society faces problems of a complexity and magnitude beyond the boundaries of any single discipline—problems of population control, food distribution, development and use of energy resources, human relationships during periods of rapid and widespread change, and others. Each of these involve issues of economic, political, social, psychological, ethical, and religious significance. For example, valuable insight into the problem of distributing the world's food resources could follow from examining, say, the ethical implications of a specific proposal. But detached from an understanding of the economic or political consequences of any given plan, ethical thought would be addressed to less than the total problem at hand. To develop a more comprehensive understanding of these and other complex problems and to find realistic, consequential solutions, interdisciplinary approaches seem desirable.

To carry out such research and discussion, the framers of IGPH believed at least two requirements to be propaedeutic. First, students of the program must be informed of the origin of the problem of interdisciplinarity and the various solutions that have been proposed. This undertaking includes an appreciation for the special methods and techniques associated with interdisciplinary research. Second, concrete illustration of how these methods and techniques should be applied to important problems and issues must occur to bring about genuine interdisciplinary research and transdisciplinary dialogue.[22] Apart from these two considerations, IGPH does not attempt to impose a singular framework upon the investigations or dialogues conducted within the program.

Whereas a discipline will have a set of axioms, postulates, theorems, and theories that its specialists are expected to know, broadly conceived research and discourse occurring across disciplines does not lend itself to such formulations. Hence IGPH does not derive its coherence from any single set of knowledge claims, but instead from its orientation toward problems rather than disciplines. It tries to organize a nondisciplinary setting in which scholars and students from the humanities and social sciences whose interests are problem-oriented and whose research problems range over more than one discipline can study and teach outside their regular departments. Those affiliated with the program are convinced that in this way newly acquired knowledge can augment a scholar's disciplinary understanding of a problem. Interdisciplinarity in IGPH exists as a means to problem-oriented research and discourse, not as an end in itself.

Operation
The rationale outlined above requires that the program maintain as much flexibility in its mode of operation as is reasonably possible. It would defeat its objectives to establish a fixed sequence of courses, since problems of interdisciplinary interest know no fixed boundaries. It would not be feasible for the program to have a faculty of its own, since there is no guarantee that such a faculty would be competent to meet the needs of students pursuing interdisciplinary problems at any given moment. It would be impossible to grant a degree, since no single degree could encompass the varied interests of students involved in nondisciplinary research and graduate study.[23] Furthermore, were such reflections put aside, there remains the hard reality of fiscal constraints now facing higher education that make all of these features costly beyond the means of Penn State and most other educational institutions.

As an alternative to the more traditional characteristic elements of graduate programs (a continuing faculty, a curriculum of courses ideally coherently interrelated, students admitted, and degrees granted), IGPH attempts to develop and promote interdisciplinary research and discourse with a minimum of bureaucratic structure. When possible, it works within existing College and University structures.

The program is administered through the College of the Liberal Arts. It maintains relations in the form of faculty support, student affiliation, and cosponsored colloquia with all departments in that college and with the departments of Art History and Art Education housed outside the College. Participating departments are represented on the program's Steering Committee. Because those who serve on the committee value interdisciplinary research and discourse, they tend not to represent parochial departmental interests, but rather serve more as liaisons representing the programs to their departments. This committee makes all major policy decisions, within guidelines acceptable to the Dean of Liberal Arts. They solicit faculty to develop and teach courses, select pre- and postdoctoral fellows, arrange colloquia, and map future plans. The committee's policy decisions are implemented by a Program Director and Associate Director.

Faculty are recruited from those among the professoriate who manifest an interest and demonstrate competence in interdisciplinary graduate education in the humanities and social sciences. Most develop and offer a relevant transdisciplinary course or seminar, some participate only in faculty seminars, others contribute advice or direction to graduate students working on transdisciplinary problems. Some, because of their particular research interests, are involved with the program on a continuing basis. Others, because of changes in their research interests or because of variations in student needs, have temporary active involvement with the program.

Students affiliated with IGPH are usually enrolled in the College of the Liberal Arts, though some from the Colleges of Arts and Architecture, Education, and Science also associate with the program. Typically, in the final phases of their graduate course work, students will take a year to study outside their regular department. At that time they examine intensively a problem that ranges over more than one discipline. With the advice of their graduate mentor and the Associate Director of IGPH, they schedule course work, directed study, or other involvement in ongoing research projects relevant to their own research focus. Each year eight of these students have been supported with fellowships provided by the University as part of its responsibility under the terms of the NEH grant. When the grant expires, continued student support will come from participating departments in the form of teaching or research assistantships.

Courses sponsored by the program fall into four broad problem areas: the problems, theories, and methods of interdisciplinarity per se; humanistic problems of an interdisciplinary character, such as comparative examinations of civilizations to determine those factors that contribute to their respective world views; relationships between social sciences and humanistic concerns, for example, the use of sociological, psychological, and anthropological constructs to explain the effects of rapid change on social and personal relations and development; linguistic and literary considerations related to social problems. Most of the IGPH-sponsored sources were developed through use of NEH funds for faculty release time. Some courses included in the program were developed previously, however. Each year from twelve to sixteen courses are scheduled in these areas. Representative are such courses as "Interdisciplinarity and General Science Theory," "Artist, Herald, and Poet in the Thirteenth Century," "Mapping the Two Cultures," and "Adolescence in a Changing World."

Instruction and discourse of a nondisciplinary sort occurs also in faculty seminars. These seminars are problem-oriented and are developed from one of three perspectives: the social sciences, the linguistic disciplines, and the philosophico-historical disciplines. Frequently they are related to the problem area under consideration in an IGPH-sponsored seminar or course. However, some faculty members have generated topics of interest to colleagues independently of any connection with the course structure of the program. Each seminar meets at least ten times during a period of time convenient for those involved.

Finally the program, with the co-sponsorship of departments in Liberal Arts, Arts and Architecture, and Education, organizes and presents an annual colloquium on an interdisciplinary topic. Through this it attempts to reach a broad-based audience of faculty and students in ways that demonstrate and promote the efficacy of interdisciplinary research and discourse.

Program Development

Developing a new graduate program in a university with well over 100 currently functioning degree granting programs presents difficult problems. Not least among these are ones of budget. Since graduate education is so expensive, it is not feasible for the university to fund new programs under normal circumstances. To do so, funds must be taken from some existing program. Even if strong evidence and compelling arguments suggest the value of such an undertaking, justification for reallocating internal funds is problematic at best. In the case of IGPH there are several added complications. First, there are a number of interdisciplinary programs already in existence at Penn State and in the Liberal Arts College. Most of these are undergraduate programs in narrowly defined content areas, such as Asian Studies, Medieval Studies, and the like. The need for interdisciplinarity that IGPH wished to address is of a special sort not considered by existing programs. Second, the program is concerned with the relevance to contemporary social needs of graduate education in the liberal arts. Participants share the conviction that such relevance requires contact with the Humanities. Third, IGPH is committed to interdisciplinary education and research based on a disciplinary foundation. Its objective in this respect is not to create new fields of study so much as to help students and scholars become better disciplinarians. All of these factors combined IGPH interests with existing disciplinary efforts and, necessarily, departmental structures appropriate to graduate education at Penn State.

These considerations were significant in shaping guidelines for the program's development.

1. Students would be expected to fulfill the Ph.D. requirements of their regular department. Admitting students for graduate study, establishing degree requirements, or granting graduate degrees would fall outside the program's preserve. It presupposes the necessity of a disciplinary foundation for conducting nondisciplinary study and research. In most cases students with the equivalent of an M.A. would have sufficient training to seriously and profitably undertake systematic study outside of but related to disciplinary problems.

2. Students gradually would do increasing amounts of nondisciplinary work. By the end of their second year, students would be sufficiently trained in their own disciplines to undertake a year of intensive study outside their departments. In principle this program should culminate in a dissertation project of an interdisciplinary nature.

3. The students' programs of study and dissertation topics would be reviewed and assessed by their graduate committees. Since these students would study outside their departments for at least a year, appropriate representation from outside their disciplines would be required on these committees.

4. Faculty would be drawn from existing staff in participating departments. They would be given release time, purchased through IGPH developmental funds, to develop a team-taught seminar or course on an interdisciplinary subject of relevance. IGPH maintained that in its initial stages interdisciplinary instruction required persons from more than one discipline to conduct courses. This was essential if courses were to overcome the limitations imposed by examining a complex problem from a single point of view, however broadly that point of view may be defined. Release time was granted for preparation to permit the coteachers to discuss and reflect upon their subject. Typically a team-taught course has each instructor present his discipline's analysis of a common problem. While some instruction of this kind no doubt is necessary, IGPH is interested more in the development of new perspectives through transdisciplinary discourse. These newly developed perspectives hopefully would provide focus to the course when taught. The following term, each instructor would be released from a normal teaching assignment in his department to offer the developmental course.

5. Once a course was offered, the faculty involved would determine whether they wished to continue teaching it. If the course was regarded as worth repeating periodically, they would propose that the offering be made permanent by their respective departments. In this way the course structure of the program would gradually feed itself back into the departments. The courses would have status within existing structures as regular offerings. Enrollments would accrue to the departments involved. Scheduling interdisciplinary instruction could be incorporated into normal departmental course scheduling plans. Importantly, the Interdisciplinary Program would avoid competition with the departments for student enrollment and faculty time.

6. Eventually courses developed by the program, as well as existing ones of an interdisciplinary nature, would form a pool of offerings that would introduce the student to problems, methods, theories, and practices relevant to interdisciplinary scholarship. They would not, however, form a sequence of systematic studies. As a problem-oriented program IGPH recognized that students must discover what other fields have to say about the problems they are investigating. In other words, it is not developing offerings to create an alternative course structure but to augment, in relevant ways, existing ones.

7. Finally, wherever possible, IGPH should avoid competition between itself and the departments. It should foster an attitude of

cooperation to permit and encourage continued transdisciplinary discourse on complex problems.

Results
After four years the program appears to have reached a number of its objectives, failed to realize others, and encountered several unanticipated problems and opportunities. It is still in its developmental stages and will continue so for several years hence. Still some assessment of its impact on Penn State is possible.

There are approximately 900 students enrolled in Liberal Arts graduate programs at Penn State. Approximately fifty of these are affiliated with IGPH. These students are committed to developing their understanding of problems beyond the limits now possible within the boundaries of their regular departments. This commitment typically extends to undertaking dissertation projects of an interdisciplinary nature. Those students who have progressed to the dissertation stage of their programs usually have been successful in incorporating their nondisciplinary work in their thesis writing. Representative studies include the investigation of social, historical, and linguistic forces on a French-speaking community in Maine, and the religious, philosophical, and anthropological dimensions of Oedipal rituals in Kapiristan. At this point five students have completed requirements for the Ph.D. All have secured positions relevant to their area of research competence.

Prior to the inception of IGPH there were some interdisciplinary courses at the graduate level, but hardly enough to be noticeable. The program has developed fifty new courses. While some of these will not be offered a second time, most will. Of those not offered again, their content has been incorporated into other continuing offerings, altering in important ways the manner in which students are exposed to such subject matter. While all of its courses were developed by a team of instructors, few are team-taught on a regular basis. Typically one member of the team has remained interested in continuing the course, and these members have arranged with their departments to do so. The obstacle faced in team-teaching on a recurring basis is cost. Some have argued that the absence of continued widespread team-teaching is a sign of weak support from departments and faculty. Given the structural necessity of working through regular departments, it is likely that budgetary or other considerations will at times receive priority in decisions affecting interdisciplinary course offerings. If department heads regularly refused to permit these courses to be repeated, or if faculty seldom expressed interest in repeated offerings of their courses, the objection would carry weight. But the fact of the matter has been that when interdisciplinary research and teaching are a regular part of the faculty member's work life, and when they are interested in continuing this work in affiliation with IGPH, then arrangements satisfactory to all parties can usually be worked out with their department heads.

Prior to the inception of IGPH, only one department in the College required a minor of its Ph.D. candidates. While it would be an overstatement to claim that our program was responsible for an apparent shift in the attitudes of disciplinarians on the virtues of nondisciplinary work, we were at least one among those factors that have contributed to the adoption of strong minor requirements by a majority of departments in the College.

Prior to the program's inception, interdisciplinary study and discourse were conducted largely at the undergraduate level. Persons interested in transdisciplinary discourse tended to gravitate to programs such as American Studies, Latin American Studies, or Medieval Studies. Yet these structures, for the most part, made no visible impact on graduate education at Penn State. At the urging of IGPH, some of these undergraduate options, which already have an established constituency of faculty and students, are in the process of petitioning for graduate status.

Prior to the inception of IGPH, the Graduate School permitted students interested in nondepartmental degrees to petition for special committees to serve as ad hoc departments guiding their graduate programs. However, this rule was seldom if ever invoked. Since IGPH became active, there has been a marked increase in the number of students requesting such degree programs. There are six Ph.D. students and two M.A. candidates who are working or have completed work outside disciplinary boundaries. While they are not pursuing degrees through IGPH, the presence of this program has prompted their inquiries and subsequent negotiations to establish their programs of study.

Prior to the inception of this program, departments would occasionally co-sponsor a guest lecturer. Each year it has coordinated a jointly sponsored colloquium with several departments in the university. This new development has created a different sense of relationship to common research problems. While there is no guarantee that these jointly sponsored programs will continue after the expiration of IGPH's developmental grant, the fact that departments have been willing to contribute substantial financial support is an encouraging sign.

At a large university like Penn State, faculty members are frequently insulated from one another's ideas by departmental boundaries. Through faculty seminars IGPH has started to remove these barriers. Each year at least three seminars have been successful in providing a setting outside departments in which interested faculty and occasionally graduate students may increase their knowledge in areas relevant to problems they are now examining. Establishing and maintaining transdisciplinary discourse will be essential if the program is to continue to develop productively.

Conclusion
The flexible structure of IGPH was designed purposely to permit maximum adaptation to attitudes toward interdisciplinarity as reflected in research, curriculum, and the general environment for nondisciplinary discourse at Penn State. Such flexibility requires strong administrative support and persistent faculty effort. The danger of fiscal constraints and diminished energy is constant. This program attempts to be sensitive to the objection that graduate programs train specialists rather than *educate* human beings sensitive to the range of experiences outside their areas of competence. To train graduate students who fail to understand the implications of their work in terms of broad and human horizons creates and maintains a class of "experts" doomed to partial perspectives on the most pressing concerns of our age. Such limitations are overcome through meaningful dialogue between faculty and graduate students who are well trained in their respective disciplines, and who also are able to integrate their disciplines in framing solutions to common problems. Such solutions are, however, difficult to formulate. For IGPH to succeed, it is apparent that it must continue to devote a significant portion of its energies to maintaining an environment in which such research and discourse may occur. Only through supportive attitudes and actions from the administration and departments in the Liberal Arts College can the program remain viable in contributing to the education of graduate students and in enhancing the role of the humanities in resolving socially relevant problems.

Notes

1. Gary Woditsch et al., "Assaying the Great Cargo Cult: Recent Research on Learner-Centered Curricula." Prepared for the 30th National Conference on Higher Education. AAHE, March 24, 1975.

2. *The Realms of Meaning* (New York: McGraw-Hill, 1964), p. 4.

3. Philip Phenix, "The Use of the Disciplines as Curriculum Content," *Educational Forum* 26 (March 1962): 280.

4. T.J. Sergiovanni and Robert Starratt, *Emerging Patterns of Supervision: Human Perspectives* (New York: McGraw-Hill, 1971), pp. 236–37.

5. Ibid., p. 237.

6. Special Report of the University Committee on General Education. *The Present State and Future Direction of General Education at Columbia* (New York, Columbia University, 1977).

7. Ibid., p. 2.

8. Ibid., p. 1.

9. Unless otherwise indicated, the discussion of activities that follows is based on information derived from the *Report of the University Committee on General Education* (New York, Columbia University, 1976).

10. Ibid., p. 6.

11. Ibid., p. 7.

12. Ibid., p. 8. Italics added.

13. Goodwin Watson, "Individualized General Education" (Union, N.J.: Newark State College, Laboratory for Applied Behavioral Science, 1967).

14. Ibid., p. 3. Italics added.

15. Ibid., p. 4.

16. Ibid., p. 7.

17. Ibid., p. 8.

18. Ibid., p. 9.

19. Ibid., p. 11.

20. Ibid., p. 18.

21. Ibid.

22. *Interdisciplinary* here and below refers to research and discourse (including instruction) that attempts to integrate parts of two or more disciplines into a new perspective. Such a perspective may eventually become a new discipline, e.g., social psychology. *Transdisciplinary* refers to research and discourse that attempts to solve a problem shared by two or more disciplines and beyond the scope of any single discipline, and that does not attempt to integrate the disciplines involved into a new discipline.

23. *Nondisciplinary* refers to the general framework of research and discourse (including instruction) of both an inter- and transdisciplinary nature, without specifying or limiting the disciplines involved nor the form their interaction may take.

APPENDIX

A Selective Listing of Interdisciplinary Programs

The following lists just a few of the interdisciplinary education projects currently in progress in Canada and Western Europe. It has two purposes: to give an impression of the kinds of concerns that exist in interdisciplinary education, and to provide addresses and related information for those wishing to pursue the topic in greater depth. The entries encompass various degrees of interdisciplinarity because no attempt has been made to limit the definition of that term.

There were limitations in our resources, however, and the initial list was quite restricted. To the entries in this list were sent questionnaires requesting current information relating to title, location, administration, purpose, and nature of each project. From the generous number of replies this appendix was compiled. It was necessary to eliminate some of the responses that were duplications or that described projects of a noneducational nature. We are nonetheless grateful for the interest shown and would like to thank everyone who gave us his time and consideration.

Originally it was intended that the Appendix include American projects also, and a great deal of information was gathered accordingly. We learned, though, that there are other more comprehensive sources of American interdisciplinary information available. For the United States we refer readers to *Interdisciplinary Studies in the Humanities: A Directory,* edited by Elizabeth Bayerl (Metuchen, N.J.: Scarecrow Press, 1977); The Grant Information System, 205 Temple Street, Fredonia, N.Y. 14063; and *Science, Technology, and Society: A Guide to the Field. Directory of Teaching, Research and Resources in the United States,* compiled and edited by Ezra D. Heitowit, Janet Epstein, and Gerald Steinberg (Ithaca, N.Y.: Cornell University, Program on Science, Technology, and Society, s.a. [1976]). In addition, work is in progress on a directory of all interdisciplinary programs in the United States; this work should be published soon.

All entries are in alphabetical order according to program title within any one country (also alphabetically ordered). The information on address and administration is as current and accurate as possible. Each entry contains a brief description of the nature and purpose of the project, and we have included mention of the disciplines it involves to further designate its nature. Descriptions are distilled from comments written on the questionnaires and from various kinds of printed matter supplied by respondents. In the process of abbreviating, translating various languages, and deciphering handwriting, it is possible that errors or inadequate statements may have been made. We regret any of these but hope that the reader, with his interest stimulated, will use the Appendix as intended and contact individual projects for further information.

For a few entries no descriptions are supplied. There are several recently founded universities in Europe, particularly in England, France, and Germany, in which concern for interdisciplinarity is reflected in the very structure of the institution. Therefore it appeared undesirable to describe some particular programs only. Those wishing further information concerning a specific program in one of these universities should address themselves directly to that program.

Austria

Psychiatric University Clinic, Vienna
Lazarettgasse 14
A-1090 Vienna

Director: Prof. Dr. Peter Berner

Level: postdoctoral

The Clinic sponsors various training programs, primarily for postdegree students. Two examples are a training program in forensic psychiatry and another for behavior therapists. Besides psychiatry and psychology, the Clinic draws upon nursing and justice in its training programs.

Belgium

Golden Delta Symposia
Instituut voor Dierkunde
Rijksuniversiteit Gent
Ledeganckstraat 35
B-9000 Gent

Chairman: Prof. Dr. H. Gysels

Level: postdoctoral

The symposia are conducted to study environmental planning issues connected with the Rhine, Meuse, and Scheldt estuarine region. Participants come from ecology and environmental sciences, geography, and physical planning. Goals are to convince the Dutch and Belgian governments of the immediate need for environmental planning and to implement the results of the symposia studies.

Canada

Department of Man-Environment Studies
University of Waterloo
Waterloo, Ontario

Chairman: Dr. George Priddle

Level: undergraduate

This Department emphasizes interdisciplinary problem-solving in three areas: energy and the trend toward a conservation-oriented society; environmental assessment and management; environmental issues and the Third World. It utilizes sociology, anthropology, geography, economics, communication, biology, physics, and chemical engineering.

Kinesiology
Simon Fraser University
Burnaby 2, British Columbia V5A 1S6

Chairman: Prof. E.W. Banister

Level: undergraduate, graduate, postdoctoral

Kinesiology is concerned with human movement and all aspects of human structure, function, and performance. Information is drawn from medicine, physiology, psychology, biochemistry, bioengineering, and other disciplines. Particular emphases of the program are: applied physiology and health sciences; sports science, aesthetic movement, and recreation; health maintenance and rehabilitation. B.Sc., M.Sc., and Ph.D. degrees are offered.

England

General Honours Degree in Arts
University of Exeter
Queen's Building
The Queen's Drive
Exeter EX4 4QH

Director: Prof. K.W. Slater

Level: undergraduate

A student in this program engages in a comparative study of English literature and history for the period 1500–1960; in addition he studies a third subject from the following list: English, French, German, Italian, history, economic history, politics, sociology, philosophy, theology.

Interdisciplinary Higher Degrees Scheme
University of Aston in Birmingham
Gosta Green, Birmingham

Director: Dr. D.J. van Rest, currently (directorate rotates)

Level: graduate

This program concentrates on practical solutions to real problems as it prepares graduates for careers in industry and commerce. It demonstrates the validity and benefit of "action-oriented applied practical research" at the doctoral level. Interdisciplinary collaboration and academic-industrial sharing of information, with the goal of commercial exploitation of scientific knowledge, are emphasized. Participating disciplines include engineering, natural science, management, social science, and humanities.

School of Environmental Sciences
University of East Anglia
University Plain, Norwich
Norfolk NR4 7TJ

Dean: Dr. J.R. Tarrant

Level: undergraduate, graduate, postdoctoral

The School is a self-contained unit within the University designed to provide interdisciplinary education in the environmental sciences. Some of the disciplines involved are biology, ecology, geography, geology, chemistry, meteorology, agriculture, social science, planning, and resources management. Degrees offered are B.Sc., M.Phil., and Ph.D.

Social History
Department of History
University of Lancaster
Lancaster LA1 4YG

Director: Dr. G.A. Phillips (Prof. H.J. Perkin is Head of the Department of History)

Level: undergraduate

This interdisciplinary degree scheme, leading to a B.A. in Social History, emphasizes history and sociology primarily, and to a lesser extent economics, educational studies, politics, English, philosophy, and religious studies.

University of Sussex
Falmer, Brighton, Sussex

France

Bio-neurophysiological Basis of Sociological Behavior
Laboratoire d'eutonologie
Hôpital Boucicaut
78 Rue de la Convention
Paris 75015

Director: Dr. Henri Laborit

Level: postdoctoral

This study is concerned with interdisciplinary relationships in human behavior and biological structure—an integrated view of the biological, neurophysiological, psychological, and social natures of man. It draws from the disciplines of biology, neurophysiology, behavioral sciences, sociology, economics, and political science.

Management and Improvement of Regions
Institute for the Sciences of Behavior and the Environment
Université de Rennes
Avenue du Général Leclerc
35031 Rennes Beaulieu

Directors: Profs. P. Trehen, J. Cl. LeFeuvre, J.J. Chauvel

Level: undergraduate

This program engages in studies of rural and coastal areas, pollution, tourism, and animal behavior in captivity. Disciplines that may be involved include biology, ecology, ethology, geography, geology, rural sociology, economics, and pedology.

Theater Department
Université de Paris VIII
Route de la Tourelle
75571 Paris (Cédex 12)

Director: Prof. André Veinstein

Level: graduate

Within this Department the following interdisciplinary problems are studied: comparison of theater to the other arts, including the way in which it is integrated with other arts; theatrical techniques outside theater proper; a theatrical approach to different points of view in the human sciences. Participating disciplines include theater, music, plastic arts, motion pictures, aesthetics, literature, education, sociology, political economics, and psychology.

Sports, Culture, and Human Science
Université de Lille III
Lille SP 18
59650 Villeneuve d'Ascq

Director: Prof. Bernard Jeu

Level: undergraduate

Drawing from sports and physical activities, history, sociology, literature, philosophy, ethnology, statistics, and accounting and management, this interdisciplinary program is concerned with the historical, social, and cultural significance of sports. It is aimed primarily toward the formation of administrators or managers of professional or amateur sports rather than of educators or trainers.

Université de Grenoble II
(Sciences Sociales)

Domaine Universitaire
38040 Grenoble (Cédex)

Université de Lille III
Domaine Universitaire
59650 Villeneuve d'Ascq

Université de Nantes
U E R de Sciences Humaines
Chemin de la Sensive du Tertre
44000 Nantes

Université de Paris VIII
Vincennes
75012 Paris

Ireland

Department of Town Planning
University College, Dublin
Earlsfort Terrace
Dublin 2

Chairman: Prof. Kevin I. Nowlan

Level: postgraduate

Utilizing economics, social science, geography, architecture, and engineering, this Department sponsors research projects of an interdisciplinary nature and provides comprehensive training for those entering town planning as a profession in Ireland.

Joint Honors in Ecology
University College, Dublin
Belfield
Stillorgan Road
Dublin 4

Directors: Profs. J. Bracken and J.J. Moore

Level: undergraduate

Final-year students in this honors program have two primary goals: discussion of some advanced aspects of ecology, and an understanding of the importance to ecology of input from nontraditional disciplines. In this respect the disciplines studied include botany, zoology, chemistry, physics, and pharmacology.

The Netherlands

Institute for Social Medicine
Catholic University of Nijmegen
Verlengde Groenestraat 75
Nijmegen

Director: Prof. A. Mertens (and others)

Level: undergraduate, graduate, postdoctoral

The Institute's aim is to study various fields of social medicine, including sociomedical gerontology, medical and health education, industrial medicine, health organization, and epidemiology. Psychology also plays an important role in these studies.

Institute of Educational Sciences
Katholieke Universiteit
Erasmuslaan 40
Nijmegen

Director: Prof. Dr. E. Velema

Level: graduate

The purposes of this Institute are to prepare educational scientists in instructional techniques, for educational management, for guidance and counseling activities, and for continued research. In addition to educational sciences, the study program involves psychology, sociology, and philosophy.

Northern Ireland

Environmental Science
School of Biological and Environmental Studies
New University of Ulster
Coleraine

Director: Prof. P.J. Newbould

Level: undergraduate

The goal of this program is to generate a student understanding of the major environmental systems and their mutual interactions. A student may study ecology, geography, geology, meteorology, and to a lesser extent physics, chemistry, and economics.

Scotland

Centre of African Studies
University of Edinburgh
Edinburgh EH8 9LL

Convenor of Committee: Dr. D.N. McMaster

Level: graduate

The Centre offers two degrees in African Studies—Diploma or M.Sc. In pursuing one of these a student will be involved in interdisciplinary studies involving Arabic, economics, educational studies, geography, history, political science, social anthropology, and social medicine.

Science Studies Unit
University of Edinburgh
34 Buccleuch Place
Edinburgh EH8 9JT

Director: Prof. David Edge

Level: undergraduate, graduate, postdoctoral

This is an interdisciplinary program focusing attention on those areas in which scientific activities overlap more general concerns of human society. Studies include sociology, sociology of scientific knowledge, history, and philosophy of science. An undergraduate spends his first two years in a more traditional program in the natural sciences.

Technological Economics
University of Stirling
Stirling FK9 4LA

Directors: Profs. F.R. Bradbury and B.J. Loasby

Level: undergraduate, graduate

The purpose of this program is to explore and develop the area between technology and economics with particular reference to decision-making in science- and technology-based industry and resource management. This may involve the disciplines of economics, engineering and technological studies, physical science, and management science.

Sweden

Centre for Interdisciplinary Studies of the Human Condition
University of Gothenburg
Mölndalsvägen 85
S-412 85 Gothenburg

Chairman: Prof. Karl-Erik Eriksson

Level: undergraduate, graduate, postdoctoral

The Centre serves as a forum for interdisciplinary contacts within the University and is oriented toward the solution of broad problems. Various undergraduate and graduate courses are offered, and its participant members, who may come from any of the disciplines of the University, often engage in postdoctoral research projects.

Nordplan (continuing training program and research training program)
Nordic Institute for Studies in Urban and Regional Planning
Skeppsholmen
111 49 Stockholm

Director: Prof. Per Andersson

Level: graduate, postdoctoral

The main emphasis of the program is interdisciplinary understanding and teamwork training leading to an "advanced knowledge of planning methodology." Disciplines that may be involved are physical planning, transportation, economic geography and planning, architecture, history of architecture, sociology, regional and local economy, applied mathematics, administration, and natural resource management.

Switzerland

International Centre for Genetic Epistemology
Université de Genève
3 Place de l'Université
1211 Genève 4

Director: Prof. Jean Piaget

Level: postgraduate

Drawing on psychology, logic, physics, biology, and mathematics, the Centre is oriented to the epistemological study of dialectics and development.

West Germany

Centre for Interdisciplinary Research
University of Bielefeld
Wellenberg 1
4800 Bielefeld 1

Directors: Prof. Dr. Norbert Horn, Prof. Dr. Helmut Satz, Prof. Dr. Reinhart Koselleck, Prof. Dr. Klauss Immelmann

Level: postdoctoral

Participants come from the entire University and engage in research projects, which take one of two broad forms: "research groups" in which residents of the Centre participate in a common local effort or in individual projects; "working groups" in which interested parties come together for short conferences or symposia on a common problem. The Centre's activities are international in scope.

Freie Universität Berlin
1 Berlin 33

Institute for Consumer and Behavioral Research
Universität des Saarlandes
6600 Saarbrücken

Director: Prof. Dr. Werner Kroeber-Riel

Level: graduate

Utilizing physiology, psychology, and economics, this psychophysiological (laboratory) program attempts to measure and explain emotional behavior and its relations to cognitive behavior, and then apply the results to marketing and advertising.

Interdisciplinary Center for Didactics in Higher Education
University of Hamburg
Sedanstrasse 19
D 2000 Hamburg 13

Director: Prof. Dr. Rolf Schulmeister

Level: undergraduate, graduate, postdoctoral

The Center engages in curriculum revision, reform of learning situations and examination structure, and integration of various areas of studies in professional and practical education. Participating disciplines are education, psychology, philology, natural sciences, medicine, economics, and law. The goal is a more interdisciplinary approach to higher education.

Rheinisch-Westfalische Technische Hochschule
51 Aachen

Ruhr Universität Bochum
463 Bochum-Querenburg
Universitätsstrasse

Universität Bielefeld
4800 Bielefeld 1
Herforderstrasse

Universität Konstanz
755 Konstanz
Sonnenbüll

Universität Trier
55 Trier
Schneidershof

Selected Bibliography

In keeping with the title and aim of this anthology, the bibliography contains only those publications that are directly concerned with interdisciplinarity as an issue pertinent to higher education. Within this large area those publications have been selected in particular that deal with the *quaestio juris*. Technical publications and those that address issues of a rather limited scope have not been included here.

Adkins, Douglas L. *The Great American Degree Machine: An Economic Analysis of the Human Resource Output of Higher Education.* Berkeley: Carnegie Commission on Higher Education, 1975.

Apostel, Leo. "Conceptual Tools for Interdisciplinarity: An Operational Approach." In *Interdisciplinarity: Problems of Teaching and Research in Universities.* Paris: OECD, 1972, pp. 141–80.

Ashby, Eric. *Any Person, Any Study: An Essay on Higher Education in the United States.* New York: McGraw-Hill, 1971.

Axelrod, Joseph, et al. *The Search for Relevance.* San Francisco: Jossey-Bass, 1969.

Becker, E. *The Structure of Evil: An Essay on the Unification of the Sciences of Man.* New York: George Braziller, 1968.

Bell, Daniel. *The Reforming of General Education.* New York: Columbia University Press, 1966.

Berger, Guy. "The Interdisciplinary Archipelago." In *Interdisciplinarity: Problems of Teaching and Research in Universities.* Paris: OECD, 1972, pp. 35–72.

Bernal, J.D. *The Social Function of Science.* Cambridge, Mass.: MIT Press, 1965.

Bertalanffy, L. von. *General System Theory: Foundations, Development, Applications.* New York: George Braziller, 1968.

Bird, Otto A. "Humanities." *Encyclopedia Britannica.* Macropedia, vol. 8, pp. 1179–83. Chicago, 1974.

Bledstein, Burton. *The Culture of Professionalism: The Middle Class and the Development of Higher Education in America.* New York: Norton, 1976.

Boisot, M. "Discipline and Interdisciplinarity." In *Interdisciplinarity: Problems of Teaching and Research in Universities.* Paris: OECD, 1972, pp. 89–97.

Booth, W.C., ed. *Knowledge Most Worth Having.* Chicago: University of Chicago Press, 1967.

Bönig, E., and Roeloffs, K. *Three German Universities: Aachen, Bochum, Konstanz.* Paris: OECD, 1970.

Briggs, Asa, and Michaud, Guy. "Problems and Solutions." In *Interdisciplinarity: Problems of Teaching and Research in Universities.* Paris: OECD, 1972, pp. 185–252.

Brinker, Paul. "Our Illiberal Liberal Arts Colleges: The Dangers of Undergraduate Overspecialization." *Journal of Higher Education* 31 (1960): 133–38.

Carmichael, Oliver. *Graduate Education: A Critique and a Program.* New York: Harper and Brothers, 1961.

Clark, Burton. *Educating the Expert Society.* San Francisco: Chandler, 1962.

———. *The Distinctive College.* Chicago: Aldine, 1970.

Crane, R.S. *The Idea of the Humanities.* Chicago: University of Chicago Press, 1967.

"Curriculum: Interdisciplinary Insights." *Teachers College Record* 73 (1971), no. 2.

Diversity by Design. San Francisco: Jossey-Bass, 1974.

Dressel, Paul. *College and University Curriculum.* Berkeley: McCutcham, 1968.

———. *The New Colleges: Toward an Appraisal.* Iowa City: Iowa University Press, 1971.

Education for the Professionals. Chicago: University of Chicago Press, 1962.

Feldman, K., and Newcomb, T. *The Impact of College on Students.* 2 vols. San Francisco: Jossey-Bass, 1969.

Freedman, Mervin. *The College Experience.* San Francisco: Jossey-Bass, 1967.

Freire, Paulo. *Education for Critical Consciousness.* New York: Seabury Press, 1974.

———. *Pedagogy of the Oppressed.* New York: Seabury Press, 1973.

Frey, Gerard. "Methodological Problems of Interdisciplinary Discussion." *Ratio* 15(1973): 153–72.

Gaff, Jerry, and Wilson, Robert. "Faculty Cultures and Interdisciplinary Studies." *Journal of Higher Education* 42 (1971), no. 3.

———, et al. *The Cluster College.* San Francisco: Jossey-Bass, 1967.

General Education. Chicago: University of Chicago Press, 1961.

Greenberg, David S. *The Politics of Pure Science.* New York: New American Library, 1967.

Greene, Th.M., ed. *The Meaning of the Humanities.* Princeton: University Press, 1940.

Gusdorf, Georges. "Humanistic Scholarship." *Encyclopedia Britannica.* Macropedia, vol. 8, pp. 1170–79. Chicago, 1974.

———. "Interdisciplinaire (Connaissance)." *Encyclopedia Universalis,* vol. 8, pp. 1086–90. Paris, 1970.

———. *Introduction aux sciences humaines.* Paris: Les Belles Lettres, 1960.

———. *Les sciences humaines et la pensée occidentale.* 6 vols. Paris: Payot, 1966–73.

Heckhausen, Heinz. "Discipline and Interdisciplinarity." In *Interdisciplinarity: Problems of Teaching and Research in Universities.* Paris: OECD, 1972, pp. 83–89.

Hefferlin, J.B. von. *The Dynamics of Academic Reform.* San Francisco: Jossey-Bass, 1969.

Heiss, Ann. *Challenges to the Graduate School.* San Francisco: Jossey-Bass, 1969.

Hentig, Hartmut von. *Magier oder Magister? Über die Einheit der Wissenschaft im Verständigungsprozess.* Stuttgart: Klett, 1972.

Hofstadter, Richard, and Smith, William, eds. *American Higher Education: A Documentary History.* 2 vols. Chicago: University of Chicago Press, 1961.

Holzhey, Helmut, ed. *Interdisziplinär. Philosophie Aktuell, 2.* Basel: Schwabe, 1974.

————. "Interdisziplinarität (Nachwort)." In *Interdisziplinär,* edited by H. Holzhey. Basel: Schwabe, 1974, pp. 105–29.

Huxley, Aldous. *Literature and Science.* New York: Harper and Row, 1963.

Ikenberry, S., and Friedman, R. *Beyond Academic Departments.* San Francisco: Jossey-Bass, 1972.

Interdisciplinarity: Problems of Teaching and Research in Universities. Paris: OECD, 1972.

Jacob, Philip. *Changing Values in College.* New York: Harper and Row, 1957.

Jantsch, Erich. "Towards Interdisciplinarity and Transdisciplinarity in Education and Innovation." In *Interdisciplinarity: Problems of Teaching and Research in Universities.* Paris: OECD, 1972, pp. 97–121.

Jaspers, Karl. *The Idea of the University.* Boston: Beacon Press, 1959.

Jochemsen, Reimut. "Zur gesellschaftspolitischen Relevanz interdisziplinärer Zusammenarbeit." In *Interdisziplinär,* edited by H. Holzhey. Basel: Schwabe, 1974, pp. 9–35.

Jones, W.T. *The Sciences and the Humanities.* Berkeley: University of California Press, 1965.

Kapp, William K. *Toward a Science of Man in Society: A Positive Approach to the Integration of Social Knowledge.* The Hague: Nijhoff, 1961.

Katz, Michael B. *Class, Bureaucracy and Schools: The Illusion of Change in America.* New York: Praeger, 1971.

Laszlo, E. *Introduction to System Philosophy.* New York: Gordon and Breach, 1972.

Leavis, F.R. *Two Cultures? The Significance of C.P. Snow.* London: Chatto and Windus, 1962.

Lee, Calvin. "Knowledge Structure and Curriculum Development." *Educational Record* 47 (1966): 347–60.

Levi, A.W. *The Humanities Today.* Bloomington: Indiana University Press, 1970.

Luszki, Margaret Baron. *Interdisciplinary Team Research: Methods and Problems.* Washington D.C.: The National Training Laboratories, 1958.

Luyten, Norbert A. "Interdisziplinarität und Einheit der Wissenschaft." *Int. J. Interdis. Forschung* 1 (1974): 132–53.

————. "Interdisciplinarité: un impératif de la recherche scientifique." *Civitas* 29 (1973–74): 221–42.

Mayhew, Lewis, and Ford, Patrick. *The Changing Curriculum.* San Francisco: Jossey-Bass, 1972.

McKeon, Richard. "Character and the Arts and Disciplines." *Ethics* 18 (1968): 109–23.

Michaud, Guy. "General Conclusions." In *Interdisciplinarity: Problems of Teaching and Research in Universities.* Paris: OECD, 1972, pp. 281–88.

Milton, Ohmer. *Alternatives to the Traditional.* San Francisco: Jossey-Bass, 1972.

Morgan, George W. "Disciplines and Interdisciplinary Research and Human Studies." *Int. J. Interdis. Forschung* 1 (1974): 263–84.

Pantin, C.F.A. *The Relations Between the Sciences.* New York: Cambridge University Press, 1968.

Phenix, Philip. "Use of the Disciplines as Curriculum Content." *Educational Forum* 26 (1962): 273–80.

Piaget, Jean. "L'Épistémologie des relations interdisciplinaires." *Int. J. Interdis. Forschung* 1 (1974): 154–72.

———. *Main Trends in Inter-Disciplinary Research.* New York: Harper and Row, 1973.

———. "The Epistemology of Interdisciplinary Relationships." In *Interdisciplinarity: Problems of Teaching and Research in Universities.* Paris: OECD, 1972, pp. 127–39.

Prior, M.E. *Science and the Humanities.* Evanston: Northwestern University Press, 1963.

Quick, Robert, ed. *A Guide to Graduate Study: Programs Leading to the Ph.D. Degree.* Washington, D.C.: Association of American Colleges, 1969.

Ravetz, J.R. *Scientific Knowledge and Its Social Problems.* Oxford: Clarendon Press, 1971.

Recurrent Education: A Strategy for Life-Long Learning. Paris: CERI, 1973.

Rogers, Carl. *Freedom to Learn.* Columbus, Ohio: Charles Merrill, 1969.

Rohrer, John H. and Sherif, Muzafer, eds. *Social Psychology at the Cross-Roads.* Freeport, N.Y.: Books for Libraries Press, 1970.

Rudolph, Frederick. *The American College and University: A History.* New York: Knopf, 1962.

Schwab, Joseph. *College Curriculum and Student Protest.* Chicago: University of Chicago Press, 1969.

Schwartz, Richard, ed. *Internationales Jahrbuch für Interdisziplinäre Forschung.* Vol. I: *Wissenschaft als Interdisziplinäres Problem.* Berlin: de Gruyter, 1974.

———. "Interdisziplinarität der Wissenschaften als Problem und Aufgabe heute." *Int. J. Interdis. Forschung* 1 (1974): 1–131.

Sherif, Muzafer, and Sherif, Carolyn, eds. *Interdisciplinary Relationships in the Social Sciences.* Chicago: Aldine, 1969.

Snow, C.P. *The Two Cultures and the Scientific Revolution.* New York: Cambridge University Press, 1963.

Steffen, Hans, ed. *Bildung und Gesellschaft.* Göttingen: Vandenhoeck & Ruprecht, 1972.

Storr, Richard J. *The Beginnings of Graduate Education in America.* Chicago: University of Chicago Press, 1953.

The Graduate Study of Education. Cambridge, Mass.: Harvard University Press, 1966.

Thwing, Charles F. *The American and the German University.* New York: Macmillan, 1928.

Veach, H.B. *Two Logics.* Evanston: Northwestern University Press, 1969.

Wilden, Anthony L. *System and Structure: Essays in Communication and Exchange.* London: Tavistock, 1972.

Wilson, John. "Orthodox, General, or Integrated?" *University Quarterly* 21 (1967): 445–52.

Wise, Gene. "Integrative Education for a Disintegrated World." *Teachers College Record* 67 (1966): 391–401.

Name Index

Subject Index